D0997419

Critical acclaim for Anthony Holden:

Charles, Prince of Wales

'A work of considerable confidence . . . I am willingly convinced that this is as near the truth as we are ever likely to hear it.' Hugo Vickers, *The Times*

'Holden is a major shareholder in the Charles industry, but the kind who raises intelligent questions at the AGM . . . Although Holden is part of the rat-pack, he is at least the thinking man's rat.' Mark Lawson, *Independent*

'Holden is *la crème de la crème*.' John Mortimer, *Sunday Times*

Olivier

'This superb book . . . witty, spellbinding, definitive.' Anthony Sher, *Observer*

'An important biographer and a major subject . . . a substantial achievement. Future writers will be hard put to do better.' John Peter, *Sunday Times*

Big Deal

'I read at a sitting Anthony Holden's vivid and funny account of his well-spent (in every sense) year as a professional poker player. And I will read it again when I'm next seized by an urgent desire to buy a plane ticket to Las Vegas.' Jonathan Raban, Books of the Year, *Independent on Sunday*

'Vivid, engrossing, superb . . . the best description of world-class poker we've been given.' Salman Rushdie, *Times Literary Supplement*

The Oscars

'A tale of greed, revenge, vanity, megalomania, chicanery, sibling hatred, betrayal and double-crossing, high finance and low morality . . . This has to be a definitive work. It would take a superman merely to dip into it. Being of mortal clay I gorged myself and loved every fat, cholesterol-choked page.' Hugh Leonard, *The Times*

The Tarnished Crown

'The most significant work ever written about the House of Windsor.'
Jonathan Cooper, *Daily Express*

'Will fan the flames of royal debate like no other publication since
Andrew Morton's *Diana: Her True Story*.' *The Times*

Tchaikovsky

'A perfect blend of accessibility and erudition.' *Daily Telegraph*

'One of the most readable and engrossing musical biographies
for many years.' Derek Parker, *The Author*

'Arguments so persuasive as to be overwhelming . . . this confident,
expertly disciplined account . . .'
Jonathan Keates, *Observer*

CHARLES: A BIOGRAPHY

CHARLES

A BIOGRAPHY

ANTHONY HOLDEN

BANTAM PRESS

LONDON · NEW YORK · TORONTO · SYDNEY · AUCKLAND

TRANSWORLD PUBLISHERS LTD
61–63 UXBRIDGE ROAD, LONDON W5 5SA

TRANSWORLD PUBLISHERS (AUSTRALIA) PTY LTD
15–25 Helles Avenue, Moorebank, NSW 2170

TRANSWORLD PUBLISHERS (NZ) LTD
3 William Pickering Drive, Albany, Auckland

Published 1998 by Bantam Press
a division of Transworld Publishers Ltd
Copyright © Anthony Holden Ltd 1998

The right of Anthony Holden to be identified
as author of this work has been asserted in accordance
with sections 77 and 78 of the Copyright Designs and
Patents Act 1988.

A catalogue record for this book is available from the British Library
ISBN 0593 024702

All rights reserved. No part of this publication may
be reproduced, stored in a retrieval system, or
transmitted in any form or by any means,
electronic, mechanical, photocopying, recording,
or otherwise, without the prior permission of
the publishers

Typeset in 11/13pt Sabon by Falcon Oast Graphic Art
Printed in Great Britain
by Clays Ltd, Bungay, Suffolk.

To
Arsène Wenger
a true prince among men
and the 1997–8 Arsenal squad
whose double
kept me going
through my treble

CONTENTS

LIST OF ILLUSTRATIONS

PROLOGUE AND ACKNOWLEDGEMENTS

THIS IS MY THIRD BIOGRAPHY OF THE PRINCE OF WALES IN AS MANY decades, a bizarre and relentless punctuation to both our lives.

Written to mark his thirtieth, fortieth and fiftieth birthdays, hard on the heels of my own, this dogged trilogy now consists of three different books about three completely different men. The first was a lonely, confused bachelor, still living at home with his parents as he entered his thirties; the second was a driven but still troubled husband, the father of two sons, claustrophobically trapped in an unhappy marriage. The third is a divorced widower, looking older than his years, and facing a stark choice between his children, the love of his life and the throne – or, by trying to have all three, playing a dangerous long-term game that could threaten the future of the very institution which gives his tortured life any meaning.

Neither of us could have imagined that it would all come to this when I first met the Prince of Wales in the cocktail bar of a Canadian hotel, the Four Seasons in Calgary, Alberta, in July 1977. It was an amiable encounter, the first of many all over the world before I ventured to voice a note of dissent. 'What on earth are *you* doing here?' were the first words he ever addressed to me, as indeed they were the last, rather less kindly meant, in a Melbourne park during Australia's bicentennial celebrations eleven years later.

Between those two landmarks, and indeed since, we have both been on a long and fascinating, if at times bumpy, journey. I was married before he was, had children before he did, got divorced before him, and am now very happily remarried. At each stage, until he stopped speaking to me, he plied me with questions about married life. 'Fun, is it?' – one of the remarks quoted in these pages – was an early, endearingly direct example. Had we remained on speaking terms – we were never, as is still alleged, often in print, friends – I might have been able to offer him the same comfort and advice as other male friends our age who have been down the same road, desperately trying to ensure that their children do not suffer from their own mistakes.

The first prince I chronicled, at the time of both our thirtieth birthdays, was a young man full of idealistic promise, whom I admired but did not envy. The second, ten years later, was a prematurely middle-aged man, whose admirable public aspirations belied his less than admirable private conduct. No doubt the same could be said of me; but I harboured no ambitions to become the nation's moral figurehead, let alone titular head of its established Church. I was, frankly, disappointed in the promising prince I had once known, and intimated as much in a book that spelt out his public work in uniquely positive detail, while also suggesting – four years before Andrew Morton – the parlous state of his marriage. As it happened, I did not share his taste in architecture, nor think it an appropriate use of his unelected office to put British architects out of business; so I said so. But it was the marital chapter that did it. Through his aide and friend Tom Shebbeare, director of the Prince's Trust, the prince denounced my book as 'fiction from beginning to end', protesting that it had 'ruined' his birthday.

I was none too happy to turn forty, either. But I was naïvely unprepared for the invasion of my own privacy that followed, as the tabloids declared open season on a fellow journalist who happened to be living with someone who was not then his wife (but who now, I am happy to say, is). Today, towards the end of this dire decade for the Windsors, it seems hard to imagine that, just ten years ago, these were still the days of devout deference, when any mention of the royal family still suspended all critical faculties, and a hint of royal disapproval was enough to unleash the dogs of tabloid war.

Indignantly I consulted lawyers, who told me I had a prima facie case for defamation against the Prince of Wales, but advised me not to proceed, as no jury in the land would take my side against the heir to the throne. Knowing they were right, I had no option but to learn to live with his economy with the truth.

It was, perhaps, a salutary lesson in giving me a glimpse of life as the kind of public figure I had never sought to be. Clearly, however, I did not succeed in summoning quite the degree of insouciance to which I aspired. Accusations of 'sour grapes' have pursued me ever since, as my public pronouncements about the Prince of Wales have grown increasingly harsh. I am aware of this, and unabashed by it – as unabashed as one of my literary heroes, the poet and journalist Leigh Hunt, who was imprisoned in 1813 for describing the fifty-year-old Prince of Wales, recently appointed Prince Regent, as 'a violator of his word . . . a despiser of domestic ties . . . a man who has just closed half a century without one single claim on the gratitude of his country or the respect of posterity.'

Nearly two centuries later, more loyal commentators have occasionally suggested my own incarceration in the Tower. I recall the 1988 episode here only to reassert my credentials as a writer who has studied the prince for twenty years, who has made many lasting friends among those around him, and who shares their disappointment in the way that he appears to have betrayed his early promise. If the present volume is dominated by analysis of his private life, at the expense of his well-meaning, if often misjudged, public work, it is really his fault, not mine. I regret it as much as he must.

Ten years on from that quasi-marital spat between prince and biographer, the injustice was finally righted. At, of all places, a Spice Girls concert in Johannesburg, South Africa – graced by the presence of HRH the Prince of Wales and his son Harry – the instrument of his revenge, Tom Shebbeare, came over to me and, to his credit, in front of my colleagues in the press corps, apologized. 'I owe you an apology,' said the man who had denounced me in the prince's name in 1988. 'You were right and I was wrong.' I thanked him, I hoped, with all the grace he himself had displayed. An honourable man, devoted to his master, he nevertheless had the decency to acknowledge that a wrong had been done, and to attempt to put it right. There are, I am sorry to say, few others around the prince of whom this is true. If Shebbeare loses his job within months, even years of this book's publication, because I have made that moment public, I trust the entire nation will join me in suing for wrongful dismissal.

Shebbeare and I subsequently enjoyed, at my suggestion, a private, off-the-record lunch – not a word of which appears in these pages – at which we candidly discussed the man who had haunted both our lives for many years. Our conversation that day has since proved very helpful to me in the writing of this book. If he of all people can accept as genuine my informed disillusion with the prince to whom I once warmed, I devoutly hope that the reader of this book, if not others around Charles, let alone the man himself, can be as fair-minded. Three-quarters of this third book post-dates my second study of the prince, not least because, as last time around, the most recent ten years of his life have been the most eventful, and by far the most significant. I have attempted to tell the tale as objectively as possible, from the respective points of view of its three main players: Charles, Diana and Camilla. As a professional biographer, if intermittent royal-watcher, I know that the reader would expect no less.

As my previous two studies of the prince have become standard works of reference, whose early pages are summarized in this third volume, it seems appropriate to reassert their credentials here. The section on Charles's days at Hill House and Cheam schools were checked for accuracy by their respective headmasters during his schooldays, Colonel Henry Townend and Peter Beck; the section on Gordonstoun read and approved by the teacher closest to the prince, Robert Waddell, and discussed with a subsequent headmaster, Michael Mavor; the section on his university years by the late Lord Butler, master of Trinity College, Cambridge; Dr Dennis Marrian, senior tutor; Dr Anil Seal; and by his tutor at the University College of Wales, Aberystwyth, Edward Millward. The entire text of the first volume was read by the prince himself, whose fascinating marginal annotations I still treasure – and have never made public – and other members of the royal family, as well as senior members of his then staff.

Others whose help with the earlier volumes are reflected in this one include: Edward Adeane, private secretary to the Prince of Wales, 1979–85; Ronald Allison, press secretary to the Queen, 1973–8; the late Stephen Barry, valet to the Prince of Wales, 1970–82; Melvyn Bragg; David Campbell; Canon Sebastian Charles, former secretary, Inner City Aid; Sir David Checketts, private secretary to the Prince of Wales, 1970–9; Lt.-Col. David Cox, former director, the Prince of Wales's Committee; Sir David Frost; the late Sir Martin Gilliat, private secretary to Queen Elizabeth the Queen Mother; General Sir Ian Gourlay, director-general, United World Colleges, 1975–90; Rod Hackney, president of the Royal Institute of British Architects, 1987–9; Sir Harold Haywood, director of the Prince's Trust, 1977–88; Sir William Heseltine, private secretary to the Queen, 1986–90; Maxwell Hutchinson, president of the Royal Institute of British Architects, 1989–91; Hywel Jones, Cambridge friend of the prince; Charles Knevitt, founder-director, Inner City Aid; Sir Tom McCaffrey, press secretary of the Prime Minister, 1976–9; John Maclean, royal protection officer; Sir Philip Magnus, official biographer of King Edward VII; Michael Manser, president of the Royal Institute of British Architects, 1983–5; the late Sir Iain Moncrieffe of that Ilk; Lord Mountbatten; Paul Officer, royal protection officer; Stephen O'Brien, chief executive, Business in the Community, 1983–92; George Pratt, founder-director of the Prince's Trust; (Lord) Richard Rogers; Michael Shea, press secretary to the Queen, 1978–87; Tom Shebbeare, director of the Prince's Trust, 1978–; Lord Snowdon; Nicholas Soames MP; the late Viscount Tonypandy; the late Lord Wilson of Rievaulx, prime minister 1964–70 and 1974–6; the Rt Revd Robert Woods, Dean of Windsor, 1962–70.

Among experts in the prince's specialist fields, some of them his close friends, who have helped me to a better understanding of his preoccupations, I must thank: Peter Ahrends, Ashley Barker, Christopher Booker, Tony Clegg, Phil Collins, Theo Crosby, Dan Cruickshank, Sir Philip Dowson, Trish Evans, Richard Frewer, Paul Greetham, Ernest Hall, Stuart Lipton, John Lockwood, Jules Lubbock, John Simpson, Deyan Sudjic, John Thompson, Richard Wade, Dr Elizabeth Whipp and Lady Roisine Wynne-Jones.

Among writers, journalists and photographers, some of whom earn their living watching the prince's every move, and other friends and colleagues whose assistance has informed this book, I thank: Bryan Appleyard, (Lord) Jeffrey Archer, Harry Arnold, Michael Barratt, Richard Barber, Sally Bedell Smith, Tony Benn MP, Ross Benson, the late Basil Boothroyd, William Boyd, Sarah Bradford, Tina Brown, Beatrix Campbell, Nigel Dempster, Peter Dunn, Anne Edwards, Bob Edwards, Kent Gavin, Tim Graham, John Grigg, Philip Hall, Prof. Stephen Haseler, Prof. Peter Hennessy, Christopher Hitchens, Anthony Howard, Anwar Hussein, Robert Jobson, Richard Kay, Kitty Kelley, Robert Lacey, Elizabeth Longford, Brian MacArthur, Stryker McGuire, Suzy Menkes, Peter Osnos, John Pearson, Prof. Ben Pimlott, Howell Raines, Charles Rae, Fiametta Rocco, Anthony Sampson, Alan Scales, Ingrid Seward, Andrew Stephen, David Thomas,

Hugo Vickers, James Whitaker and Christopher Wilson.

It is customary in books like this to thank the Prince of Wales's office for its courteous co-operation, etc., as I myself have done in the past. On this occasion, alas, it is not appropriate.

At the time of my previous volumes, the press office of Buckingham Palace was more than helpful. Over the years I have enjoyed close relations with a succession of press secretaries to the prince, some of whom have become my close friends: John Dauth, Warwick Hutchings, the late Victor Chapman, Philip Mackie and Dickie Arbiter. This time around, however, I have reason to thank few beyond Geoff Crawford, formerly press secretary to HRH the Princess of Wales, now press secretary to HM the Queen, who has remained his unfailingly courteous self, despite my occasional public criticisms of his employers. Only two others have consistently displayed the same civility: Sir Robin Janvrin, private secretary (designate at the time of writing) to the Queen, and Patrick Jephson, formerly private secretary to the Princess of Wales.

A charm offensive of my own, at much the same time as the prince's with the media in the wake of his ex-wife's death, meanwhile failed to soften the hearts, or clear the heads, of Charles's current staff, who have rejected all my proffered olive branches: Stephen Lamport, private secretary; Mark Bolland, deputy private secretary; and Sandy Henney, press secretary. Henney went to some lengths, in vain, to prevent me joining the Prince of Wales's 1997 trip to South Africa, despite my accreditation on behalf of a national newspaper, and was as obstructive as possible while we were there, excluding me from the chartered aircraft on which the prince chatted with other members of the press for the first time in ten years. The most recent, and most sophisticated, member of the prince's private staff, Mark Bolland, declined my invitation to lunch on the grounds that it would be a waste of my time. 'I come with no axes to grind,' he wrote, 'but . . . we do not start from the best of wickets. I am sorry not to be more positive.' Translating this as 'Sod off', the *Guardian* of 26 May 1998 further reported Bolland as having told royal reporters two months earlier, while on tour in Canada, 'We are always polite when someone approaches us with a book project. Except for Tony Holden. We don't bother being polite to him.'

The Prince's ex-wife was rather more gracious. In all three of her incarnations, as Lady Diana Spencer, HRH the Princess of Wales and subsequently ex-HRH Diana, Princess of Wales, I am lucky enough to have known the mother of Charles's children – to the point of enjoying several candid lunches with her, in public and private places, over the last five years of her life. After careful thought, I have decided to include in this book some of her confidences at those times, which began with a meeting at the Knightsbridge restaurant San Lorenzo in 1993 while I was writing *The Tarnished Crown* ('Perhaps,' she giggled, 'it should be called *The Tarnished Tiara*') and ended with a long lunch at Kensington Palace – just the two of us – in October 1996, ten months before her death. The various different conversations, dates and venues are clearly flagged in the source notes.

That last Kensington Palace lunch, which would not have been possible before her divorce became final, was a very happy occasion; relaxed, gossipy, full of laughter. Her habitual candour was delightful. The princess had recently returned from a trip to Washington, and was full of praise for her hostess, Katharine Graham, and for Hillary Clinton, with whom she was planning a series of joint initiatives. Her cattiest remarks were reserved for the Queen Mother, with whom she had come to share a strong mutual antipathy. She spoke with distaste of Kevin Costner, who had just been on the phone trying to persuade her to appear with him in a movie, and with admiration of General Colin Powell, who had recently talked her out of launching a Margaret Thatcher-style foundation ('too much bureaucracy'). In a conversation which ranged far and wide, high and low, we also spoke at length of the nuances of bringing up children after divorce. She permitted herself a few withering remarks about her ex-husband, and the 'third person' in their marriage – referred to throughout as 'you-know-who' – but tended by then to err on the side of generosity. She spoke with great passion of her public work, and with adoration of her children.

In the absence of any input from the prince or his staff – if not of other friends and associates sensible enough to realize that whatever I wrote might make some impact – Diana's memory has been my guiding star in the writing of this third and, I devoutly hope, last in my series of interim reports on the man who would be king.

PART ONE

Winning his Spurs

CHAPTER ONE

'IT WAS NOT TO BE'

SOON AFTER MIDNIGHT ON SUNDAY, 31 AUGUST 1997, AS FORTY-EIGHT-year-old Charles, Prince of Wales slept at Balmoral Castle, the rest of his life was being brutally rewritten by a freak sequence of events 1,000 miles away in Paris. At 12.45 a.m. Charles was awoken by a phone call telling him that his former wife, Diana, had been gravely injured in a car crash that had instantly killed her companion, Dodi Fayed. By dawn the prince was waking his sons, William and Harry, to tell them that their mother was dead.

The scale of the ensuing public grief took Britain and the world, especially Charles and the Windsor family, utterly by surprise. During the week leading up to Diana's funeral, amid scenes unprecedented in modern British history, daily life ground to a halt as millions made flower-laden pilgrimages to Kensington Palace to pay their last respects in wholly unEnglish ways: publicly weeping and wailing; sobbing in the arms of total strangers; lamenting the loss of a tragically young mother as vulnerable as she was inspirational, dead at the age of only thirty-six.

Four months after the landslide election of a populist new government, the mass mourning betokened the loss of a public figure who had somehow remained 'one of us', while ready to rock the boat to knock some sense into 'them'. Diana's crusades for the sick, the suffering and the underprivileged had contrived to transcend politics, and indeed her own fallibility, striking a chord in all but the hardest of hearts. Even those who had never met her felt personally bereaved. Many families the world over mourned as if they had lost one of their own.

At first, Diana's death looked like very bad news for Charles. As he and his family remained in seclusion at Balmoral, apparently reluctant to share the nation's grief, the crowds outside Buckingham Palace grew angrier by the day. This, after all, was the princess the Windsors had banished a year earlier, stripping her of her royal rank and expelling her from the family when her divorce from Charles had become final. Far from retreating in disarray, Diana had since carved her own niche in the life of the nation, leaving Charles an almost marginal figure, rapt in puzzled contemplation of an uncertain future, with only his mistress to console him.

Diana had shown that royalty could be human, could move among its people, could even touch them by way of lending solace to their woes. So stark was the contrasting silence from Scotland that events soon moved beyond royal control. Even when the prime minister persuaded the Windsors finally to come south, after five days of mounting public unrest, and the Queen made an emergency broadcast to show her subjects that she cared, 'Diana's Army' – the millions who loved her even more in death than in life – found it hard to forgive. From the beginning of the week, Charles had been the main target of their rage. 'How dare he?' asked one woman in the crowd outside Buckingham Palace on the very day of Diana's death, when her ex-husband flew to Paris to escort her coffin home. 'How dare he go to Paris? He's the man who ruined her life.'[1]

Charles's problems were largely of his own making. Only six weeks before Diana's death, he had taken his public life in his hands with an overt demonstration of his affection for the woman he had loved before, during and after his marriage – the 'third person' in their marriage, as Diana herself had famously called Camilla Parker Bowles. On the evening of Friday 18 July the prince hosted a fiftieth birthday party for Camilla at his Gloucestershire home, Highgrove, where she had long since replaced Diana as chatelaine. Was she also to replace the princess on the future King's arm, perhaps even on the throne? The party was the climax of a long-term strategy to win public acceptance for Camilla as his consort, dating back to his televised confession of adultery with her in June 1994.

Mrs Parker Bowles had since become the most reviled woman in the land, so unpopular that fellow housewives pelted her with bread rolls in their local supermarket; but there were signs that Charles's game plan was finally beginning to work. With unfortunate timing, as it transpired, the Camilla question had been manipulated to the top of the national agenda during the weeks before Diana's death. It became the subject of opinion polls, radio phone-ins and TV debates, and it dominated public discussion in bars, pubs and clubs, even after Diana herself took up with the scion of one of the country's most controversial families.

The polls still showed a large majority against Camilla replacing Diana as Charles's future queen, but the tone of the debate was beginning to soften. As one participant put it in a BBC television debate, 'If the state of the nation prevents the marriage of two fifty-year-old divorcees, who have apparently been in love for some twenty-five years, when other such couples get married every day, then there is something wrong with the state of the nation.'[2]

But Diana's death changed all that. Camilla, as one friend put it, promptly 'crawled under her bed with a bottle of whisky and a packet of cigarettes, and wondered when, if ever, she would be able to come out again'.[3] Charles had long since declared Mrs Parker Bowles a 'non-negotiable' part of his life. Even during the week of Diana's funeral, he called her several times a day on his mobile phone, and told friends he needed her 'now more than ever'. But his first priority then, and for the foreseeable future, had to be his two bereft sons.

For the first time in his life, to warm public approval, the prince began to cancel or postpone public engagements to be with them. That November, during the half-term break Prince Harry had been due to spend with his mother, Charles took him to South Africa to meet Nelson Mandela and the Spice Girls. There, for the first time, Charles paid brief tribute to his ex-wife's public work, and for the second time thanked the world for its expressions of condolence. To his surprise, he found himself riding a wave of public sympathy – directed primarily at his sons, but washing over him as their father – which saw his public popularity begin to climb for the first time in nearly two decades. By Christmas 1997, four months after Diana's death, a poll for *The Times* officially declared him as popular as prime minister Tony Blair, then still enjoying an extended honeymoon with the electorate after his historic election victory the previous May.[4]

Still the old, insular Charles would occasionally resurface – defiantly going out fox-hunting, for instance, within days of a huge parliamentary vote for its abolition, amid polls showing overwhelming opposition among his future subjects. But the plight of his sons was disarming criticism. By February 1998 he was cutting back on his charity work to devote more time to them. The following month he took them with him to Canada to brave their first public engagements, amid scenes of mass hysteria, before a photocall on the ski slopes. Prince William, it became clear, could bring his mother's charms to the rescue of the ailing British monarchy. At the age of only fifteen, 'Wills' – far more than his father – was the House of Windsor's hope for the future. Or was it the House of Spencer's?

Charles looked on happily as William donned a back-to-front baseball cap and played to the cameras. This time around, he did not resent the comparisons. Where once he had been jealous of Diana's greater popularity, now he could only breathe a huge sigh of relief as their son picked up where she had left off. At the supreme court of the House of Windsor – his mother, also his monarch – Charles might at last be relieved of the blame for bringing the Crown into such disrepute.

In his ex-wife's lifetime, Charles would have been appalled at the idea of a 'Dianified', baseball-cap monarchy. Deep down, he still was; but even he could see that this was the only realistic way forward, the key to the monarchy's survival in an increasingly sceptical age. It was time, he was advised, to assert a leadership role by appearing to become the family's prime 'modernizer'. If that involved public disagreements with his father, who had caused him such grief over the years, then, as far as Charles was concerned, so much the better. It was time for him to escape from Philip's shadow – the bullying father of his childhood, whom he had blamed for 'pushing' him into his luckless marriage, and whose wrathful disapproval could still, even as he approached fifty, reduce him to tears.

Diana's disappearance from the scene, in short, was proving Charles's salvation. Now he could reclaim the role of 'caring, compassionate' prince, in which he had been cast before Diana arrived in his life, but which she had hijacked and played so much better. Suddenly there was a spring in the prince's step, despite another painful knee operation, as he chatted amiably with the 'reptiles' of the press for the first time in ten years. In their instinctive decency, the British people were giving him another chance. Moreover, in their loyalty to the monarchy, they were allowing the Windsors surreptitiously to reclaim in death the princess they had banished in life. Even the excesses of the posthumous Diana cult, with her Memorial Fund sanctioning her autograph on margarine tubs and scratch cards, began to work in the prince's favour. All that was left was to win public acceptance for Camilla.

On the weekend of 14–15 March 1998 – after his return from Canada, and with the boys safely back at boarding school – Charles hosted a 'cultural' weekend for a dozen loyalists at Sandringham, his mother's country estate in Norfolk, and let it be leaked that Camilla had acted as hostess. The tacit approval of the Queen, who tactfully spent the weekend at Windsor, could be assumed. Among the guests was Peter Mandelson, the government's master manipulator, who was helping his friend Charles to assume the guise of a leadership role in the battle to modernize the monarchy.

To those who knew the private prince – whose true conservatism in matters royal had been laid bare by his attitude to his marriage – it seemed wholly out of character that he would wish to preside over a slimmed-down, Scandinavian-style monarchy bereft of the splendour of its post-imperial rituals. It was he, after all, who had led the vain fight to save the royal yacht *Britannia*, long after the polls had showed a daunting majority of taxpayers unwilling to finance such post-imperial extravagances. But the fortunes of the House of Windsor had sunk so low that both the Queen and the prince were forced to adapt to Tony Blair's newly 'cool' Britannia, gritting their teeth through walkabouts and photo opportunities with pink-haired, nose-ringed rock stars.

And the tactic seemed to be working. On her golden wedding anniversary, ten weeks after Diana's death, a 'rebranded' Queen walked around Whitehall laughing and chatting, even clutching a heart-shaped balloon for photographers. New Labour, new monarchy. By February 1998, when Britain was contemplating war with Iraq and the Northern Ireland peace talks seemed in danger of collapse, the television news and newspaper front pages were dominated by the Queen Mother's hip operation and Princess Margaret's stroke. Normal British values seemed to have been restored.

*

Over the last century, since Disraeli masterminded the widowed Queen Victoria's rebirth as Queen-Empress, the British monarchy has survived as the world's pre-eminent hereditary institution by continually reinventing itself. In a secular age, when constitutional monarchs were obliged to sign government legislation whether they liked it or not, the Saxe-Coburg-Gothas changed their awkwardly German name to the cosier-sounding Windsor and cast around for a new role. During the reign of the present Queen's father, King George VI, they found their twentieth-century niche as a 'family' monarchy – a living exemplar of Christian family values, strong enough to survive another world war.

Charles's own mother has played a major part in the royal family's iconography, sitting for portrait painters over tea at Windsor with her father, mother and sister – for all the world like any other British nuclear family, albeit a pampered and privileged one that seemed to speak a different language from its subjects, as well as living a different way of life. As Elizabeth II, fast approaching Victoria's record as Britain's longest-reigning monarch, she has kept the theme going strong, encouraging the nation to bill and coo over her children, surrogate offspring of every house in the land. As *ex officio* head of the Church of England, the monarch was content with the role of custodian of the nation's moral values, and the job of setting an exemplary model for decent-minded citizens to follow.

Throughout the 1980s, as the younger generation came to the fore, the British love of its royals – reflected in the slavish sycophancy of the press – reached a crescendo with a succession of royal weddings and births. Amid the harsh realities of Thatcher's every-man-for-himself, devil-take-the-hindmost Britain, the royals fulfilled their primary function by offering some much-needed good news amid all the bad. No wonder, when all those marriages collapsed within a decade, the backlash was all the mightier. The British people had made a huge investment of affection and goodwill – not to mention money – in Charles and Diana, Anne and Mark, Andrew and Fergie. As they abused their privileges, broke the sacred vows of marriage, then offended bedrock monarchists by opting for divorce, all viewers of the royal soap opera felt cheated, even angry. What was the royal family for, if not to provide a symbol of stable family life?

Charles took the brunt of the backlash. He was, after all, the future king; but he had also two-timed Britain's most popular princess, the world's most famous woman, loved as much for her faults as for her strengths. The prince who at thirty had promised to be a 'New Age' husband – present at the birth of his sons, changing his fair share of nappies, sharing the upbringing of the children – had reverted to royal type, marrying Diana as a brood mare, and expecting her to take charge of the nursery while he openly kept a mistress. Had Diana been the brainless bimbo he thought he had married, so in love with being a princess that she would turn a blind eye, Charles might have got away with it. But she turned out to be a thoroughly modern woman, and at the same time a deeply traditional one, by insisting on her own rights within the ideal of a strong family unit. Unlike some of her predecessors as royal brides, she was not prepared to look the other way. When this Cinderella stamped her glass slipper, with a crash that echoed around the world, she transformed herself from mere jet-set clothes horse to potent feminist icon. Diana became the potential instrument of Charles's destruction.

Now, realizing the scale of the mistake he had made, the prince looked on helpless as his wife set about attempting to remove him from the line of succession, winning public support for a direct transition from his mother to their son. The law, of course, was on the prince's side; it would take a constitutional upheaval, plus his mother's agreement, for the succession to be altered. But he was in serious danger of losing the public consent by which any monarch reigns. He had forfeited respect and affection – the two public gifts indispensable to a successful monarch. Diana was at her most vengeful in the second half of 1991, when she made the tape recordings that blackened Charles's name via Andrew Morton's book *Diana: Her True Story*. Since the divorce she had softened, working out a *modus vivendi* with her ex-husband for the sake of their sons. She had agreed to make a joint appearance with him aboard *Britannia*, the scene of their ill-fated honeymoon, during the royal yacht's poignant farewell voyage around Britain in the autumn of 1997. It would have symbolized the civilized way in which they were rebuilding their separate lives; and it would have boosted Charles's public ratings, then largely in Diana's control. But Dodi Fayed and fate intervened.

Now that she is dead – and Charles has a chance to regain the respect, if not the affection, of the nation – it becomes forlornly clear what might have been, what Britain and the Commonwealth might have had. 'We would have been the best team in the world,' as Diana herself put it, only weeks before her death. 'I could shake hands till the cows come home. And Charles could make serious speeches . . . But' – she shook her head sadly – 'it was not to be.'[5]

What kind of man could throw away such a pearl, such a rare combination of private happiness and public triumph? Even before her death, a friend of Diana spoke with equal eloquence of what might have been:

> His indifference pushed her to the edge, whereas he could have romanced her to the end of the world. They could have set the world alight. Through no fault of his own, because of his own ignorance, upbringing and lack of a whole relationship with anyone in his life, he instilled this hatred of himself.[6]

The turnaround in the fortunes of the monarchy during the half-century of Charles's lifetime is stark to behold. Three weeks before Diana's death, during the dog days of August 1997, an ICM opinion poll showed its popularity at an all-time low, commanding the support of less than half the Queen's subjects for the first time in British history. 'Solid support' for the royal family, according to the poll, would 'literally die out' with the over-sixty-fives, the only age group to show a clear majority in believing that Britain would be worse off without them.[7]

Yet when Charles was born, in November 1948, the thousand-year-old institution was as popular as it ever had been, with a third of Britons believing the monarch was personally chosen by God. The prince himself must shoulder much of the responsibility for the decline in the fortunes of the institution that he was born to serve. Another poll in August 1997, just before Diana's death, showed 46 per cent of Britons were 'dissatisfied' with his performance as Prince of Wales, 4 per cent more than professed themselves 'satisfied'.[8] A majority wished him to step aside, for the throne to pass to his son Prince William.

They will, more or less, get their wish. The best Charles can hope for is a brief reign as a caretaker king for the last decade or so of his life. As he turns fifty, his mother is seventy-two years old, twenty-six years younger than her own mother, who is as old as the century and showing every sign of making it to the millennium. All his life Charles has known he will spend most of it waiting in the wings – 'the longest apprenticeship ever', as it has been called[9] – and has consequently tried to win his place in history as a crusading Prince of Wales.

He can point to a record of achievement in helping disadvantaged youth via the Prince's Trust. His admirers would point to his campaigns for more traditional architecture, alternative medicine, the environment, ecumenism, literacy standards; his detractors would say they have achieved little, and in some cases done positive harm. Here, it appears, is a well-meaning man, decent and civilized, anxious to make something of his position rather than merely living a life of idle self-indulgence, like many of his predecessors. Yet he has made minimal impact, and is best known for two-timing one of the most-loved women of the twentieth century.

What is it about Charles that seems to have made him his own worst enemy? The seeds of the introspective, melancholy soul with a depressive streak, intensely proud of his heritage, yet unable to adapt it to a changing world, can be traced to his childhood and youth in a cold, distant family, bereft of the normal human interaction which fuels most mortal lives. Add the privilege that went with his birth, a cocoon of deference and sycophancy blocking out the real world, and you have all the ingredients of a tortured soul unable to treat other human beings as equals, to appreciate his own frailties, to understand that he can occasionally be wrong.

But if the public Charles has been undone by the private Charles, it is really because he has never been in sympathy with the age in which he lives. Beam the prince back to any previous century and he would be entirely at home, capable of appreciating its public and private values, its art and architecture, its morality and Zeitgeist – a popular future King with a beautiful wife and two fine sons, whose mistress would have remained a well-kept secret among his intimate circle. Land him in the twentieth century, where he has the misfortune to belong, and Charles is a displaced person, restless and discontented, out of synch with his contemporaries, unhappily resigned to being unappreciated and misunderstood.

The outstanding princes of Wales in British history have been those in tune with the spirit of their times – patrons of the arts, public benefactors, inspirational and much-loved figures,

regardless of their private lives. Charles, by contrast, stubbornly
resists even understanding the notion. 'Whatever that might be!' he
has said of the phrase 'the spirit of the times', just as he famously
said 'Whatever that means!' of another notion he took too casually
– marital love.[10]

During his one brief spell in the real world, at university, he was
'proud to be square', regarding his fellow undergraduates as 'hairy
unwashed student bodies . . . long-haired, bare-footed and perspiring'.[11] Has Charles ever been a man of his time? Even his most
sympathetic and like-minded biographer, granted access to his
private journals and correspondence, seems confused. At one point
the prince is dubbed 'a child of his times' (by virtue, ironically, of
not wishing to be unfaithful to his wife); at another he 'stands outside the age in which he lives', raging 'too much at the folly of the
world to be wise'.[12]

As Charles himself put it on entering his forties:

> The fear of being considered old-fashioned seems to me to be so
> all-powerful that the more eternal values and principles which
> run like a thread through the whole tapestry of human existence
> are abandoned under the false assumption that they restrict
> progress.[13]

Has Charles's contrary pride in being considered old-fashioned
hampered his own progress through the twentieth century? Has the
institution he embodies – clinging defiantly, like him, to the past –
outlived its rational lifespan? Can Diana's death now help him, via
his sons' popularity, to find his feet in a new century, a new
millennium, bringing new meaning to his birthright as a successful,
if short-lived, king? Perhaps. But can Charles manage all this,
unlike his great-uncle David, Duke of Windsor, without the 'help
and support' of the woman he loves?

CHAPTER TWO

'NO, NOT YOU, DEAR'

THE ODDS, PERHAPS, WERE AGAINST HIM FROM THE START. NO previous Prince of Wales has been obliged to act out the office's ancient duties in the age of the mass media – self-appointed tribunes of the people – whose criteria of what is interesting or important rarely coincide with his. This uniquely twentieth-century accountability, as unwelcome as it is unwonted, has shaped his life so completely as to transform it.

Had he lived in an earlier age, when he could have retained greater control of what remained private and what became public, the world might now have very different perceptions of Charles Philip Arthur George, Prince of Wales and Earl of Chester, Duke of Cornwall and Rothesay, Earl of Carrick and Baron Renfrew, Lord of the Isles and Great Steward of Scotland. But even before he was born, even before his gender was known or his name chosen, he was the object of global speculation and media curiosity. Even as an embryo, back in glamour-starved, rationed and couponed, post-war 1948, the child growing inside twenty-two-year-old Princess Elizabeth, Duchess of Edinburgh, excited the world and its press to fever pitch.

Charles's story begins, as almost fifty years later it will climax, outside his future kingdom, in Paris. During a visit in May 1948 by Princess Elizabeth, elder daughter of King George VI, those who saw her told each other she did not seem herself. At Divine Service in the British church she looked tired and listless, rarely raising her eyes from the ground. At a British Embassy reception in her honour that evening, she had met only half the guests when her husband led her from the room to rest. It was less than six months since she had married Lieutenant Philip Mountbatten RN, the former Prince Philip of Greece, but that was time enough. Paris decided that Elizabeth, heir presumptive to the British throne, must be pregnant.

Back in the reign of her father, King George VI, pregnancy was still a word Buckingham Palace could not quite bring itself to utter. A coded announcement on 4 June, the eve of Derby Day, stated simply that 'Her Royal Highness The Princess Elizabeth, Duchess of Edinburgh, will undertake no public engagements after the end of June.' Left to draw its own conclusions, the public remembered that the same wording had been used eighteen years earlier of the Duchess of York, Elizabeth's mother, four months before she had given birth to Princess Margaret Rose. No announcement at all had been made during the Duchess's previous pregnancy; the first Britain had known of Princess Elizabeth Alexandra Mary, whom it little thought would one day be its Queen, was when she entered the world by Caesarean section on 21 April 1926.

With Elizabeth's baby expected in mid-November, the princess and her husband were still living in Buckingham Palace while Clarence House was made ready for them, but much of their time was spent at Windlesham Moor, their rented country house near Sunningdale, Berkshire. There were those who suggested this might be the most peaceful place for her accouchement, but the princess herself decided she would like to have her baby at the Palace.

On the first floor, overlooking the Mall, a suite centres on the Buhl Room, which the Windsor matriarch Queen Mary, widow of George V, had converted into a makeshift surgery. Within a few months, this was to be the scene of the first of her son George VI's arterial operations, saving him the loss of his right leg. During the latter stages of his daughter's pregnancy, the King was first made aware of the seriousness of his condition: arteriosclerosis, with a grave danger of gangrene. He was diagnosed in the Buhl Room only two days before Charles's birth, but he gave strict instructions that his daughter was to be told nothing. For the time being, it was thus for a happy event that the room was transformed into a lavishly equipped operating theatre.

By 14 November 1948, the comings and goings of a posse of distinguished doctors at Buckingham Palace were the only clues that the birth was imminent. Crowds lingered outside the Palace throughout that rainy Sunday, the lack of news doing little to dampen their ardour. But some spirits within the Palace itself did begin to flag. By early evening the expectant father had grown impatient; Prince Philip took his private secretary and close friend, Lieutenant-Commander Michael Parker, for a game of squash on the Palace court. After a swim in the adjacent pool, they were back on the squash court at 9.15 p.m. when the King's private secretary, Sir Alan Lascelles, ran in with the news that a prince had been born.

Shortly before midnight, an announcement was secured to the Palace railings by the Colville cousins: Sir John ('Jock'), private secretary to Princess Elizabeth (and previously to three prime ministers: Neville Chamberlain, Winston Churchill and Clement Attlee, at No. 10 Downing Street), and Commander Richard, press secretary to the King, and later to Elizabeth II. Richard Colville had proudly written the announcement in his own precise handwriting:

> Her Royal Highness the Princess Elizabeth, Duchess of Edinburgh, was safely delivered of a Prince at 9.14 o'clock this evening. Her Royal Highness and the infant Prince are both doing well.

By that time, word of mouth had already drawn Londoners from their homes, restaurants and nightclubs to swell the crowd outside the Palace to some 3,000. The announcement on BBC radio had been nicely timed to launch closing-time celebrations in pubs all over the country, to start guns firing and bonfires blazing, to turn the fountains in Trafalgar Square blue for a boy (as they stayed for a week) and to draw 4,000 telegrams of congratulation to the Palace post office that night.

The first the growing crowd outside the Palace knew of the birth came very soon after it happened, when those who had climbed to the top of the Victoria Memorial saw a blue-liveried footman emerge to whisper in the ear of a policeman – one of the many trying (ironically enough) to protect the Palace guard, then still on the pavement outside the railings, from being trampled underfoot. Every car going in and out was fiercely scrutinized, none more so than that of the King's formidable mother, the eighty-one-year-old

Queen Mary, who arrived at 11 p.m. to inspect her first great-grandchild. Despite the after-effects of a bout of influenza, the old lady stayed until after midnight, by which time the crowd outside had grown larger and noisier than ever.

Up on the first floor of the Palace, on the Mall frontage, was a young woman exhilarated by the birth of her first child and the enthusiasm of her family, but in need of sleep. The well-wishers outside were keeping her awake. At the princess's behest, Mike Parker and a colleague walked across the forecourt to try to quieten them. As they struggled to make themselves heard over the hubbub, the first recipient of the princess's message was none other than the film star David Niven, a friend of Prince Philip. 'I was pinned against the railings and, being unable to move, I was the recipient of the message hissed in my ear by the man from the Palace. I had my coat collar turned up and was huddled inside the garment, hoping not to be recognized and asked for autographs at that particular location. However, I turned round and did my best to shush those nearest to me, which did little good as everyone was far too excited and happy.'[1] The crowd was eventually dispersed by loudspeaker vans – a bizarre lullaby for the exhausted princess.

The 7lb 6oz infant so warmly welcomed was the first royal child to be born at Buckingham Palace for sixty-two years, and the first royal baby in direct succession to the throne since the birth of the future King Edward VIII in 1894. Princess Elizabeth was only the fourth heiress presumptive in British history to have given birth to a male child. The prince, as yet unnamed, was fifth in descent from Queen Victoria, thirty-second from William the Conqueror and thirty-ninth from Alfred the Great. He was the most Scottish prince since Charles I and the most English since Henry VIII. Eleventh in descent from the Electress Sophia, through whom the present royal family's title to the throne is established under the 1701 Act of Settlement, he could claim descent from the Yorkist kings through Richard II and the Lancastrian kings through John of Gaunt. Thirteenth in descent from James I and VI, his Scottish ancestry included Robert the Bruce and St Mary of Scotland through James's mother, Mary Queen of Scots; through Henry Tudor, his Welsh ancestry could be traced back to Llewelyn-ap-Gruffydd, the last native prince of all Wales. Through his maternal grandmother, he was the first potential Prince of Wales ever to be a direct descendant of Owen Glendower; through his father, he had the blood of Harold, last of the Anglo-Saxon kings. Genealogists stretched the line almost to the crack of doom: on one side Charlemagne, Cadwallader and Musa ibn Naseir, an Arab sheikh born in Mecca in 660; on the other plainer names such as John Smith, Frances Webb, Mary Browne and Peter Checke, a sixteenth-century innkeeper.[2]

The following morning's events are a striking reminder of how much the world has changed in the intervening fifty years, as Charles's birth was heralded rather more extravagantly than that of another potential king, his own son William, would be some three decades later. The British fleet, wherever it happened to be, was dressed overall; in Australia, the Melbourne town hall carillon somewhat prematurely played 'God Bless the Prince of Wales' (not yet among his titles); forty-one-gun salutes and peals of bells awoke New Zealand and South Africa; in Kenya the news was broadcast in seven native languages; from Key West, Florida, President Truman sent a message of congratulations; and from South Africa, President Jan Smuts cabled, 'We pray that the prince will be a blessing to our Commonwealth and to the world.' In republican America, radio stations across the nation interrupted their programmes with the news; in New York, the *Herald Tribune* declared that freedom in Britain had 'grown and been safeguarded under the ancient institution of the monarchy'. In Athens, where it was not forgotten that Philip had been born a prince of Greece, hundreds of his compatriots carried their greetings to the British Embassy; on the island of Tinoa, where she was engaged on charitable work, his mother, Princess Andrew of Greece, was aroused from sleep by the arrival of her telegram.

In London, the King's Troop, Royal Horse Artillery, rode in full dress from St John's Wood to Hyde Park, drawing six guns to fire a forty-one-salvo salute. The bells of St Paul's pealed almost without interruption from 9 a.m.; those of Westminster Abbey took three hours to complete a peal of 5,000 changes, then did it all again. On the Thames, barges and small craft were gaily festooned with flags and bunting; at the top of the Mall, cars and taxis passing the Palace kept up a constant hooting of horns. At Plymouth, the US warships *Columbus* and *Hamel* joined with the battleship *Vanguard* in a twenty-one-gun salute; guns were fired in Edinburgh and Rosyth, Cardiff and Windsor; a chain of beacons was lit along the mountain ranges of Wales. In towns the length and breadth of the kingdom, the day was marked by the constant firing of guns and pealing of bells.

The BBC marked the event by commissioning 'Music for a Prince' from three prominent British composers, Gordon Jacob, Herbert Howells and Michael Tippett, to be performed at a Royal Albert Hall concert two months later. No less speedy in his inspiration was the Poet Laureate, John Masefield, whose quatrain 'A Hope for the Newly Born' bore the Laureateship's authentic limp:

> May destiny, allotting what befalls,
>   Grant to the newly born this saving grace,
> A guard more sure than ships and fortress-walls,
>   The loyal love and service of a race.

Hearing a news vendor's cry of 'It's a boy!', the Labour politician Hugh Dalton, then chancellor of the exchequer, presciently wrote in his diary: 'If this boy ever comes to the throne . . . it will be a very different Commonwealth and country he will rule over.'[3] Other political reflections were more conventional. The prime minister, Clement Attlee, rose in the Commons to speak in sombre tones of the 'great responsibilities' ahead of the young prince, adding sentiments with which not even Labour's republicans were going to quibble in the mood of national exhilaration: 'We shall watch him growing to manhood with lively interest, knowing that in his own home he will receive a training by example rather than mere precept, in that courtesy and in that gracious and tireless devotion to the manifold duties of constitutional monarchy which have won the hearts of the people.'[4] The moment was then marked in rather more ringing terms, as was his wont, by the leader of His Majesty's opposition, Winston Churchill:

> Our ancient monarchy renders inestimable services to our country and to all the British Empire and Commonwealth of Nations. Above the ebb and flow of party strife, the rise and fall of ministries and individuals, the changes of public opinion and fortune, the British monarchy presides ancient, calm and supreme within its functions, over all the treasures that have been saved from the past and all the glories that we write in the annals of our country. Our thoughts go out to the mother and

father and, in a special way today, to the little prince, now born
into this world of strife and storm.[5]

A week after the prince's birth Palace staff were allowed in to
inspect him in groups of five, as were select members of the Privy
Council. His mother had already begun to breastfeed him, as she
did for several weeks. Though the princess did not leave her bed
for ten days, her son was soon being walked in a second-generation
pram, which Elizabeth had sought out in Royal Lodge, her parents'
Windsor retreat. It was so enormous that Charles claims he can
still remember lying in its vastness, overshadowed by its high
sides.[6]

Information as to his looks was at a premium. The first word
came from the Queen's sister, Countess Granville, who told a convention of Girl Guides in Northern Ireland that 'he could not be
more angelic looking. He is golden-haired and has the most beautiful complexion, as well as amazingly delicate features for so young
a baby ... The Queen says that she thinks the baby is like his
mother, but the Duke is quite certain that the baby is very like himself.'[7] Princess Elizabeth, whom the Countess described as
'wonderfully well and radiantly happy', wrote to her former music
teacher:

> The baby is very sweet and we are enormously proud of him.
> He has an interesting pair of hands for a baby. They are rather
> large, but fine with long fingers quite unlike mine and certainly
> unlike his father's. It will be interesting to see what they will
> become. I still find it hard to believe I have a baby of my own![8]

The photographer Cecil Beaton, commissioned to take the first
official photos of mother and child, noted that the infant prince
was 'an obedient sitter ... He interrupted a long, contented sleep
to do my bidding and open his blue eyes to stare long and
wonderingly into the camera lens, the beginning of a lifetime in the
glare of public duty.'[9]

Not for a month, until the day of his christening on
15 December, was any announcement made about the child's
names. The unusual delay prompted some criticism – it was a first
move, pleaded his parents, to protect him from undue publicity –
which quickly turned to surprise when the names were revealed.

Elizabeth and Philip were the first royal generation in a hundred years to defy Victoria's wish that all her descendants should bear her or her husband's name.* Though said by the Palace to have been made for 'personal and private reasons', the choice of Charles Philip Arthur George, with the emphasis on Charles, caused widespread surprise. The two English kings of that name had enjoyed such miserable reigns that it had been abandoned by the royal family for nigh on 300 years; its only other royal holder, Bonnie Prince Charlie, was notorious for his insurrection against the House of Hanover. The choice was widely interpreted, especially when the prince's younger sister was christened Anne almost two years later, as a deliberate revival of the names of the royal Stuarts; to the Queen's sister, Princess Margaret, one of the godparents, it meant something else entirely: 'I suppose I'll now be known as Charley's Aunt.'

The names were duly registered by Prince Philip with Mr Stanley Clare, senior registrar of Caxton Hall in the City of Westminster, who called at the Palace on the morning of the christening. The ceremony that afternoon would have been held at Windsor, where all such family occasions usually take place, had it not been for the King's health. As it was, the Palace Chapel had been destroyed by Nazi bombers in 1940, so the baptism was performed in the white and gold Music Room, whose great crimson-curtained bow windows looked out on to a wintry Palace garden.

The ceremony was followed by tea in the White Drawing Room, where the guests presented their lavish array of christening presents. Queen Mary's gift seems (no doubt as intended) to have stolen the show: 'I gave the baby a silver gilt cup and cover which George III had given to a godson in 1780, so that I gave a present from my great-grandfather to my great-grandson 168 years later.'[10]

The Archbishop of Canterbury, Dr Geoffrey Fisher, officiated, assisted by the Precentor of the Chapels Royal. The golden Lily Font, designed by Prince Albert for the christening of his and Victoria's children, had been brought up from Windsor for the occasion. By Dr Fisher's account, the infant prince, dressed in a robe of Honiton lace and white silk, again used by all Victoria's children, remained 'as quiet as a mouse' as he was bathed in water

*They remedied the matter in 1960 by naming their second son Andrew Albert Christian Edward.

specially brought from the River Jordan. Apart from his aunt and grandparents, the King and Queen, Charles's godparents were the Queen's brother, David Bowes-Lyon; the King of Norway; the Duke of Edinburgh's grandmother, the Dowager Marchioness of Milford Haven; his uncle, Prince George of Greece; and his cousin, Earl Mountbatten's elder daughter, Lady Brabourne.

Thus Prince Charles of Edinburgh formally entered the Protestant Church of England, of which he was destined one day to become Supreme Governor, and with which he would be drawn into a series of uncomfortable conflicts in middle age. At the same time, as a newborn, post-war 'baby boomer', he was duly allotted his state ration card and milk allowance.

The new Prince Charles's first few years were to be acted out against two dark and dismal backdrops, which were to make a lasting impression on his psyche: the constant absence of his parents, and the worsening health of his grandfather, the King. The boy's first Christmas and New Year, for instance, six weeks after his birth, were the last for several years he would spend with both his parents at his side. It was the first, and hardest, lesson in learning that he had not been born as other boys.

Before Charles's birth, Elizabeth had said, 'I'm going to be the child's mother, not the nurses.' Even before she became Queen, however, Charles's mother was always wife first, mother second. The midwife's work complete, she was replaced in the nursery by two Scottish-born nurses, Helen Lightbody and Mabel Anderson. Miss Lightbody had been recommended to the princess by her aunt, the Duchess of Gloucester, whose two sons she had brought up; as the senior of the two Palace nurses, she was given what was then quaintly considered the courtesy title of 'Mrs'. Miss Anderson, the daughter of a policeman killed in the Liverpool blitz, had placed an advertisement in the situations wanted column of a nursing magazine, only to find herself summoned to Buckingham Palace for an interview with the princess. In time she was to find herself in charge of Anne, Andrew and Edward as well, and later of Anne's own children, Peter and Zara.

Five days after the christening, Dr Jacob Snowman of Hampstead, London, then in his eighties, visited the Palace to circumcise the baby. On his doctor's advice, the King had cancelled a projected Commonwealth tour of Australia, New Zealand and

Canada. Christmas, most unusually, was spent in London, also on medical orders. By January, however, the King was sufficiently recovered to lead a family shooting expedition to Sandringham, so Miss Lightbody found herself back in familiar territory, having spent hours in the country nursery with Charles's cousins, the princes William and Richard of Gloucester. For three weeks she was in sole charge of Charles as his mother succumbed to a bout of measles.

By March the family was back in London, and the princess was able to resume her round of engagements. For her father, however, the prognosis was more dispiriting. Since the November diagnosis he had led the life of a virtual invalid; his doctors now advised that he must continue to do so, or face an immediate operation to ease blood constriction in his right leg. George chose the operation, which was performed in the Buhl Room on 12 March and which proved so successful that two weeks later he was able to preside at a meeting of the Privy Council, and by May he was back on a full schedule of public duties. But he and his wife, if not their daughters, now realized that he could not have long to live.

By July, when her father seemed in much better spirits after a week's rest at Balmoral, Princess Elizabeth was at last able to move out of Buckingham Palace with her husband and child and into their first family home. The renovation of Clarence House, a few hundred yards away down the Mall, had dragged on much longer than expected, and it was a great relief to leave the draughty vastness of the Palace for a more compact, centrally heated home with all mod cons. The former home of the Duke of Clarence, before his accession as William IV in 1830, the house had been used as Red Cross offices during the war. Now it boasted a chintz-curtained nursery, with white walls and blue-for-a-boy mouldings, which looked out across its own walled and private garden over the Mall to St James's Park, around which the two nurses could wheel the infant prince with little fear of recognition, or, in that era of respectful restraint, much press intrusion.

Though the infant prince's daily routine has been described in meticulous detail, it comes down to an unsurprising round of playpens, teddy bears, torn-up books and regally soiled nappies. One of its few distinguishing features was that enormous pram, which would sometimes be wheeled to nearby Marlborough House, where visits to Queen Mary (whom he called 'Gan-Gan', as

Edward VIII had called Queen Victoria) provide another of Charles's earliest memories. He has a vivid picture of the dignified old lady sitting bolt upright, her legs culminating on a footstool, surrounded by the array of precious objects which formed her famous collection (much of it filched from subjects too timid to say no). Whereas the previous generation of royal infants, even Elizabeth and Margaret, had never been allowed to go near the jade, the silver and the crystal in their splendid display cabinets, Charles was allowed to play around with whatever priceless object took his fancy. Since her grand-daughters' infancy, the *grande dame* of Windsor had lived through the deaths of her husband and two sons, and had seen another abandon the throne for an American divorcee. Now another son, she knew, lay dying. In the child by her footstool lay all her hopes for the dynasty of which she was undisputed matriarch.

Only for the first year of Charles's life was his mother spared most royal duties, while his father was based at the Admiralty in London rather than on active naval service. By his first birthday in November 1949, however, the normal working life of what the King called 'the family firm' had been resumed. Charles's father was away in Malta, where his mother flew to join him less than a week after their son's birthday. Both his parents were also away for Christmas, which Charles spent with the King and Queen at Sandringham. Over six weeks away from her infant son, Elizabeth missed out on his first steps and his first teeth. His first word was not 'Mama' but 'Nana', as in the person closest to him, his nanny. It was a depressing portent of what was to come: the most solitary of childhoods, deprived of a large degree of the parental love and warmth that most children enjoy, to the lasting benefit of their sense of self and security.

Even when Elizabeth returned to London at the end of December 1949, she seemed in no particular hurry to see her year-old son. Just as the long separation had not caused her 'any obvious consternation', in the words of the best of her biographers, nor did she 'find it necessary to rush back to him' as soon as she returned home. Instead, she spent four days at Clarence House, apparently 'attending to engagements' and 'dealing with correspondence' before going to the races to watch a horse she owned jointly with her mother. 'Only then was she reunited with her son, who had been staying with her parents at Sandringham.'[11]

For another six months, Charles's parents kept to themselves a new family secret: that during her wedding-anniversary visit to her husband in Malta, spent at the Mountbattens' Villa Guardamangia, Elizabeth had conceived her second child. Charles was one year and nine months old when his sister arrived the following summer, on 15 August 1950. Photographs of the period show the signs of bewilderment on the face of a young boy no longer the centre of his parents' intermittent attention. Charles's young world was already, as it was to remain throughout his childhood, a world much more of adults than of children his own age; and it may not have been merely wishful thinking on his parents' part that credited him with 'a most watchful, protective interest' in his sister from the first.

With two children installed, and their parents' lives again busy and public, the royal nursery settled into a rigid daily regime in the care of the two nannies, 'Mrs' Lightbody and Miss Anderson. Charles and Anne were got up each day at 7 a.m. sharp, dressed, fed and played with in the nursery until nine, when they enjoyed a statutory half-hour with their mother. They rarely saw her again until teatime, when Elizabeth would try to clear two hours in her day. She liked to bath the children herself whenever her schedule permitted, after which they were often dressed up again to be introduced to distinguished visitors. Even before his third birthday, Charles had learned to bow before offering his cheek for a kiss from 'Gan-Gan', Queen Mary, and not to sit down unbidden in the presence of his grandfather. It was a formidable introduction to the complexities of any child's life – basking but sporadically, and unpredictably, in the attentions of his mother, with his father all but a stranger.

Already a pattern was being set that would come to haunt Charles's life even in adulthood, even at times of his greatest need. Neither of his parents saw any great problem or indeed emotional wrench in leaving him to the care of his nannies for the majority of the time. Philip assumed there was little he could contribute at this stage of his son's life; that would come later. Elizabeth, meanwhile, was merely raising her child the way she herself had been brought up by her own parents: putting duty first, withholding physical affection as somehow demeaning, and trusting in the servants.

Given the values of the age, and her class, she knew no better. But it would deprive Charles of the intimacy with his parents on which most children are able to rely, not just in childhood but throughout life. Even in adulthood Charles would communicate with both his parents largely by letter or internal Palace memo; few topics of any substance were felt appropriate for discussion face to face, in the family context. The coldness and distance in Charles's lifelong relations with his parents were sown at this tender age, when he was far too young to grasp what was happening – thus preventing him at a maturer age, when most men can finally work such things out, from understanding or appreciating the lasting effect upon him.

Charles's third Christmas, in 1950, saw his father still stationed in Malta, now with his own naval command. His mother chose to spend the holiday alone with her husband, again leaving her children behind in the care of their grandparents at Sandringham. Even their attention, however, was frequently denied Charles. The young prince enjoyed an early and somewhat brutal experience of constitutional monarchy that Christmas, when the Lord President of the Council, Herbert Morrison, shut the door of a Privy Council meeting in his face. 'Sorry, young fellow-me-lad,' said Morrison, 'but I'm afraid you can't go in there. We've got a meeting with your grandfather and it's very, very secret.'[12]

Charles was visibly happier when the domestic routine settled back to comparative normality at Clarence House that spring. And so might what passed for family life have continued for another ten or fifteen years, before being further blighted by the burden of monarchy. But the King's health was growing worse. His wife and daughter now knew, though as yet he did not, that he had cancer. By July, an increase in the young couple's royal duties on the monarch's behalf forced Philip to give up his one brief naval command. In October, their departure delayed for two weeks by another operation on the King, Charles's parents left for a tour of North America and Canada. Included in Princess Elizabeth's luggage was a sealed envelope of documents, which she would have to sign if her father died during her absence.

So Charles's parents now missed his third birthday, which was spent with his grandparents and Aunt Margaret at Buckingham Palace. On their return the King made the Duke and Duchess of Edinburgh members of the Privy Council. It was all by way of momentous preparation, which to Charles only meant another

Christmas spoilt by the news that his parents would soon be off travelling again. At the time of his birth, his grandfather's health had forced him to cancel a Commonwealth tour; by Christmas 1950 it had been rescheduled for early 1952. Now, because of the King's increasingly rapid decline, it was to be undertaken by his daughter and her husband. The pictures of George VI waving them off at London airport, a frail and shadowy figure seemingly buffeted by the breeze, were a shock to his affectionate subjects.

On 6 February 1952, at Treetops, a hunting lodge overlooking the Sagana River in Kenya, Charles's mother learnt that overnight she had become Queen. Monarch at twenty-five, Elizabeth that day lost what little there was of her restricted freedom and family life. Her father was dead at only fifty-six – fourteen years younger than his own father, George V, and, as it was to prove, twenty-two years younger than his brother, Edward VIII – though both were equally heavy smokers. Less prepared for accession than on her last tour, Elizabeth left for the urgent flight home in a brightly patterned dress and hat. As she said goodbye to the servants at the door of the lodge, her chauffeur knelt on all fours to kiss her shoes.

Heir apparent at three years old, Prince Charles was not yet Prince of Wales, but already Duke of Cornwall, Duke of Rothesay, Earl of Carrick and Baron of Renfrew, Lord of the Isles and Great Steward of Scotland. 'That's me, Mummy,' he was heard to whisper when the Duke of Cornwall's name was mentioned in church among the prayers for the royal family. But, from his point of view, little else had changed. He was scarcely aware that flags would now fly throughout the land on his birthday. His daily routine was much the same, apart from the absence of his grandfather, from whose funeral rites he was carefully excluded, though he had been staying with him at Sandringham on the night he had abruptly 'disappeared'.

Soon after Easter 1952, a subdued holiday with the court still in mourning, Charles was confronted with the first outward sign of change in his family life. His grandmother and aunt moved into Clarence House, the family home refurbished only two years earlier for him and his parents, who in turn moved back into Buckingham Palace. The second-floor nursery suite had been carefully redecorated to seem as much like the Clarence House nursery as possible. There was his box of toy soldiers, his cuckoo clock, his ten-foot-high mock-Tudor doll's house, his toy cupboard, and he had a new, full-sized bed, made for him by students of the Royal College of Art. But his mother's study on the floor below was now declared out of bounds.

Passing it one day, Charles urged his mother to come and play. 'If only I could,' said the Queen, gently closing the door against him. As the months went by, this was not the only reason he had to think his childhood different from that of other boys. When he joined his family on the Palace balcony, or at the Trooping the Colour, Charles's eyes were those of an excited member of the crowd, watching the colourful displays. What puzzled him was that some people seemed to prefer to look at him.

As far as they knew how, his parents tried to mitigate the potential corruptions of privilege. All the Palace staff, at the Queen's insistence, called the prince simply 'Charles' (as indeed they did until his eighteenth birthday). When he misbehaved he was duly punished, the palm being administered to the royal hindquarters as much by his nannies as by his father. Philip once spanked him for sticking his tongue out at the crowd watching him drive down the Mall. In such painful ways did Charles begin to learn about the accident of his birth.

Nor was he allowed to take deference for granted. When the prince omitted to call his detective 'Mister', simply using his surname, as he heard his mother and father do all the time, he was told to apologize. When he slipped an ice-cube down a footman's back he was punished. When he left a door open and a footman rushed to shut it, Philip stopped the servant, saying, 'Leave it alone, man. The boy's got hands.' His father also found Charles pelting a Sandringham policeman with snowballs, while the hapless officer silently took his punishment, unsure whether to reply in kind. 'Don't just stand there,' shouted Philip, 'throw some back!' It was also at Sandringham that the Queen once sent Charles back out of the house, not to return until he had found a dog lead he had lost in the grounds, with the memorable royal rebuke, 'Dog leads cost money.'

Such was the pattern throughout his childhood. But in the later months of 1952, as he began to master the rudiments of the Queen's English, Charles began, almost by accident, to discover the meaning of the lavish home life he otherwise took for granted. No longer could he ride around London in the back of the family car with his father at the wheel. These popular excursions had suddenly stopped, and now, aged three, he had his own car and chauffeur. He also had his own footman, an eighteen-year-old Palace servant called Richard Brown (whom he once 'knighted' with his knife when Brown stooped to pick up some food Charles had dropped). 'Why haven't you got a Richard?' Charles asked when visiting the home of another well-born boy his own age. His friend didn't have a Mr Kelly, either – Sergeant Kelly, to be precise, Charles's newly assigned private detective, the first in a long line who would shadow him for the rest of his life. It was thanks to Kelly that Charles soon had another change of routine: he could no longer go for walks through Green Park and St James's Park, across the road from his home.

Part of growing up, as Charles's character began to emerge, was to develop some sort of working relationship with his sister. The Queen, looking back, is emphatic that all four of her children showed very different personalities at the earliest ages, and it was already clear that Charles and Anne were totally unalike. Charles was much more like his father in appearance, already aping some of Philip's public mannerisms: the hands behind the back, the erect bearing, the habit of looking an interlocutor fixedly in the eye, often causing a certain unease. Anne was much more like her father in character: extrovert, self-confident to a fault, occasionally temperamental. Charles took after his mother, who in turn took after her father: instinctively shy and retiring, yet overcoming it with an effort of will, which in time sowed the seeds of a driving sense of duty.

The solemnity of Charles's face in some early photographs, contrasting with the mischievousness of Anne's, is that of the shy, not of the humourless, child. It was Anne, the crowds in the Mall noticed, who waved confidently, after the fashion of her mother, long before her older brother could summon the confidence to do the same. It was Charles, by contrast, who kept reminding his sister, often in vain, that she must curtsey when entering their grandmother's drawing room. It was Charles who pulled Anne along the platform to say thank you to the engine driver when the royal train delivered them to Sandringham. But it was Anne who first discovered, and duly exploited, the wonderful Palace game discovered by her aunt and mother before her: if you walked past a sentry, he would make a satisfying clatter coming to attention and presenting arms. To walk back and forth past a sentry box provided hours of childish entertainment (to the chagrin of the long-suffering guards on duty). When he discovered that he, too, was one of the privileged few who could produce this startling effect, Charles steered clear of sentry boxes. As yet, he found it embarrassing.

The prince's fourth birthday was the first his father ever spent with him. Preparations were already under way for the Queen's coronation the following June. Ancient ritual called for the Duke of Cornwall, as senior royal duke and head of the peerage, to take an oath of allegiance to the new monarch; but it was the first time in British history, at least since the creation of the dukedom in 1337, that a sovereign with so young an heir was to be crowned. With his mother reluctant to put Charles through such an ordeal, he instead watched with his grandmother from a gallery of the Abbey. That afternoon, when his parents returned home after a triumphant progress through London, they led their son onto the balcony of Buckingham Palace, to a wave of renewed cheering. It was Charles's first experience of mass adulation, which might be thought to have turned the head of a four-year-old child. But scarcely anything of that day has lodged vividly in his memory.

For the bewildered young boy, all the coronation really meant was that his parents would soon be going away again – this time, for longer than ever. For a few months his mother's presence was interrupted only by trips around the country to show herself to her new subjects. But in late November, soon after Charles's fifth birthday, she and Philip were again to undertake that interrupted Commonwealth tour, this time in their own right. They would be away for six months.

The coronation had led to the first full flush of publicity about the royal children, which their mother decided was not in their best interests. Charles and Anne had never been allowed to see many of the newspapers that carried their photographs; now the Queen began to impose further restrictions, for her children's own good. In late June, following an absurd number of requests for his presence, the Palace officially announced that Prince Charles, still only four, would not yet be undertaking any official engagements. By way of confirmation, the Queen cancelled plans for the youngest member of the Duke of Cornwall's Light Infantry to present him with a set of model soldiers to mark the regiment's 250th anniversary.

No more photographs of the royal children were issued for several months. There had been criticism that they were already becoming overexposed to the public's unremitting interest; the *Daily Express* calculated that in the twenty-three weeks of 1953 up to June, it alone had published fifty pages of royal pictures, (suggesting, *en passant*, that today's tabloid obsession with the royal family, especially its younger members, is nothing new).[13] Nor was there any special celebration of Charles's fifth birthday that November. His parents stayed away at Sandringham, finalizing their plans for the tour, while the crestfallen boy spent the day at Windsor with his grandmother and Aunt Margaret.

A week later – once the Queen had ordered some toys from Harrods, to be stored away for her son's Christmas presents – came the moment of parting. Charles wept copiously; but as much as he disliked these separations, he was already aware of the need for them. 'Mummy has an important job to do,' he told a friend who asked where she was. 'She's down here.' He pointed out Australia on the globe that had been newly installed in the nursery, on which he followed his parents' progress around the world. His nannies testified that he felt his mother's absence very keenly. Upon their reunion aboard the royal yacht at Tobruk, it was only with difficulty that Charles was restrained from joining the line of dignitaries waiting to shake hands with the Queen as she was piped aboard. 'No, not you, dear,' were his mother's first words to her son after six months apart.[14]

After this latest prolonged separation, the young prince seemed to his mother to have grown up almost beyond recognition. For a five-year-old he was still very shy, woefully unsure of himself and almost impossibly serious. As they sailed home, the Queen decided it was time for her son's education to begin in earnest.

CHAPTER THREE

'A THOROUGHLY AVERAGE PUPIL'

'FROM HIS CHILDHOOD THIS BOY WILL BE SURROUNDED BY SYCOPHANTS and flatterers by the score, and will be taught to believe himself as a superior creation.'[1] The words of the Labour leader James Keir Hardie, on the birth of the future King Edward VIII in 1894, have echoed with equal resonance through the life of the next Prince of Wales.

Even as a child, Charles was insulated from life's verities by the in-built deference of life at court, to the point where his distaste for his schooldays can be seen as that of a superior being compelled to fend for himself amid the lower orders. As an adult, his many qualities have always been tempered by unseemly expectations of those around him, eminent or menial, who displease him at their peril. No-one, in short, can be considered his equal. In middle age, Charles's central, and somewhat surprising, flaw is that he has come to take his unearned station in life as his due, permitting the ex officio respect he requires to override normal, civilized human values. In this respect, as in so many others, his troubles stem from a conscious, almost wilful, failure to adapt to changing times.

As a child, still comparatively unspoilt, he seems to have been rather charming. The main force in shaping his young character, and thus those emergent values, was much less his mother than his father. If this seems ironic in hindsight, as Charles has embraced spiritual values so alien to the less reflective Philip, it is due partly to a hereditary stubborn streak, partly to his father's crude attempts to stiffen the spine of a young son who seemed to him distinctly unmanly. Even as a small child, Charles already appeared to his father to lack his sister Anne's 'panache'; the boy was 'soft', and needed toughening up.[2] Boarding school might do the trick – preferably, to Philip, the same ones he himself had attended – after a brief induction at a local day school.

On his fifth birthday, in the November following his mother's coronation, Charles had reached the age at which English law requires every child to begin a formal education. Although his parents had already discussed altering the traditional patterns of royal tutelage – strictly in private, behind Palace walls – their plans as yet remained secret. Philip was not alone in worrying about his son's gentle, rather repressed nature. Even to his mother Charles did not seem ready to be sent to school with other children, let alone, as some Labour Members of Parliament were demanding, to the nearest state primary school. For a five-year-old, the rather plump little boy was socially mature, as was only to be expected of one living in a world of formal adult behaviour. But he did not seem particularly bright.

He could write his own name, in carefully etched capital letters; he could count to a hundred; and he could tell the time. But he could scarcely read at all, despite hours of enjoyment being read – and committing to memory – the works of Beatrix Potter, A. A. Milne and the *Babar the Elephant* books. The prince liked his dancing classes, for which a mixed group of young aristocrats joined him at the Palace each week, and his riding lessons at Windsor, though he was already displaying less enthusiasm than his sister. He attended a London gym class and had started piano lessons, showing promise of some musical aptitude. But, as yet, the only formal instruction Charles had received for the arduous royal years ahead was to be made to stand still for long periods of time.

Before leaving for her Commonwealth tour, the Queen had engaged a governess for her son – a spry Scotswoman in her mid-forties named Catherine Peebles. Though Miss Peebles had previously had charge of the widowed Duchess of Kent's two younger children, Princess Alexandra and Prince Michael, she had no formal training, no degree and no revolutionary ideas on the upbringing of children. It was enough for the Queen to have noticed in 'Mispy' a mixture of common sense and strictness that echoed her own instincts. The one rule Charles's mother imposed on her son's governess, knowing the child's in-built uncertainty of himself, was 'No forcing'.

The Queen had considered inviting other children to join Charles's classes, but decided that his temperament urged against it. If the boy's world so far had been one of adults, it had also been one of female adults, and distinctly genteel ones at that. Apart from his father, who was so often away, Charles had spent most of his time with the Queen, the Queen Mother, Princess Margaret, his two nurses and his sister. The difficulty of establishing normal dealings with other children just now might distract him. It was decided that Charles would, for the present, take his lessons alone. Even Anne was forbidden to disturb her brother's mornings with Miss Peebles in the Palace schoolroom, where a desk and a blackboard had now joined the more familiar globe. When the time came for 'Mispy' to teach Charles's three young siblings, other children did join the classes. Looking back, the Queen felt sure she judged the difference in Charles correctly.

Miss Peebles now became one of the select few to receive a copy of the Queen's daily engagement card. Each morning at nine o'clock, when possible, Charles still spent half an hour with his mother. Then the day's instruction began, lasting initially until eleven-thirty; noon when he was a little older. Miss Peebles confirmed the Queen's own concern that Charles's unnatural start in life had rendered him a nervous, highly strung child of unpredictable sensitivity. 'If you raised your voice to him, he would draw back into his shell, and for a time you would be able to do nothing with him.' His nurse, Mabel Anderson, agreed: 'He was never as boisterous or noisy as Princess Anne. She had a much stronger, more extrovert personality. She didn't exactly push him aside, but she was certainly a more forceful child.' Anne could always find some way to amuse herself, while Charles always needed to be entertained. She was also better with her hands; Charles, as yet, was 'all fingers and thumbs'.[3]

Charles's shy, almost timorous nature was due in part to his growing awareness of his position. He knew how he was expected to behave, if not yet exactly why. When he visited a friend's farm, it was noticed that he took a polite interest in everything to be seen – almost as if he were on a royal visit – rather than showing a child's quick and selective enthusiasms. At times the spectacle of a little boy so aware of proprieties became almost pathetic: when encouraging his corgi or another of his many pets to perform their tricks, he would always add a most polite 'please'.

On a rewards-for-effort system, Miss Peebles began to draw out the boy's special interests. After beginning each day with a Bible story, Charles was allowed to indulge his fondness for painting. Geography was another natural source of fascination; thanks to the globe on which Charles followed his parents' travels, he was soon able to tell visiting ambassadors the whereabouts of their country. History was more of a problem, when trying to educate a potential king to think of himself as a normal child. But the canny Miss Peebles developed a course she called 'Children in History', in which great figures were traced right back to their origins, whether regal or humble. The only subject that completely baffled Charles, as it has done ever since, was maths.

The afternoons were taken up with educational excursions: down the Mall to the shipping offices in Cockspur Street, for a talk from Miss Peebles on the trade routes; up Highgate Hill to trace the steps of Dick Whittington and his cat before a visit to the pantomime; to the Tower, to be shown round by the Beefeaters; to St George's Chapel, Windsor, to see Winston Churchill installed as a Knight of the Garter; to Madame Tussaud's, to laugh at the wax effigies of himself and his parents.

In that first year Charles quickly learnt to read, but he still had some difficulty with his writing. After Christmas 1955 – celebrated with a party for forty children at the Palace, and a visit to Harrods to ask Father Christmas for a bicycle – he began to learn French. The afternoon excursions became overtly instructive, with visits to the various London museums. But by now the press had caught on to the routine, and the outings had to be abandoned for a straight-forward nature walk through Richmond Park. Even they, in time, became uncomfortable obstacle courses.

The Queen began to doubt whether it was possible for her son to enjoy anything approaching a normal education. If the press would not allow him to visit the British Museum in peace, what chance of privacy would he have at a 'normal' school? And would his presence disturb the education of the other children? Her plans seemed in danger, but she was determined not to abandon them lightly. On 11 April 1955 her press secretary, Richard Colville, sent the first in what was to prove a long series of such messages to British newspaper editors:

I am commanded by the Queen to say that Her Majesty and the Duke of Edinburgh have decided that their son has reached the stage when he should take part in more grown-up education pursuits with other children. In consequence, a certain amount of the Duke of Cornwall's instruction will take place outside his home; for example, he will visit museums and other places of interest. The Queen trusts, therefore, that His Royal Highness will be able to enjoy this in the same way as other children, without the embarrassment of constant publicity. In this respect, Her Majesty feels it is equally important that those in charge of, or sharing in, the instruction should be spared undue publicity, which can so seriously interrupt their normal lives. [4]

The request caused a lull, albeit temporary, in press attention. Charles and 'Mispy' remained unmolested when they visited London Zoo and the Planetarium; the boy was soon an expert in recognizing constellations, proof to his mother that, like her, he was 'at heart a country person'. They even managed a ride on the underground, the prince passing unrecognized as the son of inconspicuous parents (Miss Peebles and Sergeant Kelly). Extracurricular activities now included charades, field sports, more riding and Charles's first games of cricket and soccer – neither of which, though the national sports of his future subjects, was to prove an abiding enthusiasm. Team sports, apart from polo, have never much appealed to him. It is striking that even at so young an age, he took with much more passion to the solitary pursuit of flyfishing, under the guidance of one of the Balmoral stalkers. His father also began to teach him boxing, but reluctantly, and with some irritation, abandoned the idea after a chorus of public protest.

By the autumn of 1956 the Queen was sufficiently pleased with Charles's progress to take the next major step she had in mind. In October, soon after the start of the school term, Colonel Henry Townend, founder and headmaster of a smart London day school for boys, was pleasantly surprised to find himself invited to tea with Her Majesty at Buckingham Palace. Hill House, the Colonel's small establishment in Hans Place, just behind Knightsbridge (conveniently near the Palace), had been recommended to Charles's parents by friends and acquaintances who had sent their own sons there. One Hill House mother had particularly pleased the Queen by informing her that it was the only school in London outside which the pavement was washed and the railings dusted every day. The school's rather spartan manifesto – very much that of Charles's father – was trumpeted on the busy noticeboard beside its front steps, open for inspection to any casual passer-by:

> A sense of rivalry has to be encouraged and a boy must be led to discover something in which he can excel. He must be trained to react quickly in an emergency, have a good sense of balance and control, have the strength and ability to extract himself from a dangerous situation, and the urge to win.

Though naturally flattered when the Queen asked him to accept her son as a pupil, Colonel Townend was alarmed by the daunting double responsibility, both to the heir to the throne and to his other pupils. It was mutually agreed that, for the present, Charles would join the other boys only for their afternoon recreation. Lessons with 'Mispy' continued in the mornings; Charles would then don his school uniform and be taken to Hill House to join the crocodile along the King's Road into Chelsea. School games were played in the grounds of the Duke of York's Headquarters, the military depot named after that very duke who marched his men to the top of the hill and marched them down again. Newspaper editors, of course, also marched their men towards the playing fields, once the prince's new afternoon schedule was discovered. But one picture of Charles playing soccer looked much like another, especially as he didn't join in with much enthusiasm, and the novelty soon wore off.

As his mother and headmaster had hoped, Charles soon merged into the crowd of schoolboys walking in line down the street, recognizable only when politely raising his school cap to passers-by. His eighth birthday passed unremarked; it was not as if he were yet a fully fledged schoolboy. That, amid tight security, was being planned for the New Year.

Christmas, which again saw his father abroad on official duties, also marked the end of Catherine Peebles's supervision of Prince Charles. Although 'Mispy' would stay at the Palace to take charge of Princess Anne, Charles was to miss her sorely. With the retirement not long after of Helen Lightbody – Miss Anderson also stayed on to look after Anne – he was suddenly deprived of the two main guardians of his childhood, with whom he had spent considerably more time than with his parents. As he moved into a suite of his own in the Palace, Charles kept in close touch with both, but the shock of their departure renewed his sense of isolation. The approach of that first day at school with other children, away from the security of home, is difficult enough for any child, most of whom face it at the age of five. For eight-year-old Charles the prospect became positively awesome. Although his parents had striven to prepare him for it, the young prince was simply not equipped to be wrenched from his sheltered environment.

For all his parents' good intentions, by no stretch of the imagination was Prince Charles an ordinary child. He had grown up in palaces and castles. Ships and soldiers, objects of fantasy to other boys of his age, were to Charles everyday realities. British history was the story of his own family. He had seen his parents, often himself, treated with awe and reverence even by the high and mighty. People became nervous and ill at ease in their presence. At the ring of a bell, his nanny – and he had no reason to suppose that all children didn't have nannies – would drop whatever was happening and take him to see his mother. At the age of four he had been named one of the world's Top Ten Best-dressed Men, alongside Marshals Tito and Bulganin, Adlai Stevenson, Billy Graham, Fred Astaire and Charlie Chaplin.

The prince had never handled money; when occasionally he saw some, this supposedly potent substance turned out to be pieces of paper, or lumps of metal, bearing a picture of his mother. He had never been shopping. He had never been on a bus. He had never got lost in a crowd. He had never had to fend for himself.

Nevertheless, on 28 January 1957 Charles made royal history by becoming the first heir to the British throne ever to go to school. At 9.15 a.m. a black Ford Zephyr driven by a Palace chauffeur, with Charles and his governess (not his mother) in the back, pulled up at the school entrance, where Colonel Townend was waiting to greet him. In the school uniform of cinnamon-coloured jersey and corduroy trousers, Charles ran up to the man he had previously known as a football referee. Inside he hung up his coat – distinctive for the velvet collar so admired in his Best-dressed Man citation – and plunged with stiff upper lip into the morning's routine.

The new boy was number 102 on the school roll of 120, the sons of well-to-do professional men, lawyers, doctors, military men and politicians. One fellow pupil was the grandson of the new prime minister, Harold Macmillan. There were a number of foreign children, the sons of diplomats stationed in London; the school, which boasted a sibling establishment in Switzerland, aspired to share its places equally between English and non-English pupils. Hill House was a school for privileged children, still young and self-interested enough not to be too much in awe of the prince. The headmaster had warned them to make no special fuss of the familiar new face in their midst, who would be required like everyone else to wash up and sweep the classroom floor; but their upbringing had anyway taught them otherwise. Charles's new peers were more than equipped to take his arrival in their stride.

Opened only five years before, Hill House very much reflected the personal philosophy of Colonel Townend, a former Gunners officer in his late forties who had been an Oxford football blue and England athlete. There was no corporal punishment, and the predominately female staff taught a syllabus broad by pre-preparatory school standards. It even included elementary anatomy lessons from Townend's wife, Beatrice, a state-registered nurse, who had once been theatre sister to Sir John Weir, an assistant at the prince's birth. The doors were equipped with automatic devices to prevent trapped fingers, all the furniture had rounded edges and the school motto was taken from Plutarch: 'A boy's mind is not a vessel to be filled, but a fire to be kindled.'

It had been decided that the new boy would be 'Prince Charles' to the staff, but plain 'Charles' to his fellow pupils in Form Six of Middle School. Given no special escort that first morning, but left to make his own way, he decided that the highlight was a visit to the school 'madhouse' – a gymnasium with padded walls – for a game of basketball. After a lunch of boiled beef and carrots followed by apple pie, he painted a picture of Tower Bridge and signed it Charles. At three-thirty it was time to go home, and the chauffeur-driven Zephyr was waiting at the door. As Charles told his mother all about it, she felt a great sense of relief. The experiment, it seemed, was going to work.

Next morning, however, the crowd outside Hill House was so enormous that she hesitated to let him go. It wasn't just that the press had set up a constant vigil; local residents who had read of the new recruit in their morning papers were all but choking the street. After telephone consultations with Townend the Queen relented, and Charles arrived at school thirty-five minutes late. He had to run the gauntlet of sightseers and photographers to get inside. It was the same when he left, and again the next morning. Already it was clear to both the headmaster and the royal parents that this could not go on. Unless the newshounds and thus the gawpers could be moved on, the monarchy's bold experiment in liberal education would have to be called off.

The Queen kept her son at home while her press secretary again went into action. A detective reported back to him with the identities of all the journalists waiting outside the school, and their stated intention to wait all day. Colville then telephoned each of the newspaper editors involved, reminding them of the Queen's plea of eighteen months before. Within an hour Fleet Street had recalled its hounds and Charles was able to get on with his education.

Before long he had settled into everyday school routine more smoothly than those watching over him had reason to hope. Swimming and wrestling – which took the place of boxing at Hill House – became his favourite pastimes, and he continued to show promise with watercolours. In the classroom he remained something of a plodder, which worried nobody. The purpose of sending Charles to school was not to sow the seeds of a giant intellect, but to help him meet people his own age and learn to live among them. His parents would be more than happy with merely 'ordinary' progress.

His end-of-term report was certainly ordinary. Hill House made a practice of not sending exam results to parents; they were posted on the board and could be viewed by those who wished. The royal parents refrained, but it is the unenviable fate of princes to have their school reports preserved for posterity. Apart from arithmetic, where the verdict was still 'below form average, careful but slow, not very keen', Charles's report for the Lent term of 1957 contained its standard quota of 'fair', 'good', 'shows keen interest' and 'made a fair start'.[5] Hidden behind the vernacular of the schoolteacher, anxious not to cause too much trouble at home, was what appeared to be a reassuringly average start.

The summer term began, like the first, with an attack of tonsillitis, but this time the tonsils lost. After their removal in the Buhl Room at the Palace by James Crooks of Great Ormond Street Hospital for Sick Children, Charles insisted on keeping them in a jar on his bedroom mantelpiece. By the end of term, despite further absences through illness, the assessment remained much the same: determined but slow. Charles was, perhaps generously at that stage, credited with 'above-average intelligence', and showed continuing signs of a creative bent scarcely evident in either of his parents.

By August he was enjoying his first yacht racing at Cowes, though seasickness made his first outing in his father's yacht, *Bluebottle*, something of an ordeal. Once he got over it, however, he shared Prince Philip's exhilaration at the closeness to sea and wind – and the distance from the press. Earlier that summer his father had stumped up ten shillings (50p) after betting Charles that he couldn't swim two lengths of the Palace pool; later that summer he ticked him off, in front of a crowd of 20,000 people, for fidgeting at the Highland Games at Braemar. The prince was wearing his first kilt, of Balmoral tartan – to the Scots a sure sign that he was growing up. The nation received another sign of his maturity that summer, with the announcement that HRH Prince Charles of Edinburgh was soon to be sent away to board at a preparatory school.

Well aware that she herself had met few beyond the Palace walls before the age of eighteen, when she had persuaded her father to let her sign on as a second subaltern in the wartime ATS, the Queen was conscious of the disadvantages of sequestering her son at home. But she and her husband had equal evidence that it was no use expecting him to blend inconspicuously into the life of a boarding school, like any other child. Simpering royal commentators were already cooing that Charles and Anne were 'ordinary' children being brought up in a 'normal' way; but it was now obvious, even to their parents, that this was impossible.

'The Queen and I', said Philip, during a visit to the USA in 1956, 'want Charles to go to school with other boys of his generation and learn to live with other children, to absorb from childhood the discipline imposed by education with others.' The royal couple had already been making a series of visits, private and public, to British boys' schools, and had entertained a number of headmasters socially at Buckingham Palace. But Philip's announcement brought forth a predictable shower of advice.

In the forefront was the writer Lord Altrincham, whose attack on the monarchy in the August 1957 edition of his journal, the

National and English Review, earned him a televised slap in the face, excrement through his letterbox and lasting public obloquy. His title, which he later disclaimed, to revert to plain John Grigg, became synonymous with sedition; but it is now forgotten that Altrincham wrote as an ardent monarchist, protesting that he made his loyal criticisms in the Queen's own interests. There were few who bore this in increasingly apoplectic mind as they read how the monarchy had 'lamentably failed to live with the times', and that the court, unlike the society it was supposed to reflect, remained 'a tight little enclave of English ladies and gentlemen'.

The Queen's decision that her son would go to a private 'prep' school was another topic to which Altrincham addressed himself:

> Will she have the wisdom to give her children an education very different from her own? Will she, above all, see to it that Prince Charles is equipped with all the knowledge he can absorb without injury to his health, and that he mixes during his formative years with children who will one day be bus drivers, dockers, engineers etc., not merely with future landowners or stock-brokers?[6]

A minority of Labour MPs used Altrincham's strictures to renew their plea that the heir to the throne should attend a state school, to mix with the less wealthy and privileged of his future subjects as a symbolic beneficiary of the welfare state. But his parents were adamant: a boarding school, and a private one, it was to be. Charles was too young to be consulted about the choice of his first school, and had anyway made it more than clear that he was reluctant to leave home at all. Besides, his lack of self-confidence was 'so inhibiting that . . . [his] qualities were not yet easy to discern behind the carapace of diffidence and reserve with which he habitually protected himself'.[7]

The Queen and Prince Philip had looked over a number of preparatory schools, including the one Philip had himself attended. It had moved since the 1930s, and was scarcely the same place, but it seemed to provide everything they were looking for. Like many other conservative-minded British fathers, Philip found the idea of sending his son to his old school downright satisfying. He was also pleased of the chance to offer a posthumous salute to a favourite ancestor. Just before the First World War, Prince Louis of Battenberg, then First Sea Lord, had occasion to be impressed by the polished manners of two midshipmen under his command. On discovering that they were both ex-pupils of Cheam preparatory school, the Duke of Edinburgh's grandfather decreed that henceforth all male members of the Battenberg family would go there.

Cheam claims to be England's oldest prep school, founded in 1645 'for the sons of noblemen and gentry'. Its long roll of headmasters included William Gilpin, the model for the schoolmaster in Smollett's *The Adventures of Peregrine Pickle*, and one Robert Stammers Tabor, who in the mid-nineteenth century devised intriguing modes of address for the aristocratic pupils the school has always attracted: a peer was called 'my darling child', the son of a peer 'my dear child' and a commoner 'my child'.[8] Tabor would have enjoyed working out a new category for the eight-year-old pupil who joined the school on 23 September 1957: Charles, Duke of Cornwall, the first heir apparent to have been sent to a preparatory school in British history. At his mother's request the joint headmasters, Peter Beck and Mark Wheeler, continued the style established at Hill House: the new pupil would be 'Charles' to his fellow pupils and 'Prince Charles' to members of staff, whom he in turn would address normally as 'Sir'.

The school's most distinguished old boy was the new recruit's father, whose educational credo later prefaced its official history: 'Children may be indulged at home, but school is expected to be a spartan and disciplined experience in the process of developing into self-controlled, considerate and independent adults. The system may have its eccentricities, but there can be little doubt that these are far outweighed by its values.'[9] Philip's cousin, the Marquess of Milford Haven, had also been there. Among other former pupils were one prime minister, Henry Addington (later Viscount Sidmouth); one speaker of the House of Commons; two viceroys of India; Sir Iain Hamilton, military commander of the ill-fated Gallipoli expedition; Lord Dunsany, the Irish writer; and Lord Randolph Churchill, father of Sir Winston, who, according to his son, was 'most kindly treated and quite contented' at the school.[10]

Charles had already visited Cheam with his parents and his sister. 'You won't be able to jump up and down on these beds,' his mother had told him as he gazed with dismay upon the 200-year-old springless wooden frame and its unyielding hair mattress. As the royal family roamed the school grounds, the peace disturbed only by jets from the nearby US airbase, they felt reassured that Cheam's sixty-five acres should offer due insulation from the outside world of sightseers and pressmen. Its copious undergrowth, however, would also provide excellent cover for intruders, so it was decided that the young prince's detective should accompany him and live in the grounds.

Before term the headmasters had sent a letter to all parents, noting the 'great honour' Charles's parents had conferred on Cheam, while passing on their wish that there be 'no alteration in the way the school is run'. Charles was to be treated in 'exactly the same way as other boys'.[11] Again, however, it was impossible to expect Charles to merge inconspicuously into the beginning-of-term throng. As a young man, he remembered those first few days at Cheam as the most miserable of his life. His mother recalls him shaking with horror as they began the long overnight train journey from Balmoral to London, to be followed by the sixty-mile drive to Headley. On arrival, in his grey school uniform, Charles raised his blue school hat politely to Mr Beck, then watched his parents drive away. A few hours later the maths master, David Munir, who had been detailed to keep a special eye on the prince, looked out into the school grounds. One small boy, 'very much in need of a haircut', stood conspicuously apart, a solitary and utterly wretched figure.[12]

Cheam boys were that much older than Charles's fellow pupils at Hill House. Despite – perhaps because of – their parents' urgings, they simply could not accept the heir to the throne as just another of the twelve new boys. Charles himself had no experience at all of forcing his way into a group of strangers and winning the acceptance of his peers. For his first few nights at Cheam he cried himself to sleep. Like most other boys sent away to school at so tender an age, he was desperately homesick.

Cheam had 100 pupils between the ages of eight and fourteen; Charles's school number was eighty-nine. For the first time in his life he was sharing an uncarpeted room with other boys, making his own bed, cleaning his own shoes, waiting on others at table and keeping his clothes in a wicker basket under his bed (known to the boys as 'the dog basket'). The day began at 7.15 a.m. with the rising bell, followed by Matron's cleanliness inspection, prayers at

7.45 and breakfast at eight. Lessons began at nine, and continued with one break until lunch at one. There were half-holidays on Wednesdays and Saturdays, and on Sundays there was an extra half-hour in bed before the school parade to the nearby parish church of St Peter's.

Charles wrote the obligatory minimum of one letter home per week, and was always among the first to snap up his weekly half-pound allowance of sweets. Though he was losing his puppy fat, he was still a plumpish boy. When the change to the school diet prompted a few stomach upsets, he confided to his first-year teacher, Miss Margaret Cowlishaw, that he wasn't used to 'all this rich food' at home.

According to Peter Beck, Charles's unwonted need to fend for himself soon helped him become a good mixer. In fact, Charles's loneliness may have been partly in his own mind. He was already aware that other children might befriend him for the wrong reasons. It was often the nicest boys, he recalls, who hung back, not wishing to be seen to be 'sucking up' to him; those who forced their attentions on him were often those he liked least. His peers soon marked him down as a bit of a lone wolf – a description he would not himself deny. He seemed happier on his own or with just one other person rather than as part of a group. By his own account and that of others, he did not find it easy to make friends.[13]

As a schoolboy, furthermore, Charles was haunted by another shadow which has pursued him ever since: that of his father, an outgoing, gregarious man who had never had to cope with such problems. At Cheam, after all, Philip was Prince of Greece and Denmark, not of England or Wales. The press were not pursuing him from bush to bush, and the boys looked on him with no awe. While academically undistinguished, Philip had shone on the sports field – First XI goalkeeper and captain of the cricket team – and Charles knew all too well that his father was looking for similar achievements from him.

The prince's lessons at Cheam were geared to the Common Entrance exam taken before admission to most British public schools (although, as it transpired, he was to attend one that didn't require it). History remained an abiding interest, not least because he now knew that it largely concerned his ancestors, and was uneasily aware that it might be waiting to receive him. In geography he also shone, again because his parents' tours had made the globe a familiar place. Maths remained an utter mystery, closely followed by Latin and Greek. Before the afternoon lessons there were games, about which he remained unenthusiastic – despite evidence to the contrary in his end-of-term reports – or other outdoor activities, such as camping or wildlife study.

As at Hill House, the gym became one of his favourite haunts, where athletic rough-and-tumble often developed into a mild schoolboy fracas. Charles soon had a reputation for giving as good as he got. He was particularly sensitive to jokes about his plumpness, and took days to recover after hearing the boy beneath a collapsed rugby scrum cry, 'Oh, do get off, Fatty.' The school was visited regularly by a barber from Harrods, Cecil Cox, who once saw an older boy douse Charles's head under a cold tap; the visitor watched impressed as the prince filled a bath with cold water, wrestled with his assailant and finally forced him in fully clothed, only to be pulled in himself.

This was one of many Cheam anecdotes, some truer than others, which found their way into the press during Charles's first term. 'Even the school barber was in the pay of the newspapers,' snorted Prince Philip.[14] It did not help the 'normality' of Charles's education, or his standing among his peers, that all too often there had to be complex inquiries before school crimes, apparently to be laid at his door, were found to be the work of others. Within a week of his arrival, for instance, Charles's name had been carved in the back of a pew in the parish church. This was one story the papers did get hold of; with help from the Palace, Beck persuaded them to print corrections when other boys eventually admitted their guilt.

In an attempt to head off journalists' intrusions, Beck and Wheeler had held a press visit to the school before term began and made a special plea to be left in peace thereafter. But of the eighty-eight days of term, there were stories in one newspaper or another on sixty-eight. Again the effects were unpleasant, not least for the pupil at the centre of it all. Rumours abounded of boys and staff accepting bribes from pressmen. They were never proved true, but a tense atmosphere of mutual suspicion developed, and morale at the school began to suffer. Although the prince's detective coped with most intruders, there were occasionally more dramatic incidents. One night he aroused the headmaster after seeing a prowler on the roof of Charles's dormitory; a lengthy search was conducted, but no-one found. Only much later did a boy confess to getting back into bed seconds before the search party arrived. Even schoolboy pranks were becoming worthy of the police incident book. Once again, the Queen decided to safeguard her son's education, not to mention his sanity, by direct action.

In the Christmas holidays her press secretary invited all British newspaper editors to a meeting at Buckingham Palace. Peter Beck told the gathering of the disruption their employees were causing at his school. Bribes had been offered, though none, to his knowledge, had been accepted. Everyone felt themselves under constant surveillance. Charles's first term had ended unhappily for all, not least for the boy himself. Recalling the pleas he had made before and during Charles's time at Hill House, Colville spoke plainly to the editors. Either it stopped, and the press printed only stories of genuine significance, or the Queen would abandon her plan to educate her son outside the Palace, and withdraw him behind its walls and into the care of tutors. History would record that the failure of the great royal education experiment had been entirely the fault of the press.

Years later, it would become apparent that this moral blackmail of the press was somewhat unfair on the Palace's part. If Charles had been withdrawn from Cheam, it would really have been because he was 'utterly miserable' there. As the Queen wrote to her former prime minister, Sir Antony Eden, early in 1958: 'Charles is just beginning to dread the return to school next week. So much worse for the second term!'[15]

Six months later, Charles's mother herself brought down blanket press coverage on her nine-year-old son's head. It was the summer term of 1958, the end of Charles's first year at Cheam, and the Commonwealth Games were being held in Cardiff. The Queen had been due to perform the closing ceremony at Cardiff Arms Park on 26 July, but a sinusitis operation enforced her absence. Her husband took her place and introduced a tape-recorded message from the monarch, which was played over the loudspeakers of the packed stadium.

Charles and a few friends, who had filed into Peter Beck's study to watch the event on television, heard the Queen's disembodied voice say:

I want to take the opportunity of speaking to all Welsh people, not only in this arena, but wherever they may be. The British Empire and Commonwealth Games in the capital, together with all the festivities of the Festival of Wales, have made this a memorable year for the principality. I have therefore decided to mark it further by an act which will, I hope, give as much pleasure to all Welshmen as it does to me.

There was a buzz of anticipation as many in the arena had guessed what she was going to say: 'I intend to create my son Charles Prince of Wales today.' The tape had to be stopped as an enormous cheer convulsed the stadium and 36,000 Welsh voices broke into 'God bless the Prince of Wales'. When the clamour died down, the Queen's voice continued: 'When he is grown up, I will present him to you at Caernarfon.'[16]

The scene in Beck's study at Cheam might have given her a moment's pause. The headmaster, who had known what was coming, watched a look of dire unease cloud the prince's face as the other boys spontaneously joined in the clapping and cheering. Charles himself remembers being 'acutely embarrassed . . . I think for a little boy of nine it was rather bewildering. All the others turned and looked at me in amazement. And it perhaps didn't mean all that much then; only later on, as I grew older, did it become apparent what it meant.'[17]

For a mother trying to bring up her son as far as possible like other boys, aware that his own emergent character was far from self-confident and far from mastering its environment, it was an odd piece of timing. The Queen has since confessed that she now numbers this moment among the few mistakes she made in Charles's upbringing.[18]

In the headmaster's study that afternoon Charles also automatically became Earl of Chester and Knight Companion of the Most Noble Order of the Garter. They go, as it were, with the job. The earldom of Chester is the oldest of all the dignities of the heir to the throne, dating from 1254, when it was bestowed on the future Edward I. Since then it has always been conjoined with the title of Prince of Wales, though both, unlike the dukedom of Cornwall, are life peerages, which merge into the Crown when their holder becomes monarch, to be bestowed at his discretion upon his eldest son.

The monarch and the Prince of Wales are the only two ex officio of the twenty-six Knights of the Garter, Europe's oldest order of chivalry. Reflecting that her son was still young for his years, Elizabeth decided that it was too soon for the formal ceremony installing Charles in his Garter stall at Windsor; this ancient ritual was, in fact, to wait ten years, by which time it was part of the build-up to another major ordeal – his investiture as Prince of Wales at Caernarfon – and thus his emergence into full-time public life.

Those days remained mercifully distant as Charles enjoyed his summer holidays at Balmoral before continuing his steady if un-distinguished progress at Cheam. 'He is still a little shy,' his first end-of-term report read, 'but very popular . . . passionately keen on and promising at games . . . academically, a good average.' Beck later summed up with the verdict that the prince was above average in intelligence, but only average in attainment. By this he did not mean that the boy was bright but idle; he was pointing out the natural advantage Charles possessed in general knowledge. The new Prince of Wales was much better informed about the outside world and its ways than his contemporaries. By this time, after all, he had met many of the people who ran it, and engaged them in polite conversation.

This strange species of maturity, fostered by the formal conduct around him at home, also meant that Charles spoke and wrote the Queen's English with above-average clarity and style, at times tend-ing to a precocious use of long words. In other ways, he was much less mature than his fellows, and remained so for many years. But he joined with a will in many of the school entertainments devised by David Munir; like his mother, who with her sister had starred in the wartime Windsor pantomimes, he seemed to find such enforced public display one method of conquering his shyness. In a way, it was an apt preparation for many of the more bizarre public roles required of royalty.

One such Cheam production certainly was: a Shakespeare com-pilation under the title 'The Last Baron', which told the tale of the Duke of Gloucester, later King Richard III. The time-honoured understudy's dream came true when the boy cast as Richard fell ill and Charles hurriedly took over the part. In front of an audience of parents, he had to deliver with due gravity such lines as, 'And soon may I ascend the throne.' The drama critic of the *Cheam School Chronicle* wrote, 'Prince Charles played the traditional Gloucester with competence and depth; he had a good voice and excellent elocution, and very well conveyed the ambition and bitterness of the twisted hunchback.'[19]

The Queen was not in the audience that night, 19 February 1960, as she had been the previous Christmas for her son's minor début in a Munir entertainment called *Ten Little Cheam Boys*. The headmaster interrupted the performance to come onstage and announce that Richard III's mother had given birth to another son, Prince Andrew. Cheam staff were accustomed to boys being somewhat dashed by the news of the arrival of a younger sibling. They were struck by Charles's delight at having a baby brother and the almost excessive enthusiasm with which he relayed the latest news from home – evidence to the teachers who now knew him well that he would always be much happier in the protective bosom of his family. As Mabel Anderson said of Charles, 'He felt family separation very deeply. He dreaded going away to school.'[20]

His only link with home was the unlikely figure of his detective, DC Reg Summers, who provided a reassuring presence around the school grounds and behind the Sunday crocodile to church. Though the Queen largely resisted the temptation to call her son home for royal occasions, a special dispensation was granted that summer for him to attend the wedding, in Westminster Abbey, of his aunt Margaret to the photographer Antony Armstrong-Jones (later ennobled as the Earl of Snowdon).

The Queen visited her son no more frequently – three times a term – than other parents, and asked for no special privileges beyond cameras being put away in her presence. Princess Anne enjoyed coming for the annual sports day and always entered the younger sisters' race, unfortunately achieving no higher a position than fourth. But she could take comfort in her brother's generally undistinguished record on the sports field. Never much of a team player, Charles was bored by cricket, although he eventually made the First XI, and not the most mobile of rugger players. 'They always put me in the second row,' he complained, 'the worst place in the scrum.'

His reluctant best was soccer, and in his last year at Cheam he was made captain of the First XI. Unhappily, the team lost every match that season, with a final tally of four goals scored against their opponents' eighty-two. This time, the *Cheam School Chronicle* was not so kind: 'At half,' wrote the soccer coach, 'Prince Charles seldom drove himself as hard as his ability and position demanded.'[21]

Looking back, the staff remember Charles primarily for his uncertainty of himself and for a few little incidents that showed promise of the reflective man in the making. 'Most of the time,' said one of Charles's teachers, 'he was very quiet. He never spoke out of turn. Sometimes his voice was so low that it was difficult to hear him. But he was a boy who preferred action to noise. When there was a task to do, he got on with it quietly. No fuss.' David Munir remembered once catching Charles downstairs, finishing off his daily chores, when he should long since have been in bed. Munir warned him that he would get into trouble with Matron. 'I can't help that, sir,' the boy replied. 'I must do my duties.'[22]

Charles's extreme gentility was particularly marked on the football field, where he caused amusement by his habit of apologizing chivalrously to anyone he felled with a perfectly proper tackle. But it was endearing to find him so embarrassed by the standard prayer for the royal family, including the Prince of Wales, at Sunday morning service in St Peter's. 'I wish', he said, 'they prayed for the other boys, too.' He took his corporal punishment with the self-discipline of one who would rather get things over with. 'I am one of the people for whom corporal punishment actually worked,' he said years later. 'We had two headmasters [who] took turns at beating us . . . I didn't do it again.'[23] On at least one occasion, his crime was experimentation with cigarettes in the Cheam hedgerows – the beginning of a lifelong aversion to smoking.

By the end of his time at Cheam, despite such unnerving distractions as an IRA plot to kidnap him, which had the school grounds swarming with police, Charles had emerged a thoroughly average pupil. That he was made head boy says more about his standing in the outside world than within the school itself, although his good manners and sense of decorum may in themselves have been cause enough. In the holidays, meanwhile, his father encouraged his enthusiasm for field sports. From taking him out shooting to teaching him to drive a Land-Rover while still only twelve, Philip was intent on advancing his son beyond his years. At Christmas 1958 they went off on their first expedition together, to a coot shoot at Hickling Broad, near Sandringham. It turned into a minor rite of passage when their rented bungalow was flooded, and the royal pair caused some local excitement by applying for a room at the nearby Pleasure Boat Inn.

That same Christmas, Charles toured the British Sugar Corporation plant in King's Lynn – his first look inside a factory, and his first solo public engagement. His parents were pleased with his progress, if concerned about his continuing shyness and lack of self-confidence, especially in contrast with his sister. In the spring of 1962, in his father's absence abroad, the Queen asked Charles to take Philip's place as host at one of the luncheon parties she had introduced as a way of meeting a broader cross-section of her subjects. The thirteen-year-old prince, earnest for his years, held his own in conversation with a dozen guests, including the editor of the *Church Times*, an industrialist, a trade-union leader, a choreographer and the chairman of the BBC.

While at Cheam, Charles had disposed of a number of child-hood's other chores: his first broken bone (his ankle, falling down the school stairs), measles, chickenpox and his appendix. But the school had never quite won his wholehearted enthusiasm. The jolt of leaving home bequeathed bruises he still nursed. If he had grown accustomed to life away from home, he was still miserably aware that he was not, and never could be, one of the boys. Beck em-phasized that 'the job of a preparatory school is what it says: to prepare and not to produce a finished product'.[24] But Charles had only just mastered his new environment when he was abruptly removed from it. Even his mother acknowledged, via the Arundel Herald of Arms, that 'his first few years at Cheam had been a misery to him'.[25] The last thing Cheam had prepared him for, in short, was an unwelcome translation even further from home, to the chilly wastes of the north of Scotland.

CHAPTER FOUR

'HE HASN'T RUN AWAY YET'

PRINCE CHARLES WAS 'A VERY SENSITIVE LITTLE BOY, VERY KIND, VERY sweet', according to friends and relatives of his parents. But they worried that the Queen was too distant a mother. 'She's not very tactile. A child wants a mother to be emotional, hugged, kissed – and that's not what the Queen is good at.' But if his mother was 'tough, totally unsentimental', his father could be brutal. 'Philip misinterpreted Charles on many occasions. His attitude was based on himself. Here was this child – he would have to make his way in the world. People spoiled him. He needed to counteract the spoiling.'[1]

At the age of thirteen Charles had little choice but to gratify his father's whims by following in his footsteps. At twenty-one he felt bound to justify it: 'He had a particularly strong influence, and it was very good for me. I had perfect confidence in his judgement.'[2] But bringing up Charles in Philip's mould was not a logical exercise. Where Philip was outgoing, Charles was introspective; where Philip was gregarious, Charles was awkwardly sociable; and where Philip had been an obscure European prince, of the kind not unfamiliar to many British public schoolboys, Charles was the heir to the British throne, the first to be sent away to any school, let alone his father's remote alma mater on the Moray Firth. Charles's fears that Gordonstoun sounded 'pretty gruesome' were confirmed shortly before his arrival when Lord Rudolph Russell, son of the Duke of Bedford, ran away from the school, declaring, 'Gordonstoun is no place for me.'

Was it the right choice of school for a shy and hesitant child, in most respects a late developer? Those involved in the decision, among them the Queen Mother, Lord Mountbatten and the Dean of Windsor, Dr Robin Woods, remained divided ever after. Charles himself, though he tactfully opined in later life that Gordonstoun had been 'good for me', absolutely hated the place.

The school has been painted as a remote spartan outpost providing some sort of Germanic assault course towards manhood. Its life is tough, to be sure, with an unusual emphasis on outdoor and physical attainment. Its pupils are drawn more heavily than those of most comparable schools from a curious mix of the old-school upper classes and the social-climbing self-made. But Gordonstoun's ideology is based on a rigorous ethical code, founded in pacifism – formulated in the wake of the First World War by Prince Max of Baden, last chancellor of the Kaiser's Imperial Germany, and refined by his private secretary and disciple, Kurt Hahn. It may provide a more eccentric, narrowly aristocratic education than most other British public schools, but Gordonstoun parents are well aware of what they are letting their sons in for.

The school is modelled on that founded in 1920 by Prince Max in his castle-monastery at Salem, on the north shore of Lake Constance, in southern Germany. Max, who had been intimately involved in the collapse of Germany, set himself the personal task of rebuilding his nation's manhood. 'Let us train soldiers,' he said, 'who are at the same time lovers of peace.' The prince was given to somewhat grandiose statements, which he expected Hahn to put into effect as the school's first headmaster: 'Build up the imagination of the boy of decision and the will-power of the dreamer, so that in future wise men will have the nerve to lead the way they have shown, and men of action will have the vision to imagine the consequences of their decisions.'

In the Germany of the 1930s, after the death of Prince Max, Hahn was accused of anglicizing German education. He also happened to have been born Jewish. In 1933, when Hitler took power, he was arrested and the school closed. He took up an uncompromising stand, calling on all old boys active in the SA or SS to 'terminate their allegiance either to Hitler or to Salem'. The rise of Nazism made Hahn feel more urgently 'the need to educate young people in independence of judgement and in strength of purpose when following an unfashionable cause, to teach the protection of the weak, the recognition of the rights of the less fortunate, and the worth of a simple human life'.

On his release Hahn fled to England, where he fell ill. An Oxford friend invited him to recuperate on his estate in Morayshire, where he met up again with another university contemporary, Evan Barron, owner-editor of the *Inverness Courier*. When Hahn told them of his plans to recreate the Salem experiment in Britain, they took him to see the Gordonstoun estate, near Elgin. A lease was available on the eighteenth-century mansion house and its 300 acres. Hahn took it, and in the summer of 1934 opened the school with a clutch of masters and just thirty boys, among them Prince Philip.

Although the Gordonstoun philosophy was overtly based on that of Salem, Hahn added two significant new dimensions. One was to import from Germany the altruistic traditions of the Cistercian monks, who had ministered to the vicinity of Salem centuries before. The other was to counteract the scholastic emphasis of other British schools. 'I estimate', he said, 'that about sixty per cent of boys have their vitality damaged under the conditions of modern boarding schools.' His aim was 'to kindle on the threshold of puberty non-poisonous passions which act as guardians during the dangerous years'.

To protect his pupils from their increasingly urbanized home environments, he also wanted them to pit their young physical resources against the forces of nature on land and sea. Like Baden-Powell, he aimed to inspire a sense of purpose and self-reliance, aligned with one of duty and service. Boys, said Hahn, should be taught 'to argue without quarrelling, to quarrel without suspecting and to suspect without slandering'. Apart from a special concern for late developers – a boon to its new recruit – the school's purpose, enshrined in its motto, *Plus est en vous* ('There is more in you'), was not markedly different from the traditional British public school ideal.

But its methods were – as were the fees, higher even than Eton. Physical fitness was something of a cult; it remains so with the Prince of Wales to this day. Boys were frequently dispatched on testing expeditions, over land and water, designed to stretch initiative and physique to their limits. A sense of public service was instilled by joining in four local activities: fire fighting (the school's auxiliary service is a recognized branch of the Elgin fire service);

manning a coastguard station, complete with rockets and life-saving equipment; a mountain-rescue team, which has in its time saved climbers' lives; and an ocean-rescue team. Hahn introduced the Moray Badge as a selective reward for achievement in these fields. It proved the inspiration for the Duke of Edinburgh's own nationwide award scheme, whose silver medal Charles was to win in his last term.

Hahn's precepts are now as evident in Charles's beliefs and pronouncements as in his father's. It was a bold Prince of Wales, for instance, who suggested in 1987 that a form of compulsory community service might take the place of national service in Britain, the only European country in which it had been abolished. As the leader writers sharpened their pens, none traced the notion back to the immense influence of Kurt Hahn on both father and son. On the very day that it was announced that Charles was going to Gordonstoun, Hahn was delivering a lecture in Glasgow: 'A sick civilization', he said, 'is throwing up five kinds of young people: the lawless, the listless, the pleasure and sensation addicts, the angry young men and the honourable sceptics.' The antidotes were 'simple physical training, expedition training and rescue-service training'.[3]

Uncannily similar phrases can be found – increasingly, as he grows older – in many of Charles's own speeches. Back in 1962, with garbled versions of Hahn's philosophy and Gordonstoun's regime appearing in the British press, it was no wonder the teenage prince felt daunted. On a visit to the school with his parents, he found conditions even more spartan than at Cheam: unpainted dormitories with bare floorboards, naked lightbulbs and spare wooden bedsteads. Life appeared to be lived in huts, as exposed to the North Sea gales as were the boys' knees in their short trousers. Inside each pupil's locker was a chart, to be filled in each evening, with daily columns for 'Teeth Brushed, Rope Climbed, Skipping, Press-ups, Shower' etc. All in all, it was a cheerless place, leaving Charles distinctly unenthusiastic about what he called his 'imminent incarceration'.

Philip flew his son north on the first of May. The locals could tell they were coming; on the school gates stood naval guards with fixed bayonets, who required tradesmen (and parents) to produce passes to gain admission. The Queen's consort, not the new boy, was accorded an official welcome by the school's headmaster,

Robert Chew, a founder-member of Hahn's Gordonstoun staff, who had previously taught at Salem, flanked by the chairman of the governors, Captain Iain Tennant, and the head boy, Peter Paice. The only privilege accorded the new boy was a quiet lunch with his father and the headmaster before Philip left. He drove back to his aircraft at Lossiemouth, then flew over the school before heading south again, dipping his wings in a farewell salute to his son, who watched with sinking heart.

Charles's arrival at Gordonstoun, he remembers, was even more miserable than at Cheam. As he was shown to Windmill Lodge, the asbestos-roofed stone building he was to share with fifty-nine of the 400 other boys, the prospect seemed even worse than he had expected. One Gordonstoun old boy, the novelist William Boyd, has written with 'retrospective revulsion' of 'the concrete and tile washrooms and lavatories, the pale-green dormitories with their pale wooden beds'.[4] One of Charles's contemporaries, the journalist Ross Benson, reports that the windows were 'kept open throughout the night, which meant that those closest to them were likely to wake up with blankets rain-soaked or, in winter, covered with a light sprinkling of snow'.[5]

Not only had Charles been rudely yanked from the one external environment to which he had grown accustomed; all his dogged progress up the Cheam hierarchy had now come to naught. He was an unprivileged new boy again, at a school where the boys' older years altered their attitude to him. Where at Cheam he had found diffidence, at Gordonstoun he came up against adolescent malice. Boyd paints a vivid picture of a 'reign of terror', with gangs of marauding thugs 'beating up smaller boys' and 'extorting food and money'. New boys, according to Benson, were welcomed 'by taking a pair of pliers to their arms and twisting until the flesh tore open. In all the houses boys were regularly trussed up in one of the wicker laundry baskets and left under the cold shower, sometimes for hours'. Although apparently spared this indignity, Charles was immediately picked out for bullying 'maliciously, cruelly, and without respite ... He was crushingly lonely for most of his time there'.[6]

The only boys he knew, apart from Lord Mountbatten's grandson, Norton Knatchbull, were his cousins Prince Welf of Hanover, whom he had recently visited with his father in Germany, and the exiled Prince Alexander of Yugoslavia. Even they, for befriending him in his first few days, were labelled 'bloodsucker' and 'sponge' by their contemporaries.

The Gordonstoun day began with the cry of the 'waker' at 7 a.m., followed by a run around the garden in shorts and singlet. Then came the first of the day's two cold showers; Charles and his fifty-nine housemates shared a washroom containing six showers and one bath. He had to make his own bed and clean his own shoes before breakfast. The rest of the new boys' day, in an official summary prepared for public consumption by the headmaster, went beyond the normal stint of classwork to 'a training break (running, jumping, discus- and javelin-throwing, assault course, etc.) under the Physical Training Master' and 'seamanship, or practical work on the estate'. They would also see active service as coast-guard watchers, sea cadets, army cadets and scouts, with the fire service, mountain rescue and/or surf life-saving teams.

When not occupied by this formidable schedule, boys were at liberty to wander at will around the countryside and down to the sea, though the nearby town of Elgin was strictly out of bounds. Charles eagerly took full advantage of this freedom; visitors noticed with interest that he tended to take them for walks round the countryside rather than show them round the school. He developed nodding acquaintanceships with the fishermen and shopkeepers of the village of Hopeman, and occasionally, but only occasionally, for fear of singling himself out, he accepted invitations to Sunday lunch or a day's shooting with family friends among the local worthies, such as Captain Tennant, who doubled as the Lord-Lieutenant of Morayshire.

Charles desperately wished he could use his position to bend the rules and escape more, but this would have involved braving the wrath of his father as much as the staff and fellow pupils. Conforming to the school regime, like any other underprivileged member of its society, was gradually to become claustrophobic. It was in the countryside that Charles preferred to relax; he didn't much enjoy school games, and he felt obliged to shun his peers' illicit activities in Elgin's Pete's Café.

But he quickly took to all maritime activities. He and Welf teamed up as a life-saving unit, receiving their proficiency certificates on Charles's fourteenth birthday in November 1962. One of his earliest exercises, a canoe expedition from Hopeman Beach to Findhorn Bay, turned ugly even by Gordonstoun standards when a storm blew up shortly after they were out at sea. The twelve-mile journey took all day, and the prince arrived back at school exhausted. In true British public-school spirit he recovered in time to go out to dinner that night with Captain Tennant, and mustered enough sang-froid to claim he was eager to repeat the adventure as soon as possible.

Other early duties included emptying the school dustbins and tidying up their trail of refuse. By the end of his first term Charles had qualified (in one of Gordonstoun's many unique hierarchical rituals*) to wear the standard school uniform of grey sweater and shorts, rather than the blue uniform that distinguished new boys. He also qualified for a ritual ducking, fully clothed, in yet another cold bath; but the prince was apparently spared this ordeal. It may seem strange that Gordonstoun boys hesitated to put the heir to the throne through a ritual humiliation; but Charles's limited success at 'blending in' – or, perhaps, the full extent of what he was up against – was soon evident from the testimony of one school-leaver, who was not slow to sell his story to a Sunday paper:

> How can you treat a boy as just an ordinary chap when his mother's portrait is on the coins you spend in the school shop, on the stamps you put on your letters home, and when a detective follows him wherever he goes? Most boys tend to fight shy of friendship with Charles. The result is that he is very lonely. It is this loneliness, rather than the school's toughness, which must be hardest on him.[7]

It was. 'It's near Balmoral,' his father told him. 'There's always the Factor there. You can go and stay with him. And your grandmother goes up there to fish. You can go and see her.'[8] Charles did, whenever he could. At Birkhall, her home on the Balmoral estate, the Queen Mother listened to Charles's plaintive outpourings about his loneliness, his homesickness, the impossibility of blending into school like other boys. She provided a sympathetic shoulder to cry on, often literally, and was especially moved by the

---

* Upward progress at Gordonstoun is a process so arcane that it may best be summarized by Prince Charles's graduation through all stages: School Uniform, Junior Training Plan, Senior Training Plan, White Stripe, Colour Bearer Candidate, Colour Bearer, Helper, Guardian. Colour Bearers (prefects) are elected by their fellows; from their number housemasters appoint Helpers (heads of houses), from whom the headmaster chooses the Guardian, or head boy.

gentle qualities of her late husband so evident in her favourite grandchild. More than either of Charles's parents, perhaps, his grandmother understood the ordeal of the quiet, uncertain child in a harsh and alien world. 'He is a very gentle boy, with a very kind heart,' she said, 'which I think is the essence of everything.' But she would not, as he asked, intercede with his parents to take him away from Gordonstoun. She would try, she said, to help him through a trial he must face. It was another early lesson in the duty which went with his birth.

Charles was utterly miserable, and did not hide the fact, even from a father unlikely to feel, let alone show, much sympathy. 'Well, at least he hasn't run away yet,' was all Prince Philip would say, asked how his son was getting on at Gordonstoun. At the end of Charles's first term, however, the headmaster was able to report to his parents that their son was 'well up . . . very near the top of his class'. The Christmas holidays, after family festivities at Sandringham, provided the first in a new and traumatic wave of trials-by-press. It was New Year 1963, and Charles travelled alone to Bavaria for a winter-sports break with his 'uncle', Prince Ludwig of Hesse, and his family. But the crowd of press photographers, which in turn attracted crowds of sightseers, ruined it for him. After two or three chaotic days in the resort of Tarasp, he was forced again to retire into an artificial world: the private slopes of the Hesse *Schloss*. Even there, he needed a bodyguard of Swiss police, themselves patrolling the property on skis.

His resentment was forgotten only the following summer, when a much greater ordeal overwhelmed him. The Cherry Brandy Incident, now a fondly remembered, mildly amusing milestone in Prince Charles's childhood to most Britons, was much more than that to the boy at the time. It upset him deeply, leaving scars which lasted several years – notably a bewildered mistrust of the press which has never left him, though it is now more contemptuous than bewildered.

On his arrival at Gordonstoun another appeal had been made for the press to leave him in peace:

> The added strain and burden of publicity upon a young boy of the Prince of Wales's age, on joining a public school for the first time, can readily be understood by all parents. For this reason, Her Majesty and His Royal Highness hope that editors

personally will be able to cooperate . . . When publicity was
reduced at the end of the first term at Cheam School, it became
possible for the whole school to function in the normal way,
and therefore the Prince of Wales was able to receive a normal
education. This was only possible because neither he nor any of
the other boys and staff were subjected to publicity, which is
most unsettling and which, of course, singles His Royal
Highness out as different in the eyes of all other boys of the
school.[9]

By his third term at Gordonstoun Charles remained utterly unrec-
onciled to the place. 'It's absolute hell,' he wrote home,[10] but at
least press coverage of his progress was minimal. By then, June
1963, he had won further promotion within the school, entitling
him to more freedom of choice over outdoor training activities,
including expeditions aboard the school yacht, Pinta, one of which
took him to Stornoway, on the isle of Lewis, on Monday 17 June.
As usual his detective, Donald Green, accompanied the party of
Charles and four other boys ashore. Green went off to make
arrangements at the local cinema – Jayne Mansfield was to be the
subject of their scholastic attentions that evening – leaving the boys
to wait in the Crown Hotel. Once word of the prince's arrival got
around, a crowd quickly gathered, and Charles found a sea of faces
pressed against the hotel windows, peering and pointing at him.

> I thought 'I can't bear this any more' and went off somewhere
> else. The only other place was at the bar. Having never been
> into a bar before, the first thing I thought of doing was having
> a drink, of course. And being terrified, not knowing what to do,
> I said the first drink that came into my head, which happened
> to be cherry brandy, because I'd drunk it before when it was
> cold out shooting. Hardly had I taken a sip when the whole
> world exploded around my ears.[11]

Into the bar, as he took that first sip, had walked Frances
Thornton, a young freelance journalist known ever after to Charles
as 'that dreadful woman'. At fourteen, unknown to him, the Prince
of Wales was under the legal age for purchasing alcoholic liquor.
Within twenty-four hours the story had gone round the world.
Coming soon after other public criticisms – of Charles shooting his

first stag and 'invading the Lord's day' by skiing in the Cairngorms on a Sunday – it caused uproar. Even the Profumo Affair, the government sex scandal then at its height, could not keep the unfolding saga of Charles's misdemeanour off the front pages. To make matters worse, Buckingham Palace at first issued a denial, after misunderstanding Green's telephoned account of the incident. The following day, after further inquiries, the Palace press office was forced to retract the denial, thus keeping the story bubbling along. There followed the carpeting of Green by the Queen's senior detective and his subsequent resignation, while the entire nation felt entitled to discuss the question of suitable school punishment for Charles. Even *The Times* felt moved to inform its readers that the headmaster of Gordonstoun kept a cane in his study, at the ready, for just such moments.

As leading articles called on the head to act, Mr Chew summoned Charles to his study and withdrew his recent school promotion. It was a punishment much more devastating than the cane. Reduced to the ranks, Charles had again had his life complicated by undue and unwelcome attention. For so trivial an incident to have had so disproportionate an effect now seems absurd. The Queen was able to laugh it off; but Charles, though a more human and endearing figure to most newspaper readers, was thoroughly unsettled and unable to laugh about it for several years. When boys made puns on the name of the school yacht, *Pinta* – 'Drinka Pinta Milka Day' was then the Milk Marketing Board's popular slogan – he somehow failed to appreciate the joke.

As his Gordonstoun life grew more varied – a stint at HMS *Vernon*, the naval training camp at Portsmouth, his first archaeological digs around Morayshire, a bout of pneumonia after a fishing trip – he won his way back up the Junior Training Plan and further up the scale. A year later he proved something to himself and his family by passing five GCE O levels, in Latin, French, history, English language and English literature, though maths and physics still eluded his grasp. The summer of 1964 was a particularly happy one, at Balmoral and Cowes, with the bonus of an excursion to King Constantine's wedding in Athens, where Charles had the satisfaction of ducking a raftload of French photographers. By the time he returned to school that September, his life seemed to have found a new equilibrium. But it was very soon to turn sour again, as an exercise book went missing from his classroom.

This sort of thing had happened before: forgeries had been hawked around Fleet Street, and one genuine one, culled from a waste-paper basket, had turned out to be the work of another boy. Name tags from Charles's clothes had proved popular on the school's 'black market', and textbooks inscribed with his name had disappeared. These were the everyday realities of his 'normal' school life, with which he had learned to live, albeit uncomfortably. But this time the olive-green book in which Charles wrote his essays had been stolen from the pile on his form-master's desk. The headmaster issued an appeal for what he called 'a collector's item'.

It was too late: the book had already reached Fleet Street. A Gordonstoun boy (who was never identified) was reputed to have got £7 for it from an old boy, an officer cadet, who had then sold it on to a Scottish journalist for £100. Rumours of offers as high as £5,000 abounded in London until it was traced to St Helen's, Lancashire, and the offices of Terence Smith of the *Mercury Press*. It took Scotland Yard six weeks to get the book back, by which time the German *Der Stern*, the French *Paris-Match* and the American *Life* magazines all possessed photocopies. Convinced by the Scotland Yard seizure of the document's authenticity, *Stern* published the essays in full, in German, illustrated by the hand-written text in English, complete with the form-master's comment: 'Quite well-argued.' It was 'highly regrettable', said Buckingham Palace, 'that the private essays of a schoolboy should have been published in this way'.[12]

So it was; but it could have been much worse. Charles emerged with credit from worldwide exposure that would have daunted any schoolboy. Though published under the lurid headline THE CON-FESSIONS OF PRINCE CHARLES, what little the essays revealed showed the sixteen-year-old prince a liberal and original thinker, mature for his age. *Stern* managed to miss the point of the piece about which it got most excited: a dissertation on the corrupting effects of power. Its views were not those of the future King, but of the nineteenth-century historian William Lecky, a section of whose *History of England in the Eighteenth Century* the class had been told to précis.

The Times quoted with approval from another piece on the sub-ject of democracy. Charles professed himself 'troubled by the fact that the voters today tend to go for a particular party and not for the individual candidate, because they vote for the politics of a party'. He thought it wrong, for instance, that a below-par Conservative candidate should win votes simply because he toed the party line against nationalization or the abolition of public schools. In another essay, on the press, he emerged from his recent ordeals surprisingly unsoured, arguing that a free press was essential in a democratic society 'to protect people from the government in many ways, to let them know what is going on – perhaps behind their backs'.

A fourth essay was a ten-minute exercise to name the four items he would take to a desert island if – a sign of the times – evacuated during a nuclear crisis. Charles opted for a tent, a knife, 'lots of rope and string', and a radio, both to keep in touch with developments and to monitor any hope of rescue. He did add, with his now familiar archness, that such an emergency would have him 'in a frightful panic'.

The matter might have ended there, had not *Stern* thought of adding a last, gratuitous passage: 'Prince Charles became short of pocket money at Gordonstoun at the end of August. It then occurred to him that some collectors paid good money for original handwritten manuscripts and sold the work to a schoolmate for thirty shillings.' *Time* magazine decided to follow up this intriguing titbit, and the following week published its version of the saga under the headline THE PRINCELY PAUPER. Now the Palace lost patience and issued one of its extremely rare denials. Colville wrote to *Time*:

> There is no truth whatsoever in the story that Prince Charles sold his autograph at any time. There is also no truth whatever in the story that he sold his composition book to a classmate. In the first place he is intelligent and old enough to realize how embarrassing this would turn out to be, and second, he is only too conscious of the interest of the press in anything to do with himself and his family. The suggestion that his parents keep him so short of money that he has to find other means to raise it is also a complete invention. Finally, the police would not have attempted to regain the composition book unless they were quite satisfied that it had been obtained illegally.

Far from printing a retraction, the editors of *Time* headlined the letter MONEYED PRINCE CHARLIE, with the rider, 'The royal family's press officer mounts a princely defence in his belated offer to clarify the case.'[13]

Charles's national notoriety did nothing to endear him to the school bullies. During his second year he was still pleading for release from the 'hell' that was Gordonstoun. Charles's letters home about his night-time ordeals, and his suffering at the hands of the 'foul' people in his dormitory, make grim reading. He complained that he had slippers thrown at him, and was hit with pillows and punched at all hours of the night. He hated the school, which he called a 'HOLE', and his school fellows. He longed to go home.[14]

For the first, if by no means the last, time in his life, Charles was also subjected to merciless teasing about his large and prominent ears. Mountbatten had already urged his parents to get Charles's ears 'fixed', bluntly telling the boy, 'You can't possibly be King with ears like that.' But nothing had been done. Now he found himself the mortified victim of newspaper cartoonists as much as his Gordonstoun contemporaries. In the most affecting terms, he bemoaned the bad manners of his contemporaries, who had the 'foulest natures' he had ever come across. He was stunned to find that people like them existed.[15]

The school rules were widely ignored. Smoking and drinking, even openly in the pubs of Elgin, were as 'commonplace' as pilfering from the local shops, even 'joy riding' in 'borrowed' cars. All mention of sex was taboo at Gordonstoun, naturally encouraging a thriving trade in pornographic magazines, sexual banter 'of the vilest and coarsest sort' and 'male lust at its most dog-like and contemptuous' when it came to the local girls, including 'consenting kitchen maids'.[16] Ever the innocent, and already rather priggish about the ways of his contemporaries, Charles does not seem to have got involved. Far from cavorting in Elgin with his peers, Charles was even shocked by their 'horrid' language, which he attributed to lazy-mindedness.[17]

The following month, March 1964, saw the birth of another brother for Charles, Prince Edward. The Gordonstoun inmate tried to use it as an excuse to escape for a few days. His hopes that his mother would ask the headmaster to let him return to London to meet his new brother proved vain. But that autumn offered a different diversion from Gordonstoun's routine strains in the shape of a 'mock' election – a common practice in many British schools – to coincide with the general election of October 1964. Charles was to be seen wearing a Scottish Nationalist Party rosette around Gordonstoun, and speaking vehemently in favour of devolution. When one opponent gently reminded him that he was Prince of Wales, he cried, 'Independence for Wales, too! That's for the next election!' It is a measure of the background of British public schoolboys that the Conservative Party romped home with 140 votes; the Scottish Nationalists polled 129; but Labour, with a mere sixteen votes, trailed way behind the Liberals and the Irish Independents, at a time when the party was winning its first British general election for thirteen years.

The Christmas holidays were marked by the delivery to Windsor Castle of a 'beat group kit' – an electric guitar with amplifier, and an electric organ – to complement Charles's 'much-worn' Beatle wig; at this early stage of his life, he was not yet entirely immune to the tastes of his contemporaries. After New Year at Sandringham, he and Anne were again dogged by the press on a skiing holiday in Liechtenstein. Through his hosts, Prince Franz Josef and Princess Gina, he reached an accommodation with the photographers, who were mostly foreign; British editors were still attempting to respect the Queen's wishes. They would be welcome on the slopes in the afternoons if they would leave him alone in the mornings. To universal surprise, it seemed to work, and he was able to continue his progress towards becoming the proficient skier he is today.

Back at Sandringham it was the usual round of field sports, in unusually severe winter weather. 'The whole family', said Miss Anderson, 'goes out in weather most would think mad.' That Easter, Charles was due to be confirmed at Windsor. Though his young seriousness took on, for the first time, a contemplative air which today is very familiar, the episode is primarily remembered for the attitude of his father, who took a dim view of the entire proceedings.

Prince Philip thought his son too young, at sixteen, for solemn acceptance into the Church of England, and had indeed been undergoing a period of doubt about his own religious beliefs. Philip's tortured progress from the Greek Orthodoxy of his childhood through Salem's German Protestantism to the formal Anglicanism of his adopted life had bred a disenchantment, even a cynicism; there had been a time, though he had now in middle age reverted to Anglican orthodoxy, when he had classed himself agnostic, perhaps even atheist. Again, Charles was in a different mould. During pre-confirmation talks with the Dean of Windsor, Robert Woods, he displayed a sound grasp of his undertakings – and his faith, while becoming more complex, has not wavered since. His father, at the time, was intent on making his protest felt, and considered the then Archbishop of Canterbury, Dr Michael Ramsey, a very tiresome preacher. Throughout his son's confirmation service in St George's Chapel, Windsor, Philip conspicuously read a book. 'Come and have a drink,' said Woods to Ramsey afterwards. 'Thank you,' said the outraged Archbishop. 'Bloody rude, that's what I call it.'[18]

Charles's progress at Gordonstoun had been interrupted by only one recall to London on official duty that year, for the state funeral of Sir Winston Churchill. He was nearing the end of his fourth year, had advanced from Senior Training Plan to Colour Bearer (prefect), and had finally managed to satisfy the O level examiners of a modest grasp of mathematics. He had graduated from piano to trumpet, taking part in several concerts in Elgin town hall and St Giles's Cathedral, Edinburgh. He had also enjoyed his first taste of two contradictory passions, polo and the cello, only the first of which was to prove enduring. He was to crown his last full year at the school with boldness in a field in which his father had never shone. For the school play at Christmas 1965, Charles undertook the role of Shakespeare's Macbeth; thirty years before, Prince Philip had qualified only for the role of an attendant lord.

The production was to be directed by Eric Anderson, a new arrival from Fettes School in Edinburgh – where he had recently directed the future prime minister, Tony Blair, as Mark Antony in *Julius Caesar*. Later headmaster of Eton and rector of Lincoln College, Oxford, Anderson and his wife Poppy were to become close lifelong friends of the prince, sharing his secrets with a sensitivity apparent from their first encounter. On his arrival at Gordonstoun the previous year, Anderson had pinned up a notice seeking volunteers for a production of *Henry V*. At auditions, in his view, the best candidate for the title role was the Prince of Wales. But Anderson was reluctant to take such a risk with the prince's fragile self-confidence; the production would be attended by the Morayshire squirearchy, and any embarrassment might well reach the press. After talking it over with his wife, he had instead cast the prince in the lesser role of Exeter. Twelve months on, Anderson decided that the prince had matured enough for them both to take the risk of a truly royal Macbeth.

Charles took the part very seriously, treating his six weeks of research into the character as a further expedition into those realms of human nature explored at the time of his confirmation. A fortnight after their son's seventeenth birthday, his parents flew north to see Charles strut and fret his few hours in the Gordonstoun art department's re-creation of Glamis Castle (ancestral home of his maternal grandmother's family, the Strathmores). A schoolboy's photo of the false-bearded prince performing the famous dagger soliloquy went around the world, swelling the coffers of the school's Photographic Society.

Anderson deemed it necessary to make one small amendment to Shakespeare's text. Out of consideration for the Queen, it was decided to dispense with the stage direction 'Enter Macduff, with Macbeth's head.' Otherwise, Charles's satanic thane stoutly endured the eloquent nagging of fourteen-year-old Douglas Campbell as Lady Macbeth, and raised an inappropriate laugh only when the three witches cried, 'All hail, Macbeth, that shalt be King hereafter!' The *Gordonstoun Record* did him proud:

> Prince Charles was at his very best in the quiet poetic soliloquies, the poetry of which he so beautifully brought out, and in the bits which expressed Macbeth's terrible agony of remorse and fear. In the second part of the play, he equally well expressed the degenerative hardening of Macbeth's character, the assumption of cynicism in an attempt to blunt the underlying and too painful moral sensitivity.

A local triumph, it was the high point of a year during which school life had become, after those early trials, merely monotonous. That Christmas, the question of a university career was already under discussion in royal circles. Charles had not yet completed his span at Gordonstoun; but he was in the mood for a change, the familiar mood of school-leavers who take a year out in the wide world between school and university. As this would not be available to him, his parents for once agreed that his position might now be used to afford him a privilege allowed few other schoolboys. On condition that he would return to Gordonstoun to finish the work he had begun there, he could take a break at a school somewhere in the Commonwealth.

During her coronation tour of Australia, the Queen had promised that she would 'send my son to visit you too, when he is older'. The promise seemed long overdue in that autumn of 1965, when the Australian prime minister, Robert Menzies, seized the chance of a visit to London to persuade the Queen that the ideal choice would be Geelong Grammar School – the so-called 'Eton of Australia' near Melbourne, in his own state of Victoria. It was the Australian high commissioner, Sir Alexander Downer, himself a Geelong old boy, who suggested the idea of Timbertop, Geelong's mountainside outpost 200 miles to the north of Melbourne and 2,000 feet above sea level, in the remote but accessible foothills of the Victorian Alps.

All Geelong boys undergo a year of exercise and 'self-reliance' at Timbertop, which at first made Charles fear that it sounded like an Australian Gordonstoun. In fact, the school's philosophy is far less heavy-handed, more homespun. By self-reliance, Geelong meant literally that: there was a handful of masters *in loco parentis*, but the boys were mainly younger ones in the care of their seniors, who would appeal to the staff only in the event of emergency. Theirs was a rural life of comparative self-sufficiency, each boy having considerable freedom to spend his time as he pleased. It was above all an exercise in getting to know people and displaying leadership qualities, from which the young Prince of Wales, still far from sure of himself, could only benefit. Being of the age of the older boys, he would undertake the responsibility of having a younger group in his care. Unlike his fellows, he would have to spend some time working for his GCE A levels in history and French, scheduled for his return to Gordonstoun, but the rest of the time would be more or less his own, in fine fishing and walking countryside. Though made famous by Neville Shute in *The Far Country*, the gum-tree forests around Mount Timbertop were otherwise relatively uncharted territory.

In December 1965 Charles had received a letter at Gordonstoun from a man he knew well, his father's equerry, thirty-five-year-old Squadron Leader David Checketts, who had been chosen to escort him to Australia. 'You are probably, and quite naturally, apprehensive about going to Australia, and if I can be of any help with any doubts or fears you might have, please let me know. I give you my word they will go no further than me.' Though hand-picked for the role by Philip, Checketts clearly knew of the tensions between father and son, and was going to kindly pains to reassure Charles that he would be more approachable, and more sympathetic to doubts and fears. 'I couldn't be more delighted to be going with you,' he added, 'and sincerely hope you will feel free to ask me any questions and for any advice or help, which, unless you wish otherwise, will remain purely between us.'[19] Again, Charles could be in no doubt that it was not the press to whom Checketts was referring, but his father. The boy need be in no fear that any signs of human frailty would be relayed home.

Charles flew out to Australia with Checketts at the end of January 1966. Though just seventeen, he had still not entirely conquered his fear of new, unknown situations, and again remembers feeling highly apprehensive. He had heard that Australians were 'critical' and expected a mixed reception. Even more unnervingly, it was his first trip abroad without either of his parents, though he had reassuring company in the shape of Checketts and Detective Inspector Derek Sharp.

A former public relations man with a distinguished RAF record, Checketts was to prove a mainstay of Charles's life for the next thirteen years. He set up home with his wife and family at Devon Farm, 120 miles from Timbertop, and acted as a kind of business manager to the prince. The farm became a headquarters for dealing with press enquiries, and for entertaining Charles over many a down-to-earth weekend. The prince would muck in like a member of the family, making his own bed, coming down to breakfast in his dressing gown, doing his share of the household chores and acting as an elder brother to the Checkettses' young children. It was the beginning of a lasting friendship; in time Checketts was to become his equerry, and later his first private secretary.

Checketts has said of those seven months in Australia, 'I went out there with a boy and came back with a man.'[20] Many others, including Charles himself, have since testified that this was the period in which he at last shed his perennial burden of 'late development' and grew into manhood. If the Australian public at first received him warily, it was the acceptance of his schoolmates which the prince was more concerned to win. One night at Timbertop, after taking a walk in the rain, he knew he had succeeded. As he strolled back to his dormitory carrying a rolled umbrella, every inch the English gentleman abroad, he was delighted to be greeted by a chorus of 'Pommy bastard!'

Timbertop boys live together in a compound of nine huts, each containing about fifteen, and each supervised by an older boy described as 'a sort of NCO'. One such was Charles, who shared a room in the masters' quarters with a sheep-farmer's son named Stuart Macgregor, a former head boy of Geelong who had come out to Timbertop to study in peace for his university entrance. Here Charles, too, studied for his A levels. He did not attend what few classes there were, but spent time supervising the younger boys in such chores as wood-cutting, boiler-stoking and (again) dustbin-emptying. He joined in the strenuous hikes and cross-country runs that were compulsory most afternoons and weekends, and earned popularity by rather neglecting his studies for the life of the out-back; entranced by its natural beauties, he was occasionally late with the essays he sent down to the supervisors at Geelong. His Australian hosts were introducing him, quite deliberately, to a university style of tuition, not knowing whether he would ever again have the chance to enjoy this type of academic life.

Excursions further afield became increasingly exotic: sheep-shearing and pig-swilling, gem-hunting and panning for gold. Charles felled trees, took part in a scheme to help war widows and was introduced to the local ornithology. He was thoroughly enjoying himself. Timbertop, he found, was as stimulating as Gordonstoun had become tedious. He was popular among his fellows for himself, not his rank, and he had never known such freedom to wander the great outdoors at will. He had originally come to Australia for one term, but the Queen had directed that he might stay for a second if he so wished. The choice left entirely to him, Charles decided without hesitation to stay.

In a vivid account for the *Gordonstoun Record*, under the heading TIMBERTOP: OR BEATING ABOUT THE BUSH, Charles himself chronicled the joys of each day at Timbertop with boyish enthusiasm. Wood-chopping, for instance, was:

> . . . essential, as the boys' boilers have to be stoked with logs and the kitchen uses a huge number. The first week I was here

I was made to go out and chop up logs on a hillside in boiling hot weather. I could hardly see my hands for blisters . . . Each afternoon after classes, which end at three o'clock, there are jobs which . . . involve chopping and splitting wood, feeding the pigs, cleaning out fly-traps (which are revolting glass bowls seething with flies and very ancient meat), or picking up bits of paper round the school . . .

Of weekend expeditions into the bush he wrote:

You can't see anything but gum-tree upon gum-tree, which tends to become rather monotonous . . . You virtually have to inspect every inch of the ground you hope to put your tent on in case there are ants or other ghastly creatures. There is one species of ant called Bull Ants which are three-quarters of an inch long, and they bite like mad! Some boys manage to walk fantastic distances over a weekend of four days or less, and do 130 or even 200 miles. The furthest I've been is 60–70 miles in three days, climbing about five peaks on the way. At the camp-site the cooking is done on an open fire in a trench. You have to be very careful in hot weather that you don't start a bush fire, and at the beginning of this term there was a total ban in force, so you ate all the tinned food cold.[21]

An unexpectedly important moment in the prince's life came at the end of that first term, when he joined a party of thirty other boys on Geelong's annual visit to the missionary stations in Papua New Guinea. They landed at Port Moresby – after a flight that had taken them over Prince of Wales Island – to find that a large crowd had gathered at the airport to see the prince, who had never before encountered such a throng in his own right. His instinct was to stay on the plane, in the hope that it would take off again as soon as possible. Checketts, as both remember it, had to 'more or less kick the prince off the plane'; Charles walked across the tarmac towards the ecstatic assembly in a state of high anxiety. Once he reached them, however, and found how easy it was to talk to people, even in such difficult circumstances, he began to enjoy the experience. Since that day, he says, he has never again been nervous of big crowds.

Again the prince wrote his own account of the trip, this time for

the Geelong school magazine, and one extract reveals not only his
dawning interest in anthropology, but also the beginnings of a
personal philosophy which would later take firm root:

> I can't help feeling that less and less interest is being taken by
> the younger Papuans in the customs and skills of their parents
> and grandparents, because they feel that they have to live up to
> European standards, and that these things belong to the past
> and have no relevance to the present or future . . . I was given
> one or two presents by young people, and when I asked if they
> had made them, they said their mothers or aunts had. No
> doubt, however, in the years to come, when there are new
> generations of Papuans, they will consider these ancient skills of
> use . . .[22]

In Sydney more than twenty years later, during Australia's bicentennial celebrations in 1988, Charles told its people that his time at
Timbertop had provided some of the most genuinely happy
moments of his life. His second term there confirmed his love of the
great outdoors and for ruggedly masculine pursuits. He was to
revisit the country frequently, even attempting to spend a prolonged period there as governor-general.

'Australia', he said at the time, 'opened my eyes. Having a title
and being a member of the upper classes as often as not militates
against you there . . . Australia conquered my shyness.' Thanking
the Australian people for their kindness, he promised to return as
soon as possible, saying, 'I am very sad to be leaving.'[23]

By way of repaying the compliment, the headmaster of Geelong,
Thomas Garnett, said that before the prince's visit 'most
Australians had very hazy and possibly erroneous ideas of him . . .
as just a distant and uninteresting figurehead. In future most of
them will know him as a friendly, intelligent, natural boy with a
good sense of humour, who by no means has an easy task ahead of
him in life.'

Three terms back at Gordonstoun were an unwelcome extension to
his schooldays, though he had the consolation of becoming
'Guardian', or head boy (like his father before him), and of passing
two A levels (a Grade C in French and a B in history). To his relief
as much as his satisfaction, Charles had done enough to prove that

he could win a university place in his own right, the first heir to the throne in British history to do so. His last year at Gordonstoun showed the increasingly earnest young prince also developing a fondness for the arts; inspired by hearing Jacqueline du Pré play the Dvořák concerto, he persisted with regular cello lessons, and sang the Pirate King in Gilbert and Sullivan's *The Pirates of Penzance.*

Unlike his father, he showed little interest in matters scientific or technological. His preoccupations already seemed to lie more in the past than the future, and the time he spent in the caves of Morayshire, bats fluttering around his head, was to be followed up with a close interest in archaeology at Cambridge and thereafter. He had played his last team games – apart from polo, which is more of an individualist's sport anyway – and had no more than a broken nose to show for his time on the rugger field. His natural introspection had much more to feed on.

At home, too, there had been significant advances. The prince had spent his eighteenth birthday in November 1966 studying for his A levels, barely aware that bells were tolling all over the country in honour of the occasion and that judges at the Old Bailey were wearing their finest scarlet robes. Upon that day he had reached the age when he could reign as king in his own right. If any disablement befell the sovereign, there would no longer be any constitutional need for his father to act as regent. Now Charles began chairing his first meetings of the Duchy of Cornwall and undertaking his first full-scale public engagements with his parents. A date had also been set, in the summer of 1969, for his investiture as Prince of Wales at Caernarfon.

Charles had just two more years before his emergence, fully fledged, into public life. He was to spend them sampling a brief taste of a unique kind of freedom – university life, which to most who have known it retains a distinctive flavour throughout all their subsequent metamorphoses. Charles was more than ready for it. He may have declared himself 'glad' that he went to Gordonstoun, but he was even more glad to leave. 'He's looking forward to leaving school,' said his father. 'There comes a time when you've had enough of it.'

For his own part, the prince summed up that 'I might not have enjoyed school life as much as I might have, but that is because I am happier at home than anywhere else.' He gave thanks that

Gordonstoun had 'developed my will-power' and 'helped me to discipline myself'. For self-discipline, he declared – 'not in the sense of making you bath in cold water, but in the Latin sense, of giving shape and form to your life' – was surely 'the most important thing' any education could instil.[24]

He has since proved even more of a traditionalist than his parents in his attitude to bringing up his own children – seeing no problem, for instance, in abandoning them to nannies in the school holidays while going off to play polo or hunt, shoot or fish without them. All that was to change after their mother's premature death. But it was due to Charles as much as Diana that William and Harry were not subjected to those same remote Scottish miseries.

CHAPTER FIVE

'THEY DON'T KNOW WHAT I'M LIKE'

AMID THE HOUSE OF WINDSOR'S PROLONGED WOES IN THE LAST decade of the twentieth century, it is often forgotten that the 1960s were an equally challenging decade for the monarchy. After thirteen years of patrician Conservative rule, the advent of a young, ambitious Labour government created the same sense of expectation as it would some thirty years later in May 1997. The new liberalism of the 'Swinging Sixties', with its heady mix of pop culture and youth protest, conspired to render the institution of monarchy as distant from, and irrelevant to, contemporary British life as at any time since the war.

While the Windsor machine at Buckingham Palace was still driven by a heedless, complacent 'old guard', some younger, sharper heads in the royal employ began to worry. With the next generation in mind, plans were laid for a royal relaunch, centred on the young man who symbolized the monarchy's future, using some orchestrated publicity to portray him as a 'strongly contemporary figure'.[1] Charles would soon be twenty-one, the age at which the Queen had promised to invest him as Prince of Wales at Caernarfon. It would make the ideal launch pad for a new era of monarchy, more accessible, more human. With the enthusiastic support of Charles's father, ambitious plans were laid by David Checketts and a brash young Australian in the Palace press office, William Heseltine.

Twenty years on, in the late 1980s, Heseltine would become private secretary to the Queen, the most powerful figure in

Buckingham Palace besides the monarch herself, advising on constitutional matters, liaising with government, and presiding over a
vast nexus of power, influence and patronage. In the mid-1960s he
was her assistant press secretary, already on his second stint in
royal service. Private secretary to the Australian prime minister at
the age of twenty-five, he had spent two years as an assistant press
officer at the Palace before returning to Australia as right-hand
man to the governor-general. During those few years back home,
in the heart of the Commonwealth, he had pondered the difference
between the reserved, po-faced, almost sullen monarch in the
popular mind and the shrewd, jaunty, often witty woman he had
come to know. On his return to her employ in 1965, he determined
to do something about it.

Back at the Palace, the new press secretary found Checketts
musing in similar fashion over the immediate future of Prince
Charles. Traditionally, royal press officers had regarded their role
as keeping the press at bay; they saw it as their function, unlike
most press or public relations officers, more to discourage journalists than assist them, more to prevent anything being printed than
to promote their corporate product. But these two progressive
thinkers, still young for the royal positions they held, had more up-
to-date ideas. As Heseltine set about improving the monarch's
'image' – itself a word newfangled enough to bring a curl to courtly
lips – his thinking dovetailed with Checketts's proposals for some
quiet orchestration of the Prince of Wales's launch into public life.

Together they devised a four-year plan, which amounted to the
unprecedented 'packaging' of a prince, and was to pave the way
towards a bold, often volatile new era in relations between the
monarchy and its people. By the time Heseltine unveiled the centrepiece of his new iconography – the joint BBC–ITV film *Royal
Family*, shown on the eve of Charles's investiture at Caernarfon –
he had opened up to an insatiable public a Pandora's box of royal
goodies which could never again be slammed shut.

His employers, as yet oblivious of the Palace revolution being
hatched below stairs, were meanwhile proceeding along rather
more orthodox lines. On 22 December 1965 Charles's parents
hosted a dinner party at Buckingham Palace with the express purpose of discussing his future. Gathered around the table were the
prime minister (Harold Wilson), the Archbishop of Canterbury
(Michael Ramsey), Lord Mountbatten (representing the Services,

as Admiral of the Fleet), the Dean of Windsor, the chairman of the Committee of University Vice-Chancellors, and the Queen's private secretary, Sir Michael Adeane. Adeane had briefed all the guests beforehand on the subject for discussion – who was not himself invited, thus rather giving the lie to Philip's proud protestations that his son was involved in all decisions over his upbringing.

At breakfast next morning, Charles learned from his parents that the conversation had continued into the small hours. As the prince had already indicated his own wish to go to university, the party had gone through the pros and cons of ancient, 'redbrick' and modern. These in turn were weighed against the Services: Dartmouth, Cranwell, Sandhurst. Soft drinks and beer were served after dinner, plus a brandy for the prime minister, who urged Mountbatten to speak his mind. 'Trinity College, like his grandfather,' said Charles's great-uncle Dickie, 'Dartmouth like his father and grandfather, and then to sea in the Royal Navy, ending up with a command of his own.'[2] The traditional pattern, thought Charles's parents, seemed hard to resist.

But there would again be marginal innovations. If he were to go to university, Charles was intent on living in college – like Edward VIII at Oxford, but unlike Edward VII and George VI at Cambridge, both of whom had lived in large town houses, their tutors travelling to them. None of them had stayed the full three years, nor taken a degree. This remained a matter of vexed debate between Charles and his parents, who for now postponed a decision. The prince himself at first favoured a multi-disciplinary course of studies, perhaps including a dabble in medicine and other such curiosities, which would have made a final examination impossible. But a cautious Philip kept his son's options open for him: 'I don't think his course should be constrained by the absolute need to take a degree.' Wary advisers wholeheartedly agreed, telling his parents, 'For God's sake, don't let him risk exams.'[3]

Charles himself opted for Cambridge, always preferring the old to the new wherever possible, and valuing his family's links with the university. Edward VIII had been the only Prince of Wales to choose Oxford, where he had won a reputation as a none too studious devotee of the high life. The more academically minded Charles had no such aspiration; he wanted, as far as he could tell, to seize the chance for some peace and quiet, to devote his last years free from royal duties to the kind of studies for which he would never again have time. Besides, Cambridge was closer to Sandringham, where he now had his own home in the shape of Wood Farm, the ideal retreat for the shooting weekends to which he was increasingly devoted.

The obvious choice of college was Trinity. The Dean of Windsor's son Robert, whom the prince already knew, was an undergraduate there, and his younger son Edward would be a contemporaneous freshman. But Trinity was also the college of Charles's grandfather, George VI, and of King Edward VII, quite apart from Bacon and Dryden, Marvell and Thackeray, Byron and Tennyson, Newton and Rutherford, Balfour and Baldwin, Melbourne, Grey and Campbell-Bannerman.

Its newly installed master, moreover, was another senior politician, a valued and trusted friend to Charles's parents: R. A. Butler, the Conservative chancellor, foreign secretary and home secretary, often described as 'the greatest prime minister we never had'. 'Rab' Butler, it was universally agreed, would be the perfect figure to shoulder *in loco parentis* responsibilities that bore unusual resonance.

Butler's genial independence of mind was to cause some problems over the next few years. He began at once, over tea with Charles at the Palace in December 1966, earning the wrath of some courtiers when he urged the prince not to bother as yet with any specific study of the British constitution. There would be plenty of time for all that later, argued 'Rab'. This was a chance to study something in which Charles was genuinely interested; archaeology and anthropology, as the prince himself was suggesting, sounded fine. It was also a time to develop some understanding of the structure of British society, perhaps even of the tribal adulation offered a monarchy by its people. Butler's young protégé agreed enthusiastically. In words which would return to haunt him, Charles relished the prospect of 'three years when you are not bound by anything, and not married, and haven't got any particular job'.[4]

He duly arrived in Cambridge in October 1967, to embark on the part one tripos course in 'ark and anth' under the supervision of Trinity's senior tutor, Dr Denis Marrian, who agreed to leave future options open. The only overt privilege to set the prince apart from other freshmen, on Butler's recommendation, was the telephone on his study desk. Workmen from Sandringham had already furnished his first-floor 'set' of rooms, number six on Staircase E of New Court, while the college found itself obliged to protest that the new kitchen installed during the summer vacation had been scheduled long before the prince's arrival.

The chance to cook for himself was to prove a boon when Charles's hopes of dining with his fellow undergraduates in the college hall fell foul of a new version of an old problem. As at Cheam and Gordonstoun, people tended to hang back, even to avoid him. At Cambridge, moreover, this was 1968; as opposition to the Vietnam War provoked diverse forms of student protest on campuses the world over, it was not always fashionable to be seen in the company of a hereditary princeling. On one occasion Charles found himself locked out of the college late at night, along with another nervous young freshman; together they had to ring the porter to let them in. It was the kind of modest little adventure that sometimes sparks undergraduate friendships; but the following night in hall, as Charles wandered down the aisle looking for someone to sit with, he saw the face of his co-conspirator turn away in acute embarrassment. Nobody wanted to be thought too anxious to become his friend.

In letters home Charles is shown musing in a melancholy way about his preference for the companionship of trees or hills over that of human beings, with whom he had to put on a self-conscious show of enjoying himself. But there may have been other reasons why his contemporaries hung back. He was 'unbelievably strait-laced', according to one. He was 'always dressed in corduroys, and rather well-polished, rather heavy shoes'. Very reserved, he 'never let down his guard'.[5]

To Butler's disappointment, Charles's initial circle of Cambridge chums centred on the polo-playing fraternity – he quickly won his half-blue – and fellow public schoolboys from the military and landed gentry rather than the grammar-school products who comprised three-quarters of the college's undergraduate population. One working-class boy whom he did befriend, largely because they shared rooms on the same staircase, was a Welsh economics student called Hywel Jones, an impassioned young socialist destined to become president of Trinity's student union. It was Jones who persuaded Charles that it might broaden his outlook on things to follow him in joining *all* the university's political clubs, including Labour – a notion Butler smartly scotched.[6]

The master had by now introduced a pleasant little ritual, which was to prove an important part of Charles's maturing process. Butler set aside half an hour each evening for a private chat before dinner, giving Charles his own key to a side entrance to the master's lodge, which led by way of what he liked to call 'my secret staircase' directly into the master's study. He found Charles 'talented – which is a different word from clever, and a different word from bright'. Though still a plodder academically, the prince had a relentless curiosity about the ways of the world, which the master was more than qualified to gratify. 'He grew here,' Butler said later. 'When he arrived he was boyish, rather immature, and perhaps too susceptible to the influence of his family.'[7]

But if Butler had to explain patiently to the Prince of Wales why he must not be seen to show allegiance to any one political party, he was also shrewd enough to urge Charles to continue his exploration of socialist ideas with Hywel Jones behind closed doors. Both prince and republican moderated each other's views; and in later years, when he became a pinstriped member of one of Britain's leading economic think-tanks, Jones remained a regular dinner guest of the prince as he sought to deepen his understanding of matters economic, both macro and micro.*

Those evening chats with Butler over Charles's three years at Trinity made perhaps the most important single contribution in his young life so far to broadening his experience and understanding of his fellow man. As the prince entered his twenties, the grand old man of the Tory Party was quite as much a personal guru to the young Charles as Mountbatten or, in later years, Laurens van der Post. But it is sadly characteristic of the older Charles to have disavowed Butler's influence, after it was detailed in the author's 1979 volume, *Charles, Prince of Wales*. This may be due partly to the excitement caused by Butler's revelation that he had encouraged a sexual liaison between the innocent young prince and his research assistant on his memoirs, Lucia Santa Cruz, daughter of the then

---

* Twenty-five years later, after Hywel Jones had appeared in a couple of TV programmes about him, Charles rather gracelessly disavowed their youthful friendship, suggesting that the relationship was 'not as close as [Jones] allowed himself to believe'.[8]

Chilean ambassador to London, who has subsequently gone down in history as the woman who took the Prince of Wales's virginity.[9] But it also shows an ungrateful streak in Charles, a man quite as prepared to disown specific influences as to cultivate them. All too aware that he is easily led, but meanwhile wishing to project himself to the world as his own man, an independent thinker, he is increasingly capable in middle age of such virulent bouts of *amour propre*.

His immaturity at the time was another ghost the prince did not care to see returning to haunt him. Did he really think, for instance, that a false beard and spectacles would enable him to escape recognition while watching a student demonstration 'to see what they're like'? It is commendable that he was keen to take a look, and a sad comment on his plight that he felt unable to go disguised as himself. But it is no surprise, for all his hours of conversation with Hywel Jones, that the natural conservatism of his upbringing prevailed. 'I do try and understand what they're getting at,' said the first-year prince as the Sorbonne students' siege of Paris sparked similar protests on campuses all over the world, including Cambridge, 'but I can't help feeling that a lot of it is purely for the sake of change, which from my point of view is pointless.'

In studious mood, Charles was otherwise little in evidence round the streets of Cambridge that first summer. 'He writes useful and thoughtful essays, although sometimes they are a little rushed,' reported his director of studies, Dr John Coles, to Dr Marrian. 'He is interested in discussion and likes to draw parallels between the people we study and ourselves.'[10] It was a victory for dogged effort over natural ability when the summer vacation brought the news that he had won a 2:1 in his first-year exams – not in the top league, in other words, but the upper half of the second division. A thoroughly average result, it gave him the self-confidence to spurn Butler's advice, switch to a course in history and embark on an overt study of the British constitution.

'But why?' asked Butler.

'Because,' the master recalled him replying (though the prince himself subsequently denied it), 'I'm probably going to be King.'[11]

After an idyllic summer at Balmoral, Charles was none too keen to return to Cambridge with its 'hairy, unwashed student bodies', as he put it in a letter to Mountbatten.[12] His second year at Trinity is remembered more for his performance in student cabaret than in his history tutorials with Dr Anil Seal, his new director of studies. Charles's arch sense of humour – typified by his love of *The Goon Show*, a long-running, anarchic BBC radio programme – was very much at home in undergraduate revue, where funny voices, painful puns and lavatorial jokes tend to be the prime index of wit. Though the Cambridge Footlights has produced several generations of Britain's most talented recent comedians, notably most of the personnel of *Beyond the Fringe* and Monty Python, the attempts of individual colleges to emulate them have always limped several leagues behind. The best-remembered image of the Prince of Wales's second year at Cambridge is that of him sitting onstage in a dustbin – a lasting icon of how easy it can be for royalty to set the nation on a roar. By the time his younger brother Edward aped these antics on television in 1987, roping in his siblings to enact his own version of undergraduate humour for charity, the Prince of Wales was high on the list of the embarrassed and unamused. Only narrowly did he manage to dissuade his wife from joining in, along with her friend Fergie, Duchess of York.

At Cambridge, the unequal struggle to keep the outside world at bay was also, alas, beginning to flag. Perhaps it had always been a pipe dream to expect the student prince's parents to leave him in peace to enjoy university life, whether getting on with his studies or cavorting onstage for the cameras. But Butler found himself increasingly annoyed by the number of 'balcony jobs' (as he scathingly called state occasions) for which Charles was 'needlessly' summoned back to London. Then came an announcement that caused Butler as much rage as it did Charles dismay. To the historian A. J. P. Taylor it was 'a sordid plot to exploit Prince Charles ... made for political reasons, and what is worse, for reasons of party ... Mr Wilson is imposing on Prince Charles a sacrifice he would not dream of imposing on his own son.'[13] Welsh nationalists, too, were outraged by the news that Charles would be spending the summer term of 1969, immediately prior to his investiture as Prince of Wales at Caernarfon Castle, studying Welsh at the University College of Wales, Aberystwyth.

Since the death of Llewelyn-ap-Gruffydd in 1282, at the hands of the English invader, Edward I, Welsh nationalists have always had understandable difficulty taking English Princes of Wales to their hearts. Edward's installation of his son two years later started a line of English princes whom this vociferous minority of Welshmen still cannot abide, more than 700 years on. By the time Charles arrived at Aberystwyth he had passed his twentieth birthday, delivered his first public speech, attended his first royal garden party and given his first radio interview (to Checketts's old friend and business colleague Jack de Manio, the longstanding host of BBC radio's *Today* programme). It was all part of the gathering momentum of the Heseltine–Checketts 'launch' package; and in the process he had begun to square up to the demands placed on him by his hereditary fate in life. But nothing had prepared him for overt hostility ranging from crude student abuse to bomb attacks, hunger strikes and even assassination threats.

The timing proved, to say the least, unfortunate: 1969 was the last year of Harold Wilson's second Labour government, a period of unpopular public austerity, which boosted the resurgence of a fierce strain of nationalism around the principality. As a spate of bomb attacks was mounted on public buildings, a Special Branch security squad was assigned to mount a twenty-four-hour watch over the prince. The men of violence were universally denounced, but there was widespread English sympathy for Welsh resentment of this token term learning a half-dead language at, ironically enough, this most English of Welsh universities. Even the English-born president of the Aberystwyth student union declared the forthcoming investiture 'a cheap, shoddy political gesture . . . If I were Welsh, I would feel incensed.' As one of his Aberystwyth lecturers put it, 'We wouldn't have minded if he was coming for a full three years, but we don't like him popping over for a quick academic wash and brush up before Caernarfon.'[14]

On the day of Charles's arrival, students tried, in vain, to saw the head off a statue of the last Prince of Wales, Charles's great-uncle, on the town's promenade. All Charles could do was confess to 'misgivings' and make the best of a bad job, burying himself in the university's language laboratory, with only eight weeks before a speech in Welsh at an eisteddfod. It was an anxious and lonely period – 'I haven't made many friends, there haven't been many parties' – but the fact that even his tutor, Edward Millward, was a Welsh nationalist helped him grope towards some understanding of Welsh grievances and aspirations. 'If I've learnt anything in the last eight weeks,' he said as term ended, 'it's been about Wales and its problems.' Mindful of the Papuans who had caused him such concern while at Timbertop, he had discovered that the Welsh were 'depressed about what might happen if they don't preserve their language and culture, which is [*sic*] unique and special to Wales. And if something is unique and special, I think it's well worth preserving.'[15]

Gradually Charles's new subjects found it in their hearts to warm to him. By the time he had spoken his first few public words of reasonably elegant Welsh, they were beginning to call him 'Carlo bach' – a term of endearment as significant in Wales as 'Pommy bastard' had been in Australia. His display of resolution in the face of ugly threats had led to a modest personal triumph, much admired by his father – 'He came, saw and conquered the Welsh,' a proud Philip confided to a friend – and a source of great relief to David Checketts, whose pride in his young master was growing fast. As Checketts prepared for the next phase of the 'unveiling' process, he realized he had an unexpected ace up his sleeve. By hitherto protecting the prince from much direct personal publicity, he had also concealed the fact that his earnest young charge was showing himself perfectly equal to the tasks ahead of him. He was alert, shrewd and solemnly aware of his destiny. All of which would come as something of a surprise to the great British public, who in the Palace's view could have been forgiven for thinking, after the Cherry Brandy Incident, the Goonish theatricals and the initial inability to handle Welsh protest, that this prince was just another chinless upper-class halfwit.

Charles may have survived Aberystwyth, but he had as yet won only half the battle. He now knew enough local history to appreciate the significance to the Welsh of Caernarfon Castle, captured by the English invader in 1282. It was there that King Edward I, after killing Llewelyn-ap-Gruffydd – and hanging, beheading, disembowelling and quartering his brother for good measure – had declared his infant son the first English Prince of Wales. And it was there, nearly 700 years later, that Charles himself was now to be installed as the twenty-first.

There were times when the Queen regretted the commitment she had made back in 1958, just as she had regretted creating Charles Prince of Wales so young. The decline of the British economy, the rise of Welsh nationalism and the advent of an era of violent protest all conspired to make such a ceremony seem at best a political blunder, at worst a danger to its protagonist's life. There was no historical obligation for such a ritual; the legend that Edward I displayed his infant son from the battlements had long been adjudged apocryphal, and the only precedent for a public investiture in six centuries was that of the last Prince of Wales, the future King Edward VIII and Duke of Windsor, who had found himself the unhappy victim of some unashamed political chicanery by David Lloyd George, then chancellor of the exchequer.

For more than 650 years, well aware that Caernarfon Castle remained a symbol of English usurpation of Welsh sovereignty, most monarchs had been content to invest their sons in Parliament, palaces or safe English county towns. In 1911, however, during the painful disestablishment of the Welsh Church, Lloyd George had talked George V into a ceremony supposedly designed as a demonstration of Anglo-Welsh unity, but in truth to enhance his own political prestige and appease the opponents of his regular assaults on inherited privilege. The King was duly persuaded that the 'mini-coronation' of his seventeen-year-old son would be an apt climax to his own coronation tour of Britain; and the ceremony went ahead despite the prince's strenuous protests that the 'preposterous rig' he was required to wear would make him a laughing-stock among his friends in the Navy.

The episode was a momentous political triumph for Lloyd George, who stands to this day in aggressive bronze splendour in the Castle Square, his back turned on the bloodstained battlements. For Wilson to attempt the same legerdemain half a century later, in a more cynical age, was perhaps a risk not entirely worth taking. The investiture of Prince Charles in 1969 turned out, in the judgement of the Queen's biographer Ben Pimlott, Professor of Politics at the University of London, to be 'the first major royal ceremonial of the century about which it was politically respectable to argue that it should never have taken place'.[16]

As Lord Snowdon, Constable of the Castle, made elaborately artistic preparations for the world's first major outside broadcast in colour, the political protests mounted. Emrys Hughes MP launched a sustained Commons campaign against a ceremony to be held 'in a castle built by Welsh slave labour under the orders of the intruder, the conqueror'. He was better supported in his protests against the mounting costs of the investiture – a cunning ploy, he believed, to facilitate an increase in the Civil List. Plaid Cymru, the Welsh nationalist party, dissociated itself from this 'piece of English trickery', while the more extreme Welsh Language Society daubed revolutionary slogans in Welsh over roads, bridges and traffic signs throughout the country.

Both groups disavowed the sterner forms of protest which began on 17 November, when a time bomb exploded in the unhappily named Temple of Peace in Cardiff, just as Snowdon and the secretary of state for Wales, George Thomas, were arriving for a planning meeting with 450 Welsh delegates. It was the first in a succession of fifteen bomb attacks on government and military buildings, post offices and pipelines, which moved the Chief Constable of Cardiff to declare, 'If this doesn't stop, someone is going to get killed.' He was to be proved right on the morning of the investiture itself.

Its approach was giving a new lease of life to a thin red line of anarchists calling themselves the Free Welsh Army, who claimed close relations with the IRA, then a year into its renewed campaign of violence in Northern Ireland, but mercifully they were less well organized. As Plaid Cymru voted to boycott the ceremony, and a poll found that 44 per cent of the Welsh people thought it all 'a waste of money', Charles himself sought to pour princely balm on what he recognized as a 'friction point' for many people:

> I don't blame people demonstrating. They've never seen me before. They don't know what I'm like. I've hardly been to Wales, and you can't expect people to be over-zealous about the fact of having a so-called English prince come amongst them and be frightfully excited about it.

Echoing his great-uncle, he said that he would be 'glad when it was over'.[17]

Not until a decade after the ceremony did George Thomas – by then speaker of the House of Commons, later Viscount Tonypandy – reveal how near the investiture's planning committee had come to calling it off. By early 1969, six months before the appointed date, the atmosphere had grown so ugly, and the threats against the prince's life so realistic, that an emergency meeting was called at the Welsh Office to discuss postponement. Thomas himself, his Welsh eloquence adding an extra edge to his natural political cunning, argued that, in truth, postponement would mean cancellation. No part of the United Kingdom, he said, should be allowed to become a no-go area for the royal family. 'It will require great moral courage from that young man, but he has already displayed it in considerable quantities.' Over the months of preparation Thomas had become a close, almost avuncular figure to Charles. When he passed on the prince's wish that the ceremony should go ahead, the meeting was finally swayed – and officially declared never to have taken place.[18]

It was only three weeks before the investiture, at the dreaded post-Aberystwyth speech, that Charles himself transformed the atmosphere. Three hundred tolerably well-pronounced, unfluffed words of Welsh to Urdd Gobaith Cymru, the Welsh League of Youth, were enough to still the noise of protesters. A respectful reference to Llewelyn-ap-Gruffydd, and a promise to work for the preservation of the language, proceeded to reduce hardened nationalists to tears. Plaid Cymru called for an end to the graffiti protest campaign and voted to rethink its boycott. Suddenly, after all the bluster, the open-hearted Welsh people saw what a difficult position Charles had been placed in, and how decorous an exit he had managed to make. With a truly Welsh flourish the Mayor of Caernarfon, Ifor Bowen Griffiths, declared Charles 'the ace in our pack ... When he stood up at the eisteddfod and started to speak in Welsh, he wasn't just a boy. He was a prince. You could have put a suit of armour on that lad and sent him off to Agincourt.'

On investiture eve, however, the Queen's progress north with her family in the royal train was delayed for an hour outside Chester, as bomb-disposal experts dealt with a sinister cardboard box found beneath the bridge that was to carry them over the river Dee. It turned out to be a hoax. But only hours later, around dawn on 1 July itself, a real bomb exploded in Abergele, thirty miles from Caernarfon, killing the two men who were attempting to position it against the wall of a government office. In London the previous afternoon, unknown to the Prince of Wales, Jack de Manio, Denis Marrian and others had foregathered in a BBC television studio to record personal tributes to Charles, to be broadcast in the event of his assassination.[19]

The atmosphere in the coach carrying the prince, Checketts and Thomas through the crowds to the castle that morning was decidedly tense. 'What was that?' Charles asked Thomas, after a loud bang in the distance, which both recognized as the sound of another bomb. 'Oh, a royal salute, sir,' replied Thomas. 'Peculiar sort of royal salute,' said Charles uneasily. 'Peculiar sort of people up here,' replied the southern Welshman of his northern compatriots.[20] As they passed the harbour they could see two mine-sweepers grimly patrolling the entrance, where Charles had hoped the royal yacht *Britannia* would hover regally. Above them heli-copters scrutinized the crowd, relaying the watching faces to a police control centre. A banana skin was thrown under the hooves of the horses drawing the Queen's carriage. Even Princess Margaret was asked for proof of her identity.

Once inside the castle, according to Thomas, everyone felt safer and began to relax. A couple of hours later it was at last all over, as Charles solemnly declared to his mother, before a worldwide television audience of 200 million, 'I, Charles, Prince of Wales, do become your liege man of life and limb and of earthly worship, and faith and truth I will bear unto you to live and die against all manner of folks.'

At the same moment, across the world, three men were preparing to land on the moon. But this archaic ritual in a coastal corner of Wales – watched with mixed emotions by the aged Duke of Windsor in his Paris home – had a greater contemporary sig-nificance than was immediately apparent. The previous evening had seen the first broadcast of Heseltine's 'humanizing' backdrop, the television film *Royal Family*, giving the British people an unprecedented peek into the private lives of their royals. The majestic hands now raising Charles to his feet had last been seen wielding a barbecue fork; Philip, watching solemnly in his field marshall's uniform, had been rowing a protesting Andrew into the Balmoral sunset; Her Majesty's new liege man of life and limb had reduced his kid brother Edward to tears by accidentally snapping a cello string in his face.

Through that film, and a series of television interviews, Charles had been discovered in every British home to be every mother's ideal son. The royals may not be quite like any other family, but they were a family who at least some of the time did relatively normal things in relatively normal ways. For once, the pomp and circumstance of royalty in full-blown ceremonial took second place, in the minds of those watching, to the sight of a private family cracking jokes around the breakfast table.

For all its success at the time, providing a much-needed boost to the monarchy's flagging ratings, Heseltine's brainchild would soon grow into a Frankenstein's monster, reinforcing the 'family monarchy' theme that would rebound with such venom, and creating a public demand for royal titbits far in excess of supply. Curiosity would gradually grow so insatiable that cynical invention would become the only way many national newspapers could continue to capitalize on royalty's contribution to their profits. The main victim, in his own eyes, would be the young man for whom the whole master-plan had been invented. But he himself had yet to live out a drama far more baroque and self-destructive than anything the most lurid tabloid paper could invent.

Paradoxically, the antique royal ritual in Caernarfon that day crystallized a new era of family monarchy, to reach one climax in the Queen's silver jubilee eight years later, and another in the national outpourings over the Prince of Wales's wedding in 1981. That it was subsequently, and so swiftly, to unravel was the last thing anyone could predict – from the twenty-one-year-old prince at the centre of it all to the wistful young schoolgirl who that day spent her eighth birthday watching his investiture with her friends at Silfield School in Norfolk, near the Windsors' Sandringham estate. For Diana Spencer, the national holiday was a welcome break from the greyness of life without her mother, who had walked out on her husband and children eighteen months earlier.

It was to be another decade before Charles would see Diana as a potential bride – a rootless, somewhat heedless decade of drift, while he used his life in the Services to follow Lord Mountbatten's advice to 'sow some wild oats'. Charles's quest for a wife was to be long, complex and fraught with near misses. His eventual proposal to Diana would not be the first he would make; by then he would also have met the one woman whom he will always believe he should have married, and without whose continuing presence in his life his marriage might have survived.

But all that lay way ahead in his thirties; as he embarked on his twenties, under no immediate pressure to marry, Charles was intent on having some fun while he still could. Mountbatten, after all, had told him he would not be able to make a sound choice of bride until he had played the field.

In a case like Charles's, Mountbatten believed that a young man should sow a few wild oats – by which he meant having as many affairs as possible before choosing a bride purely on the grounds of breeding, looks and character. It was crucial, he argued, to find this paragon before she fell for anyone else, as a husband would always have difficulty regarding a sexually experienced wife with un-qualified affection.

Back at Cambridge after his investiture, amid those 'long-haired, bare-footed, perspiring' students,[21] Charles pursued a new romance with Sybilla Dorman, daughter of the governor-general of Malta. Sybilla had been the prince's guest aboard *Britannia* at Caernarfon, before taking him back to her father's Mediterranean fiefdom for a brief recuperative break. Both were studying history, and shared an enthusiasm for amateur dramatics. At Cambridge Charles would collect her for dinner in a mud-stained Sandringham Land-Rover, and was reputed to have climbed the walls of her college, Newnham, after out-staying its midnight curfew. Journalists who pursued the couple to Malta watched with quivering pen as the comely Sybilla applied the prince's suntan oil. But this was to prove the first of innumerable false trails. Charles was soon escorting another girl, Lucinda Buxton, the daughter of the naturalist Aubrey Buxton, a friend of his father, to a Trinity May Ball. Sybilla was one of Charles's many girlfriends who married someone else while the prince was still 'playing the field'; Lucinda, who went on to become an intrepid explorer and documentary film-maker, opted to remain single.

There would be more, many more, before Charles eventually met the girl he would marry. But none would compare with the next to bewitch him, barely a year after he left Cambridge. Of all the girls he would bed and discard over the coming decade, 'one – and one alone' had 'an immediate and indelible effect upon him'. Eighteen months his senior, and far more sexually experienced, she was not the best-looking of Charles's *innamorate*; but she had down-to-earth charms and a direct, unstuffy manner which captivated the unworldly young prince. He particularly liked the way Camilla Shand smiled with her eyes as well as her mouth. She was 'pretty . . . bubbly . . . affectionate . . . unassuming . . . and – with all the intensity of first love – he lost his heart to her almost at once'.[22]

PART TWO

Enter Camilla

CHAPTER SIX

'SO HOW ABOUT IT?'

OF ALL PEOPLE, ACCORDING TO CHARLES, IT WAS LUCIA SANTA CRUZ
who first introduced him to Camilla, with the sixth sense that this
high-spirited and highly sexed if homely ex-debutante was 'just the
girl' for him.[1] As with the Duke of Windsor's first meeting with
Wallis Simpson, the precise details of that momentous encounter
have since become shrouded in mystery and myth. But Lucia seems
an incongruous candidate for matchmaker, as Camilla moved in
the upper-class, polo-playing, hunting-shooting-and-fishing, far
from bookish circles to which the prince needed no introduction
from the blue-stockinged (if herself hot-blooded) daughter of the
Chilean ambassador.

It was in precisely those circles that Charles first registered
Camilla Shand in the summer of 1971, at Smith's Lawn, the
Guards' polo ground near Windsor. A year his senior, twenty-three-
year-old Camilla was the girlfriend of one of his polo-playing
chums, Andrew Parker Bowles, a handsome young Guards officer
and amateur jockey who broke women's hearts as fast as his peers
spent their parents' money. Apart from Camilla's fellow debutantes
such as Lady Caroline Percy, Parker Bowles had already romanced
Charles's own sister, Princess Anne, another libidinous young
equestrian who had yet to fall for her fellow Olympian, Captain
Mark Phillips. As the scion of one of Britain's leading Catholic
families, Parker Bowles could never have married the Queen's only
daughter; but his pursuit of her during his leaves from an army
posting to Germany in 1969–71 certainly put his girlfriend on her

mettle. When Camilla discovered he was two-timing her with two other women at once, she responded by seducing the banking heir Rupert Hambro. It was as if they needed to play musical beds to sharpen their own mutual passion. 'When I was with Andrew,' said Lady Caroline Percy, 'Camilla would come up to me at parties and ask what I was doing with her boyfriend. She was always doing this to girls at parties. I got fed up with it, and said to her, "You can have him back when I've finished with him." '[2]

Almost a decade older than Camilla, and most of his other conquests, Parker Bowles undoubtedly held the whip hand. So volatile was his romance with Camilla that friends thought she went after the gullible young Prince of Wales just to show him that she too could bed royalty. She certainly had the credentials. 'My great-grandmother was your great-great-grandfather's mistress – so how about it?' she is said to have asked the prince soon after their first meeting. It proved an offer Charles could not refuse. A mutual passion grew to the point where, one October evening in 1972, Charles surprised fellow revellers at Annabel's nightclub by his intimacy with Camilla on the dance floor, before spending the night at her modest flat in London's Belgravia.

Only two months remained before Charles was due back on naval duty. Having already discovered Camilla's charms during furtive forays to Broadlands, Mountbatten's home in Hampshire, he was anxious to make the most of the little time he had left with her – anxious enough to take risks he would normally avoid. Even his protection officer knew better than to ask questions as he kept all-night vigil outside Camilla's humble ground-floor flat in Stack House, Cundy Street, around the corner from Victoria Station.

Camilla was said by previous boyfriends to be 'obsessed' with the royal credentials in her family's sexual pedigree. 'She was always mentioning it, as if it were something talismanic,' said her first lover, Kevin Burke.[3]

Camilla's great-grandmother, Alice Keppel, was the youngest daughter of Sir William Edmonstone, a descendant of the Stuart kings of England. In 1891, at the age of twenty-two, Alice married George Keppel, third son of the Earl of Albemarle, and an officer in the Gordon Highlanders. Though not a great beauty, Alice had wit and charm enough to attract the attention of the Prince of Wales, Queen Victoria's son 'Bertie', while he was inspecting the

Norfolk Yeomanry, of which he was colonel-in-chief and Keppel a serving officer. When they met again at Sandown races, the prince asked Alice's escort, Sir John Leslie, to leave him alone with Mrs Keppel. Leslie noted 'that certain look, blending appraisement and admiration, that crossed the prince's face as his eyes travelled over Mrs Keppel's lovely face and fashionably curved figure'.[4]

On 27 February 1898 the prince came to dinner at the Keppels' home in Portman Square, Belgravia, very close to the scene of Charles's tryst with Alice's great-grand-daughter sixty-five years later, and, in the words of his official biographer, 'an understanding arose overnight'.[5] The prince was fifty-seven, Alice only twenty-nine, but they were to be intimate companions for the twelve years left to him, nine of them as King Edward VII. 'That evening changed the rest of his life,' by one account, 'for he had found the most perfect mistress in the history of royal infidelity.'[6] Known to the King's friends as 'La Favorita', Mrs Keppel was 'attractive enough to interest him sexually, entertaining when he was bored, patient when he was cantankerous, sympathetic when he was ill, unobtrusive when he appeared in public . . . Like all successful mistresses, Alice was part-lover, part-wife, part-mother.'[7]

'My job', said Alice, 'is to curtsey, then jump into bed.' Every inch a colonel, as Sir Harold Acton described him, George Keppel accepted the situation 'as if it were perfectly natural to share his wife with his sovereign'. Like another royally cuckolded colonel three generations later, George 'made his own arrangements elsewhere'.[8]

For her part, Edward's wife, Alexandra, displayed 'almost superhuman charity and forbearance', recognizing Alice's importance in her husband's life to the extent of inviting her to visit him on his deathbed. With some reluctance, the Queen even granted her husband's dying wish that she kiss his mistress as 'an act of reconciliation'. After Edward's death in 1910 his close friend Viscount Hardinge, diplomat and statesman, privately praised not merely Mrs Keppel's 'good looks, vivacity and cleverness', but her 'wonderful discretion' and the 'excellent influence' she always exercised upon the king.

> There were one or two occasions when the King was in disagreement with the Foreign Office, and I was able, through her,

to advise the King with a view to the policy of the government being accepted. She was very loyal to the King and very patriotic at the same time. It would have been difficult to find any other lady who would have filled the part of friend to King Edward with the same loyalty and discretion.[9]

Three kings later, seventy-eight-year-old Alice was still alive when her great-grand-daughter Camilla was born in King's College Hospital, London, on 17 July 1947. She died just two months later, and her husband, George, after only a few more weeks. By then their daughter Violet had achieved her own brand of notoriety on the edge of royal circles: as Violet Trefusis, she was the lesbian lover of Vita Sackville-West, wife of Sir Harold Nicolson, official biographer of Edward VII's son, King George V.

But the Keppels had another daughter, Sonia, born two years after Alice's affair with the Prince of Wales began, and widely believed to be his child. She it was who married into the Cubitt family, which had struck it rich building the Grosvenor estates around Belgravia and other fashionable areas of central London, while also constructing Osborne, Queen Victoria's house on the Isle of Wight, and renovating Buckingham Palace.

In 1947, the year of her sister Alice's death and her grand-daughter Camilla's birth, Sonia divorced the third Lord Ashcombe, descendant of the master builder Thomas Cubitt. She later called her memoirs *Edwardian Daughter*, a title laden with innuendo about the identity of her true father. If Camilla's grandmother were indeed King Edward VII's daughter, it would make Camilla herself a second cousin of the present Queen, and second cousin once removed of her lifelong lover, the Prince of Wales.

Like Charles and Camilla seventy years later, Bertie and Alice hosted dinner parties together, travelled Europe together, and used the mistress's complaisant husband as a screen for their extra-marital activities. Like the Parker Bowleses, the Keppels were frequent guests at Sandringham, and at the homes of discreet mutual friends. Sir Philip Magnus's description of Mrs Keppel's appeal to Bertie precisely pre-echoes Camilla's to Charles: 'The truth is that in Alice he had found not only a woman who would excite him physically, as well as relaxing him mentally (a rare combination in itself). On top of that he had found a mistress who could cherish him as fondly as a wife. No man, not even a monarch, could ask for more.'

The one significant difference, as it transpired, was that Charles's wife, unlike Bertie's, was not prepared to turn a blind eye.

It is on her mother's side that Camilla Parker Bowles is descended from Alice Keppell. Her mother was Sonia's daughter by Lord Ashcombe, Rosalind Cubitt, who in 1946 met and married a dashing young war hero named Bruce Shand. Twice awarded the Military Cross, a prisoner-of-war at Spangenburg, and the author of a volume of war memoirs entitled *Previous Engagements*, Major Shand came from a colourful family of Scottish merchants who had squandered as much money as the Cubitts had amassed.

His grandfather was Alexander Shand, Eton-educated friend of the original Fabians, Sidney and Beatrice Webb, and briefly engaged to Constance Lloyd, who chose instead to marry Oscar Wilde. By the first of his four wives, Augusta Mary Coates, Alexander had a son named Philip, also educated at Eton, who went on to become an influential writer on architecture, a friend of Walter Gropius and Le Corbusier. Marital stability was never one of the Shand family's strengths; Philip's marriage broke up in the infancy of his son, Bruce, who was raised by his grandparents. Bruce never really knew his parents, but garnered an interesting array of step- and half-siblings from his father's marital adventures. Bruce's stepsister from Philip's last marriage was to marry the architect James Stirling; his half-sister, Elspeth, was to marry the Conservative politician Sir Geoffrey Howe, who, as Camilla's uncle, has been as generous with his advice as another politician from the next generation, New Labour's Peter Mandelson.

After Camilla's birth in 1947, Bruce and Rosalind Shand soon had two more children, Annabel and Mark. Like Camilla, Mark seems to have inherited the family taste for sexual adventure; before his marriage to Clio Goldsmith, daughter of the ecologist Teddy and niece of the financier Sir James, his name was linked with Princess Lee Radziwill, sister of Jacqueline Kennedy Onassis, and twenty years his senior; Caroline Kennedy, daughter of the assassinated US president; Bianca Jagger, ex-wife of Mick; and the American actress Barbara Trentham, who later married Monty Python's John Cleese.

Camilla's own eye for the opposite sex seems to have focused as soon as puberty permitted. At her first school, Dumbrells, near her parents' home on the Sussex Downs, she was described as 'a lively child who made friends easily'. At her second, Queen's Gate in London, near their town house in South Kensington, she was envied for her precocious sex appeal, despite clinging to twinsets and tweeds while her friends were followers of Sixties fashion in miniskirts and hot pants. One such was Lynn Ripley, alias the future pop star Twinkle, who thought Camilla was 'the coolest girl in the school . . . [at] fifteen, a very hoity-toity little madam who always looked great . . . A Sloane Ranger type, she had a confidence that I envied. She was someone who didn't need to be anything other than she was.'

Among Camilla's teachers was Penelope Fitzgerald, later to become a Booker Prize-winning novelist, who remembered, 'Our girls were so beautiful, but those who were less lovely were allowed to wear a little make-up.' Allowed to wear make-up, Camilla seemed to hold an animal attraction for the opposite sex: 'When a boy hove into view, she could turn on the headlights.'[10] At the time, Queen's Gate was trying to improve on its reputation for 'breeding Foreign Office wives' by teaching girls 'how to write cheques and play bridge'. Academic standards were 'improving'.[11]

Any such improvement seems to have been lost on Camilla, who left without risking any A levels. After an old-fashioned 'grand tour' of Europe she embarked on the usual post-debutante round of London parties and balls, proving a hot date among the upper-crust military and polo-playing set. Camilla's own 'coming-out' party in March 1965 earned the accolade of a mention in Jennifer's Diary, the social jottings of the legendary Betty Kenward in *Harper's* magazine. The following year, in the midst of her affair with Kevin Burke, she first met Captain Andrew Parker Bowles, recently promoted to captain in the Royal Horse Guards, a division of the Household Cavalry popularly known as 'the Blues', famous for mounting guard for the tourists in Whitehall. They were introduced by his younger brother, Simon, who had himself been pursuing Camilla while Andrew was absent in New Zealand on a tour of duty as aide-de-camp to its governor-general, Sir Bernard Fergusson.

Burke was summarily dumped as Camilla and Andrew embarked on what friends described as 'a very hot affair'. Among Parker Bowles's fellow officers was Lord Fermoy, brother of Diana

Spencer's mother Frances. Like their mother, Lady Fermoy, Andrew Parker Bowles's father, Derek, was one of the Queen Mother's closest friends. His mother, Dame Anne, was a close friend of the Queen. In 1953, at the age of fourteen, Andrew had been a page at her coronation. Through his connections, Camilla was already beginning her steady climb up the social ladder towards her royal destiny.

Camilla's passionate if turbulent affair with Parker Bowles was into its fifth year when she first met Charles at Smith's Lawn. Far more mature than the prince, she wasted little time in seducing him. There was never much question that Camilla harboured any hope of marrying Charles; apart from the obvious excitement of bedding the heir to the throne, she was merely using him to bring the wayward Andrew to heel.

That night after Annabel's was not the first they had spent together, merely the first time they had paraded their passion in public. For months Mountbatten had been indulgently tucking them up together at Broadlands. Throughout Charles's twenties, the bisexual sea dog acted as a lecherous old pander, offering his 'honorary grandson' the time, place and seclusion to sow those wild oats. By one inside account, Mountbatten offered Charles the use of Broadlands to entertain 'a number of potential *inamoratas* [*sic*] . . . taking care that they were left alone with the prince'.[12] To Charles, Broadlands had become a much-loved second home, as he wrote to Mountbatten after a series of visits in the early 1970s. [13]

By the autumn of 1972 Camilla had supplanted all her predecessors at Broadlands, to the point where she accompanied Mountbatten aboard Charles's ship, *Minerva*, for a guided tour and lunch with the prince. She returned alone the following weekend, a fortnight before Christmas, to say her farewells before Charles set sail. 'The last time I shall see her for eight months,' he wrote forlornly to Mountbatten.[14]

During his trysts with her at Broadlands, Charles had contemplated proposing marriage to Camilla Shand. She seemed to offer everything he wanted in a wife: relaxed in his presence, full of admiration for his qualities, witty, sexy and, above all, deeply loyal. But the prince was still awestruck by the commitment he was asking any potential bride to make: a surrender of her own privacy, and to some extent her own identity, to put public duty before private inclinations, perhaps even private happiness. It was not yet a question he was ready to ask anyone, though Camilla was the nearest anyone had come to tempting him.

Charles was barely twenty-four, and also mindful of Mountbatten's advice – though not, as yet, of his hidden agenda – to 'play the field' awhile. He was still a serving officer in the navy, with long stints at sea ahead of him. Not until he was back on terra firma for good, the prince decided, could he reasonably ask anyone to commit herself to him. On the positive side, there was no immediate pressure for him to marry; and any girl worth waiting for would surely wait for him.

So it came as all the more of a blow just three months later, in March 1973, when Camilla announced her engagement to Andrew Parker Bowles (who spent the day convalescing in a Berkshire nursing home after yet another riding accident). Charles was devastated by the news, which reached him thousands of miles away in the Caribbean, where he had been transferred from *Minerva* to a brief posting aboard a coastal survey vessel, HMS *Fox*. He wrote mournfully to Mountbatten about the end of what he saw as an idyllic relationship. Now he had 'no-one' to go back to in England. But he concluded glumly that the feeling of emptiness would eventually pass.'[15]

His feelings were intensified a month later, when a letter from his father advised him of the imminent announcement of his sister Anne's engagement to her fellow Olympic equestrian Captain Mark Phillips. This news quite unmanned Charles, who confessed to 'a spasm of shock and amazement' and was deeply depressed for days. Convinced that his sister had made 'a ghastly mismatch', with a man who 'has no idea whether he is coming or going', he was also bereft at the thought of losing his special relationship with Anne, mainstay of his childhood and youth, an irreplaceable confidante, whose prime loyalty now lay with another man. At the same time, Charles knew all too well, the marriage of his younger sister would only increase the pressure on him to do likewise. 'I can see I shall have to find myself a wife pretty rapidly, otherwise I shall get left behind and feel pretty miserable!'[16]

As a former girlfriend of Andrew Parker Bowles, Princess Anne attended his wedding to Camilla Shand that July in the Guards' Chapel in Birdcage Walk, next door to Buckingham Palace. The bride wore white. The Queen Mother, a distant relative of the

Parker Bowles family, also attended the subsequent reception at another royal palace, St James's (eventually to become Prince Charles's London home). Reports reaching a miserable Charles, back aboard *Minerva* in the Caribbean, told of Camilla looking radiant in 'lashings of tulle, with diamonds in her hair'. After seven storm-tossed years, she had finally landed her man, one of the most eligible bachelors in town.

Four thousand miles away, the most eligible bachelor on earth suffered another wave of emotional trauma, as he realized that this was what Camilla had really wanted all along. There was little point in regretting his failure to propose to her; she might well have turned him down anyway. To Camilla, as mutual friends would later explain to him, Charles had been just 'a nice young boy' with whom she had enjoyed an unusually interesting fling. Eighteen months older than him, and far more mature, she had always had her sights set on the more dashing Parker Bowles. Camilla, as her friend Carolyn Gerard Leigh told reporters, 'never wanted to be Queen'.[17]

When his lost love bore her first child the following year, and named him Thomas Charles after the prince, who also agreed to be his godfather, there were inevitable rumours in the polo set and beyond – which persist to this day – that Charles was the boy's father. A modicum of research would show that in March 1974, nine months before Tom Parker Bowles's birth on 18 December, the Prince of Wales was at the other end of the earth, as far away as he could possibly be, serving as communications officer aboard HMS *Jupiter*, prior to joining his parents in New Zealand at the opening of the Commonwealth Games. Both the Parker Bowles children – a daughter, Laura, soon followed – were to know untold suffering when the full extent of their mother's liaison with the prince became public knowledge twenty years later. But Tom was at least spared the taunts of his contemporaries until he was out of his teens, and a student at Oxford, when the prince failed to consult him before confessing to the world on global television that he had committed adultery with Tom's mother over many years.

For now, as the Parker Bowleses set up house at Bolehyde Manor in Wiltshire, Charles had to write off what might have been and content himself with following his great-uncle's advice to bide his time. In retrospect, the rest of Charles's twenties and early thirties were to prove rootless and aimless years during which he continued to suffer woefully from parental neglect. 'He was a gentle, melancholic soul,' observed one female friend at this time. 'There seemed to be such a loneliness, a strange desolation trapped inside him.' It has been perceptively suggested that his 'haunting search for alternative philosophies and remedies' between 1972 and 1980 was 'simply an outlet for his feelings of being unloved'.[18] Unloved, that is, by his own generation as much as that of his parents and their advisers, who had drawn up agendas for the heir to the throne's public activities but none for his private contentment.

By his thirtieth birthday in November 1978, Charles would still be a bachelor, dancing the night away at a Buckingham Palace ball with the voluptuous British film star Susan George, best known for baring all (prior to being brutally raped) in Sam Peckinpah's cult movie *Straw Dogs*. Throughout his twenties the prince openly enjoyed the company of several such racy celebrities, as well as innumerable blue-blooded English roses. But many girls seen on his arm had long since given up on their indecisive prince to marry others and start families of their own. Several genuine romances had crumbled under the pressure of pursuit by paparazzi, who were not above pitching camp round the clock on the doorstep of their current favourite. A despairing Charles was forced at times to use decoys, such as Penelope Eastwood, then the girlfriend (later the wife) of his friend Norton Knatchbull, Lord Romsey, to divert attention from an authentic passing fancy.

As he entered his thirties Charles told his staff he had three priorities for the decade ahead: to learn more about the nation over which he would one day reign; to step up his work overseas as unofficial export salesman for British industry; and, most urgently, to find the nation and Commonwealth its future Queen.

It was not just politics that had cheated Charles of his most cherished recent ambition. The absence of a bride, to act as his hostess, had been as powerful an argument as any constitutional embarrassments against his becoming governor-general of Australia, the Queen's representative in her Commonwealth dominion, seen as apt on-the-job training for the constitutional role ahead of him. The notion had been discussed several times throughout the 1970s – at the suggestion, ironically enough, of

Gough Whitlam, the Australian Labour prime minister who had abolished the national anthem and launched the country down its long march to millennial republicanism. It was Whitlam's abrupt dismissal in 1975 by the then governor-general, Sir John Kerr, in the Queen's name, that had brought the office too close to politics for princely comfort.

Whitlam's successor, Malcolm Fraser, was already hinting on the royal grapevine that he might be able to 'fix' things, thus, *en passant*, shoring up his own political security with a sizeable proportion of the Australian electorate. Fraser's own political fragility, and the upsurge in republican sentiment as Australia approached its bicentenary in 1988, were in time to make these promises hollow, but in 1978 they were, in any case, conditional upon the Prince of Wales finding himself a princess.

Apart from his immediate predecessor, whose eventual choice of bride led him to renounce the throne, Charles was the first Prince of Wales to have reached the age of thirty unmarried since James Stuart, the Old Pretender, in 1718 (and even he took a wife the following year). Of those Princes of Wales who became Kings of England, only Henry V and Charles II were unmarried at thirty; but each remained so for only two more years, and each, already on the throne, had enjoyed a singularly busy youth.

Charles had known no Agincourt, no exile from a republican government, to occupy his twenties. The decade had proved a long, troubled period of slow drift, for which his parents and their advisers must, in retrospect, take heavy responsibility. After his baptism of fire at Caernarfon, launching him with reluctance towards the arms of a rapaciously waiting world, there had been brief respite in the shape of a return to Cambridge for his final year at Trinity. Despite the distractions of more student theatricals, he won himself a thoroughly average BA honours degree, Class II Division II, before disappearing into Her Majesty's Services for what turned out to be a six-year stint.

From the moment of his arrival at Cranwell, the RAF training college, the prince displayed a natural talent for flying; besides, he welcomed the unwonted sense of freedom afforded by the solitude of the cockpit. He won his wings effortlessly before moving on, again in his father's footsteps, to the Royal Naval College, Dartmouth – the springboard to five years' service as an officer aboard Her Majesty's warships *Norfolk*, *Minerva*, *Jupiter* and

Hermes. Life out at sea with the Navy was as 'normal' as it ever would be – no press, no sightseers, no red boxes, not even a private detective – and Charles relished his rare chance to become 'one of the lads'. For a while he even felt relaxed enough to sport a beard, which lent him a striking resemblance to his great-grandfather, King George V, though it had to come off, on the Queen's orders, before his next appearance at a state occasion. The prince began to savour the communal bravado of Service life just as it had to end, with a chance to combine his love of both air and sea as a helicopter pilot in the Fleet Air Arm, the airborne arm of the Royal Navy.

To his mother's occasional dismay, he ducked none of the more hazardous aspects of training, from underwater escape practice in a 100-foot training tank to royalty's first-ever parachute jump – a 'somewhat hairy' experience, as his feet got caught in the rigging. So he was not best pleased to learn that two Mark V jet Provosts set aside for his personal use had been specially modified, or to be told that Buccaneer strike aircraft and Sea King anti-submarine helicopters were too dangerous for him to fly. 'I'm stupid enough to like trying things,' he said at the time, 'though perhaps I do push myself too hard.'

There were shudders between the Palace and Whitehall when the heir to the throne's training course in Wessex V helicopters involved him in a rapid succession of three emergency landings, due respectively to computer failure, engine failure and a broken fragment of metal lodging in his engine. But he survived, and finished his Navy days in style with a command of his own, albeit of the smallest ship in the British fleet, the wooden-hulled minesweeper HMS *Bronington*.

But even his North Sea patrols aboard *Bronington* – 'routine to the point of tedium' – were not without their alarms. In March 1976 two sea cadets were nearly lost in freezing waters when a landing operation went badly wrong; they nobly agreed to take the blame to spare the disciplinary blushes of *Bronington*'s skipper. That July, during routine exercises off Holyhead, Charles gave the order to lower anchor without noticing the underwater cable marked on his chart; on trying to raise it again, he found he had snagged the telecommunications cable linking Britain and Ireland. During his ensuing attempts to dislodge the anchor, 'conditions were so bloody that we nearly lost two divers'.

After twenty-four hours he was forced to give up and commit the cardinal naval sin of slipping anchor, sourly observing, 'I've got to live with the GPO [the General Post Office, then the national telecommunications agency] for the rest of my life. What happens if I break the damn thing? I've had enough of this.' The incident earned him 'a stern rebuke' from his superiors at the Ministry of Defence.[19]

Amid recurrent suggestions that a military training was no longer appropriate for the heir to the throne, the prince remained mindful of the words of Lord Mountbatten's father, Prince Louis of Battenberg, to the future King George V: 'There is no more fitting preparation for a king than to have been trained in the Navy.'[20] The criticism, to Charles, was 'pointless and ill-informed'. The Services attracted 'a large number of duty-conscious people'; military service was 'a worthwhile occupation which I am convinced will stand me in good stead for the rest of my life'.[21]

These swashbuckling years may have provided him with some of his most down-to-earth moments to date, amid the hearty camaraderie of Service life, but their temporary status had also accentuated his sense of purposelessness. Charles's twenties were to end on a high note, with his chairmanship of the Queen's Silver Jubilee Appeal in 1977. But this particular decade, for most other mortals one of the most vividly enjoyable of their lives, proved for the earnest young Prince of Wales a period of increasingly agonized introspection – the beginning of a long voyage of self-discovery that continues to this day.

He launched, in embryonic shape, his first charity, the Prince's Trust, and took over from Mountbatten as president of the United World Colleges, an international network of schools founded on principles similar to those of Kurt Hahn's Gordonstoun. At thirty, Charles was president or patron of some 200 charities, clubs, committees and organizations. But there was no cohesive purpose to his public activities, nor indeed to his private life. With few friends beyond the small circle he could trust, mostly his staff and the back-slapping polo brigade, he remained a solitary and somewhat tortured figure. Few Englishmen of thirty, after all, still live at home with their parents. Unable to go out on a whim, Charles spent many of his evenings alone, eating a solitary meal off a tray with a glass of milk, with the television as his only companion.

Even he began to see that, for personal as much as constitutional reasons, he needed a wife.

As yet, in his own eyes, he had simply failed to meet the right girl at the right time. A late developer sexually, as in other ways, again because of the artificiality of his upbringing, Charles was still rather clumsy with women. Beyond the obvious pulling power of his station in life, the prince's gentle and caring nature was his main appeal to the opposite sex; but he was a gauche and rather awkward beau, often disappearing without explanation from his girlfriends' lives as abruptly as he had entered them.

It did not help that his sense of propriety obliged all his escorts to call him 'Sir', even in moments of intimacy; nor that his detective had to remain with him everywhere he went, somewhat cramping his style in his beloved Aston-Martin. As many a girlfriend came and went, Charles grew more and more depressed, almost desperate.

For a while his parents even grew concerned that their oldest son might 'go the way of the Duke of Windsor'. His attitude to women also worried the otherwise doting Mountbatten, one of the few who could get him to listen to candid advice, who now warned him against heading towards the slippery slope which wrecked his Uncle David's life, precipitating his ignominious abdication and rendering the rest of his life a wasteland. When Thames TV's series *Edward and Mrs Simpson* was screened in 1978, members of the royal household were struck by the degree of sympathy Charles showed for his great-uncle's plight. Were all the well-meant reforms of his upbringing to prove the prince's undoing?

The reasons Charles hesitated so long over his choice of a bride, disappointing matrons and tantalizing maidens the world over, were many and various: personal and public, domestic and constitutional. For no other man in the world was his quest for a life-partner so complex, so fraught with potential pitfalls, so hedged around with restrictions. Anxious to recreate the stable family circle of his own childhood, he considered himself in need of a paragon among women – prepared to be privately loving, supportive and long-suffering, the sole confidante of a man with many confidences to share, as well as publicly conscientious and dutiful. And yet there were so many constraints on his choice, some of them legal, and quite out of synch with the multi-ethnic, multi-denominational country his future kingdom had rapidly become.

Under the 1689 Bill of Rights, enshrined in the 1701 Act of Settlement, by which his family's legal claim to the throne is established, the heir to the throne was forbidden to marry a Catholic. Under the Royal Marriages Act of 1772, he was barred from marrying without the consent of his mother or Parliament. As the future Supreme Governor of the Church of England, he could not marry a divorcee, or indeed any girl with what the British like to euphemize as 'a past' – which, in the permissive 1970s, narrowed the field considerably. The Queen, as custodian of the royal blood line, was keen for her son and heir to marry a princess; but eligible, let alone desirable, non-Catholic European princesses without a past were in somewhat short supply.

As a private citizen, Charles could of course marry whomsoever he chose. But a match with an ineligible or even unsuitable girl would have obliged him to renounce his right to the throne, a course that militated against every instinct bred into him. Constitutional niceties take little note of social change, and a late-twentieth-century prince was quite simply and forlornly stuck with a set of rules devised for his eighteenth- and nineteenth-century ancestors. There were times when his mother considered repeal of the ancient laws governing royal marriages; but, as usual, her deep-dyed conservatism prevailed.

Charles's cousin, Prince Michael of Kent, had only recently been obliged to surrender his place in the line of succession in order to marry a Catholic divorcee, Baroness Marie-Christine von Reibnitz. Elizabeth II's reign had otherwise seen the monarchy to some extent catch up with the social mores of the times. In 1953, when divorcees were still barred from the royal enclosure at Ascot – which today would exclude most of the royal family – the young new Queen Elizabeth II had felt obliged to talk her younger sister out of marrying a divorcee, Group Captain Peter Townsend. Twenty-five years later she permitted her to divorce the man she had married instead, Tony Snowdon. It was the closest divorce had come to the throne since the reign of King Henry VIII.

But Margaret was way down the line of succession, and the Queen felt very differently about her own children, both as their mother and as their monarch. As they too headed towards married life, she envisaged no such relaxation in the royal rules for the Prince of Wales or his siblings. When, in later years, Princess Anne thought her aunt Margaret's divorce might smooth her own passage towards a separation from Mark Phillips, she was at first firmly told otherwise. Prince Philip was himself the product of a broken marriage; but Charles knew there was no way he could contemplate marrying a divorcee, or making anything other than a lifetime commitment to whomever he did finally choose. 'In my position,' as he put it at the age of twenty-six, 'obviously the last thing you can contemplate is divorce.'[22]

These private agonies were only worsened by remorseless pressure from public, press and parents. Throughout his twenties, Britain's tabloid newspapers heard wedding bells every time the prince was seen out and about with any member of the opposite sex. But the British press had been marrying Charles off since he was three. In 1952, on his mother's accession to the throne, the Sunday papers were already printing the first of countless lists of suitable brides for a prince who, mercifully enough, could not yet read them. Twenty years later they were still publishing regular photomontages of scores of glamorous, pouting candidates, from titled daughters of the English aristocracy to less comely, often ineligible, obscure foreign royalty.

Not least because he was so set in his bachelor ways, and felt little personal inclination to marry, the prince's reluctant quest for a bride became a less than comfortable obsession. 'Married, aren't you?' he would ask people. 'Fun, is it?'[23] The perennial bachelor sadly told a friend, 'Whenever I invite people to a dinner party these days, they *all* seem to have got married.' To his small circle of intimates, he talked of little else. In his mid-twenties, he had told an interviewer that he thought thirty was 'about the right age to marry'; now that remark returned to haunt him with a vengeance. His parents had long tried to remain understanding, but his father began to grow characteristically impatient. 'You'd better get on with it, Charles,' said Philip, 'or there won't be anyone left.'

Charles had already spelt out his own criteria for marriage:

> Whatever your place in life, when you marry you are forming a partnership which you hope will last fifty years. So I'd want to marry someone whose interests I could share. A woman not only marries a man; she marries into a way of life – a job . . . She's got to have some knowledge of it, some sense of it, or she wouldn't have a clue about whether she's going to like it. If I'm

deciding on whom I want to live with for fifty years – well,
that's the last decision on which I would want my head to be
ruled by my heart.[24]

By his own account the prince had 'fallen in love countless times'
– though he had yet to add his notorious rider 'whatever love
means'. Over the decade between Cambridge and his eventual
wedding, Charles enjoyed enough liaisons – most consummated, a
few not – for members of the royal household to worry about an
inappropriate promiscuity.[25] In truth, it was more a case of a little
boy lost in a grown-up world, in search of he knew not what, combined with a built-in selfishness that eventually drove away even
the most socially ambitious of passing partners.

During his intermittent leaves at home, amid sundry adventures
ashore around the world's more exotic ports, the prince fell first for
Georgiana Russell, daughter of the British ambassador to Spain,
Sir John Russell, kinsman to the Duke of Bedford. Eighteen months
older than him, and already embarked on a worldly career at
Vogue magazine, Georgiana was the first in a long line of brief
liaisons to observe that the prince had 'long lost the art of
unselfishness'. After a sudden declaration of love, as befits a self-
styled 'incurable romantic', Charles expected his girlfriends to fit in
with his own bachelor agenda, assuming that his rank would
guarantee meek compliance. It was his misfortune, if not theirs,
to have reached adulthood in an age when women had begun to
expect rather more of a man, not least some acknowledgement of
their own independent identity and aspirations. This was not an
aspect of life for which Charles had been trained; quite the reverse.
Despite an unusual bond in their shared Greek heritage – her
mother, unlike her contemporary Prince Philip, had been brought
up in Greece – Georgiana lasted a mere nine months before moving
on to marry another.

The last straw, it seems, was a fishing trip to Balmoral, where
Charles evidently saw no need to adjust his usual routine to accommodate his guest. According to his valet, the late Stephen Barry,
Georgiana was 'freezing cold and eating scraps because the prince
was on one of his economy drives. I think she thought the week
would be rather glamorous – a romantic interlude in the Highlands
with her prince. Nothing of the kind. He was standing with his feet

in icy water all day, while she was going bored out of her mind. I thought then that she was not going to last the course, and I was right.'[26]

Next came Lady Jane Wellesley, daughter of the eighth Duke of Wellington, who had known Charles since childhood, when she had been a sprightly presence at some of his Buckingham Palace birthday parties. Jane was the first of the prince's true loves who was also an eminently suitable candidate – unlike Camilla, whose blood was not a deep enough blue – to become Queen. Daughter of one of England's noblest families, she was quite at ease at court; she also shared the mischievous nature of Charles's youth, but was prepared to behave with due decorum when necessary.

Jane's father, moreover, owned ancestral estates in southern Spain: 30,000 acres at Molino del Rey, near Granada, won for the family by the Iron Duke's peninsular campaign. They made an ideal retreat. On one of several sojourns there, during a break from his duties aboard *Minerva*, Charles became so exercised by the attentions of the press that he pleased his father, for once, by swearing at them. Despite denials issued (along with an apology for his bad language) via his private detective, neither press nor public wished to discount the comely Lady Jane as their future queen. That autumn, when she attended morning service at Sandringham as a guest of the royal family, 10,000 people defied both royal denials and a petrol shortage to turn up and gawp. 'Such was their obvious conviction that what they had read was true,' said Charles in a rare public reference to his private life, 'that I almost felt I had better espouse myself at once so as not to disappoint so many people.'[27]

Whereas the press had filed touching reports from Spain of Lady Jane 'playfully throwing watermelons at the prince', however, the truth is that he and his friend Nicholas Soames had been throwing them at her. As intelligent as she was beautiful, the serious-minded young Jane Wellesley could not believe how immature her coeval was in his early twenties, when she herself was already forging a career in television (then on the staff of the *Radio Times*, now as a successful independent programme producer, a founder-director of Warner Sisters).

Lady Jane, who has never married, was less likely than people imagined to want to be Charles's or indeed anyone's queen. Again, the prince was unlucky to grow up in an age when women could find such a fate far from irresistible, and royal proposals of marriage could not assume automatic acceptance. Although she has been cited as turning him down, Jane Wellesley has remained a loyal enough friend to the prince never to have revealed publicly whether he even got as far as proposing; the likelihood is that, fearful of such a fate but well versed in protocol, she was smart enough not to have given him the chance.

Throughout 1973–4, nevertheless, Lady Jane remained the bookies' favourite in the royal marriage stakes, peaking when she accompanied the Queen Mother and Princess Alexandra to the 1974 royal film première – a sure sign of family approval. But later that year her odds lengthened briefly when a glossy American blonde was spotted among the dignitaries in the Strangers' Gallery of the House of Lords to hear Charles make his maiden speech. She was Laura Jo Watkins, the daughter of an American admiral, to whom the prince had taken a shine that March when she was among the reception committee for HMS *Jupiter* at San Diego, California.

Mountbatten was a friend of Laura Jo's father, Admiral James Watkins, whom he had met in Malta while serving with the US Sixth Fleet. With Charles's wild oats in mind, he had invited both father and daughter to London for a farewell dinner for the American ambassador, Walter Annenberg. Throughout the week Laura Jo popped up at various functions, and newspapers were already waxing lyrical about an unmarried Wallis Simpson when she just as abruptly disappeared again. Unusually large crowds converged on Cowdray Park polo ground that weekend to see the prince at play, but they were disappointed. 'You don't think I'm such a bloody fool as to bring her here today, do you?' he laughed, in unwontedly paternal mode. And that, it seemed, was that, until four years later, in the summer of 1978, when his friend Guy Wildenstein flew Laura Jo over to the French resort of Deauville as a surprise present during Charles's annual polo visit.

It was, ironically, over dinner at Jane Wellesley's in the summer of 1975 that Charles met the next young woman to capture his heart, the beautiful but star-crossed Davina Sheffield – someone for whom the prince could not disguise his yearning, even in public. A soldier's daughter and an ex-debutante, blonde and dramatically attractive, Davina was one of the few girlfriends with whom Charles contentedly allowed himself to be photographed. That summer he took her up to Balmoral, where she charmed his family. But Davina was committed to spending the autumn in Vietnam, to work in an orphans' hospital during what turned out to be the last stage of the war. Forced to flee by the Vietcong advance, she returned home to more tragedy: the brutal murder of her mother by raiders at their Oxfordshire home.

As she turned to the prince for solace, Davina was publicly arm in arm with him again by the autumn of 1976. The nation endured a momentary *frisson* when she was reported to have been seen naked in the men's changing room during a surfing expedition to Bantham, a quiet Devon cove frequented by Charles and his friends. In the ensuing furore one of her ex-boyfriends, an Old Harrovian named James Beard, chose to reveal that they had enjoyed 'a full sexual relationship' while cohabiting at his cottage near Winchester. In vain did Beard try to make amends by wishing the couple well: 'I am sure they will be very happy. I think she will make a magnificent wife and an extremely good Queen.' With royal protocol still demanding a virgin bride, the damage had been done. Davina went the same way as another of Charles's passing romances, Fiona Watson, daughter of the Yorkshire landowner Lord Manton – who fell by the royal wayside after a jealous ex-boyfriend alerted Fleet Street to the fact that she had once revealed her startling 38–23–35 statistics, in full colour across eleven pages, to readers of *Penthouse* magazine.

Throughout the late 1970s a dizzying succession of elaborately named, blue-blooded daughters of the aristocracy were romantic-ally linked with the prince, including Lady Leonora Grosvenor and her sister Lady Jane, sisters of the Duke of Westminster; Lady Victoria and Lady Caroline Percy, daughters of the Duke of Northumberland; Bettina Lindsay, daughter of the Conservative politician Lord Balniel; Lady Cecil Kerr, daughter of the Marquess of Lothian; Lady Henrietta Fitzroy, daughter of the Duke of Grafton; Lady Charlotte Manners, daughter of the Duke of Rutland, and her cousin Elizabeth Manners; Angela Nevill, daughter of Prince Philip's private secretary, Lord Rupert Nevill; Lady Camilla Fane, daughter of the Earl of Westmorland; and Lord Astor of Hever's daughter Louise.

By the time Charles turned thirty, he had also had his long-awaited, almost obligatory encounter with the glamorous Princess Caroline of Monaco, daughter of Prince Rainier and the former

Grace Kelly. It was an undisguised mutual sizing-up operation, and it was not a success. Caroline was forty-five minutes late for their first rendezvous – the kind of discourtesy the prince loathes – at which both soon realized they had little in common. She 'irritated' him and he 'bored' her. 'Before I arrived the world had me engaged to Caroline,' he said. 'With our first meeting the world had us married, and now the marriage is in trouble.'[28] A second meeting was cancelled, and the following year, pleading pressure of work, Charles regretfully declined his invitation to attend Caroline's wedding to the French playboy Philippe Junot. Besides, Caroline of Monaco was, of course, a Roman Catholic, and it would have taken a grand passion even to begin to contemplate ways around so formidable a hurdle.

Charles's mother, ever conscious of her duty to the purity of the blood royal, remained keen for him to marry fellow royalty if at all possible. His life might have turned out very differently had a non-Catholic virgin princess been available. 'People tend to marry within their own circles,' as Philip put it. 'There is a built-in acceptance of the sort of life you are going to lead.'[29] In June 1977 the *Daily Express* even managed, exclusively and 'officially', to announce the Prince of Wales's betrothal to Princess Marie-Astrid of Luxembourg – 'the formal engagement will be announced from Buckingham Palace on Monday'[30] – offering various bland solutions to the minor inconvenience that she, too, happened to be a Roman Catholic. By now the Palace's exasperated denials had become cries in a sceptical wilderness.

But that same year did finally see Charles embark on the romance that was eventually to lead, by a circuitous and unexpected route, to the end of his long quest for a bride. It was during the Marie-Astrid furore, at Ascot in June 1977, that he first met Lady Sarah Spencer, daughter of his mother's old friend Earl Spencer. Red-haired, vivacious Sarah was suffering at the time from anorexia nervosa, exacerbated by the end of a recent romance with the Duke of Westminster, one of Britain's richest men, who was also a close friend of Charles. To this day Sarah keeps a photograph of herself in her bikini dating from this period, when she was virtually skeletal. As she told the prince of the treatment she was undergoing with Dr Maurice Lipsedge, a London psychiatrist – who would later treat her bulimic younger sister – Charles was immensely sympathetic. As a romance began to blossom, he allowed himself to be party to one of the Spencer family's desperate ploys to nurse Sarah back to health: she was allowed to telephone the Prince of Wales every time she put on two pounds in weight.

That summer Charles invited Sarah to watch him play polo at Smith's Lawn, Windsor, the great sexual marketplace where he had first met Camilla six years earlier. A romance seemed on the cards, though he was briefly diverted by the charms of a Venezuelan beauty named Cristabel Barria-Borsage. Sarah was his nominal date that evening, but he spent most of it dancing with Cristabel, who rode back to London that night in the front of his car, a seething Sarah sharing the back seat with his detective. By some accounts, it was the Venezuelan beauty who wound up spending that night with Charles. Accustomed to his girlfriends – Sarah included – addressing the prince as 'Sir', Cristabel was not sure what to call him as they climbed into bed. 'What shall I call you, Charles or sir?' she asked. 'Call me Arthur,' came the agitated reply.[31]

Sarah was forced to grin and bear it while Cristabel proved but a passing princely fancy. By that autumn she was again Charles's 'steady' girlfriend, moving the press to proclaim her the latest candidate for Britain's next queen. In November Charles accepted Sarah's invitation to join a weekend shooting party at the Spencers' ancestral estate in Northamptonshire, Althorp. Home from boarding school for the weekend, as it happened, was her younger sister Diana – then just sixteen.

In Nobottle Wood, a ploughed field on the Althorp estate, young Diana self-consciously cut a 'nondescript' figure in her borrowed anorak, corduroy trousers and wellington boots. She had known the royals since childhood, so did not feel particularly nervous around the prince. 'Look at the life they have,' she had often thought to herself. 'How awful.'[32] That day she was also aware, of course, that her sister would not welcome any attempt on her part to make an impression on her potential prize catch. But Charles took enough notice of Diana to observe that she seemed a 'very jolly and amusing and attractive' 16-year-old – 'full of fun'.[33]

As Sarah danced attendance on the prince at a party in his honour that evening, Diana deliberately kept out of the way. 'I remember being a fat, podgy, no make-up, unsmart lady, but I made a lot of noise and he liked that.' After dinner, Charles upset Sarah by asking her younger sister to take him on a guided tour of the Spencer picture gallery, then one of the finest private art collections in Britain outside his own family's. She was about to comply when Sarah came up and told her to 'push off', moving Diana to score a stylish revenge: 'At least let me tell you where the [light] switches are, because you won't know.' Then she duly made herself scarce.

Diana, to her sister's dismay, had clearly made an impression on Charles. The same was not true, as yet, the other way round. Diana's main memory of the prince, looking back at that fateful weekend, was: 'God, what a sad man.'[34]

CHAPTER SEVEN

'SOMEBODY TO LOOK AFTER YOU'

DIANA KNEW ALL ABOUT SADNESS. IT HAD BLIGHTED HER LIFE SINCE she was six years old – and the day she had sat forlornly alone on the cold stone floor of the house where she was born, watching the domestic staff loading her mother's worldly goods into a waiting car. There was a scrunch of feet on the gravel, the slam of a car door and the sound of an engine starting, then slowly receding into the distance as the whole house fell ominously silent. Diana's mother was gone, never to return. 'Mummy', as her daughter later put it, had 'decided to leg it.'[1]

It was that scrunching sound on the gravel, Diana used to say, that she could still hear thirty years later. It haunted her every day thereafter, and kept her awake at night. As soon as they were old enough to understand anything, the four surviving Spencer children – Sarah, Jane, Diana, Charles – knew that their parents' marriage was not the field of dreams they had fondly imagined. They grew up to a descant of raised voices, which may have ended at home that dark day in 1967, but continued through the law courts for two more years in one of the bitterest high-society divorce cases of the day. Johnny Spencer countersued his wife on the grounds of her adultery with Peter Shand Kydd, a wallpaper heir into whose arms she had fled. Feelings in the family ran so high that Frances's own mother, the Queen Mother's friend Ruth, Lady Fermoy, testified against her daughter.

Her parents' divorce case was about as painful for Diana as these things can possibly be. Like the rest of the nation, the eight-year-old girl could only watch via the national newspapers as her father mobilized sufficient character witnesses from the British aristocracy to render her mother's case hopeless. Custody of the children, most unusually, then as now, was granted to her father.

The Spencer marriage had started, as it was to end, in a blaze of publicity. In 1954 Frances had been the youngest bride this century to have married in Westminster Abbey, with the young new Queen and her husband Philip among the guests. By the birth of her fifth child ten years later, Frances had grown so weary of life with Johnny Spencer, whom she subsequently sued on the grounds of cruelty, that she was prepared to surrender not merely her title, but her children, to escape him. 'Suddenly,' as one of the servants put it, 'she just wasn't there any more.'[2]

As Diana was transplanted to a country boarding school, her mother removed herself to the remote north-west of Scotland, where she settled into a happier new domesticity as Mrs Shand Kydd. Henceforth, as her brother Charles recalled in his tribute at her funeral, Diana and her siblings would spend their school holidays shuttling the 500 miles between Norfolk and Oban. Subsequent relations with her mother, however affectionate, would always be shot through with tension. It was much the same with her father. Diana loved both her parents as much as any dutiful child; but their love for her and her siblings, in their different ways, was scarcely unconditional. In later life she was able to make light of it all. 'Being third in line was a very good position to be in – I got away with murder,' she said. 'I was my father's favourite, there's no doubt about that.'[3] But scars had already been etched on Diana's young psyche.

Lady Diana Frances Spencer had been born into a family more English than the royal family, and arguably more royal. Towards the end of the Middle Ages, when wool was so important to England that the Lord Chancellor first saw fit to preside over the House of Lords while sitting, as he still does, on the Woolsack, the Spencers were among a handful of old English families to make a huge fortune simply by owning sheep. In 1506, under the Tudors, they acquired the estate of Althorp in Northamptonshire, where they built the handsome pile which is, to this day, their family seat – larger than any of the royal residences except Buckingham Palace. A century later Sir Robert Spencer was reputed to be the richest man, in terms of ready cash, in the kingdom. In 1603 he was made Baron Spencer, one of the first peers of England created by the new Stuart King, James I. The line of descent has remained unbroken ever since.

To her future husband and his parents Diana began life, quite literally, as the girl next door. She was born on 1 July 1961, at Park House, a former hunting lodge on the royal estate at Sandringham, Norfolk, which her father was renting from the Queen while waiting to inherit his earldom. Edward John, Viscount Althorp, heir to the seventh Earl Spencer, and his wife Frances (née Roche), younger daughter of the fourth Baron Fermoy, were familiar figures at court. Diana's father had been the Queen's equerry on her coronation tour of Australia in 1954, and her grandmother was one of the Queen Mother's few lifelong intimates.

After losing one son in infancy, the couple already had two daughters, Jane and Sarah. At the fourth attempt, Viscount 'Johnny' Althorp had gone to the lengths of lighting bonfires to greet a male heir to the 200-year-old title in his charge. Amid the natural joy of childbirth, however, a note of dismay greeted the arrival of another girl. The pressure on her mother to produce a male heir was a pressure Diana herself would one day know. Already it was causing irreparable damage to her parents' marriage – the same hurtful, creeping corrosion she too would one day endure, though for very different reasons. Diana herself was to outdo her mother by effortlessly breeding male heirs to a far grander title, with all the natural magic she seemed to bring to every task she undertook – a gratifying corrective to the way she herself came into the world.

The man she was eventually to marry, heir to the loftiest hereditary title on earth, was one of the first to lay eyes on the little blonde bundle who would play so fateful a role in his own life. Charles, Prince of Wales, even at twelve the magnanimous landlord, swiftly dropped by the Althorps' home with a celebratory bottle of champagne. Perhaps, with his own heritage in mind, he also offered a word of sympathy to the frustrated earl-in-waiting, who was soon to order gynaecological tests on a wife who did not seem capable of breeding him male heirs. It would be three more years before the Althorps at last had a son to ensure the Spencer succession. Proudly they won royal permission to name him Charles, after their illustrious young neighbour.

Charles and Diana Spencer were only four and seven years old when the end of each week signalled a train journey to London to spend the weekend with their mother. By Saturday evening – 'standard procedure' said Diana – Frances would already be in tears. When the children asked what was wrong, she told them, 'Oh, I don't want you to leave tomorrow.' Their older sisters, Sarah and Jane, were already away at boarding school, so Charles and Diana took more of the brunt of their parents' separation – 'a very wishy-washy and painful experience' for them both, in Diana's words. 'I always looked after my brother, really. My sisters were very independent.'[4]

At night Diana would hear her brother crying in his bed, but was too scared of the dark to go and comfort him. In the absence of the nuclear family she craved, Diana created an alternate one of her own: a collection of twenty stuffed animals whom she hugged in bed each night. 'That was my family,' she said, and most of them were still with her, on the sofa of her bedroom at Kensington Palace, until her dying day.

Divorced parents were then much more unusual in Britain; and schoolfriends can be cruel. Starved of hugs, Diana retreated within herself. Hard though her soft-hearted father tried to create a loving family atmosphere, he was traditional-minded enough to maintain firm discipline. Charles Spencer has revealed that he and his sisters were physically punished by a succession of nannies. One of them, Mary Clarke, testified: 'The children were very strictly brought up in a very old-fashioned way, as if they were still living at the beginning of the century.'

Mrs Clarke was one of the few Spencer nannies to last very long. If Charles and Diana decided they did not like a new arrival, 'we used to stick pins in her chair and throw her clothes out of the window. We always thought nannies were a threat because they tried to take mother's position.'[5] Mrs Clarke's two years looking after Diana left her in no doubt that it was her parents' divorce that forged the complex character the world came to know. 'I can see her now, this child with fair hair down to her shoulders, rosy cheeks and downcast eyes, talking about love. She always needed to be loved.'

Nanny Clarke also remembered Diana saying, 'I shall only get married when I am sure I am in love, so that we will never be divorced.' This became 'something of a theme for her. The abiding ambition of this child was simply to marry happily and have children.' She described her former charge as 'beautiful, obsessive, every bit an actress, astute, devious, strong-charactered, nonetheless sympathetic, genuine and sensitive, in tune with ordinary folk'. The child's sincerity, she said, came from her father, 'whom she adored'.[6]

Diana was fourteen when her father became the eighth Earl Spencer in 1975 on the death of his own father, Jack, and moved his family into the ancestral Spencer seat at Althorp. A 450-year-old, 1,500-acre stately home boasting a fine collection of Old Masters, it also conferred on the new earl the less welcome legacy of crippling death duties. Less than a year later, in the midst of dire financial difficulties, he remarried – another divorcee, and a somewhat exotic one in the shape of Raine, Countess Dartmouth, much-loved by British gossip columnists as an outspoken London politician and the daughter of the prolific, rose-tinted romantic novelist Barbara Cartland.

Raine Dartmouth's arrival as their stepmother caused dismay among the growing Spencer children. Her flamboyant style grated on them, and the sleepy halls of Althorp were not accustomed to her brand of new-broom dynamism. Raine was soon applying her celebrated energies to sprucing the place up, and generating new sources of income. Though some rejuvenation was long overdue, her brisk personal style offended both family and local sensibilities, as she dismissed some longstanding members of staff, opened the house to the paying public and herself ran a gift shop in the stable block.

Although Raine undoubtedly made Johnny Spencer happy, her pushy, domineering ways were anathema to his children, who took to calling her 'Acid Raine'. Photographs of the period already show a telling dislocation in the young Diana's eyes. Now her father too had betrayed her. When he suffered a near-fatal stroke in 1978, just a week after celebrating Althorp's return to solvency, Diana and her siblings were astonished to find Raine coming between them and their father, preventing them from visiting him in hospital. But they were eventually placated by the care and affection she lavished on him, gradually nursing him back to health.

From her preparatory school, Riddlesworth, Diana had been transplanted to West Heath School in Kent. She won cups for swimming and diving, even for the best-kept guinea pig, but little else. 'In the academic department,' she laughed, 'you might as well forget about it!'[7] Although by her own account a bit of a trouble-maker – 'I always had this thing inside me that I was different, I don't know why' – she was regarded as a thoroughly average pupil, 'a perfectly ordinary little girl who was always kind and cheerful'. Though she still saw the younger royals during vacations, she was beginning to make lasting friendships of her own, including the two girls who would enjoy fleeting fame as her Chelsea flatmates. There was a little gentle teasing as she exchanged letters with the Queen's second son, Prince Andrew, of whom she hung a photo over her bed. Andrew was just a year older than Diana. One day, giggled her friends, there might even be a romance.

But it was Andrew's older brother whom she now studied closely in Nobottle Wood, while handing round drinks to members of a visiting shooting party, including the thirty-year-old Prince of Wales. Only once, since visiting the youngest Spencer daughter in her cradle, had Charles made any significant gesture towards Diana. In the summer of 1969, after his investiture at Caernarfon, on what happened to be her eighth birthday, the prince had relaxed at Balmoral by writing a children's story for his younger brothers Andrew and Edward, then aged nine and five. Entitled *The Old Man of Lochnagar*, it was eventually to be published, in 1980, with drawings by his friend Sir Hugh Casson. At the time, on returning to Sandringham, Charles ran off an extra copy for the little girl next door who sometimes played with his brothers.

During the sixth months after the day she met him again in Nobottle Wood, Diana would leave school at sixteen, without one O level to her name, to travel the well-worn path of well-born girls to a finishing school in Switzerland: the Institut Alpin Videmanette, near Montreux. She lasted only six weeks, fleeing abruptly, pleading homesickness. 'When I went to finishing school, I wrote something like 120 letters in the first month,' she recalled. 'I was so unhappy there . . . It was just too claustrophobic . . .'[8] All she brought back with her from Montreux was a smattering of French and some early experience on the ski slopes.

Her sister's romance with the Prince of Wales meanwhile appeared to be flourishing. After that November weekend at Althorp, Charles invited Sarah to join his New Year skiing party in Klosters, causing some lip-smacking press innuendo about the number of bedrooms in the rented chalet they shared with the

Gloucesters. Trying to be helpful, Sarah went out of her way to tell a journalist that her relationship with the prince was 'purely platonic', explaining, 'I think of him as the big brother I never had.' But she made the mistake of adding, 'I wouldn't marry a man I didn't love, whether it was a dustman or the King of England. If he asked me I would turn him down.'[9]

Not merely had she broken the cardinal rule of speaking to the press; Sarah had also hurt Charles's sensitive feelings, bringing on a princely sense-of-humour failure. His ardour immediately cooled, and he withdrew to his usual distance. Not for want of her trying, Sarah received no invitation to join him on his polo expedition to Deauville, in northern France, that summer; nor was she pleased to hear that the Prince of Wales had danced the night away in a disco that weekend with a French girl named Chantal.

By April 1978, when her middle sister Jane married Robert Fellowes – son of the royal land agent at Sandringham, who had recently become the Queen's assistant private secretary and would later rise to the top job of her private secretary – Sarah was no more than just another member of Charles's circle of acquaintances. At least she was high enough on the list to be invited to his thirtieth birthday ball at Buckingham Palace that November. But so, to Sarah's annoyance and her own delighted surprise, was her little sister Diana – just a year after that first brief encounter with Charles in Nobottle Wood.

Chief bridesmaid at Jane's wedding to Fellowes, soon after her return from Switzerland, Diana had been deemed too young to be allowed to live in her own London flat and was sent off to Headley Borden in Hampshire, the home of Major Jeremy Whitaker, a photographer, and his wife, Philippa. During her three months with the Whitakers she cleaned and cooked for them and helped look after their daughter, Alexandra. But still Diana ached for the bright lights of the big city, where most of her schoolfriends were already prototype 'Sloane Rangers'; and eventually her parents agreed on a compromise whereby she could live in her mother's London *pied-à-terre* in Cadogan Square. As Mrs Shand Kydd spent most of her time in Scotland, it was as good as having her own place. In the year she spent there, Diana took in paying flatmates, including her schoolfriend Laura Greig, later one of her ladies-in-waiting, and Sophie Kimball, daughter of a Tory MP.

To pay her way, Diana signed on with upper-crust employment

agencies and took jobs as a waitress at private functions, even as a cleaning lady. In the evenings there was plenty of work as a babysitter, while she occasionally made up the numbers at one of the dinner parties hosted by Sarah, who, two years later, having given up on her prince, would marry a wealthy Lincolnshire landowner, Neil McCorquodale. Diana's London life has been described as 'sedate, almost mundane. She didn't smoke and never drank, preferring to spend her free time reading, watching television, visiting friends or going out for supper in modest bistros'. By her own assessment, Diana 'wasn't interested in having a full diary. I loved being on my own . . . a great treat'.[10] Noisy nightclubs, wild parties and smoky pubs were 'never her scene'; 'Disco Di' existed 'only in the minds of headline writers with an appreciation for alliteration'. In truth, Diana was 'a loner by inclination and habit'.[11] Her weekends were equally prim and proper, spent at Althorp with her father, at her sister Jane's cottage on the Althorp estate, or at the country-house parties of her circle of upper-crust friends.

By September 1978, when her father suffered his stroke, Diana had signed on to a cookery course run by Elizabeth Russell in Wimbledon. Soon she was also working part time as sister Sarah's 'charlady', cleaning the flat and doing household chores for a pound an hour. So it was an all but literal Cinderella who went to the Buckingham Palace ball celebrating Charles's thirtieth birthday that November. But there was no glass slipper on offer as yet. Eighteen months were to pass before Charles even noticed Diana again, a year before he made her his bride.

For now, aware that she was lucky to be there at all, she rested content that night, watching him dance with Susan George, with her sister Sarah, with old flames like Lady Jane Wellesley and Lady Leonora Grosvenor (by then the Countess of Lichfield), and with two married women widely known to be his close friends, Dale, Lady Tryon, and Mrs Camilla Parker Bowles.

The following day Charles lunched at Windsor with a friend of his mother's, a sixty-five-year-old viscountess who felt 'protective' towards the young scion of a family she regarded as 'under-educated and ill-informed Germans', in need of the help of 'old aristos' like her. 'Poor Charles', she said, 'was never more endearing than on that day after his thirtieth birthday.' The prince apologized for the meagre lunch, given his mother's absence, which at least meant that they were spared her 'perfectly dreadful' corgis. Then he launched into a *cri de cœur*, telling her that he was so set in his bachelor ways that he would never find a wife who would 'fit in' and want to share his life.

'Sad, isn't it?' he confided. 'What woman would ever put up with all this? With me?' After lunch his older, wiser companion left feeling more protective than ever about her future king. 'Charles is very sweet, but not too bright. He has a slender understanding of the world. Humbly nice and well-mannered, but there's a dimension missing.' To her, the future king 'seemed to have everything but actually had nothing. At least, nothing that mattered much.'[12]

The forlorn truth was that Charles's thirtieth birthday had crystallized the lack in his life of a Camilla Parker Bowles, or, to be precise, *the* Camilla Parker Bowles. All these years, since her marriage to his polo-playing friend in 1973, Charles had kept in constant touch with Camilla – mostly, to his chagrin, by telephone, though he was able to see her often enough at weekend house-parties, if rarely alone. As her husband, soon to become an aide to the Queen, remained on friendly terms with other members of the royal family, he was a regular weekend guest at Balmoral, Windsor and Sandringham; and his wife was naturally invited, too.

Or so the fiction ran. Like his liaison with Lady Tryon, the prince's friendship with Camilla was regarded for public relations purposes as a 'safe' one, conducted under the guise of a friendship with a married couple – for the world had yet to learn that Parker Bowles was a complaisant husband of the old school, one of those Englishmen sufficiently loyal to the Crown to believe it his duty to allow the Prince of Wales to exercise droit de seigneur over his wife. Or, as it is known in military and polo-playing circles, 'laying down your wife for your country'. The prince had come to regard Camilla as his 'best friend' – a 'touchstone' and 'sounding-board' who had become 'a vital source of comfort to him'.[13] And it was during this period, six years and two children into the Parker Bowles marriage, that he and Camilla became lovers again.

While giving the couple the run of Broadlands, Mountbatten was meanwhile hatching his own masterplan: for Charles to marry his grand-daughter, Amanda Knatchbull, now an attractive if earnest twenty-one-year-old, in whom the prince did indeed begin to show increasing interest. Not wishing to reveal his hand too soon, Mountbatten had to take the rough trade with the smooth as part of the price of trying to cement his name, and his genes, into the history of Britain's royal dynasty.

Charles's diary for 1978–9 shows him to have been a frequent guest at Broadlands, ostensibly for fishing and shooting purposes, but also to sow more wild oats under his great-uncle's roof, while learning to love Amanda. Where once he had consorted with Camilla Shand, and still occasionally did, he also renewed a friendship with Amanda dating back six years, when he confided to Mountbatten after a family holiday on the island of Eleuthera, in the Bahamas, that he found the fifteen-year-old had blossomed into something of a beauty. 'Most disturbing!'[14]

The following year, Mountbatten unabashedly raised the long-term question of marriage in a letter to the prince aboard HMS *Jupiter*, asssuring Charles how deeply Amanda had fallen for him. Devoted to his 'honorary grandfather', with no comparable adult to turn to for advice, Charles took the suggestion very seriously. Charles warmed to Amanda's liveliness and loyalty, as well as her love of the countryside, to the point of writing her letters which made his affection clear. He had even begun to think that she might one day make an 'ideal' Princess of Wales.[15]

Over the next five years, under Mountbatten's watchful eye, Charles and Amanda saw more and more of each other, at Broadlands or Balmoral, in London, Windsor and Eleuthera. As cousins they were able to spend time together in the family circle without arousing the suspicions of the press. By 1979 Amanda's father, Lord Brabourne, felt able to confide to his father-in-law, Mountbatten, that he thought the couple were moving slowly towards marital bliss.

Amanda had been one of the first girls to go to Gordonstoun, and could joke with Charles about the horrors of the place. As she made a more adventurous academic progress than his, through the Universities of Kent, Beijing and London, she grew genuinely fond of the prince, sharing his love of the countryside and his sense of the absurd, admiring his devotion to duty and seriousness of purpose, and touched by his closeness to her grandfather. But such sisterly devotion, in so honest and intelligent a young woman, does not necessarily translate into love – and Amanda, though nearly nine years younger than the prince, was mature enough to recognize this. She may also have noted his conspicuous devotion to Mrs Parker Bowles. When he eventually did propose marriage to her, in the romantic setting of the royal yacht in the summer of 1979, Amanda turned him down.

Whatever dismay her refusal occasioned Charles – or indeed their 'mutual grandfather' – was swept away later that month, on 27 August, when an IRA bomb exploded aboard Mountbatten's fishing boat *Shadow V* as it was leaving Classiebawn Harbour near his summer home in western Ireland. In his eightieth year, Mountbatten was killed instantly, as were his fourteen-year-old grandson Nicholas (Amanda's younger brother, who had also been named Charles after the prince) and the boatman, Paul Maxwell. Amanda's parents, Patricia and John Brabourne, were seriously injured, as was her brother Timothy, Nicholas's twin. Doreen, Lady Brabourne, Amanda's eighty-three-year-old grandmother, was also fatally injured, surviving the night but dying early the following morning.

The news reached Charles on a fishing trip to Iceland with Dale Tryon and her husband. 'I still can't believe what has taken place,' he wrote in his diary that evening. Charles simply could not believe that Mountbatten, the great survivor, would not somehow miraculously return. Overcome by a tide of emotions – 'agony, disbelief, a kind of wretched numbness' – he was also seized by an angry resolve to ensure that 'something was done about the IRA'. In the full flood of grief, moved to bitter rage, he confessed that he felt 'supremely useless and powerless'.[16]

Since staying with him in Malta at the age of five, Charles had been utterly devoted to Mountbatten. In 1958 Mountbatten had relished the privilege of being the first to take the newly created Prince of Wales to Wales, when they visited Holyhead together aboard *Britannia*. Although he had been devoted to Charles since his boyhood, he felt they had grown especially close during the prince's teens. He had come to see him as the son he had not had himself. 'One does miss sons . . .'

To Charles, Mountbatten was quite simply irreplaceable. He had said to him the previous year that he would not know what to do without him 'when you finally decide to depart'.[17] For the prince, he had combined the roles of 'grandfather, great-uncle, father, brother and friend'. His 'infinitely special' role in Charles's life had not merely been that of a uniquely trusted confidant. While immensely affectionate, Mountbatten had also been one of the few figures in the prince's intimate circle to speak bluntly to him when required, offering constructive criticism as well as avuncular advice and praise where it was due. Life would 'never be the same' without him.[18]

Charles's first reaction to Mountbatten's death was to plunge back into the arms of the only other mainstay of his life, Camilla Parker Bowles. Unhinged by grief, he also embarked on a wild, unlikely series of affairs with highly attractive but in most cases less than suitable sirens. Amid rumours that he was trying to contact Mountbatten's ghost via a Ouija board, he embarked on a romance with the most spiritual woman to have caught his fancy, Zoe Sallis, a striking Indian-born actress who had been the mistress of the Hollywood film director John Huston, by whom she had a seventeen-year-old son.

Ten years older than the prince, Zoe was a devout Buddhist with a firm belief in reincarnation. Under her spell, believing it represented the spirit of Mountbatten, Charles turned vegetarian, gave up shooting and began burbling to his staff about the transmigration of souls, speculating as to the shape in which Lord Louis might soon return to earth. Once the relationship turned emotional as well as spiritual, his dalliance with Zoe set alarms bells ringing at the Palace; his private secretary, Edward Adeane, urged several of Charles's friends to intervene, pleading, 'It's got to be stopped.'[19]

A stickler for protocol and correctness, Adeane was appalled to hear the future Defender of the Faith espousing the beliefs of another religion to the point, as he saw it, of dangerous delusion. When Charles refused to listen to his urgings that he terminate the liaison, Adeane went to the unusual lengths of threatening to protest to the Queen. That, as always, was enough to terrify Charles into submission. His copy of The Path of the Masters, a Buddhist tract extolling the virtues of nirvana, was returned to its owner, who was banished into outer darkness.

On the rebound, Charles enjoyed a brief relationship with Jane Ward, the upper-crust assistant manager of the Guards Polo Club, and the worldly girl-about-town Sabrina Guinness, previously seen on the arms of such less than royal figures as Jack Nicholson and Mick Jagger. In this case, Charles's father lost patience with his son. To Philip, quite apart from her lurid, well-publicized past,

Sabrina was the kind of social gadfly who would attract undesirable press attention. Although she was from the banking side of the celebrated brewing family, Charles himself knew that marriage into 'the Irish beerage' was out of the question. But he put up no opposition, as submissive as ever, when she was deliberately humiliated at Balmoral by both his parents. On her arrival, Sabrina observed jauntily that the vehicle that had brought her from the railway station looked like a Black Maria, to which Philip retorted, 'You would know all about Black Marias.' As she committed the unpardonable sin of sitting down unbidden in the royal presence, the Queen snapped at her that she was sitting in Queen Victoria's chair: 'Sit somewhere else!' As ever, Charles put up no resistance when his father took Sabrina aside and told her in no uncertain terms to get out of his son's life.

Charles then proceeded to bite off more than he could chew in the shape of Anna Wallace, the daughter of a Scottish landowner whom he met while hunting that November, in the autumn of his thirty-first birthday. Popularly known as the 'ice maiden' or 'Whiplash Wallace' because of her fiery temperament, Anna was one of the prince's few girlfriends who would not accept that his rank entitled him to treat her with anything less than the utmost gallantry. For six months the romance flourished, to the point where tabloid journalists caught the couple *in flagrante* on a rug beside the river Dee at Balmoral the following summer. 'Moments before the royal wick was lit,' recalled the doyen of the royal 'rat-pack', James Whitaker of the *Mirror*, 'he spotted us crawling on our bellies with cameras and binoculars. He jumped up and ran to hide in the bushes, ungallantly leaving poor Anna to cover herself up. He was a wimp that day. He hid and cowed and left the young woman unprotected. He shouldn't have done that – I was ashamed for him – but, of course, I didn't print the story. He is, after all, my future King.'[20]

No wonder Anna turned down Charles's impetuous proposal of marriage, which would never, anyway, have secured his parents' approval. She soon had further, even more public cause for complaint about her careless suitor. At a Windsor Castle ball to celebrate the Queen Mother's eightieth birthday that summer, Charles spent the entire evening dancing with Camilla Parker Bowles – safe enough, as always, given the presence of her husband – to the point where his date herself flounced out, publicly railing at the prince: 'No-one treats me like that, not even you. Don't you ever ignore me like that again!'

Alas, Charles remained too princely to heed such lessons. At a polo ball weeks later at Stowell Park, the Gloucestershire home of his friend Lord Vestey, he again let Anna watch fuming as he danced the night away with Camilla. So enraptured was he to be back in Camilla's arms that he offended protocol by failing even to dance with his hostess, Lady Vestey – whose car Anna borrowed to disappear into the night. Soon she had married Johnny Hesketh, younger brother of Lord Hesketh.

So Charles was still in somewhat bruised shape when he met young Diana Spencer again that summer, during a weekend house-party at New Grove near Petworth in Sussex, the home of his friend Commander Robert de Pass, and one of the 'safe houses' at which he had been invited to entertain girlfriends beyond the prying eyes of the press.

Not until the last minute had Diana known that Charles was going to be there. Since his thirtieth birthday party eighteen months earlier she had seen him only once – at a Sandringham shooting party that February, when she had travelled to King's Lynn with his cousin Amanda Knatchbull and had had the good sense not to intrude on the bond between them, strengthened by Mountbatten's recent death. Now – through her friend Rory Scott, a Guards officer whom she liked enough to iron his shirts – Diana had recently met de Pass's son Philip, whom she happened to see in London that week. Concerned that the prince should have a good time, Philip offered Diana a spur-of-the-moment invitation. 'You're a young blood,' he told her. 'You might like him.'

And so it came to pass, at a post-polo barbecue the following Saturday, that Charles found himself sitting on a Sussex hay-bale next to the 'jolly' and 'bouncy' teenager he remembered from Nobottle Wood nearly three years earlier, whom he had first met in her cradle at Sandringham when he was on the threshold of his teens. Diana was still awed by the prince, and mindful of his recent bereavement; but with no Amanda Knatchbull on hand to deflect her she ventured to offer her own brand of sympathy about Lord Mountbatten's death. 'You looked so sad when you walked up the aisle at the funeral,' she told him. 'It was the most tragic thing I've ever seen. My heart bled for you when I watched it. I thought, it's wrong, you are lonely, you should be with somebody to look after you.'

Professing himself 'greatly touched', thirty-one-year-old Charles found himself looking at eighteen-year-old Diana through new eyes. They talked late into the evening. Charles, in one of Diana's favourite phrases, was 'all over me like a rash'. Knowing he had just broken up with Anna Wallace, she was flattered by his attentions but firmly on her guard. 'Well, this isn't very cool,' she thought. 'I thought men were supposed not to be so obvious, I thought this was very odd.' That evening, he 'practically leapt on me'. Unsure how to cope, Diana concentrated on maintaining her honour. 'Frigid wasn't the word. Big F when it comes to that.'[21]

Next day the prince had to leave early to drive himself back to London 'to deal with some paperwork', and asked Diana to come with him. She politely declined, pleading that it would appear rude to their hosts. Charles was as impressed by her good manners as he was fired by her demureness. Nothing could be more calculated to ensure that he asked her out again soon. Even before her nineteenth birthday, Diana was a mistress of the art of feminine wiles.

Since playing Cinderella at his thirtieth birthday ball, she had known her own share of highs and lows in her ever-eventful young life. Her father's near-fatal stroke that autumn had brought to a head the tensions between his children and their stepmother, Raine, who had barred them from visiting the earl while she insisted on single-handedly nursing him back to health. Even when he suffered a serious relapse, in the month of Charles's birthday party, Raine refused to give up hope, persuading him to try a new, as yet un-licensed 'wonder drug' called Aslocillin. Even his resentful children were reluctantly impressed when two months later, in January 1979, as his wife maintained her bedside vigil to the strains of Puccini's *Madam Butterfly*, the comatose earl suddenly opened his eyes and was 'back'. Raine defiantly booked them both into London's most expensive hotel, the Dorchester on Park Lane, for a month-long convalescence.

Although her heart was not really in it, Diana spent those troubled weeks completing her Wimbledon cookery course, from which she duly emerged with a diploma testifying to her skills at everything from sauces to soufflés. Amid the continuing domestic drama, she then began to train as a ballet teacher at the Brompton Road studios of Betty Vacani, the very woman who had taught the young Prince Charles. Three months into the course, in March 1979, she had to abandon it when she tore all the tendons in her left ankle while skiing with friends in the French Alps. In plaster for three months, she helped to run the travel company managed by a group of hearty young Etonians she had met on the slopes. By July, on her eighteenth birthday, she finally achieved her ambition of owning a London flat of her own.

No. 60 Coleherne Court, soon to become one of Britain's most famous addresses, was Diana's £50,000 coming-of-age present from her father. A three-bedroomed apartment in a mansion block on London's Brompton Road, in the heart of 'Sloane Ranger' territory, it was found for Diana by her sister Sarah – then working for Savills, the upmarket estate agents, while nursing her bruises after being dumped by Charles. Diana immediately fulfilled a longstanding promise to a schoolfriend, Carolyn Bartholomew, to offer her a room when she got a place of her own. Two more high-spirited girlfriends, Anne Bolton and Virginia Pitman, soon moved in at Diana's modest rent of £18 a week. Together they redecorated the entire flat in fashionable pastel shades, while Diana organized cleaning rotas and 'clucked about the place' in rubber gloves. 'It was her house and she was incredibly proud of it,' recalled Carolyn.[22]

To supplement her income, while still doing Sarah's domestic chores, Diana found herself a part-time job at the Young England kindergarten in St Saviour's church hall in Pimlico, run by Victoria Wilson and Kay Seth-Smith. Several afternoons a week she taught the toddlers dancing, painting and drawing, and helped them invent games. Two afternoons a week she also looked after Patrick Robertson, the son of a London-based American oil executive. Blissfully happy working with young children, Diana had found a *métier* of lasting significance.

Her spare time was one long round of teenage pranks and adventures, with the girls of Coleherne Court getting up to all sorts of giggly tricks amid an ever-widening circle of male friends, most of them well-bred Hooray Henrys drawn from Eton or the Guards. Among them were Rory Scott, the handsome lieutenant in the Royal Scots Guards whose shirts she happily washed and ironed, and James Gilbey, the car dealer whose name would later reverberate through her life. Whatever sexual vibes may have lurked beneath the innocent high spirits, all her friends from this period, both male and female, testify to the innocence of Diana's undoubted charms. She was soon to survive an exhaustive press trawl through her private life, and even endure the embarrassment of her uncle publicly confirming her status as a virgin *intacta*, because of a sixth sense she firmly felt about her future. She knew that one day she was going to meet and marry someone of significance. 'I knew I had to keep myself tidy,' as Diana's young self rather charmingly put it, 'for what lay ahead.'[23]

She must have exuded such innocence to Charles that July on the Sussex hay-bale, after making that first impression on him at Sandringham in February, as he suddenly began to pepper Diana with invitations. Since Mountbatten's death, and his rejection by Amanda Knatchbull, the prince had all but abandoned the idea of marriage. Set in his bachelor ways, he gave women little reason beyond his rank and status to fall for him, expecting them to fit into his own rigid schedule of polo, shooting and fishing, standing loyally by their man while he pursued his own agenda, showing little interest in theirs.

Charles never quite realized that, regardless of his birth, his girl-friends, let alone potential brides, expected rather more than a brief, unexciting act of highly conventional sex as their reward for a boring, often freezing-cold day forcing wide-eyed admiration at his manly prowess in the field. Friends who knew better wondered if it was deliberate, sensing that Charles was one of nature's bachelors.

Were it not for his unfortunate constitutional obligation to breed heirs, the prince might well have led a long and happy life as a single man, taking his pleasures privately in the country houses of friends with discreet, well-born women, whether unattached or not. In circles so blindly loyal to the monarchy, Andrew Parker Bowles was not the only husband prepared to look the other way.

CHAPTER EIGHT

'WHATEVER LOVE MEANS'

BY THE TIME HE BEGAN TO REGARD YOUNG DIANA SPENCER AS A serious candidate for a princely proposal, Charles was deeply involved with Camilla again. In the spring of 1980, three months before the Petworth house-party, he had caused acute embarrassment in diplomatic circles by taking Mrs Parker Bowles with him to Rhodesia as his official 'escort' when representing the Queen at the ceremonies marking the country's independence as Zimbabwe.

Her husband, ironically, had just returned to Britain after a prolonged stint in Rhodesia as aide-de-camp to the former colony's last governor, Lord [Christopher] Soames, father of Charles's old friend Nicholas. Far from being at his side while the Household Cavalry colonel had been in Rhodesia, Camilla had been spotted dancing with Charles at Annabel's; now that her husband had returned home, she was travelling to Rhodesia on the Prince of Wales's arm. Buckingham Palace courtiers were apoplectic, all too conscious of the heavy innuendo behind press reports stressing the 'paradox' in Mrs Parker Bowles's travelling from the UK to Rhodesia while her husband flew in the opposite direction 'after making a great success of heading the liaison forces under Soames'. Parker Bowles would not be returning to be at his wife's side for the forthcoming ceremonies. 'Buckingham Palace officials have always been happy to see Charles in the company of happily married women,' according to a press briefing, 'because such sightings cannot give rise to rumour.'[1]

Oh, no? Unrestrained by the double-speak incumbent on the

national press, the satirical magazine *Private Eye* had already drawn gleeful attention to the royal liaison, right down to the cunning use of a well-placed question mark by its gossip columnist, 'Grovel':

> No sooner had Lord Soames been appointed Governor of Rhodesia than the subject of jobs for the boys arose. Among the lucky ones: Major Andrew Parker Bowles, now a colonel and in charge of British liaison with the guerrilla forces. Andrew, 39, is married to a former (?) Prince Charles fancy, Camilla Shand, and if I should find the royal Aston Martin Volante outside the Parker Bowles mansion while the gallant colonel is on duty overseas, my duty will be clear.[2]

When a heedless Charles insisted on taking the colonel's wife to a posting she had never bothered to share with her husband, the diplomatic patience of Lord Soames – whose daughter, Charlotte, had been romanced by Parker Bowles in his wife's absence – was stretched to extremes. 'Pray God the claret is good,' said the usually unflappable Lady Soames before a formal dinner party threatening all manner of potential embarrassments. The Foreign Office waited until after the handover to break a silence about Charles's conduct maintained through gritted teeth. 'The hauling down of the British flag was a humiliating enough circumstance without everyone knowing the royal family's envoy had brought his popsy along with him,' protested an unnamed Foreign Office source. 'The lack of tact was indescribable. It just made a joke out of the whole thing.'

Still mourning the loss of his mainstay Mountbatten, and angrily desperate about the pressure on him to marry, Charles was more openly outrageous with Camilla that summer than he has ever been, before or since. At the Cirencester Polo Club ball, a bi-annual event at which he was guest of honour, the prince again spent the entire evening dancing with his fellow officer's wife, to the astonishment of 300 black-tied, diamond-encrusted guests. Not merely was it another uncharacteristic breach of royal protocol to ignore all the other upper-class women with whom the most basic courtesy required him to dance; this time, in front of her husband and countless indiscreet witnesses, Charles was kissing Camilla passionately on the dance floor. 'On and on they went,' according to one observer, 'kissing each other, French kissing, dance after dance . . . It was completely beyond the pale.' Unsure how to react, Parker Bowles himself sat watching with a wan smile. 'HRH is very fond of my wife,' he kept saying to sympathizers. 'And she appears to be very fond of him.'[3]

That June Charles also surprised the prime minister, Margaret Thatcher, with a letter surrendering his country house in Kent and handing it back to the government. Left to the nation in 1967 by the Earl of Stanhope as a country seat for future Princes of Wales, Chevening House near Sevenoaks is today at the disposal of the foreign secretary, in much the same way as the prime minister enjoys the use of Chequers in Buckinghamshire. Chevening enjoyed fleeting fame during Thatcher's administration when used as a bargaining chip by Camilla's uncle, Sir Geoffrey Howe, in a Cabinet reshuffle. It became even better known in April 1998, when the newly divorced foreign secretary, Robin Cook, named it as the venue for his rapid remarriage to Gaynor Regan (before promptly marrying elsewhere to hoodwink the press).

In 1980 Chevening was the Prince of Wales's base outside London, as Stanhope had wished; it had been for six years, and was expected to be *sine die*. Charles offered no public explanation for abandoning it, telling the prime minister only that he would have no further need of this 'beautiful and valuable property'[4] because he intended to spend more time in the West Country, nearer his Duchy of Cornwall estates. A few weeks later it was announced that the duchy had spent the surprisingly large sum of £750,000 on a much smaller Georgian house, henceforth to be the prince's country home: Highgrove House in the hamlet of Doughton, Gloucestershire, just outside the town of Tetbury – and, as it happens, just a few minutes' drive from the Parker Bowles home, Bolehyde Manor.

Where Chevening boasted 150 rooms and 3,500 acres of Kentish farmland, Highgrove, former home of Maurice Macmillan MP, son of the Conservative prime minister, had but nine bedrooms and 350 acres. Baffled observers suggested that Charles had perhaps chosen it because his sister, Anne, lived near by at Gatcombe Park; but Charles and Anne, in truth, had been less than close since her marriage to Mark Phillips (whom Charles had given the family nickname of 'Fog' – 'because he's thick and wet'[5]). Nor was it the Michaels of Kent, also neighbours, who had drawn him west from

Kent so precipitously. 'The big cedar tree in front and the walled garden finally made up my mind,' said Charles himself, none too convincingly. The local attraction that had really made up his mind was, of course, the proximity of Mrs Parker Bowles.

For any future girlfriend or wife of the Prince of Wales the warning signs were obvious. His love for Camilla had led Charles, most uncharacteristically, to brave a diplomatic incident, tarnish his lustrous reputation amid the habitually sycophantic polo set, and alienate his duchy's management as much as his mother's courtiers with a dubious extravagance it could ill afford. Any future women in Charles's life, even the one he would eventually marry, would not merely have to be 'approved' by Camilla, who required reassurance that they would offer no threat to her own place in the prince's life. They would also have to learn, almost literally, to live with her. All too soon this would become painfully clear to the coy teenager whom Mrs Parker Bowles contentedly christened 'the mouse' – and who would in turn dub her 'the rottweiler'.

For the moment Diana Spencer had no such concerns, as she giggled with her flatmates about the sudden flurry of princely invitations. Nor was she aware of a long-running campaign by the Queen Mother, her grandmother's lifelong friend, to thwart the dynastic ambitions of Lord Mountbatten, before and after his death. There was an almost audible purr from Clarence House, the London residence of Charles's grandmother, when Diana began to replace Amanda Knatchbull in the Prince of Wales's affections.

The dutiful daughter of a hereditary earl, on the fringes of the royal circle since childhood, Diana was not as offended as other girls might have been when she was given just twenty minutes' notice of Charles's intention to take her to a performance of Verdi's *Requiem* at the Royal Albert Hall. 'We had the funniest time ever,' said her flatmate Carolyn Bartholomew, 'getting the hair washed, getting it dried, getting the dress, where's the dress? We did it in twenty minutes flat. But, I mean, how dare he ask her so late?'[6] No doubt given rather more advance notice, the elderly Lady Fermoy came along as her grand-daughter's chaperone for the evening, which ended with dinner at Buckingham Palace.

Next came an invitation for Diana to join Charles aboard the royal yacht *Britannia* for Cowes Week, in a party hosted by his father and including many other royals. Then it was Balmoral in early September, for the annual centrepiece of the Windsors' ten-week summer holiday, the Highland Games at Braemar. The pace of Charles's pursuit was suddenly intense and relentless.

'Intimidated' by the atmosphere at Cowes, where all the other guests, including Charles's friends, seemed so much older than her, and all of them, this time, were over her 'like a rash', Diana confessed herself 'terrified' of her début at Balmoral, which amounted to a thinly disguised royal inspection of Charles's latest potential bride. Meeting the Queen, she said in retrospect, was 'no big deal'; she had been 'around the royals' since childhood. But she wanted to 'get it right'. So she knew, unlike Sabrina Guinness, not to sit in Queen Victoria's chair.

But the ordeal was nonetheless unnerving, so she was delighted to be able to stay not in the main house but with her sister Jane, whose husband Robert now enjoyed the use of a grace-and-favour cottage on the estate. In a prim twentieth-century version of courtly love, Charles would telephone each morning to suggest a walk or a picnic, and Diana found herself having a 'wonderful' time. Other house-guests that weekend included the prince's skiing friend Charles Palmer-Tomkinson and his wife, Patty, who recalled being 'particularly taken' by the carefree young Diana:

> We went stalking together, we got hot, we got tired, she fell into a bog, she got covered in mud, laughed her head off, got puce in the face, hair glued to her forehead because it was pouring with rain ... she was a sort of wonderful English schoolgirl who was game for anything, naturally young but sweet and clearly determined and enthusiastic about him, very much wanted him.[7]

As Charles taught Diana to fish, and his brothers fought to sit next to her at dinner, the prince told his intimate circle that weekend that he did not yet love her, but felt that in time he might learn to. She was full of gaiety and good humour; she had no 'past'; she was young enough to be 'moulded' to the role of wife and mother according to the 'special needs' of his position; and, as her first love, he could have every reason to hope, as Mountbatten had once advised him, that he would also be her last. Charles began to take Diana very seriously, while she made no secret of her feelings for him. But these few days, less than two months since the spark had been ignited on that Sussex hay-bale, were to prove their last chance to get to know each other in private, free from public pressure.

Beside the river Dee one day that week, their idyll was suddenly shattered by the glint of a pair of high-powered Nikon binoculars. The indefatigable James Whitaker, whose self-imposed duty each summer was to perch himself all day on a rock above Balmoral to see what happened, had spotted the latest love interest in the life of his prime target. With a photographer in tow, he did some human stalking of his own, creeping ever closer to the coy couple on the riverbank until they themselves were spotted. Taking the initiative, significantly enough, Diana told Charles to go fishing alone while she hid behind a tree, cunningly using the mirror from her powder compact to track the journalists' movements while staying out of sight. Even Whitaker was impressed: 'She was very clever that day, much more so than any of his previous girlfriends.'[8] Diana managed to make her escape incognito, by hiding her head in a scarf and Charles's cap while walking away through the trees. But it was only a matter of time before she was identified as the Prince of Wales's secret new love.

It was the end of the only private life Diana would ever know. Within days an army of reporters was camped on the doorstep of Coleherne Court, following her wherever she went in her red Mini Metro, pursuing her even to the Young England kindergarten, where eventually she was persuaded to let them take their first photograph of her – too innocent, as yet, to know that standing with her back to the sun would treat the world to its first close-up, through her ankle-length skirt, of her long and elegant legs. 'I knew your legs were good, but I didn't realize they were that good,' Charles teased her. 'But did you really have to show them to everybody?'[9]

These few tender words amounted to the only encouragement, let alone assistance, Diana was to receive as her ordeal-by-press escalated. Showered with questions each time she emerged from her front door, she was careful to give monosyllabic, non-committal answers about her feelings for Charles – well aware that one word out of place could consign her, like her sister before her, to the royal out-tray. While endearing herself to the watching world, perfecting her famous art of grinning coyly through her

(*Overleaf*) Charles at fifty: the Prince of Wales in Nepal, 1998.

Maternal styles: a forlorn young Charles is ignored as his parents greet the Queen Mother and Princess Margaret on returning from Canada, 1951, while Diana has William and Harry flown out to join her in Canada, 1991.

Bored by his mother's coronation, 1953.
The reluctant schoolboy at Hill House (*right*) and Cheam.

Charles's investiture as Prince of Wales at Caernarfon, 1969.

(*Opposite*) The student prince at Trinity College, Cambridge, 1968.

A stint in all three Services offered an escape from worldly woes.

ROYAL NAVY

Lord Mountbatten, his 'honorary grandfather', was the mainstay of the young Charles, briefly bearded like his great-grandfather, King George V.

'Sowing wild oats': Pre-marital girlfriends Lady Jane Wellesley (*above*), Davina Sheffield (*opposite, above*) and Lady Sarah Spencer, sister of his wife-to-be.

'My great-grandmother was your great-great-grandfather's mistress – so how about it?' said Camilla Parker Bowles (with Charles, *below*) of Edward VII and Mrs Alice Keppel (*above*).

'Whatever love means,' said Charles at the announcement of his engagement to Lady Diana Spencer in February 1981.

'Don't worry, it will get a lot worse,' Princess Grace of Monaco told Diana at her first public engagement at Goldsmiths Hall in the City of London. Before they arrived, Charles had upset Diana by declaring her low-cut black dress unsuitable for a member of the royal family.

The 'fairytale' wedding at St Paul's on 29 July 1981 was sealed by the first kiss ever seen on the balcony of Buckingham Palace.

(*Opposite*) While Charles was courting Diana, he introduced her to his close friend Camilla Parker Bowles.

'To this day, you know – vivid memory,' said Diana of the sight of Camilla Parker Bowles among the VIP guests at her wedding (*above*).

Diana's bulimia grew worse on the honeymoon aboard *Britannia*, when pictures of Camilla fell out of Charles's diary.

The couple's apparent marital bliss at Balmoral (*overleaf*) was already a tragic sham.

eyelashes, the innocent, naïve Diana was under enormous stress. In private, she admitted, 'I cried like a baby to the four walls. I just couldn't cope with it.' When she sent out an SOS to the Palace press office, she was told there was nothing they could do to help her. Charles, similarly, was 'not at all supportive'. All Diana could do in her distress was hope he would 'hurry up and get on with it'.[10]

Still intent on behaving correctly to her prince, she bit her tongue and said nothing when his phone calls mentioned only his concern about Camilla Parker Bowles. Poor Camilla, he would complain, had all of 'three or four' photographers hanging round outside her home; Diana forbore to mention that the rest of Fleet Street was camped on hers. Already, unsurprisingly, she was beginning to wonder about the precise nature of Camilla's role in Charles's life. The Parker Bowleses had been among the house-guests that recent weekend at Balmoral; indeed, Andrew, together with Nicholas Soames, had been delegated to escort Diana home to the press furore, leaving Camilla behind with the prince in splendid Scottish isolation. Whenever Charles invited Diana to dinner at Buckingham Palace, the Parker Bowleses were usually there, too, and Camilla always seemed to know everything that had passed between Charles and Diana.

So she was far from surprised, the following month, when a trip to Ludlow to watch Charles ride in an amateur race turned into a weekend as the Parker Bowleses' house-guests. The only photographs of Diana and Camilla together date from that October day in 1980 when Charles's long-term lover 'looked after' his potential fiancée while their mutual hero came second in the Clun Handicap Stakes on his favourite horse, Allibar. The next day Charles and Andrew went out hunting, leaving Diana and Camilla to get better acquainted. So well did things go, as far as Camilla was concerned, that Charles and Diana were back to stay with them again the following weekend.

Now Charles drove Diana the short distance to show her round Highgrove, the new home he had just acquired. When he asked her to take charge of the interior decoration, she was excited but baffled. The prince said he liked her taste; but he had never been to her flat, never once picked her up himself on one of their evenings out. She was also, rather charmingly, somewhat shocked, thinking it a 'most improper' suggestion as they were not yet so much as engaged. Camilla's enthusiasm for the idea that evening told Diana just how well Mrs Parker Bowles already knew the inside of the house. Fourteen years her junior, Charles's girlfriend began to harbour suspicions about her suitor's closest confidante. But she bit her tongue and hoped for the best, confident that, were Charles eventually to propose, he was a moral enough man to leave his past behind.

The well-brought-up young girl was being careful to play the game by the rules as she saw them, not wishing to appear too eager, remaining scrupulous about what was proper and what was not. So she was genuinely distressed a few weeks later when the *Sunday Mirror* carried a front-page story proclaiming that on 5 November she had secretly driven from London to spend the night with Charles aboard the royal train in a rural Wiltshire siding.[11] Now at last, for the first time, Buckingham Palace intervened on her behalf with an angry denial; the story was 'wholly false . . . a total fabrication', protested the Queen's press secretary, Michael Shea, demanding a front-page retraction. But the paper's experienced editor, Bob Edwards, defiantly stood by his story, which was 'very reliably' sourced. In vain did Diana plead that she had spent that evening at home with her flatmates, watching TV before an early night, exhausted after escorting Charles to Princess Margaret's fiftieth birthday party at the Ritz the night before.

She even went to the lengths of speaking directly to the man she had nicknamed the 'wicked' James Whitaker, telling him, 'I am not a liar. I have never been on that train. I have never even been near it.' The vehemence of the Palace's denial, meanwhile, intrigued Edwards, weighed against his own solid evidence (later said to have come from the security services) that a blonde woman had been seen boarding the train, and had stayed 'several hours' before departing 'in the most furtive manner'. As the Palace pressed its case all the way to the Press Council, the editor remained puzzled; when the Palace suddenly backed off, saying it had no wish to pursue the matter further, he became yet more intrigued. But neither he nor the rest of the national press saw the alternative explanation staring them in the face. So in love with Diana was the whole of Fleet Street, so intent that Charles should make her his bride, that it did not cross the collective mind of the royal-loving British press that there might have been another 'mystery blonde' in the prince's life, whom he entertained aboard the train that night.

The story eventually evaporated in the euphoria of ensuing events. As the fairy tale sought by Fleet Street began to unfold, it took some years for the journalists involved to realize the truth of the story they had got so nearly right, and yet so badly wrong – the truth that Diana realized at the time, to her horror, but which Fleet Street comprehensively missed. Charles had entertained three Duchy of Cornwall officials to dinner aboard the train that evening; the telephone records also showed that a call had been made to Bolehyde Manor. Six years later, when the retired Bob Edwards was awarded the CBE in the New Year honours list – a token, as he took it, of royal forgiveness – a card from the late Lord Wyatt of Weeford, an establishment figure close to the royal family, carried the simple message: 'I think you'll find it was Camilla.'[12]

At the time, Diana had no chance to take up the matter with the prince himself. On the morning the story broke, he had left for an official visit to Nepal and India. In New Delhi, as the stand-off continued back home between Palace and paper, he chose to denounce the 'sensationalism' of the British press, bewailing the 'lack of moral values' it displayed. 'Honesty and integrity are vital factors in reporting,' he told (rather incongruously) members of the Indian Institute of Technology, 'and often get submerged in the general rush for sensationalism.' Whatever may have passed between himself and Mrs Parker Bowles on the train that evening, this was hypocrisy of truly princely proportions. 'Insofar as personal integrity goes,' as one commentator later observed, 'this was a low water mark in Charles's life.'[13]

With Diana's honour left undefended, her mother now chose to go to battle on her behalf. In early December Mrs Shand Kydd wrote a letter to *The Times* protesting at the 'lies and harassment' her youngest daughter had been forced to endure. 'May I ask the editors of Fleet Street', she continued, 'whether, in the execution of their jobs, they consider it necessary or fair to harass my daughter daily, from dawn until well after dusk? Is it fair to ask any human being, regardless of circumstances, to be treated in this way?'[14] Sixty Members of Parliament then tabled a motion 'deploring the manner in which Lady Diana Spencer is being treated by Fleet Street', precipitating an emergency meeting between national newspaper editors and the Press Council. But the siege of Coleherne Court continued unabated.

For all his indignant remarks in India, it was noticeable that

Charles seemed to avoid Diana on his return. He spent Christmas and New Year at Sandringham, she at Althorp and her London flat. Relations between the press and the royals sank to an all-time low over the festive season, as one by one the Windsors lost their composure when confronted by crowds of reporters. 'A very happy New Year to you,' yelled Charles sarcastically at a posse of reporters, 'and a particularly nasty one to your editors.' His younger brother, Edward, appeared to have fired a shotgun over the head of a *Daily Mirror* photographer. Even the Queen's patience snapped; she broke years of silence to shout, 'Why don't you go away?' That, at least, is what she was reported as saying. James Whitaker, as so often, had a slightly different version. 'Her Majesty, if you'll excuse me, behaved like a fishwife,' he recalls. 'I've never heard her use such strong language.'[15]

Such was the climate in which Diana was finally invited to join Charles at Sandringham, driving herself to Norfolk on New Year's Day. By now she was becoming skilled at evading pursuit by the press outside her front door in Chelsea, laying false trails and sneaking through side exits, even, on one occasion, knotting the sheets from her bed to lower her suitcase out of a rear window before going to meet Charles at Broadlands. On this occasion she drove herself to Kensington Palace, behind whose walls she swapped her now famous Metro for her grandmother's silver Volkswagen Golf, in which she managed to slip away undetected, only to drive into a sea of journalists at the other end of her journey.

Given her suspicions about Mrs Parker Bowles, and the true identity of the 'mystery blonde' on the royal train, Diana was in an unusually pensive mood during her reunion with Charles, already beset by the doubts that would haunt her marriage. There is no question that she was desperate to marry him, that she harboured lofty ambitions forgivable in one so young; so it appears that she now bent over backwards to give him the benefit of the doubt. The shy, rather prim teenager felt motherly towards the prince, whom she had so often heard complaining about his lot.

Friends of the period say that she echoed Charles's self-pitying strains, telling them that his parents and their staff 'work him too hard' and 'push him around'. To her, he seemed the loneliest of men; as she had told him during their first real conversation, he was in urgent need of someone to 'look after' him, and the

ambitious nineteen-year-old could think of no more suitable candidate than herself. Whatever part Camilla Parker Bowles had played
in Charles's life to date, she was married to another, and would
surely disappear after Charles too had wed. Mrs Parker Bowles
had, after all, shown nothing but kindness to Diana, who chose to
ignore warnings from Anna Wallace and others that Camilla was
the only woman the prince would ever really love.

If Charles, too, was assailed by doubts, he was unprepared to
listen to the well-intentioned warnings of friends who could
already see the scale of the mismatch. His mother, as always in personal matters, felt it inappropriate to offer an opinion; but
everyone around her was enthusiastic about Diana, including,
significantly, the Queen Mother and her friend Ruth, Lady Fermoy.
Diana's grandmother concealed her doubts about the couple's com-
patibility until she was on her deathbed, thirteen years later,
contenting herself at the time with telling Diana, 'Darling, you
must understand that their sense of humour and their lifestyle are
different, and I don't think it will suit you.'[16]

But two of Charles's closest friends were adamant that he was
making a mistake: Nicholas Soames and Penny, Lady Romsey, the
former Penny Eastwood, now wife of Mountbatten's grandson
Norton Knatchbull. Quite apart from the twelve-year age gap, she
argued, Charles and Diana had very little in common. To her it
seemed that Diana had fallen in love with an idea rather than a
person, that she acted as if she were 'auditioning for a central role
in a costume drama . . . quite unaware of the enormity of the real
undertaking that she seemed to contemplate so light-heartedly'.
When her husband endorsed his wife's views, arguing the case
against Diana with more vigour but less tact, Charles was moved
to an outburst of indignation. He was 'not willing or – at this time
– able to loosen, let alone sever, so precious a bond merely because
of the anxiety of those about him'.[17]

By now, sensing that the all too public melodrama was in urgent
need of some denouement, the prince also felt himself under
intense pressure from his father, who issued a stern warning about
Diana Spencer's honour, which Charles interpreted, rightly or
wrongly, as 'an ultimatum'. Ominously, he described to friends the
prospect of marriage to Diana as a leap into the dark. It was in his
nature, he knew, to be hesitant about giving undertakings which
might return to haunt him.

In what he confessed was a 'confused and anxious state of mind', he went skiing with the Palmer-Tomkinsons to steel himself to taking the plunge. It was barely six months since his first real chat with Diana in Sussex; the speed with which Charles had reached this point of no return was almost as if he feared this eminently suitable candidate, like so many others, might slip through his fingers. Already, in the cabbage patch behind the Parker Bowles house, he had ventured an informal enquiry, along the lines of, 'If I were to ask, might you consider . . .' But he had yet to make a formal proposal. Now, from the Palmer-Tomkinsons' Klosters chalet, he telephoned Diana to set up a meeting on his return. He had 'something important' to ask her.

Coleherne Court held its collective breath, her flatmates reassuring Diana that the prince would surely now abandon any other women in his life, as Charles returned to London on 3 February, only to disappear on manoeuvres aboard HMS *Invincible*. He was back at the Palace two nights later, having arranged to meet Diana at Windsor Castle on the Friday, 6 February. Late that evening, in the castle's nursery, he formally proposed marriage. 'I've missed you so much,' Diana remembered him saying, none too convincingly. He did not go down on his knees, or even take her hand, just came straight out with, 'Will you marry me?'

Diana's immediate response was a fit of the giggles, which did not please him at all. Charles reminded her that he was in deadly earnest, and that his offer meant she would one day be queen. While 'a small voice inside my head', according to Diana, told her she would 'never become queen', she accepted the prince without the slightest hesitation, telling him repeatedly how much she loved him. 'Whatever love means,' he replied, by her account, even then.

Charles went upstairs to telephone the Queen, and then Earl Spencer to ask formally for his daughter's hand, leaving Diana alone with her thoughts. Her natural elation, fuelled by her love for the prince and her inbred sense of duty, was only slightly tempered by anxiety. Even that was forgotten when she got home and broke the news to her flatmates, who had put champagne on ice. After excited celebrations, they took a drive around London for the heck of it, revelling in their secret.

Diana had fallen deeply in love. Few girls her age could have resisted the attentions of the world's most eligible bachelor. Whatever Charles's reasons for choosing her, she was prepared to put up with all the flummery – even to look on as the antique absurdities of the contemporary British monarchy obliged her uncle to reassure the press that she was a virgin. 'Charles's parents!' says one friend of the Windsors, looking back to that moment. 'They should have known that he needed someone more experienced than that . . . To hell with being a virgin. That was the least important consideration.'[18]

Diana was young for her years, Charles old for his. But she had every reason to hope that together they could create the happy family life she herself had been denied, the happy family life that he told her he too wanted. There are those who believe, not without reason, that Diana had set out to 'get her man' with all the determination of the proverbial Canadian mountie. But those who knew her well, from her former nanny, Mary Clarke, to her girlfriends at Coleherne Court and her sisters, also believed that Diana would never have agreed to marry Charles unless she was convinced that he loved her in return.

Two days later, her days of freedom numbered, Diana flew off to Australia with her mother and stepfather for a ten-day break at his farm in New South Wales, decamping to its nearby beach house for extra security. One of the few who knew her precise whereabouts was the Prince of Wales, for whose telephone calls his fiancée waited in vain. 'I pined for him,' as she put it, 'but he never rang me up.'[19] After several days' trying to be understanding, telling her mother to put it down to pressure of work, she could bear it no longer, and telephoned Charles at the Palace, only to be told that he was not there. Later, he did return her call. It was the only one she received from him during those ten days. On her return home, she was thrilled to answer the door to a member of his staff bearing a bunch of flowers. But there was no note from Charles, and Diana wistfully decided that they could not have come directly from her fiancé. It must have been merely a considerate gesture by his office.

Only a few days were left before the world shared their secret, as plans were discreetly laid for the engagement to be announced from the Palace the following Wednesday, 24 February. They met just once, when Diana rose at dawn to drive down to the Berkshire stables of Nick Gaselee, Charles's friend and racehorse trainer, to see him put Allibar through his paces. As she watched with his detective, the horse suddenly reared its head and collapsed beneath the prince after suffering a massive heart attack. Diana rushed to Charles's side, but the horse was dead within minutes. There was little time for her to comfort the distraught prince, as he had to leave for engagements in Wales. After a hasty farewell, Diana was smuggled away in the Gaselees' Land-Rover, with a rug over her head, to dodge the lurking photographers.

On the following Thursday, the eve of the announcement, she packed a bag, said a tearful goodbye to her flatmates, and left the real world behind at Coleherne Court to move into Clarence House, the Queen Mother's London residence. As she drove through its gates with the armed police bodyguard assigned to protect her, Inspector Paul Officer, he said, 'This is the last night of freedom in the rest of your life, so make the most of it.' His words, said Diana, 'went like a sword into my heart.'[20]

There was no-one else – no-one from the royal family, least of all her fiancé – to welcome her. 'It was', she said, 'like going into a hotel.' Far from the Queen Mother fluttering around and giving her 'a crash course in the art of being royal', as Fleet Street legend has it, Diana was shown by a servant to her first-floor room, where she found a letter waiting for her on the bed. Dated two days earlier, it was from Camilla Parker Bowles.

How did Camilla know she would be at Clarence House? Even Diana herself had not known until a few hours earlier. 'Such exciting news about the engagement. I'd love to see the ring!' gushed the letter, suggesting lunch while the prince was away. With what would turn out to be extremely bad timing, Charles was due to go on an official visit to Australia and New Zealand, returning via Venezuela and the United States. He would be gone all of five weeks. First, at least, Diana could enjoy sampling the engagement rings sent round for her inspection, in a briefcase supposedly containing a choice of signet rings to mark Prince Andrew's twenty-first birthday. She chose the biggest: 'Along came these sapphires. I mean *nuggets*! The Queen paid for it.'[21]

Diana waltzed through the engagement rituals as if in a dream. When asked in her first television interview if they were in love, she responded with a smile and an instinctive 'Of course!' to Charles's grim encore of, 'Whatever love means.' Did he make this subsequently celebrated response because he knew Camilla would be watching? If so, the supreme irony is that, thanks to Camilla, the real Charles knew just what love meant.

As Diana moved into Buckingham Palace, and realized how inadequate was her meagre wardrobe for the rigours of royal life, she sought help from a friend of her sisters, Anna Harvey, fashion editor of *Vogue* magazine. Over the days that followed, while laying the foundations of a collection versatile enough for all royal requirements, she commissioned her wedding dress from David and Elizabeth Emanuel, to whom she had been introduced by Lord Snowdon. She also asked them to design 'something special' for her first official engagement on Charles's arm – a reception at Goldsmiths Hall, in the City of London, where the guests were to include Princess Grace of Monaco.

Diana was thrilled with the black silk ballgown that the Emanuels produced, strapless and backless with a daringly deep neckline. Come the evening, and her arrival in all her finery at Charles's study door, it did not win her the compliments for which she was hoping. On the contrary, the prince was moved to spluttering protests, declaring her décolletage unsuitable for a member of the royal family. Black, the colour Diana thought 'the smartest you could possibly have', was to him to be be reserved for times of mourning. Fighting back tears, she replied simply and honestly that she possessed nothing else suitable for the occasion. So off they went in a mutually sullen silence, shattered only by the roar of the crowd and excited shouts of photographers as Diana made her highly dramatic, and typically distinctive, exit from the car and entrance into public life.

Thrilled to meet the former Grace Kelly, whom she had always admired, Diana was surprised to be taken aside by the princess and led off for a friendly chat in the powder room. The sympathetic Grace had noticed Diana's unease on her first big night out, and sensed the fuss her choice of dress was causing not just the party guests, but the watching world. She encouraged Diana to share her doubts and fears, and proved a good listener as the teenager poured her heart out about the press, the coldness of her royal reception, the constant absence and distance of her future husband. 'Don't worry.' Princess Grace finally smiled. 'It will get a lot worse!'

Days later, at the end of March, Diana drove with Charles to Heathrow Airport to see him off to Australia. As he climbed the steps and turned to wave, she was pictured through the window of the VIP suite brushing away her tears. At the time, this was taken as a touching glimpse of the love at the heart of the unfolding fairy tale. In truth, as she herself later revealed, she was weeping because her last minutes alone with the prince at the Palace had been interrupted by a phone call. It was Camilla, wanting her own fond farewell. So tender was the conversation that Diana had felt obliged to leave the room.

That moment, she said ten years later, 'just broke my heart'. Left alone in the vast emptiness of Buckingham Palace, she went into a spiral of decline from which she was never really to recover throughout the fifteen years of marriage ahead. Once it was over, she recalled, 'I missed my girls so much I wanted to go back there and sit and giggle like we used to, and borrow clothes and chat about silly things, just being safe in my shell again.'[22]

Since her arrival at Clarence House, Diana's friends had worried that she seemed to be growing dramatically thinner. They were not to know that she was already visiting the royal kitchens, making new friends among the backstairs staff as she gorged herself on whatever was to hand, only to vomit it up again later. Her increasingly regular routine, by one particularly vivid account, ran as follows:

> At lunchtimes when she did not have guests, Diana would go into the nursery kitchen. She would take down a large glass bowl engraved with the EIIR cypher which held just over half a packet of breakfast cereal. She would fill it with Kellogg's Frosties and several chopped bananas, strawberries and sometimes pieces of apple. She would add tablespoons of caster sugar and pour on Windsor cream, a thick double cream from the Jersey herd at the Home Farm at Windsor. She would then sit down on top of the spin-dryer to eat her way through the mess which she washed down with fresh orange juice. When she had finished, she would go to her lavatory, lock herself in and spew up what she had just forced down. This pattern of gorge and regurgitate would happen twice and sometimes three or four times a day.[23]

Bulimia nervosa, the eating disorder that would haunt her marriage, had already taken hold, brought on, her friends will always believe, by acute anxiety about Charles and Camilla. The prince's camp – typified by the less than sympathetic note of distaste in the description above – will always maintain the opposite: that Diana's bulimia was the 'canker' within the marriage. Friends of the Queen, such as her biographer Elizabeth Longford, testify that Charles's mother believed that 'the stress in the princess's marriage was the result of [this] precondition', dating back to her childhood.[24] Others, like Mary Clarke, who knew her from childhood, insist that Diana became ill 'because of the anger and hurt of finding out she wasn't loved'.[25]

To Diana herself, bulimia was 'a secret disease' she could confess to no-one.

> You inflict it upon yourself because your self-esteem is at a low ebb, and you don't think you're worthy or valuable. You fill your stomach up four or five times a day – some do it more – and it gives you a feeling of comfort. It's like having a pair of arms around you, but it's temporary, temporary. Then you're disgusted at the bloatedness of your stomach, and then you bring it all up again. And it's a repetitive pattern which is very destructive to yourself.[26]

To her, there was no doubt about the cause of her illness: Charles's continuing friendship with Camilla Parker Bowles, with whom she finally had that lunch during his long absence abroad. The conversation reinforced Diana's impression that Camilla felt she owned some special right to Charles. She kept saying, 'Don't push him into this, don't do that,' and she was full of wily female advice as to how to 'handle' the prince. But one recurring refrain above all others lingered in Diana's mind. Was she planning, asked Camilla, to take up fox-hunting when she moved to Highgrove? When Diana said no, that she had disliked riding and horses since an accident in childhood, Camilla failed to hide the relief on her face. It did not take Diana long to work out that hunting would be the key to Camilla's continuing hold over Charles, a way to spend time with him without arousing anyone's suspicions, including hers.

Not for the first time, Diana realized that Camilla saw her primarily as 'a threat'. If she had been a true friend, she would have stayed in touch while Charles was away, soothing her anxieties, alleviating her loneliness in the vast, unfriendly confines of the Palace. Said her flatmate Carolyn Bartholomew, 'She went to live at Buckingham Palace and then the tears started. She wasn't happy, she was plunged into all this pressure and it was a nightmare for her. This little thing got so thin. I was so worried about her.'[27] It hadn't helped when Charles put his arm around her twenty-nine-inch waist one day and chided her for being 'a bit chubby'. By her wedding day, it had shrunk to twenty-three inches.

The surface explanation was, of course, her bulimia. But the bulimia itself was fed by her continuing anxieties about Camilla, in a vicious circle which would henceforth see each side of the argument blaming the other. In Charles's absence, Diana took the chance to ask the key members of his staff – Edward Adeane, Francis Cornish, Michael Colborne – if they thought the prince would give up Mrs Parker Bowles after the marriage. But they could offer naught for her comfort. 'If they evaded the question on principle,' in the words of another Charles apologist, 'they certainly had no answer.'[28]

Charles, for his part, spent his travels wondering quite who this was with whom he had chosen to spend the rest of his life. Everywhere he went, especially in Australia, his fellow men congratulated him on his taste, with blokeish nudges and winks that appalled his royal sense of propriety. To his further distaste, Diana 'lookalikes' were laid on at each of his destinations. The real Diana's face followed him everywhere, on newspaper front pages, magazine covers and television news bulletins. To some of those travelling with him (including the present author), it appeared as if Charles was curiously content to let his mind be made up for him. If the rest of the world was falling in love with Diana so fast and so completely, then perhaps he should, too. If he could.

His return home in early May proved a desperate anticlimax for his increasingly tense bride-to-be. Clinging to the hope that her prince would come to her rescue, devote himself to easing her problems, share his time and his secrets with her, Diana was brutally disillusioned. When first they were reunited, after six weeks apart, he gave her a cursory peck on the cheek and disappeared to change for lunch.

If she needed any confirmation that Charles, like his parents, was not a tactile person, this was a bleak beginning. Occasionally he would take her hand in an avuncular way, or put his arm round her waist to steer her through a group of people; but even the servants noticed that it was more the way a brother touches a sister than a full-blooded young man embraces his wife-to-be. One night that June, so legend has it, there was a violent thunderstorm which sent a frightened Diana scurrying along the Palace corridors to her fiancé's room in the middle of the night. Although he took her into his bed, it was 'not the momentous night it might have been'. Charles merely offered her his protective arm and told her not to be frightened of the thunder. He treated her, by one cynical account, 'decorously – more decorously than she would have wished.'[29]

Nor was he around as much as she had hoped. Most of Diana's time was still spent alone in her small suite on the Palace's nursery floor, while Charles went about his business in his own suite literally hundreds of yards away. Much of the time he wasn't there at all; as often as not, Diana discovered, he had gone to the country to see Camilla. Gradually she realized how often his staff were covering up for him. 'The lies and the deceit. I was told one thing, but actually another thing was going on.'[30]

Still wondering whether he could bear to give up Camilla for this highly strung young creature who demanded his exclusive attention, Charles hid behind his inborn royal defences. He did not see that it was incumbent on him to inform Diana of his movements. Nor, in the process, did he bother to ensure that she herself was coping with her daunting new life, squaring up to the formidable ordeal of their wedding service, now just two months away.

In truth, he too was racked by doubts. 'She is exquisitely pretty, a perfect poppet,' he told a friend, 'but she is a child. She does not look old enough to be out of school, much less married.'[31] His parents were no use to him: they were uncomfortable discussing personal matters, and anyway were convinced that it was now too late to change his mind. So, too, once the engagement had been announced, was his sister Anne, even though her own marriage had already run into difficulties. 'Just close your eyes and think of England' was her helpful advice. He had no-one else to turn to but Camilla, with whom he soon had an unprecedented row. She had her own private reasons, which Charles half knew, for endorsing Diana as his bride; how could he possibly question her judgement? For a while, in an attempt to stiffen his resolve, Mrs Parker Bowles acted offended and refused to see him or to take his phone calls.

With the wedding less than a week away, a parcel arrived in the small Buckingham Palace office that Diana shared with Michael Colborne, a naval colleague of the prince who had joined his staff as financial controller. Somehow, it had managed to arrive via a separate route from the wedding presents, which were now arriving *en masse*.

Despite Colborne's helpless protests, Diana insisted on opening it herself, to find inside a gold chain bracelet bearing a blue enamel disc, on which the letters G and F were entwined. Charles had christened Camilla his 'Girl Friday', but Diana also knew that their pet nicknames for each other were 'Gladys' and 'Fred'. She had seen a card inscribed 'to Gladys from Fred' when Charles had sent Camilla some flowers while she was ill with meningitis. This was not, as she first thought, a present to her husband-to-be from his long-time lover. Worse, it was the other way round. The prince must be planning to give this keepsake to Camilla.

Diana sought out Charles and demanded an explanation. In a confrontation as uncomfortable as any he had known, the prince stood his ground, explaining that Mrs Parker Bowles had been an intimate friend for years; he felt it 'unnecessary to go into detail'.[32] But now he would be calling an end to the intensity of their friendship, and seeing much less of her. He felt it appropriate to give her a token of his affection, by way of a farewell, and wished Diana could see it the same way. He was sorry that she was so upset, but insisted on going ahead with the gift. In fact, he would be taking it to Camilla personally the following Monday, two days before their wedding. Nothing Diana could say or do, no amount of tears or hysterics, would dissuade him.

It was a defining moment, in which Diana realized for the first time that she might never be rid of the shadow of Camilla Parker Bowles. That weekend, with the wedding only a few days away, she was seen in public to burst into tears while watching Charles play polo. Pleading pre-marital nerves, she fled the scene.

On the Monday morning Charles duly drove himself off, as announced, to give Camilla her bracelet and say his farewells. In a most unusual breach of the royal rules, he did not even take along his protection officer, Chief Inspector John MacLean. When Diana found MacLean in the Palace, but Charles gone, she asked where her fiancé was. 'He's gone out to lunch,' came the reply. At her wits' end, Diana had a tearful lunch with her sisters, and told them that she couldn't go through with it, that she wanted to call the whole thing off. This marriage was going to be a disaster. 'Too late, Duch!' they said light-heartedly, using her childhood nickname to try to cheer her up. 'You can't chicken out now. Your face is already on the tea towels.'[33]

Charles was away all day, as Princess Anne had chosen that afternoon, with remarkably tactless timing, for the christening at Windsor of her second child, a daughter to be rather racily named Zara. One of the godfathers was the princess's former beau, Andrew Parker Bowles, who was naturally there along with his wife. As was Anne's brother Charles, who chose not to bring his fiancée to this family occasion.

At the wedding rehearsal in St Paul's, forty-eight hours before the ceremony, Diana alarmed her fiancé by breaking down and sobbing, 'Absolutely collapsed ... because of all sorts of things. The Camilla thing rearing its head the whole way through our engagement and I was desperately trying to be mature about the situation but I didn't have the foundations to do it and I couldn't talk to anyone about it.'[34]

Charles put it down to pre-wedding nerves. But that same evening he was relieved to see Diana put on a brave face alongside himself and the Queen in a Palace receiving line for 800 friends and family invited to the eve-of-wedding ball, from Nancy Reagan via Raine Spencer to, of course, Andrew and Camilla Parker Bowles. With a few of her own friends there, Diana was somewhat restored to her usual high spirits, dancing with Rory Scott alongside the prime minister, Margaret Thatcher, to the music of Hot Chocolate. The occasion, by royal standards, went with an unprecedented swing; as royals and commoners alike became the worse for wear, Princess Margaret attached a balloon to her tiara, Prince Andrew tied one to his tuxedo, and Diana's brother, Charles Spencer, found himself bowing to a waiter. 'It was an intoxicatingly happy evening,' recalled one of Diana's friends. 'Everyone horribly drunk and then catching taxis in the early hours ... It was a blur, a glorious, happy blur.'[35]

As she returned to Clarence House, where decorum required her to spend the eve of her wedding, Diana had no way of knowing whether Camilla Parker Bowles returned home that evening, or, as she later came to believe, spent a few last hours at the Palace in Charles's arms.* Next day, amid her continuing anxieties, she was mollified by the arrival of a gift from her husband-to-be: a signet ring engraved with the Prince of Wales's distinctive three-feather motif, with a card reading, 'I'm so proud of you, and when you come up I'll be there at the altar for you tomorrow. Just look 'em in the eye and knock 'em dead.' During dinner with her sister Jane that evening, nonetheless, Diana gorged herself before leaving the room to be sick. 'The night before the wedding,' in her own words, 'I was very, very calm, deathly calm. I felt I was a lamb to the slaughter. I knew it and I couldn't do anything about it.'[36] Back at the Palace, Charles spent much of the evening staring moodily out of the window, in contemplative mood – showing no signs of joy, according to a companion, but aware that 'a momentous day' was upon him.[37]

Next morning, 29 July 1981, Diana was awoken at 5 a.m. by the noise of the crowds already gathering in the Mall, beneath her bedroom window. Kevin Shanley came to do her hair, Barbara Daly to do her make-up, and the Emanuels to ensure that all was well with her sumptuous wedding gown. When he arrived to offer moral support, even her brother Charles considered it a fairy-tale transformation: 'It was the first time in my life I ever thought of Diana as beautiful. She really did look stunning that day . . . slightly pale, but happy and calm.'[38] Waiting for her at the foot of the Clarence House staircase, her father told her, 'Darling, I'm so proud of you,' before they climbed into the Glass Coach for their stately progress through the crowds to St Paul's – during which, as she affectionately recalled, Earl Spencer 'waved himself stupid'.

With the world watching, Diana's prime concern at the cathedral was 'to get my father up the aisle'. She was well aware that her family was worried the frail old earl might not make it. With Diana's support, in front of 750 million people, he made a slow but steady progress on his daughter's arm to Jeremiah Clarke's *Trumpet Voluntary* – slow enough for Diana to concentrate on her other main preoccupation that morning: trying to spot

---

* In his book *Diana vs Charles* (1993), James Whitaker testified that the prince's valet, Stephen Barry, told him Camilla slipped away from the party with Charles. 'It was incredibly daring,' he quoted Barry as saying, 'if not incredibly stupid.' Barry died of AIDS in 1984. As a Charles apologist noted with heavy sarcasm, 'He was therefore never able to rebut the charge against either his employer or his own integrity.'[39]

Camilla Parker Bowles. Ten years later, this was still her main memory of what should have been the happiest moment of her life: 'I spotted Camilla, pale grey, veiled pillbox hat, saw it all, her son, Tom, standing on a chair. To this day, you know – vivid memory.'

Camilla was in the third row from the front, on the groom's side, in the midst of his most senior guests, including members of the royal family. Across the aisle was the prime minister, Margaret Thatcher, with her husband, Denis, and members of the Cabinet. As Charles's bride spotted his lover, she thought, 'Well, let's hope *that*'s all over with.'[40]

PART THREE

Three in a Marriage

CHAPTER NINE

'LIKE A LAMB TO THE SLAUGHTER'

EVEN THE ARCHBISHOP OF CANTERBURY, WHO CONDUCTED THE wedding service and endorsed the media 'fairy tale' from the pulpit, was in on the secret of Charles and Camilla. 'Oh, yes,' admitted the Rt Revd Robert Runcie years later, 'I knew about that already.'

Runcie's friend Ruth, Lady Fermoy, Diana's maternal grandmother, had discreetly discussed Charles's needs with the Archbishop, confiding her own worries about the prince's craving for 'a woman to love for and be cared by'. Echoing her evidence against her own daughter in her custody case with Earl Spencer, Lady Fermoy did not dissent from Runcie's judgement that her grand-daughter Diana was 'an actress and a schemer' who would 'never be under control until she fell in love with someone'. The result, even to the Archbishop who solemnized it, was 'an arranged marriage'.

When the couple had first come to see Runcie as part of their preparation for marriage, his chaplain Richard Chartres – 'a very observant man' in Runcie's view, soon to become Bishop of London – had said of Charles, 'He's seriously depressed. You can tell from his voice.' Runcie's own, rather more blasé outlook was, 'They're a very nice couple, and she'll grow into it.' By 1996, the year of their divorce, the retired Archbishop had to admit he had been wrong. 'I don't know what will become of her. Sad, really.'[1]

Fifteen years earlier, as he consigned Diana to an uncertain fate, Runcie was not the only protagonist at the wedding to know the secret of the married woman in the third pew. The bridegroom's parents, one of whom was Supreme Governor of the Church of England, also knew perfectly well what they were letting Diana in for. 'Here is the stuff of which fairy tales are made,' they heard the Archbishop intone, echoing the famous words of the constitutional historian Walter Bagehot: 'A princely marriage is the brilliant edition of a universal fact, and as such it rivets mankind.'[2] Of no princely marriage in history were Bagehot's words to prove truer, or Runcie's more hollow.

The wedding of Charles Windsor to Diana Spencer on 29 July 1981 was the biggest media event the world had ever seen. Three-quarters of a billion people watched via television as the bride endearingly confused her husband's forenames, while the groom made the not insignificant error of endowing her with her own worldly goods rather than his. As the gloriously sunny day went off without any worse hitches, ending with the first royal kiss ever seen on the balcony of Buckingham Palace, the Prince and Princess of Wales were universally deemed a fairy-tale couple, openly in love.

The innocent young girl in whom a nation reposed its emotional hopes was the first English-born bride of an heir to the throne for more than 300 years. Diana was set to become the first English Queen Consort since the days of King Henry VIII. She also brought to the Windsor line the only royal blood it lacked, that of the Stuarts. Her first-born son would thus be the first potential monarch in British history to be descended from every British king and queen who had issue.

Diana was also on course to become the first British Queen ever to have worked for her living. The last Princess of Wales, later King George V's Queen Mary, never made a speech or used a telephone in her life. Barely a generation after Mary's death, her successor set a new style for the monarchy as a girl-next-door princess, wearing off-the-peg clothes from chain stores. For all her deep-blue blood, Diana was also a thoroughly modern young woman; though no intellectual, she was already savvy, street-wise and smart. Apparently no heart-on-sleeve feminist, either, she showed considerable Spencer pride beneath those demurely lowered eyelashes.

In a long, hot summer disfigured by race riots, the royal wedding was just the shot in the arm Britain needed. The festive street parties toasting the royal couple made a stark contrast with alarming civil disruptions all over the country – rioting and ugly street violence, looting and arson from Brixton in south London to the Toxteth area of Liverpool, from the St Paul's district of Bristol to Handsworth in Birmingham and Moss Side in Manchester. As the physical damage was counted in scores of millions of pounds, the social cost was evaluated by a growing coalition of experts anxious to identify causes and seek solutions. By the time trouble erupted again four years later, on the Broadwater Farm estate in Tottenham, north London, Charles would be involved via his Prince's Trust in attempts to improve the social conditions at the root of the problem. In that summer of 1981 not only had he at last found himself, for better or worse, the bride he had so long been seeking; he had also been offered the sharp focus he so desperately needed for his public role.

Such thoughts could not have been further from the prince's mind as he and his bride processed through the streets of London – lined by a million cheering people, many of whom had slept there overnight – to the post-wedding 'breakfast' at Buckingham Palace. Diana, too, had reason to believe that her rival, Camilla, was now indeed an unhappy memory. Just to make sure, she had struck her name off the 120-strong guest list, along with that of another rival for the prince's affections, Dale 'Kanga' Tryon. A defiant Camilla hosted a lunch party of her own, secure in the knowledge that her wedding present to Charles had been secreted into the luggage he would be taking on honeymoon. Few of the excited guests at the Palace noticed that the bride and groom, though sitting next to each other, did not exchange a word. Those who did put it down, quite rightly, to sheer exhaustion. 'We were so shattered,' said Diana herself, who was 'exhausted at the whole thing'. But she had 'tremendous hopes in my heart'.[3]

At the end of the day, for the new princess, the sight of the crowds filling the Mall as far as the eye on the balcony could see was 'overwhelming . . . so humbling, all these thousands and thousands of happy people. It was just wonderful.' Charles said much the same in a letter to a friend: 'What an unbelievable day it was . . . I was *totally* overwhelmed'.[4] As they drove away from the Palace in a horse-drawn carriage, the soldier riding escort right behind them was the ever loyal Andrew Parker Bowles, no doubt sharing the 'tremendous hopes' in Diana's heart.

But Diana's disillusion set in immediately, even during the first three days of the honeymoon, spent with the Romseys at Charles's old hideaway, Broadlands. 'It was just grim,' she recalled ten years later. All her hopes were dashed as early as 'Day Two, [when] out came the van der Post novels he hadn't read. Seven of them – they came on our honeymoon. He read them and we had to analyse them over lunch every day.'[5] The rest of the time Charles spent fishing. By the time they flew to Gibraltar on 1 August, to board *Britannia* for a Mediterranean cruise, she was already growing ill again.

Aboard the royal yacht, with its crew of 277 to get in the honeymooners' way, Diana was dismayed to find that they were never left alone. Even their evening meals were black-tie affairs in the company of the ship's twenty-one officers, where the day's events were discussed to the accompaniment of a Royal Marines band. Charles, to whom the camaraderie of the mess deck was second nature, felt very much at home; for Diana, the only woman present, it was 'very difficult to accept'. By day, as the yacht cruised down the coast of Italy towards the Greek islands, Charles was still reading van der Post or writing endless letters. 'All I can say is that marriage is very jolly and it's extremely nice being together aboard *Britannia*,' he wrote home. 'Diana dashes about chatting up all the sailors and the cooks in the galley, etc., while I remain hermit-like on the verandah deck, sunk with pure joy into one of Laurens van der Post's books . . .'[6]

Little did Charles realize it was *because* he remained 'hermit-like on the verandah deck' that Diana was 'chatting up the cooks' – and even less *why* she spent so much time in the galley. Its staff were naturally delighted by her constant visits, and amused by her apparently insatiable requests for ice-cream, without themselves realizing what was actually happening. 'Bulimia appalling,' she noted. '[Sick] four times a day on the yacht. Anything I could find I would gobble up and be sick two minutes later.' This, of course, made her very tired, leading to sudden mood swings, so that 'one minute one would be happy, the next blubbing one's eyes out'.[7] The prince professed himself 'perplexed' by all this, but relieved that she was able to hide it from the crew.

The new princess even managed to maintain her public façade when the shadow of Camilla intruded on what should have been an idyllic honeymoon in the sun aboard the world's largest private yacht. In his father's seaborne study, which Charles had hijacked as his private retreat, they were comparing schedules one day when two photographs of Camilla fluttered out of his diary onto the floor.

A few days later, when they entertained Egypt's President Anwar Sadat and his wife to dinner, Diana noticed that her husband was wearing a new pair of gold cufflinks in the shape of two intertwined 'C's. Under angry questioning, Charles admitted they were a gift from Camilla, but failed to see anything wrong in so charming a gesture from so close a friend. Diana saw things differently. For Charles to attribute her mood swings to 'the transient pressures of adapting to her new and exacting role as his consort'[8] was disingenuous, to say the least.

After two weeks at sea, the couple flew from Egypt straight to Scotland, to continue their three-month honeymoon at Balmoral. Looking radiant at a Deeside photocall, Diana told journalists she could 'thoroughly recommend married life'. The reality was already very different. 'I remember crying my eyes out on our honeymoon,' she would say later. Charles could see that something was profoundly wrong, but professed bafflement. For him this was 'a blissful interlude at his favourite home, complete with his books, his fishing rods and his friends', while his new bride was for some reason 'unable to surrender herself to his good humour'.[9] Those friends, of course, were part of the problem, as was the prince's idea of a good time. Where Diana craved his sole attention – more of those moments of intimacy which are the shared memories of most honeymoons – Charles actually seemed to go out of his way to avoid being alone with her.

Already, within weeks, a pattern had begun to emerge. Viewing his bride with dismay as young and empty-headed, Charles sought companionship elsewhere, while consumed with guilt about being unfaithful to Camilla. Diana, for her part, could see that marriage was not going to be the bed of roses she had hoped. Her new husband was not paying her as much attention as fairy-tale brides feel entitled to expect. But she was determined to try to make the marriage work: 'When you've had divorced parents like myself, you'd want to try even harder to make it work. You don't want to fall back into a pattern that you've seen happen in your own family. I desperately wanted it to work, I desperately loved my husband and I wanted to share everything together.'[10]

To her chagrin, however, Diana herself was smart enough to see that Charles really was 'blissfully happy' reading van der Post while leaving her to get on with her tapestries, as women do. The only joint activity he suggested was to go for long walks. His idea of fun was 'to sit on top of the highest hill [and] read Laurens van der Post or Jung to me' even though 'I hadn't a clue about psychic powers or anything'.

For a young bride seeking solitude, to build a relationship with a husband she barely knew, it did not help that the rest of the royal family were never far away. Diana soon perceived that Charles was 'in awe of his mama' and 'intimidated by his father', while it fell to her to be 'always the third person in the room'. In the evenings, as the family gathered for dinner in formal attire, he would ask his mother and grandmother whether they wanted a drink before he asked his bride. 'Fine, no problem,' she reflected. 'But I had to be told that that was normal because I always thought it was the wife first. Stupid thought!'[11]

The princess knew that everyone could see she was getting 'thinner and thinner and sicker and sicker'. In part, as she conceded, this was 'basically [because] they thought I could adapt to being Princess of Wales overnight'. But Charles also began to attribute her unpredictability – laughing one minute, weeping the next – to a growing 'obsession' with Camilla Parker Bowles. Diana's insecurity about his feelings for Camilla, he told friends, was 'fed by the canker of jealousy'. She simply refused to believe that her husband had, as he faithfully promised, given up his lover for good. What about those photographs, that exchange of expensive gifts? How could he wear those cufflinks during their honeymoon? As the rows escalated, Charles drew back from his bride 'in bewilderment and despondency'.[12]

The prince was right: Diana was 'obsessed' with Camilla. During their extended honeymoon at Balmoral, by her own confession, she had recurring bad dreams about the other woman in her husband's life. She was, in her own words, 'obsessed by Camilla totally'. She did not trust Charles. She persuaded herself that he was 'ringing her up every five minutes asking how to handle his marriage'.[13]

By October he was – breaking his vow of self-denial after barely three months. Diana's behaviour so baffled and alarmed Charles that he also asked his friend Michael Colborne, then his mentor van der Post, to come to Balmoral to talk to her. He could scarcely, of course, have made a worse choice of confidants for Diana. Here was one man who had tried to hide Camilla's secret gift from her, and another who had already haunted her honeymoon via his books, with which Charles had spent more time than with her. Now she was required to confide her problems to the elderly sage, who was hardly likely to take her side against his protégé. As it was, the princess proved beyond van der Post's Jungian ken. 'Laurens', she said, 'didn't understand me.'[14]

Soon, while still technically on her honeymoon, Diana had travelled secretly to London for counselling. After clandestine meetings with psychiatrists at Buckingham Palace, she was prescribed a tranquillizer, Prozac, which she took most reluctantly. Charles was appalled, being a strong, and public, opponent of such drugs, and a firm believer in hiding your emotions, gritting your teeth and getting on with things. To Diana, who had not been able to share her true worries with them, the doctors did not understand her real problem: that she craved sympathy, attention and under-standing from her husband. In its absence, there was no-one else to whom she could turn for solace. The royal family and its advisers expected her to adapt to the stresses and strains of life as a princess, including overnight global adulation, as if it were second nature.

As yet the Windsors were probably unaware of Diana's other preoccupation: Camilla. Nor did they know that her thoughts were already turning to suicide – not because she genuinely wished to die, but as one way of showing her husband and his family quite how desperate she was feeling.

At first the Prozac saw her through to the end of a honeymoon that had turned into a protracted nightmare. Her demons, thought the doctors, had been caged. 'They could go to bed at night and sleep,' as she put it, 'knowing the Princess of Wales wasn't going to stab anyone.'[15]

But when the three-month honeymoon came to an end, she returned to her downward spiral. As she and Charles set off on their first official engagement together – a three-day tour of Wales at the end of October, for the prince formally to present his bride to his principality – she was the radiant and graceful Diana whom the world was fast taking to its heart, with a natural touch un-familiar from the Windsors that would soon become her trademark. Already there were ominous signs that the crowds were far more interested in her than in Charles. 'I know my place,' he joked to crowds who groaned when they found themselves on his side rather than hers. 'If only I had two wives!'

But the crowds also noticed, close up, how pathetically thin the princess was looking, and in private she gave up trying to hide the strain from outsiders. Back in the privacy of the royal train Diana constantly broke down in tears, drained of all energy, pleading that she could not face another crowd. 'Stay close to her,' Charles told her lady-in-waiting, 'she needs your support' – still not realizing, apparently, that the support she actually needed was his. When she made it safely through the first public speech of her life – partly in Welsh – on receiving the freedom of the City of Cardiff, Diana was so upset at the lack of congratulations from Charles that she no longer troubled to conceal her unhappiness from their staff.

On the second day of the Welsh tour, however, another reason for Diana's malaise emerged with confirmation from London that she was pregnant. Charles decided that this must be reason enough for her constant sickness and tantrums, and Diana, too, cheered up for a while. 'A godsend,' she called it. 'Marvellous news, occupied my mind.'[16] It was also an excuse to give up the Prozac, for fear it might harm the baby. Maybe now, with Charles sharing her delight in the prospect of their first child, he might at last begin to take more interest in her.

On 2 November, three days before Buckingham Palace announced Diana's pregnancy, Charles went out hunting in the Gloucestershire countryside near Cirencester. At one point, as the fox went to ground beside a main road, the prince found himself riding towards a crowd of spectators, including some journalists, at whom he yelled, 'When are you going to stop making my life a misery?' As they watched him turn away to rejoin the main group, shaken by the vehemence of his outburst, they saw him ride back out of range beside a woman who 'looked suspiciously like Camilla Parker Bowles'.[17] Such was Fleet Street's euphoria about the news of a forthcoming royal birth that the incident went unreported.

So Diana, too, knew nothing about it. But her pregnancy was not proving easy. With acute morning sickness complicating her bulimia, the princess grew ever thinner and weaker. Each public appearance still won her unqualified adulation, but seemed to do little to improve her spirits. Towards the end of the year, it was all she could do to avoid being sick in public as she formally switched on the Christmas lights in London's Regent Street. Over the autumn she had embarked on a series of long, candid conversations with her husband's friends and advisers about the reasons for her unhappiness, harping on themes which they summarized as 'the loss of freedom, the absence of a role, the boredom, the emptiness in her life, the heartlessness of her husband'. Surprised by her candour, they patiently tried to explain those aspects of her new role with which she was having trouble coming to terms: her husband's frequent absences, the complex interplay between the private and the public man, the need for her to find her own separate identity in the shape of royal patronages – 'something in Wales', perhaps, or 'something with children'.[18]

Some of their staff, such as the private secretary assigned to Diana, Oliver Everett, were understandably bemused by her continuing volatility – one moment offering profuse thanks for his help, the next coldly ignoring him. Charles's own private secretary, Edward Adeane, was already losing patience with some aspects of the prince's conduct of his public life, and had even less patience for his wife. A lofty courtier of the old school, whose father and grandfather before him had been private secretaries to Windsor monarchs, Adeane and his crusty bachelor outlook had little time for the naïve young ingenue his boss had chosen to impose on the royal household. Adeane's 'stuffy' ways brought out Diana's natural playfulness, wagging her finger at him as she picked up his cigar butts, which Adeane found unbecoming. More than once, Charles confided, he had to intervene to 'soothe his private secretary's feelings'.[19]

Diana's pregnancy was at least an excuse for her to take things a little easier and cut back on public appearances; but that, of course, merely left her more time to feel lonely and to brood. Though thrilled by the prospect of becoming a mother, she became increasingly distraught at what she saw as Charles's neglect, which climaxed that Christmas at Sandringham. She had hoped that the long annual break in his public duties might at last afford them some time alone together, like most young newlyweds excitedly looking forward to the birth of their first child. Instead, predictably enough, it was offstage royal business as usual: Charles enjoying the great outdoors most of the time, walking or shooting, leaving his edgy, unhappy wife on her best behaviour, without his moral support, amid his daunting and cheerless extended family. After enduring two weeks of this apparent indifference, through Christmas and New Year, Diana finally cracked and confronted

Charles noisily with her feelings. The ensuing row could be heard all over Sandringham House. At the point of real despair, Diana threatened suicide; Charles accused her of being melodramatic, and coolly laid plans to go out riding. She had little alternative, as she saw it, but to carry out her threat.

Standing at the top of Sandringham's main staircase that day in January 1982, three months pregnant, Diana hurled herself down the stairs, landing at the feet of her horrified mother-in-law. Visibly shaking with shock, the Queen could not believe what she had seen; Charles, on hearing what had happened, went out riding as planned. As a local doctor tended Diana, pending the arrival from London of her gynaecologist, Dr George Pinker, it was clear that she had suffered severe bruising around her stomach. Mercifully, Pinker was later able to confirm that the baby had not been harmed.

Over the coming months, the princess persisted in further dramatic acts of self-mutilation: slashing at her wrists with a razor blade, throwing herself at a glass cabinet in Kensington Palace, cutting herself with the serrated edge of a lemon slicer and stabbing her chest and thighs with a penknife. She later acknowledged that these were not genuine suicide attempts, but 'cries for help'.

> When no-one listens to you, or you feel no-one's listening to you, all sorts of things start to happen . . . You have so much pain inside yourself that you try and hurt yourself on the out-side because you want help, but it's the wrong help you're asking for. People see it as crying wolf or attention-seeking, and they think because you're in the media all the time you've got enough 'attention' . . . But I was actually crying out because I wanted to get better in order to go forward and continue my duty and my role as wife, mother, Princess of Wales. So yes, I did inflict [injuries] upon myself. I didn't like myself, I was ashamed because I couldn't cope with the pressures.[20]

These 'cries for help' were also the point of no return, after barely six months, for the marriage. Charles's failure to heed them was, to Diana, the ultimate rejection. As one eyewitness of her miseries put it to Andrew Morton, the journalist through whom she eventually revealed them to the world, 'His indifference pushed her to the edge, whereas he could have romanced her to the end of the world. They could have set the world alight. Through no fault of his own, because of his own ignorance, upbringing and lack of a whole relationship with anyone in his life, he instilled this hatred of himself.'[21]

That Charles could ignore these alarming acts of desperation, dismissing them as 'fake' while going blithely about his business, may seem extraordinary. Even he has confessed that he was 'not always solicitous' and 'did sometimes rebuff her'. For his part, he too was feeling deprived of 'the emotional support at home to which, in his romantic way, he had for so long aspired'. As he saw it, though 'drained by the persistence of his wife's reproaches', he usually 'tried to console her and rarely offered any rebuke for what his friends judged to be her waywardness. If his ministrations were inadequate and – given his public duties – intermittent, they lacked neither sincerity nor compassion'. Besides, his attempts to console her were all too often rejected.

Charles's reaction to his wife's sudden spate of assaults upon herself – 'they drew blood but a sticking plaster invariably sufficed to stem the bleeding' – was as 'shocked and uncomprehending' as all those privy to them. However 'incompetent' his attempts to comfort her, he felt 'tenderness and pity for his wife when she was stricken by these apparently inexplicable moods'.[22]

Amid it all, the lower reaches of the British press did not regard the princess's pregnancy as any reason to diminish the pressures on her. In February 1982, when she and Charles were taking a break with the Romseys on Eleuthera, a group of tabloid reporters and photographers crawled hundreds of yards on their bellies through tropical undergrowth to secure a photograph of the pregnant princess in a bikini. Next day, amid uproar, Rupert Murdoch's *Sun* even had the gall to apologize for taking the photograph alongside a lavish front-page reproduction of it.

Though the vacation otherwise passed uneventfully, Norton and Penny Romsey still noticed Diana's impatience with Charles's penchant for spending his leisure time reading and painting; and, as they feared, the remaining months of her pregnancy saw little improvement in her spirits. To Charles, preoccupied with the Falklands conflict, Diana seemed to resent the fact that the press was giving a distant war priority over her. Some of his friends, meanwhile, did not help by persuading him of the bizarre conclusion that his wife 'sought to possess him, but only in order to be able to reject him'.[23]

On the evening of 21 June 1982, the gulf between husband and wife was briefly forgotten when Diana gave birth to a son in St Mary's Hospital, Paddington. At her most bitter, Diana would later say they had to find a date for William's birth 'that suited Charles and his polo'; the child was induced, at her request, in truth partly because her bulimia had left her so weak, partly because the media anticipation had become so intense that she could bear it no longer. 'I felt the whole country was in labour with me,' she said years later.[24] At the time, Charles chalked up another Windsor first by staying at his wife's bedside throughout the birth; and Diana could enjoy a joke at his expense when the Queen's first comment on seeing her new grandchild was, 'Thank heavens he hasn't got his father's ears.'

It took two days for them to negotiate the names of William Arthur Philip Louis – the three royal names were a quid pro quo for Diana's choice of William – before embarking on the first few months of uncomplicated happiness in their married life. Diana had fulfilled her side of the unspoken bargain that is an arranged marriage: she had delivered her husband a male heir, as was his constitutional duty, to ensure the royal succession. But still it seemed to her that she got little thanks for it.

The previous month, with the help of the interior designer Dudley Poplak, a friend of her mother, Diana had completed the redecoration of the apartment at Kensington Palace that was to be their home. Five weeks before William's birth, she and Charles had finally moved into the 'royal ghetto' they were to share with Princess Margaret, the Duke and Duchess of Gloucester, and Prince and Princess Michael of Kent.

All too soon, however, Diana's initial euphoria became clouded by a chronic case of post-natal depression. With it returned the sickness, the bulimia, the tantrums and the obsession with Camilla. This last was not entirely unjustified; one day she overheard Charles speaking to Mrs Parker Bowles by phone from his bath, saying, 'Whatever happens, I will always love you.'[25] There ensued 'a filthy row', and a period when Diana would become highly distressed whenever she did not know where Charles was, if he did not tell her where he was going, or if he was late home from an engagement. Soon both of them were plunged back into a corrosive cycle of mutual hostility and suspicion, abuse and recrimination. They moved into separate bedrooms.

As Diana devoted all her emotional energies to her baby, fortunate that she had chosen an extremely patient nanny in Barbara Barnes, Charles chose very different forms of consolation for his lack of emotional fulfilment. It was during this period that he first began to alarm his parents with what they saw as eccentricities: giving up shooting, and turning vegetarian ('Oh, Charles, don't be so silly,' said the Queen). While the Windsors naturally blamed Diana, they might more logically have looked into their own hearts. Their neglect during his own childhood had surely launched Charles on the long quest of self-discovery which saw him seeking consolation in religions other than his own, of which he was one day destined to become Supreme Governor. His aversion to killing, albeit short-lived, was in part a return to the Buddhist beliefs he had once shared with Zoe Sallis, as was his natural aversion to eating meat, accentuated at this time by intense conversations with his vegetarian bodyguard, Paul Officer.

The logical culmination of these thought processes was to come a few months later, that December, when the prince made his first public speech advocating 'alternative' medicine. Like their colleagues in architecture, the leading lights of Britain's medical profession were not entirely pleased to be told how to do their jobs by an unelected princeling with no medical experience or qualifications. A good doctor, Charles told them, 'should be intimate with nature . . . He must have the "feel" and "touch" which makes it possible for him to be in sympathetic communication with the patient's spirits.'[26]

It was not only the doctors who were mildly offended by this speech. So was Charles's wife, a mistress of the arts of 'feel' and 'touch', woefully deprived of any such thing from her husband. At the time, moreover, she was still afflicted by post-natal depression. Denial from her husband was the last thing she needed.

In her heart, Diana knew that Charles was ill-equipped by his upbringing to deal with a psychological disorder in anyone, let alone someone close to him. But she could not help feeling 'misunderstood' and 'very, very low'. It was quite out of character. 'I'd never had a depression in my life. But then when I analysed it I could see that the changes I'd made in the last year had all caught up with me, and my body had said: "We want a rest."' But Diana's sufferings gave her an even deeper, more lasting cause for concern. As far as she could tell, no-one in the royal family, including Charles, had any personal experience of dealing with depression. 'Maybe I was the first person in this family who ever had a depression or was ever openly tearful.' The consequences were ominous. 'It gave everybody [in the royal family] a wonderful new label: Diana's unstable, Diana's mentally unbalanced.' Unfortunately, as she soon realized, that label 'seemed to stick'.[27]

At William's christening in early August 1982, she complained of feeling 'totally excluded' amid 'endless pictures of the Queen, Queen Mother, Charles and William'. The family then repaired, as usual, to Balmoral, where she grew steadily worse. At a total loss, Charles arranged for her to return to London to see another round of counsellors and psychiatrists.

Misinterpreting her motives, the press decided that Diana had become 'bored' at the royal family's rain-soaked Scottish retreat, where there was no nightlife to suit the mythical 'Disco Di', who had fled to go shopping in Knightsbridge. For the first time, barely a year after the marriage, the tribunes of the people turned against her; the gossip columnist Nigel Dempster labelled her 'a monster and a fiend' for supposedly destabilizing the prince's staff and driving away his friends.

Later, there might have been some substance to this charge; but not yet. In letters to friends, Charles still nursed some hope that things might improve. But progress was patchy; every apparent step forward was always followed by some frustrating setback. That very day, for instance, after a 'hopeful' morning, the afternoon had seen a 'heavy feeling' descend.[28] Behind the façade, in private as in public, he too was close to despair.

There was a hopeful sign that September, when Diana volunteered to represent the Queen at the funeral of her soulmate, Princess Grace of Monaco, killed that month in a car crash. Charles disapproved; in an exchange of memos with his wife – the only way the royals see fit to discuss such matters – he argued that she was not yet ready to undertake her first solo engagement abroad on behalf of the monarchy. But Diana felt a kinship with Grace, another outsider who had endured difficulties in becoming royal, and a debt of honour for her kindness on her public début eighteen months before. She dug in her heels, and went over Charles's head direct to his mother, again by memo. No doubt taking it as a healthy sign of Diana's intent to prove herself, and relieved to find someone willing to pay the Windsors' respects to a woman she had always regarded as 'vulgar', the Queen agreed. To Charles's chagrin, Diana won universal praise for the dignity with which she graced an occasion as Hollywood as it was Monégasque.

But Diana's apparent revival did not last long. Palace staff were privy to another domestic row the following month, when Charles loudly berated his wife for her last-minute refusal to accompany him to the British Legion remembrance service at the Royal Albert Hall. On the eve of the annual ceremony at the Cenotaph, when the royal family leads the nation's homage to the dead of two world wars, the occasion is regarded as one of the most important fixed points in the royal calendar. After a seething Charles had left without her, Diana evidently underwent a change of heart; she was seen by astonished spectators to arrive in the royal box fifteen minutes late, after the ceremony had begun, looking 'grumpy and fed-up'. To arrive after the Queen was a gross breach of protocol, for which she would not swiftly be forgiven.

The incident was but the latest climax in Diana's continuing concerns: Charles's apparent indifference to her, the loneliness and boredom of royal life, her unshakeable obsession with Camilla. But the princess also felt resentful that her husband and his staff had offered her no help in coping with her new status. 'No-one sat me down with a piece of paper and said: "This is what is expected of you."' So she did what came naturally, which only exacerbated the problem. When Diana was photographed sitting on hospital beds and holding patients' hands, Charles and his staff were 'shocked . . . They said they had never seen this before, while to me it was quite a normal thing to do.'

But there had never been a royal quite like Diana before, as she herself was well aware: 'Here was a situation which hadn't ever happened before in history, in the sense that the media were everywhere, and here was a fairy story that everybody wanted to work.' It was 'isolating', yes, 'but it was also a situation where you couldn't indulge in feeling sorry for yourself. You had to learn very fast. You either had to sink or swim.'[29] Diana became determined to swim.

She had to fight to stay afloat when some indiscreet remarks by the couple's then press secretary, the Canadian Vic Chapman, suggested that she had developed other obsessions, such as demanding that her shoes be polished daily and arranged in immaculately neat straight lines. Leaks of this kind of irrational behaviour, amid further comments on her thinness, prompted the first public rumours that Diana might be suffering from an eating disorder – perhaps, like her sister Sarah, anorexia nervosa.

As an informed guess, it was only half wrong. Diana's bulimia was growing steadily worse. If she had been on an official visit around the country – what she called an 'awayday' – she would return home feeling 'pretty empty, because my engagements at that time would be to do with people dying, people very sick, people's marriage problems'. She found it 'very difficult to know how to comfort myself, having been comforting lots of other people, so it would be a regular pattern to jump into the fridge'.

Where Charles saw her illness as the source of their problems, Diana still insisted that it was the product of his dismissive attitude towards her. 'I was crying out for help,' she said, 'but giving the wrong signals.' To her, Charles was 'using' her bulimia as 'a coat on a hanger . . . [He] decided that was the problem: Diana was unstable.' At mealtimes together, far from expressing sympathy, he would accuse her of 'wasting' food. Remarks like these, of course, only added to the pressure on her. 'So of course I would, because it was my release valve.'[30]

From his viewpoint, Charles could only watch with mounting dismay as Diana thrashed around in her own private agonies, now compounded by the withdrawal of the media's unqualified support. As they prepared to embark on a year of major foreign tours together, he could only grit his teeth and hope.

When they flew to Australia the following March, for their first official foreign tour together, amounting to six weeks away, Charles and Diana took nine-month-old William with them. Seeking controversy where there was none, the press was wrong to suggest that the Queen disapproved; in fact, she had not even been consulted. Mindful of his parents' long absences during his own infancy and childhood, Charles was only too pleased to accept the thoughtful suggestion of the Australian prime minister, Malcolm Fraser, that they might enjoy the trip more if they brought their son along. Diana, of course, was thrilled.

They based themselves at Woomargama, a sheep station in New South Wales, where William was left with his nanny, Barbara

Barnes, while the prince and princess undertook an arduous schedule of public engagements. The scale of the adulation – with
millions materializing to see them from a population of only
17 million – was like nothing Charles had ever known; the clamour
and crush, apart from being dangerous, offended his sense of
decorum and stretched his nerves. To the prince, by now, these
overseas visits were more of a duty than a pleasure; in his thirty-
fifth year, he had already 'endured' more than fifty of them. For
Diana, of course, it was a whole new experience – and a daunting
one, despite her husband's supposedly reassuring presence. Thanks
to her, the crowds were bigger than Charles had ever known; in
Brisbane alone, more than a quarter of a million turned out for a
glimpse of the world's most glamorous couple. But it was 'Lady Di'
who dominated the headlines, and the pictorial coverage. It was
another forceful reminder for Charles that his future subjects,
while warm towards him, were 'besotted' with his wife.

He did not take kindly to this. Back at Woomargama, Charles
immersed himself in Turgenev and Jung while Diana relaxed with
William. But both agreed, for once, that they worked as a mutual
support system during the unusual ardours of their antipodean
journey, which took them to New Zealand for two weeks after four
in Australia. The whole thing, for Charles, had become too much
of a circus, with Diana's every twitch being photographed for
posterity. 'It frightens me,' he wrote to friends, 'and I know for a
fact it petrifies Diana.' She was 'marvellous', he reported, and
helped keep him going; for her part, the princess acknowledged
that Charles had 'pulled her out of her shell and helped her cope
with the pressure . . . We were a very good team in public, albeit
what was going on in private . . . We had unique pressures put
upon us, but we both tried our hardest to cover them up.'[31]

It was during this trip, however, that another source of tension
between them began to surface: Charles's natural resentment, as he
was candid enough to admit to friends, at being 'upstaged and out-
shone' by his wife. To a proud man, accustomed all his life to being
the centre of attention, it had at first been a relief when Diana took
some of the pressure off him; but when the spotlight showed no
sign of swinging back his way, Charles's *amour propre* began to
suffer. As she herself realized, he felt 'low about it, instead of feeling happy and sharing it'.[32] But Diana did not entirely understand
his priorities. To Charles, this was not just a matter of personal

jealousy, but of royal protocol; Diana was there as his wife and consort, not as his superior.

The same proved true on a tour of Canada a few weeks later. Though the crowds were neither as large nor as manic as in Australia, they were all there to see Diana rather than Charles. In strict terms of status, he should have been the star of the travelling roadshow; but in terms of public esteem, it was clear that the pulling power was all hers. If it was Diana's obsessions and pre-occupations that had so far undermined their chance of marital happiness, whether justified or not, Charles now had one of his own to eat away at what little hope they had left.

Back in London, they basked in universal adulation, summed up in a typically effusive tribute from the speaker of the House of Commons, George Thomas, that same devout Welshman who had fluttered around Charles during his investiture. 'Not only the royal family have gained by their success,' trilled Thomas, 'but the whole nation and the Commonwealth have received a blessing beyond measure . . . In the rapidly changing world that we have, I believe that the Prince and Princess of Wales and their son will give us the continuity that assures us stability.'[33]

Speaker Thomas could not be expected to discern the deep irony behind his rhetorical flourish. Stability, the quality the Wales marriage was supposedly going to supply to the nation, was the one thing the union itself sorely lacked. Continuity, as a result, was already in long-term doubt. The causes of their unhappiness did not vary; Diana's complaints remained the same, Charles refused to mend his ways, and they had found no way of communicating; by mutual agreement, they had failed to build 'the intimacy and mutual understanding without which the relationship could not grow'.[34]

That autumn was the worst they had yet known. While at Highgrove, Charles took to joining Camilla with the Beaufort Hunt as soon as his wife left for London. It did not take Diana long to work out what was going on; all her worst fears, still written off as her irrational 'obsession', were being realized. That November, when she joined her husband for a weekend at Highgrove, a suspicious Diana pressed the 'recall' button on the phone in his study, to find it ringing Camilla's number. There was a 'monu-mental row' in front of the domestic staff as Charles nevertheless insisted on going out hunting with Camilla, even with Diana in residence. The servants watched in horror as the princess broke down in hysterical tears; Charles, by now past caring, rode off regardless.

Both still wanted more children; and they must have called a truce over Christmas and New Year at Sandringham long enough for the princess to become pregnant again. As she relaxed her timetable accordingly, Charles had an unusually busy year ahead, with trips to Brunei in February, East Africa in March, Papua New Guinea in August, France, Monaco and Holland in the autumn. To his mind, Diana now took advantage of these absences to 'banish' some of his closest friends, including the Romseys, the Palmer-Tomkinsons, the Brabournes and Nicholas Soames.

Convinced that these pre-marital loyalists were conspiring with Charles against her, and facilitating his secret meetings with Camilla, Diana ensured that they were no longer invited to Highgrove or Kensington Palace. For all his subsequent protests, Charles chose at the time to go along with this considerable sacrifice. These friends testify that, for a period, his phone calls and letters ceased to come. Understandably hurt, but suspecting what was really happening, they did not take the matter up with the prince for fear of placing him in a difficult position.

Charles would later deny it, but Diana believed that her husband had already 'gone back to his lady'. She also knew from a scan that the child in her womb was a boy, while he was desperately hoping for a girl. For the moment, she decided not to tell him, as her pregnancy again occasioned sporadic oases of calm amid all the turbulence. Already Diana wanted out, as she confided to her friend Sarah Ferguson. But the princess knew that that was impossible then, if ever, and during that summer of her second pregnancy she managed to appear calmer and more content than at any other time in the marriage.

Charles responded wholeheartedly to Diana's welcome transformation, giving her no cause for suspicion of Camilla, and treating his heavily pregnant wife with unusual solicitude at Balmoral. 'We were very, very close to each other the six weeks before Harry was born,' she recalled, 'the closest we've ever, ever been.'[35] But it was to prove the calm before a climactic storm.

At 4.20 p.m. on Saturday, 15 September, Diana gave birth to a second son in the Lindo wing of St Mary's Hospital. She had still failed to summon the nerve to let Charles in on the secret of their child's gender. 'Oh, God,' he exclaimed, 'it's a boy.' And, he added, in a biting reference to his son's Spencer genes, 'He's even got red hair.'

With this, the prince left for Windsor to play polo. 'Something inside me closed off,' said Diana. 'It just went bang, our marriage, the whole thing went down the drain.'[36]

Charles and Diana had been married barely three years. Henceforth, as well as occupying separate beds, they would start to lead separate lives.

CHAPTER TEN

'WHY CAN'T YOU BE MORE LIKE FERGIE?'

IT WAS NOT ONLY ON THE DOMESTIC FRONT THAT CHARLES'S LIFE WAS disintegrating. Now, early in 1985, Edward Adeane chose to resign as the Prince of Wales's private secretary. Only within the Palace was the huge significance of Adeane's departure appreciated. His father, Lord Adeane, had been private secretary to Charles's mother and grandfather, Elizabeth II and George VI; his grandfather, Viscount Stamfordham, had been private secretary to Queen Victoria and her grandson, George V. It was Adeane's grandfather, indeed, who had given the royal dynasty its name of Windsor; at the height of the First World War, when George V was reluctantly persuaded to drop the German name of Saxe-Coburg-Gotha, Stamfordham suggested instead the name of the historic Berkshire town where the king spent his weekends. In 1980, a year after becoming Charles's private secretary, Edward Adeane fulfilled a cherished personal ambition by completing a century of un-broken royal service by his family.

It had thus been taken for granted, a *fait accompli*, that the bachelor Adeane would in turn devote his life to the royal family, like his father and grandfather before him, staying at his master's side for as long as it took to maintain his family's proud tradition by becoming private secretary to King Charles III. His abrupt departure signalled that something really was rotten in the House of Windsor.

Not long before, Charles had also lost the services of his long-standing naval friend, Michael Colborne, who had been supervising his personal finances, with the title of secretary to the prince's office. Three years earlier his long-serving valet Stephen Barry had been among the first of his staff to leave, within six months of the marriage. By the end of 1985, no fewer than forty members of the royal household had chosen to quit: apart from Adeane, Colborne and Barry, there was Alan Fisher, the butler the Waleses inherited from Bing Crosby; Lieutenant-Colonel Philip Creasy, comptroller (financial controller) of the prince's household; and the hapless Oliver Everett, who had given up a promising Foreign Office career for temporary secondment to the prince's office, only to wind up becoming his wife's reluctant private secretary and now the Queen's librarian. Even Charles's loyal, long-time detectives, Paul Officer and John MacLean, eventually bade their prince farewell as, in the words of her brother Charles, Diana 'got rid of all the hangers-on who surrounded Charles'.[1]

Remarks like that bolstered the public perception that the princess was systematically cleansing the Wales stables, purging first friends and now staff, while a browbeaten Charles surrendered purse strings as much as apron strings. Loyal retainers who felt obliged to quit were quoted blaming the princess and her petulant ways. 'The debonair prince is pussy-whipped from here to eternity,' an American magazine stated that year, before the couple's visit to the Reagan White House.[2] The truth was subtly different. To some extent, as her self-confidence grew, Diana did make attempts to change the climate of the alien world in which she found herself, and to construct a personal landscape in which she had a chance of taking more control. From the moment she struck the names of Parker Bowles and Tryon off the guest list for the wedding breakfast, she had made the understandable effort of many a young bride to persuade her husband to leave his bachelor world behind. She had not, of course, entirely succeeded; so the process naturally continued with the staff, many of whom anyway felt uncomfortable being privy to the couple's perpetual squabbles.

But the cases of those closest to Charles belie the suggestion that Diana's behaviour was primarily to blame. Stephen Barry, his valet for twelve years before the wedding, may not have been personally close to the prince in terms of anything like friendship, but he was the man who had woken him up every day for twelve years, taken him breakfast in bed, shared many of his most private secrets, and had thus become close to Charles in quite another sense.

'I did not have a row with Princess Diana,' Barry testified. 'Nothing of the kind happened.' He decided to quit because the prince's centre of gravity was shifting to Highgrove, and his own life was in London. After covering most of the globe with Charles, he had also lost his appetite for travel. And, as he sensibly put it at the time, 'It's quite reasonable and not surprising that anyone as young as Princess Diana would want to be surrounded by people of her own choice.'

When Barry informed her of his decision to go, Diana immediately joked, 'People will say we've had a terrible row!'

'As long as we know we haven't,' he replied, 'that's all right, isn't it?' The bulimic Diana nodded, and 'took another spoonful of yogurt'.[3]

Colborne's departure also had little, if nothing, to do with Diana. In fact, it was more Charles's fault for failing to cut through the Palace protocol that denied the title of comptroller to one of his navy chum's humble status. A key player in the administrative side of the prince's life, and a trusted friend, Colborne was a grievous, and unnecessary, loss. Like all the others who left in this lemming-like parade, he was glad to be spared the constant rows and tension between the prince and princess; but he would have stayed on, lending Charles valuable moral support, had he been promoted to a rank and salary befitting his contribution to the smooth running of Charles's life.

Adeane, too, had become weary of the marital spats; but it was not, as bruited about at the time, Diana's waywardness that drove him out of royal life. It was Charles's.

'Edward', said Diana, perhaps diplomatically, 'was wonderful. We got on so well.' She especially appreciated the candidates he proposed for her ladies-in-waiting: 'One or two [fell] by the wayside but the others remained very strong.'[4] For all the petty irritations, the princess genuinely endeared herself to this punctilious courtier of the old school by the efficiency and dispatch with which she dealt with paperwork, especially letters – a dutiful habit drummed into her in childhood. Her husband, by contrast, was notoriously slapdash about paperwork, which he had always hated.

As the prince began to assemble his portfolio of causes to champion, Adeane had made it clear that he thought some of them inappropriate, also taking a dim view of the growing army of informal advisers recruited by the prince. Even Charles's admirers concede that '[his] enthusiasms too often bore the imprint of the last conversation he had held or the latest article to have caught his eye', as well as 'his tendency to reach instant conclusions on the basis of insufficient thought'.[5]

Under the pressure of countless new initiatives, many turning out to be mere dalliances that were soon forgotten, the Prince of Wales's private office – inadequately staffed to meet the mounting flow of business – began to spin increasingly out of control, with piles of paper accumulating at random, and heaps of letters lying around unanswered. Uncomfortable with such carelessness, Adeane was even less pleased to note that his advice was increasingly being ignored. The climax came on 30 May 1984, with the prince's infamous 'carbuncle speech' at Hampton Court Palace.

When Charles criticized Peter Ahrends's design for the National Gallery extension in Trafalgar Square as 'a monstrous carbuncle on the face of a much-loved friend', and launched into a wholesale assault on modern architecture, he was not just abusing the hospitality of the Royal Institute of British Architects at a celebratory dinner on the occasion of their 150th anniversary. He was insulting the eminent Indian architect Charles Correa, whom he ignored throughout the evening, although the prime reason for the prince's presence was to present Correa with the RIBA's Gold Medal for his outstanding work for the Third World homeless – precisely the kind of work that Charles has otherwise claimed as his own. He was also causing commercial damage to a British company, and subverting statutory planning procedures. Above all, he was committing a damaging, and unjustified, slander – the kind of slur which, had it come from anyone else in public life, might well have earned them an expensive lawsuit.

His private secretary, for once, was on the side of the prince's opponents. The speech, to Adeane as to its audience, was symptomatic of Charles's failure to grasp the complexities of the architectural process, which is not merely about style, but about the handling of space and scale, interminable negotiations with planners and developers, and the immense complexities of designing modern, high-technology buildings to last centuries. Had the prince done a modicum of research before launching so vicious a public assault on a distinguished man's reputation, he would have known that the design he criticized was in fact a compromise between the gallery's trustees and the architect, then at an interim stage about which Ahrends himself was less than happy. At the request of the trustees, the architect had already made certain revisions to his original design. So when the prince questioned, for instance, the sacrifice of gallery space to office space, he was in fact attacking the brief given Ahrends by his client, the gallery's trustees (of which Charles himself would soon be one).[6]

At the time of the prince's speech a public planning inquiry was under way, at the end of which the secretary of state for the environment, Patrick Jenkin, was due to make a final ruling. But the views of the public became irrelevant from the moment Charles stood up to speak. Jenkin happened to be in the audience at Hampton Court; while the prince was still on his feet, he whispered to his neighbour, 'Well, that's one decision I don't have to make!'[7]

Peter Ahrends's distinguished career was blighted that evening. Soon his practice, one of Britain's leading architectural partnerships, was losing millions of pounds in potential commissions. Developers who feared the prince's veto no longer invited the 'carbuncle architects' to enter competitions, the meat and drink of the their profession. That night, in the heat of the moment, Ahrends gave vent to his feelings; the prince's remarks, he told journalists, were 'offensive, reactionary, ill-considered ... if he holds such strong views, I'm surprised he did not take the opportunity offered by the public inquiry to express them'. Ever since, he has shown dignified restraint by holding his peace, though described by colleagues as 'a broken man' – 'a tragic figure' who had 'every right to feel aggrieved'.*

For days Adeane had been trying to talk Charles out of the speech. Its passionate partiality, apart from constituting an abuse of hospitality, would incur the enmity of a British professional institute under royal patronage; and it would involve him in a heated public debate in an area which was wholly new ground to him. Charles listened testily, unaccustomed to internal opposition of such force. But his stubborn streak won the day; unknown to Adeane, who was still trying to talk him out of the speech in the

---

* Seven years later, in July 1991, the Prince of Wales watched his mother open the building hastily commissioned to replace the British architect's design: the new Sainsbury Wing of the National Gallery, designed by an American architect, Robert Venturi. Could Charles *really*, asked one architectural critic, admire this 'limp, sub-classical' result of his intervention? 'For those committed Classicists whose work the prince has endorsed, this building is not so much a joke as a crime – an insult to the hallowed tradition of Vitruvius and Palladio.'[8]

car *en route* to Hampton Court, he had already leaked the text to *The Times* and the *Guardian*. Telephoned for a response, the RIBA's president, Michael Manser, had been so horrified as to threaten to boycott the evening. As it was, he contented himself with a measured slap of the royal wrist. It was 'deeply unsatisfactory', said Manser, 'that the debate should become locked into the arguments of new versus old. What we need to discuss is good or bad.'[9]

For Adeane, all this fuss, in the teeth of his advice, was the last straw; he was gone within six months. For Charles, it was the start of a campaign that would earn him vigorous opposition, at times obloquy, symbolizing his painfully swift transition, in the eyes of the press and many of its readers, from caped crusader to comic crank.

Diana, meanwhile, was visibly growing in self-confidence. Her unexpected staying power as a world superstar was bolstering her self-esteem and giving her the upper hand in the relationship, publicly if not privately. As she mastered the art of the royal appearance, the princess began to take an almost sadistic pleasure in upstaging her husband. For every new speech he made, she would wear a different hairstyle or hat; the photographers, she well knew, were much more interested in her than in him – as, still, were the crowds, who continued to groan if Charles rather than Di headed in their direction. But Charles's increasing distress sprang from more than merely a bruised royal ego. The public's insatiable appetite for details of the Princess of Wales's clothes, her hair, her hats, her tiniest asides, drowned out anything he might do or say. For a man desperate to be taken seriously, the tidal wave of trivia became unbearably irritating.

As his preoccupations grew more earnest, so hers seemed to grow more frivolous. While Charles denounced the ways of the modern world, Diana frequented fashion shows and a social milieu not normally visited by royalty. Whenever Charles toured Britain's inner cities, on a social campaign that became a crusade, his wife was now rarely at his side. He did not want her there, to steal his column-inches, and she herself had no wish to be.

If Diana was exacting her revenge for what she saw as Charles's betrayals, it was also the first sign of the intuitive knack for public relations that would later prove the making of her. At this stage of her development, as well she knew, hers was a passive power, both over her public and her husband. It was best preserved by opening her mouth as little as possible, and best explained by telling delighted bystanders, 'I'm as thick as a plank.' This remark (which became a regular one-liner) suggested just how savvy Diana really was, while reinforcing the empty-headedness of which her reflective husband increasingly despaired. Inspecting the sumptuous garden of a friend's country home, he complimented his foreign hostess on her excellent English. 'My father believed in educating girls,' she explained. 'I wish', muttered Charles ruefully, 'that had been the philosophy in my wife's family.'[10]

Only now, when increasingly on her own at public functions, did Diana feel free to let her true self show through. It was during this 'cold war' of 1985 that the guests of her favourite fashion designer, Bruce Oldfield, were astonished by her extravagant behaviour at a fundraising ball, one of the first of such events that she attended conspicuously alone, leaving a moody Charles behind at Highgrove. Any doubts about recent rumours that she had been out partying alone, dancing the night away without her husband, were staunched when the princess stayed on after the appointed witching hour of midnight – on and on, until the French musician, Jean-Michel Jarre, husband of Charlotte Rampling, asked her to dance. Diana, said one witness, 'positively lit up . . . Everyone within twenty yards got the fallout from Diana's mood that night. She was suddenly aware of everything she had been missing.'[11]

As they began to go their separate ways – with the public, as yet, only barely aware of what was happening – Charles found himself unable to compete with Diana's instinctive skills as a public performer. It was now, with two pregnancies behind her and another highly unlikely, that she began to emerge as a global fashion icon, the world's most popular cover girl, besieged by designers wanting her to be seen in their wares. Charles watched helplessly, and not altogether approvingly, as the charmingly informal touches she brought to formal public occasions began to build her a huge army of followers. To him, this style of 'showbiz' monarchy was anathema, and would not last. The ancient institution to which he was heir could not survive, he believed, as a branch of the entertainment industry. Doggedly, he pursued his own more serious agenda, launching the inner-city campaign that was to bring him into conflict with the Thatcher government.

In a speech to the cream of British management, the Institute of Directors, the prince startled his audience with a *cri de cœur* about the 'inhuman conditions' endured by so many urban Britons: 'The hopelessness left in such communities is compounded by decay all around, the vandalism and the inability to control their own lives in any way beyond the basic requirements of day-to-day survival in a hostile environment.'[12] This mild flirtation with political controversy was as nothing to the explosion eight months later, in October 1985, when Charles was quoted as fearing that he would inherit a 'divided' Britain. Under the headline PRINCE CHARLES: MY FEARS FOR THE FUTURE, a Manchester paper reported that the prince was 'prepared to force his way through parliamentary red tape to ensure that his country is not split into factions of the haves and have-nots'. Charles was said to be worried that 'when he becomes king there will be no-go areas in the inner cities, and that the minorities will be alienated from the rest of the country'.[13]

From New York, where she was addressing the United Nations, an incensed Margaret Thatcher telephoned Buckingham Palace to demand an explanation. The prime minister was less than convinced by the protests of courtiers that Charles had intended no criticism of her government. But the provenance of the royal remarks was murky. They had been leaked by Rod Hackney, one of his more personally ambitious architectural advisers, after a private conversation on the royal train. Hackney, whose brand of 'community architecture' had seen him forge a post-Hampton Court alliance with the prince, was swift to apologize for the trouble he had caused. But there could be no forgiveness for so damaging an indiscretion. He received a strongly worded letter of rebuke, and was banished from the charmed circle of Charles's advisers.

The British constitution defines no role for the heir to the throne. Its unwritten rules are eloquent as to what the Prince of Wales should not do, unhelpfully silent as to what he should. Beyond staying out of party politics, the job description is a *tabula rasa*. History has thus seen some monarchs-in-waiting set themselves up as rivals to their royal parents, acting as unofficial leaders of the opposition, barely disguising their eagerness to take over; others have taken the chance to make themselves useful, as patrons of the arts or activists in other non-controversial fields. Rather more, denied any role in affairs of state, have used the position and its perks to enjoy lives of self-indulgent dissipation.

The history of the office is not, as a result, a particularly distinguished one. Charles, the twenty-first English Prince of Wales in 700 years, entered his thirties intent on changing all that. One of the better-educated heirs to the throne, endowed with a strong sense of history, he seemed by disposition more earnest, reflective and well meaning than the majority of his predecessors, if equally aloof from the daily lifestyles and concerns of his future subjects. In early adulthood, his modest intelligence appeared to belie genetic theory. Heir to the throne since the age of three, but unlikely to inherit it until he was a septuagenarian grandfather, he had spent most of his youth frustrated by the prospect of so long and tiresome a wait in the wings, and increasingly irritated by continual taunts that he should get 'a proper job' – not least from Cabinet ministers such as Norman Tebbit. In the mid-1980s Charles made a conscious decision to turn necessity to advantage by earning himself a niche as a crusader Prince of Wales, riding a populist white charger to the rescue of disadvantaged minorities around his future realm.

From architecture to conservation, employment to the inner cities, race relations to other urgent social concerns of the day, the prince boldly used his office to launch initiatives like grapeshot, and won a positive public response. The mid-1980s saw him ready to ride to the rescue of any underprivileged minority with whom he could sympathize without incurring the wrath of Thatcher, midway through her eleven years in power. Under pressure from her right-wing backbenchers, the then prime minister steered him away from tacit criticism of the government, deleting urban deprivation and inner-city blight from his agenda; but a philosophical jigsaw nevertheless appeared to be falling into place, its disparate pieces fusing the wild profusion of causes he had espoused.

While still in the navy, in the mid-1970s, Charles had founded the Prince's Trust, designed to make small financial grants to unemployed youths intent on community service. The Trust's work was worthy but dull stuff to a tabloid press then intent on chronicling the 'macho' lifestyle of the playboy prince, playing the field as he open-endedly postponed his choice of bride. Having entered his thirties a frustrated and somewhat embittered figure, he was finally liberated by his eventual marriage from the long and powerful shadow of his parents. Free to pursue an increasingly idiosyncratic range of interests, he started exploring the virtues of holistic, homoeopathic and other less conventional forms of medicine.

His attack on orthodox medicine in 1982, at the 150th anniversary dinner of the British Medical Association, had brought Charles his first, unexpected taste of criticism. When he formally opened the Bristol Centre, an 'alternative', drug-free cancer clinic, orthodox cancer specialists wrote outraged letters to *The Times* and to the prince himself, eliciting a highly defensive, almost apologetic reply. Such is the power of royal patronage that the BMA felt obliged to institute an official inquiry into the virtues of 'complementary' forms of medicine, the case for which was found unproven in its 1986 report. Some 'alternative' treatments promoted by Charles, such as herbalism, were found to be 'positively harmful'. The doctors had given the prince a taste of his own medicine; and he didn't much like it. His public pronouncements on the subject grew increasingly intermittent.

Charles had meanwhile begun to practise organic farming on the Duchy of Cornwall acreage adjacent to his Gloucestershire home, Highgrove. His attempts to make Highgrove 'a model of environmental soundness' were later proudly chronicled in a book, *Highgrove: Portrait of an Estate*. Windowsills and doorframes had been draught-proofed and disused chimneys blocked to conserve heat. Low-energy lightbulbs had been installed. Charles was frustrated in his wish to introduce straw-fired central heating, which proved impractical, but converted the swimming-pool heating system from electricity to oil. He introduced a 'reed-bed' sewage-disposal system, harnessed to solar power, and a 'short rotation coppice system' to prevent his trees degenerating through cross-breeding. All this, plus his 1,000-acre organic 'crop rotation' programme, was lovingly chronicled in a television film to promote the book. As the cameras lingered longingly on the façade of Highgrove House, a Grade I listed building, no mention was made of the fact that he had broken planning laws by unilaterally tacking on a neo-classical pediment.

Charles's habit of disappearing for a few days to 'live' the life of a Cornwall dairy farmer or Highland crofter, often with only a television crew for company, had long since earned him the tabloid nickname of the 'Loony Prince'. Throughout the 1980s – to the dismay of his father, who considered his oldest son a 'wimp' in need of 'toughening up' – the prince emerged as an embryo 'green', worrying about what he ate and drank, banning aerosol sprays from the royal residences, persuading his mother to convert the fleet of royal cars to lead-free fuel (and, since then, natural gas). From there it was but a short step towards espousing fashionable, if urgent, concerns about the planet: the ozone layer, global warming, the destruction of the tropical rain forests.

Britain, its future king believed, was becoming a selfish, consumer-oriented society in a state of increasing spiritual decay. The Thatcher years were fostering a greedy rush for wealth, elevating material over moral values. Homelessness, urban blight and inner-city decay were, to Charles, the inevitable products of a post-industrial society in which too little care was taken to regenerate once prosperous areas now fallen on hard times. He especially admired the work of an organization called Business in the Community (BiC), founded in 1981 by a group of unusually enlightened businessmen to persuade major companies to donate money, personnel or resources towards trusts, projects and enterprise agencies, designed to foster business initiatives and thus create new jobs. A catalyst for local action, inspiring rather than managing partnership projects, BiC acted as honest broker between companies and communities, creating mutual goodwill as much as mutual advantage. In 1984, after placing his diffuse array of initiatives under BiC's umbrella, Charles was persuaded to become its president – the ultimate 'enabler'.

Amid this overdue pragmatism, his speeches were still peppered with references to the decay of the modern world, its loss of spiritual values, the injuries modern man was inflicting on himself and his planet. As his marriage atrophied, Charles grew more confused than ever about the curious hand dealt him by fate. Plunging deeper into philosophy and spiritualism, his pronouncements about the meaning of life became increasingly eccentric; his trademark references to Jungian concepts learnt at the feet of van der Post were invariably lost on his listeners.

Was the Prince of Wales, in turn, losing his audience? The public figure was beginning to look as solitary as the private human being. In retrospect, it seems inevitable that Charles's public musings were infected by his domestic torments, well concealed though they still were from the world at large. For Diana was revelling in the tabloid press's cruelty to her husband, taking it as some sort of revenge for what she saw as his private cruelties to her. As far as his wife was concerned, Charles could do nothing right.

It is thanks to her, for instance, that we know of a spat between Charles and his mother-in-law, still sharing her daughter's indignation at Charles's reaction to Harry's birth. The prince did not endear himself to Mrs Shand Kydd by saying to her at the christening, 'I'm so disappointed. I thought it would be a girl.' His mother-in-law snapped back, 'You should be thankful that you had a child that was normal.'[14]

Charles's sister, Princess Anne, boycotted the occasion because she had not been chosen as a godparent – the first public sign of tension between the two princesses. The addition of a third princess, to add her own unique volatility to the equation, was heralded that summer when Diana invited her friend Sarah Ferguson to Ascot, and introduced her to her brother-in-law, Prince Andrew. Although he was still romancing the actress and photographer Koo Stark, Andrew was immediately smitten by Sarah, to whom he would become engaged within eight months.

For a while Diana's spirits had been improved by the arrival in her life of a police bodyguard, Sergeant Barry Mannakee, to whom she grew especially close. A kindred spirit who offered her a shoulder to cry on, Mannakee seemed content to become the latest repository of the princess's daily miseries. Charles noticed the unusual bond between them, and felt uneasy about it, even wondering if they were having an affair.

But Mannakee was a married man with two small children, and his rapport with Diana at least took some of the pressure off Charles. The detective's reassuring presence helped the bulimic princess through high-profile visits to Italy, Australia and America that year, which served only to enhance her international acclaim at the expense of his. To Charles's relief, she acknowledged her duty to the point of maintaining a façade of togetherness in public, whatever the state of play in private. Some of the most enduring images from this ostensibly happy mid-period in their marriage date from that April in Venice and Rome, where Diana managed to make demure Catholic black look serenely chic at an audience with the Pope.

Charles, by contrast, again found himself the subject of negative headlines when his request to take communion with the pontiff earned him the only public rebuke he has ever received from his mother. So urgent was the problem that the Queen had to use leaky government channels to convey an urgent message to her son in Rome, tartly pointing out that for him to take Communion with the Pope would constitute a breach of the terms of the 1701 Act of Settlement, by which his family's legal claim to the throne is established. Charles instantly backed off.[15]

But he remained accident prone all year. In Edinburgh that November, making his maiden speech as president of Business in the Community, he departed from his prepared Thatcherite text to declare, 'What really worries me is that we are going to end up as a fourth-rate country.'[16] The result, of course, was much tabloid hysteria and more dark looks from Downing Street.

His spirits could scarcely be lifted by the prospect of another joint visit to Australia, where Diana again proved the main attraction, leaving the prince bemoaning the 'fatuous' insults which followed him around – 'rude things shouted out, gestures made, plastic masks waved about' – while also finding his press coverage brutally hurtful.[17] They returned via the United States, where President Reagan's failure to remember Diana's name at a White House banquet, proposing a toast to 'Princess David', did not stop her again stealing the show. Charles watched ruefully as his wife took to the White House dance floor with *Saturday Night Fever*'s John Travolta.

At a very low ebb, the next day Charles took Diana to Palm Beach, Florida, for a gala dinner hosted by the octogenarian chairman of Occidental Petroleum, Armand Hammer. It was the beginning of a long association with Hammer, not untypical of the prince, who has rarely allowed dubious or controversial reputations to block his access to large amounts of money (or indeed, as in the case of the Greek shipping billionaire John Latsis, free holidays on private yachts). Hammer had been lobbying the prince for eighteen months, offering to guarantee a minimum of $1 million if he would attend the Palm Beach dinner. Charles drove a hard bargain, asking for a further donation to one of his flagging charities, Operation Raleigh, an 'outward bound'-style round-the-world ocean voyage for youngsters, then in dire financial straits.

Despite some doubts in his private office, Charles was prepared to put his royal self up 'for rent' – tickets to the dinner cost $5,000 a head – in return for the huge amounts Hammer was offering as his passport to public royal approval. In putting his wife up for rent, too, he was obliged to admit to himself (if not to her) that it was more Diana's presence than his that assured a large turnout, despite vociferous local opposition. To some residents of Palm Beach, who wrote letters of protest to the prince's office, Hammer was a Soviet 'fellow traveller' organizing 'a testimonial to himself'; Charles saw it more as 'an old man with funds in search of prestige and a young man with prestige in search of funds'.[18]

Charles had first met Hammer in May 1977, when opening a London exhibition of Sir Winston Churchill's watercolours. Hammer gave him one of the paintings as a contribution to the Queen's Silver Jubilee Appeal, of which Charles was chairman. Thus began, by one account, his 'unusual' friendship with 'one of the great frauds of the twentieth century'. Charles went on to accept Hammer's largesse on scales great and small, from painting lessons with a well-known American artist via rides in his private jet to a $5 million United World College of the American West in Montezuma, New Mexico. 'Much of the money', according to a 1998 exposé of Hammer by the American writer Edward Jay Epstein, 'came from a slush fund established to pay bribes to the corrupt middlemen who had arranged [Hammer]'s oil concession in Libya.' The prince's new friend was 'a KGB stooge', who had 'long provided a convenient conduit for the laundering of Kremlin funds used to finance Soviet espionage activities'.[19]

An even sterner view was taken by an eyewitness closer to home, the British writer Neil Lyndon, who worked closely with Hammer in the 1980s as his 'ghost[-writer], amanuensis and house-hack'. Lyndon's access to Hammer's archives convinced him that his employer was 'an active agent of the Soviet Union for most of his adult life' who was 'madly misappropriating the funds of Occidental for his own personal aggrandisement'. Beyond 'badgering younger women into sexual compromise and paying them off with corporate boodle', and 'cheating his wife out of hundreds of millions of dollars', Hammer 'believed – because his entire life had proved it – that he could do anything and get away with it. We reckoned him to be capable of evil, even murder'. Was this the kind of man with whom the prince should be associating, or the kind of money he should be accepting, even for worthy causes close to his heart?

'What does it take', asked Lyndon, 'to buy a president or a king?'[20] Charles, it seemed, never asked himself that question. He was content to present himself as 'a young man with prestige in search of funds', without enquiring too closely where they came from. But it is just as well that Diana, less enamoured of this 'rather reptilian'[21] old man, vetoed his notion of inviting Hammer to be Prince William's godfather.

On their return from the US, Charles and Diana attended a gala evening at the Royal Opera House, Covent Garden, to mark his thirty-seventh birthday. The prince failed to notice, as Diana hoped, when she slipped out of their box just before the end of the performance. Backstage she changed into a slinky silver silk dress, then caused universal surprise – and apparently universal delight – by joining the Royal Ballet star Wayne Sleep onstage for a stylish dance routine to Billy Joel's 'Uptown Girl'.

After secret rehearsals at Kensington Palace and elsewhere, Diana had planned the surprise as a birthday present for Charles. As she received eight curtain calls, to an uproarious standing ovation, she dropped a decorous curtsey to her husband in the royal box, taken by the audience as a charming birthday salute from wife to husband. But Charles was livid. For public consumption, he professed himself 'absolutely amazed' by Diana's performance; privately, at home, he told her he thought it entirely unsuitable and conduct unbecoming to a future queen. 'I don't think Charles was actually angry,' said Sleep later, 'but I remember after the show we were in the King's Smoking Room and there he was, surrounded by a semicircle of minions, looking very much the daddy going "ahem, ahem" at his naughty little girl.'[22]

If Diana could do nothing right, in Charles's eyes, he himself was scarcely faring much better. 'Brain the size of a pea, that's what I've got,' said the Princess of Wales with beguiling self-deprecation in a television interview with ITN's Sir Alistair Burnet, designed to quash the growing press speculation about their marriage. Her husband insisted that it be edited out. In the years ahead, he would wish he had done the same with one of his own off-the-cuff remarks, in a parallel TV special intended to 'humanize' his bleak public image. Whenever his worldly woes grew too much, Charles confessed, he found great consolation in talking to his plants. It was a remark that returned with a vengeance to haunt him – the joke which launched a thousand cartoons, and countless more catty one-liners. In love with Diana, blind to her faults, the British press now had a permanent excuse to mock Charles's high seriousness.

The climax came in May 1986, during a visit to the Expo exhibition in Vancouver, Canada. Diverting to open an arts exhibition in the town of Prince George, Charles waxed unusually lyrical, even by his standards, sharing his sense that 'deep in the soul of mankind there is a reflection as on the surface of a mirror, of a mirror-calm lake, of the beauty and harmony of the universe'. It was pure, half-digested Jung, reflected in the distorted mirror that was his marriage. 'So much depends, I think, on how each one of us is introduced to and made aware of that reflection within us.'[23]

Fleet Street had a field day. When Charles defiantly returned to the theme at Harvard University, the rapt attention of the American press made a stark contrast with the continuing mirth of its British brethren. 'Never has it been more important to recognize the imbalance that has seeped into our lives and deprived us of a sense of meaning,' he said, 'because the emphasis has been too one-sided and has concentrated on the development of the intellect to the detriment of the spirit.'[24] To the *Washington Post* he was 'Harvard's Prince Charming', who had 'understood his audience perfectly'; back home, to the *Sun*, he was still the 'loony' prince.

It was during that trip to Vancouver that Diana fainted in public while she and Charles were touring the giant Expo exhibition. Still bulimic, she looked dreadful and felt even worse. 'I think I'm about to disappear,' she whispered to Charles, then slid to the floor at his feet. While her lady-in-waiting and one of Charles's aides helped her out of sight to recover, the prince proceeded with his tour of the exhibition. Later, according to Diana, he berated her for this lack of royal aplomb: if she was going to faint, she should have done so in private. Not for the first or the last time, the princess broke down and sobbed. Though she was still clearly unwell, Charles rejected the pleas of their staff that she be spared the official dinner that evening. The prince insisted that she accompany him, to avoid causing 'a drama'. By the time the couple arrived in Japan, Diana looked and felt bad enough to know that it was again time to seek professional help.

On her return to London in July, her spirits were dashed even further by the discovery that her favourite bodyguard, Barry

Mannakee, had been reassigned to other duties. She suspected a conspiracy, but could not say why. Only she knew that she had been half in love with Mannakee, who had become one of her last bastions of self-assurance. To make matters worse, the public ebullience of her friend Sarah Ferguson, whose engagement to Prince Andrew had been announced in March, was highlighting Diana's own loss of sparkle. To Diana, her old friend 'Fergie' was a more than welcome addition to the royal circle; now she would have a like-minded confidante to share the unique ordeal of life with the Windsors, a soulmate to offer some light relief from her loneliness. But she had not expected to suffer by comparison. 'Why can't you be more like Fergie?' became one of Charles's recurrent refrains.[25]

Diana made the understandable mistake of taking her husband at his word. Shortly before the royal wedding in July, she and the bride-to-be tried to gatecrash Andrew's stag party dressed up as policewomen. They were denied admission, but went on to Annabel's nightclub for a few glasses of Buck's fizz before getting back to the Palace in time to flag down Andrew's car as he returned home. Again Charles did not approve, seeing fit to remind Diana that impersonating a police officer is a criminal offence. She in turn questioned his 'famous' sense of humour, urging him to 'get a life'.[26] The gulf between husband and wife was growing ever wider. It was an aching void in Charles's life, just waiting to be filled.

Andrew Parker Bowles had recently been promoted to commanding officer of the Household Cavalry, based in its ugly high-rise headquarters near Buckingham Palace. He would have less time to get away from London, leaving Camilla, never the type to be a dutiful 'army wife', more than ever alone at home. Now, to Diana's dismay, the Parker Bowleses sold Bolehyde Manor and moved even closer to Highgrove, barely fifteen minutes away at Middlewich House, in the village of Pickwick, near Corsham, Wiltshire. On their return from a Spanish vacation with King Juan Carlos and his family, Charles and a sulky Diana attended the Parker Bowleses' housewarming party, which led, unsurprisingly, to another row and a further downturn in the princess's spirits.

As Prince Andrew and his bride basked in public acclaim, a high-spirited couple very openly in love, the Waleses looked positively sombre by comparison. The nation quickly warmed to 'Fergie', Duchess of York – not as regal a figure as Diana, perhaps, but another girl-next-door princess with the natural touch, whose spontaneous effervescence won many hearts. The Queen, too, seemed to prefer her new daughter-in-law, who, unlike Diana, went riding with her, and was soon taking helicopter lessons in an effort to share every aspect of her husband's life. Suddenly the Yorks were winning all the positive headlines, while the Waleses' marriage became the subject of downbeat speculation and rumour. In private, too, as Sarah's raucous high spirits enlivened Windsor weekends, the contrast between her gaiety and Diana's moodiness became painfully evident. Charles began to envy his younger brother's obvious happiness. 'Why can't you be more like Fergie?' he asked Diana again.

Charles could not understand why his wife still could not conquer her illness. He was blind to the fact that it was Camilla's closer proximity which moved Diana to new bouts of moodiness, and an even more acute phase of 'obsessive' jealousy. He had long grown weary of their spats, preferring to avoid confrontations by walking out as she began to hurl her insults, thus making matters worse, as any amateur psychologist could have told him, by denying her an outlet for her pent-up fury. After a visit to Althorp, Diana's father let slip that there had been an 'almighty row', leaving a mirror and a window in their room smashed and the leg of a valuable antique chair snapped in half. In a wholly unexpected way, his brother's openly uproarious marriage – a much more highly charged affair, oozing overt sexuality amid much public flirtation – was proving the last straw for Charles.

By the autumn of 1986, after five years of marriage to Diana, the prince had had enough. To him, the marriage had hit a brick wall. He could find no way of penetrating Diana's intransigence, no means of persuading her that his public duties must always come before his private responsibilities. Above all, as he saw it, she had signally failed to provide the light relief he craved from his heavy public schedule; quite the opposite, as he returned home each evening with sinking heart, knowing that nothing awaited him but tantrums and recriminations. After five years without Camilla, her presence down the road became more tantalizing than ever. Charles felt imprisoned by his marriage, he told friends, and desperately longed to escape. Their incompatibility was horribly corrosive. The whole appalling saga had 'all the ingredients of a Greek tragedy'.[27]

There were, however, several acts yet to come. It was to be six more years before the couple separated, nearly ten before they divorced. But it was now that Charles decided his marriage was beyond repair, that it had, as he would later put it publicly, 'irretrievably' broken down. Now he felt free to reconvene those friends banished by his wife two years before, and to return unashamedly to the arms of Camilla Parker Bowles. 'I never thought it would end up like this,' he wrote to a friend early the following year. 'How *could* I have got it all so wrong?'[28]

CHAPTER ELEVEN

'I JUST WANT TO BE WITH HER'

THE 'FAIRY-TALE' MARRIAGE HAD GOT LOST IN THE WOODS. TO DIANA, far from being the happy home she had always sought, Highgrove was a symbol of Charles's continuing love for Camilla – the only possible explanation for his cavalier attitude towards herself, abandoning her for large stretches of time, paying scant attention to her in the little time he spent with her, failing to discover and appreciate her true qualities. To Charles, far from proving the loving, supportive wife he had craved, Diana merely emphasized what he had missed out on by failing to marry Camilla – a woman who understood and respected his deep-seated concerns about society, his determination to do his modest best to help, his ceaseless torments in trying to reconcile his unsought public role with his private quest for personal fulfilment.

In one department of their lives, at least, the unhappy couple were at one. Both Charles and Diana, after five years of corrosive domestic warfare, felt browbeaten into a very low sense of self-worth. So it was perhaps inevitable that, at much the same time, each fell into the arms of others who could rebuild their self-respect – devout admirers who could help them overdose on mental, spiritual and indeed physical affection.

It was in the summer of 1986, a few months before Charles resumed his adultery with Mrs Parker Bowles, that Diana first met a suave, flirtatious Guards officer named James Hewitt. At a London cocktail party the handsome, nattily dressed captain was introduced to the princess as one of the best horsemen in the Life

Guards' Household division. The princess confessed that she had been frightened of horses since falling off one in childhood; it was a disappointment to her husband, she confided, that she did not go out riding with him. The gallant Hewitt offered to help out.

Within months Diana's riding lessons had become a front for a passionate, five-year love affair, as she was eventually to admit on television: 'Yes, I loved him. I adored him.'[1] Whether Diana sought solace with Hewitt before Charles returned to Camilla's bed remains a matter of vexed dispute between their respective camps. The princess believed that Charles's affair with Camilla had never really stopped, that he returned to her as early as the autumn of their marriage. Charles has steadfastly denied this, maintaining that he foreswore the love of his life for all of five years after his wedding. His own televised confession of adultery dates his infidelity with Camilla from the irretrievable breakdown of his marriage in the autumn of 1986.

Bizarrely, the public record does give a precise date for the cessation of marital relations between them. The prince's remarks after Harry's birth in 1984, and his abrupt departure to play polo, had killed all thought of physical as much as spiritual love in Diana's heart and mind. Charles, for his part, had long since ceased to care, believing any kind of affection impossible in the absence of respect. Both were weary of the friction now occasioned merely by proximity. They had long since occupied separate bedrooms (as is common royal practice anyway, given the morning ministrations of domestic servants of both genders). Now, as of an official visit to Portugal in 1987, they could not even bear to occupy rooms in the same suite. No longer did the royal couple bother to pretend for the benefit of hosts, or other potential leakers to newspapers, that their aversion to sharing sleeping quarters was merely royal protocol, or anything more than it really was: a mutual distaste that had curdled beyond repair.

The spring of 1987 saw Charles so resentful of Diana's caprices as to be moved to an uncharacteristic act of real cruelty. On the Palace grapevine he learnt before his wife that, within months of his transfer to other duties after becoming 'too close' to her, the princess's much-missed bodyguard Barry Mannakee had been killed in a motorcycle accident. Yet, according to Diana, Charles waited to tell her until they were about to arrive in front of an excited crowd at an official engagement, waving regally from the

back of a limousine. 'Oh, by the way,' he said as the car drew up.
'Did you hear that Barry Mannakee has been killed?' A distraught
Diana, whose precise relationship with Mannakee Charles still
regarded with some suspicion, was forced to hide her feelings. He
was not to know that she would later describe Mannakee to her
intimates as 'the love of my life'.[2]

This was also the year in which they could no longer hide their
unhappiness from the public. Charles, as it appeared, was almost
past caring. That summer the pattern for the rest of their marriage
was set when he remained at Balmoral at the end of the school
holidays, while Diana returned to London with their sons. He was
joined there by friends – including, of course, the Parker Bowleses
– who could do little to lift his spirits, which were as low as they
had ever been. When he finally returned to Kensington Palace,
Diana's reproaches about 'abandoning' his children succeeded in
filling their father with guilt and self-reproach. By the end of the
year, he was confiding to friends that he felt wretched and dis-
heartened and could see no glimmer of light at the end of a 'rather
appalling tunnel'.[3]

The year had begun with a public row on the ski slopes of Klosters,
when Diana's horseplay with Fergie in front of photographers had
again incurred Charles's displeasure. Not until after her death
would the prince begin to appreciate how well such informality
went down with the consumer, and himself learn to unbend from
the royal correctness drilled into him by his parents. For now he
skied on moodily, opting for the advanced pistes while the young
princesses giggled their way down less demanding slopes with two
young men invited to keep them company: David Waterhouse, an
army officer, and Philip Dunne, a merchant banker. Now it was
Charles's turn to feel jealous.

Oblivious to what was happening with Hewitt, he began to suspect his wife of an affair with Dunne. The son of the Lord
Lieutenant of Hereford and Worcester, and a godson of Princess
Alexandra, Dunne became friendly enough with Diana in Klosters
for her to join a weekend house-party that summer at Gatley Park,
Herefordshire, the home of his parents, who were conveniently
away. Most of the Klosters skiing party were there, too, in what
looked like a happy reunion. But Diana chose to breach royal
propriety, in her husband's absence, by staying the night. She was

far from alone with Dunne in the house, as reported in gossip columns, but the domestic damage was done. And it was compounded at the June wedding of the Duke of Beaufort's son, the Marquis of Worcester, to the actress Tracy Ward. After a dance with one of his lost loves, Anna Wallace, Charles spent most of the evening deep in conversation with Camilla Parker Bowles. Diana took her revenge by dancing very flamboyantly with Dunne, to the point where she was mopping her brow with the hem of her dress – and continued to do so deep into the night, long after Charles had left with Camilla.

That same month, she and Fergie were pictured giggling at Ascot, in all their expensive finery, as they poked a courtier up the behind with their umbrellas.* The photo triggered a wave of public disenchantment with the young royals, which was to climax four years later at the time of the Gulf War, when their seemingly heedless hedonism provoked national outrage. It would take Diana some time to learn to dissociate herself from the royal high jinx pioneered by the irredeemably vulgar Duchess of York.

Even more worrying for Charles, Diana was beginning to carve her own distinctive niche in British public life, defying the natural caution of Palace advisers to associate herself with causes more urgent and contemporary than his yearnings for classical architecture. In April the princess opened Britain's first purpose-built ward for AIDS patients at the Middlesex Hospital, London. At the time, a multi-million-pound government advertising campaign was cryptically warning people, 'Don't die of ignorance.' Diana did a great deal more to dispel public fear and prejudice simply with a few ungloved handshakes. It was the beginning of an association with the disease and its sufferers, as patron of the National AIDS Trust, which lasted to her dying day.

In the mid-1980s, AIDS was still widely seen in Britain as 'God's revenge' for unnatural sexual practices; in some quarters Diana was reviled as 'the patron saint of sodomy'. She was reaching out to a community widely regarded as pariahs, not least in Buckingham Palace, where AIDS was seen as an unseemly issue, inappropriate for royal patronage. Well aware of widespread irrational fears about the disease, the princess pressed on regardless,

---

* The courtier in question happened to be Major Hugh Lindsay, who later died in an avalanche while skiing with Charles in Klosters.

speaking of the need to give sufferers a hug: 'Heaven knows they need one.' By enlightening millions, Diana's ungloved handshake came to be seen as a supreme example of the benevolent symbolism unique to royalty.

It made a stark contrast with Charles's long-awaited, oft-postponed visit to the Kalahari Desert that same month, for a few nights under canvas with his elderly mentor and confidant Laurens van der Post. For the prince it was a fascinating anthropological exercise, the latest stage in his long voyage of self-discovery. For the popular press, it was but the latest evidence that the heir to the throne was halfway round the bend.

Africa had always been a regular stop on the beat of any Prince of Wales – the future head of what was once the Empire, now the Commonwealth – but most of Charles's predecessors had spent their 'time off' there contentedly blasting wild animals into oblivion. The sight of this one spending four nights in a tent with an eighty-year-old Jungian philosopher, communing with the lost world of the Kalahari bushmen, made an unfortunate comparison with his wife's hospital visiting.

It was even more unfortunate that Charles's meditative retreat coincided with a scare about insanity in the royal genes; while he was away, two of the Queen Mother's nieces were discovered to have been lifelong inhabitants of a mental hospital. The revelation lay uneasily beside the tabloid picture of Charles's venture into the 'spirit world' of primitive dances beneath the desert stars, communion with the dead via bottles buried in the sand, and soul-searching campfire chats with bare-breasted natives. No doubt, cackled the tabloids, he would also be having a few words with the local plants.

The coverage, of course, was cruelly unfair. Fired by van der Post's book *The Lost World of the Kalahari*, Charles had longed to see for himself this primitive, unspoilt society, ignorant of the civilized world, into whose innocent purity his elderly friend read an unconscious illustration of Jung's teachings. By now Charles had known van der Post some twenty years. The South African-born writer and explorer spent the immediate aftermath of the Second World War with the 15th Indian Army Corps in Java, as military-political officer to Lord Mountbatten, through whom Charles first met him while at Cambridge. If Mountbatten had been role model and confidant-in-chief to the earnest young prince, van der Post took over from Zoe Sallis as a rather more spiritual guru. For all his public opposition to the 'miserable' Nelson Mandela, the writer's eloquent interpretations of the natural world moved Charles to tears. His death in 1996, at the age of ninety, would leave the prince almost as bereft as had Mountbatten's.

Amid the dispiriting satire, Charles returned to a land bleak with rumour about his marriage. Why were he and his wife spending so much time apart? She had returned ahead of him from their annual trip to Klosters; now, fresh from the African desert, the prince did not help his own cause by disappearing without her for a week painting watercolours in Italy. It was just as well the press did not discover that his party included Camilla Parker Bowles. 'I just want to be with her all the time,' he confessed to his polo manager, Major Ron Ferguson, father of the Duchess of York.[4]

The Parker Bowleses were at Balmoral again that September, after Diana's very public departure with the boys ensured that the cracks in the royal marriage could no longer be hidden from the public. Over a ninety-day period the royal couple had spent thirty-five under separate roofs, only nine of which were unavoidable because of royal duties. In private, Diana's wrath became yet more formidable, as she took to slamming doors and following Charles around Palace corridors, shrieking at him hysterically. In public, the princess still tried to put a brave face on things. 'It's very simple,' she told journalists. 'My husband and I get around two thousand invitations every six months. We can't do them all, but if we split them up, we can fulfil twice as many.'[5]

Such defiance carried a hollow ring when Charles flew back up to Balmoral on 22 September, leaving Diana in London with their sons. There was much press innuendo about the company he was keeping in Scotland, centring on the presence of his old friend Dale, Lady Tryon. At the time, in fact, 'Kanga' was in her native Australia. Again, the press had missed the true identity of Charles's companion, Camilla Parker Bowles.

In London, Diana was seen out on the town with a variety of dashing young men, while in Scotland Charles fished moodily in the Dee. Having invested so much affectionate goodwill in this marriage, the public ached for an explanation. Press speculation was reaching fever pitch, but still the Palace resisted all pressure to make a statement. Instead, Charles was talked into a disastrous publicity stunt.

The night of 15 October 1987 saw Britain devastated by a freak hurricane, the worst for 300 years (of which the television weathermen, notoriously, had given no warning). A week later, as the battered nation was still clearing up, the Prince of Wales flew from Balmoral to visit flood victims in Carmarthen, in the heart of his principality. Although he arrived with his wife, they had only hooked up at Northolt Airport, London, where she had arrived from Kensington Palace.

The tension between the couple was all too clear to the flight crew, in front of whom they bickered all the way to Swansea. Staff at Kensington Palace had been instructed to prepare for them to return together that night. After six hours beside each other in Wales, however, during which they had shared not one private moment alone, the prince took himself straight off back to Scotland and Camilla, leaving Diana to return alone to London – and thence to Devon, and James Hewitt.

Back at Balmoral, his favourite retreat among all the royal residences, Charles could see no hope for his marriage, and began to contemplate the disastrous consequences for himself and the monarchy. He poured out his heart to a friend, bemoaning the need for him to hide the truth and pretend that nothing was wrong.[6]

The prince plunged himself back into his work, with mixed results. To his surprise and dismay, the newly re-elected prime minister, Margaret Thatcher, declined his invitation to lunch at Kensington Palace to meet some of the leading lights of Business in the Community. On 12 June, the night of her third consecutive election victory, Thatcher had gone out of her way to make the inner cities a personal crusade of her own; while feeling entitled to take some of the credit for her conversion, Charles was irritated and offended to find himself frozen out of the ensuing crusade. It would take him two years to persuade Thatcher to host a lunch for his BiC colleagues at Downing Street, after which, in the prince's own words, 'absolutely nothing happened'.[7]

Under discreet pressure from Thatcher, he meanwhile allowed one of his own much-trumpeted projects, Inner City Aid, to wither and die. Launched with much fanfare in November 1986, Inner City Aid was the prince's urban answer to Bob Geldof's Band Aid. 'I wish I could be like Bob Geldof,' Charles had confided to a friend of the pop star turned glorified social worker, whose philanthropy had earned him an honorary knighthood. Inner City Aid was his attempt – an especially ambitious one, aspiring to raise £10 million ($16 million) in its first year of operation, under the chairmanship of Rod Hackney, who had been forgiven his indiscretions of the previous year.

'This is about regenerating Britain's inner cities,' proclaimed Hackney at the launch, part of his last-minute, but successful, campaign to become president of the Royal Institute of British Architects. Benefactors would be investing in nothing less than 'the renaissance of the United Kingdom from the inner cities outwards', with the Prince of Wales as 'our champion, patron and friend'. Clause two of the charter deed of Inner City Aid's parent body, the Inner City Trust, summarized its objectives as 'to relieve need, hardship and distress among persons living in deprived and decayed urban areas . . . to provide such persons with adequate housing . . . to improve their environment and to relieve poverty among such of their number who are unemployed'.[8]

Only eight hours later, at a dinner in the City of London, Charles also launched another new initiative, the Prince's Youth Business Trust, which he described as 'a scheme for job-makers rather than job-seekers . . . in catering for some of the harder-hit youngsters in the UK, it sets an example to others'. The Trust's charter was to offer grants and free professional advice to help 'disadvantaged' young people between the ages of eighteen and twenty-five start their own businesses. PYBT would offer grants of up to £1,000 per person, or £3,000 per company, and 'easy-term' loans on condition that successful applicants took compulsory counselling from two professionals.

It soon became clear that Charles and his advisers had made an elementary mistake in launching two major new projects on the same day – symptomatic of the confusion then reigning in his private office, the plethora of conflicting advice from too many different directions at once, and his own capacity for rushing into new schemes with more enthusiasm than strategic thought. Within weeks it was obvious that the two new charities could not co-exist. As Jim Gardiner, the chairman of the Prince's Trust, put it: 'We were all fishing in the same pool.' Lord Scarman, a trustee of Inner City Aid, publicly regretted that 'a great mistake had been made', and that 'enthusiasm had tended to get in the way of sensible planning'. Charles's new private secretary, Sir John Riddell, contented himself with calling it merely 'a cock-up'.[9]

Thanks to its deliberate echo of Geldof, Inner City Aid attracted much more publicity than the less glamorous PYBT, which soon seemed doomed as both chased the same sources of institutional cash, which were already being badgered by BiC, the Prince's Trust and other of the prince's charitable offspring. Geldof himself helped Inner City Aid by persuading a number of prominent architects to lend their support free of charge, despite their indignation at the prince's assaults on their profession. But it was institutional weight rather than surface glamour that won the day. Charles was urged to choose between the two by a 'dismayed' Lord Boardman, chairman of the National Westminster Bank – and of the PYBT. At an emergency meeting of the Presidents Committee, the chairmen of the nine main charities to which Charles lent his name, Boardman's forces emerged victorious. It was agreed that the two organizations could not go on fundraising simultaneously, that the same-day launch had been a momentous disaster, and that Inner City Aid would cease fundraising for at least two years.

Hackney did not give up wthout a fight. He even persuaded Geldof to escort him to a meeting with the prince at Kensington Palace, which only made matters worse. The unkempt rock star made no attempt to delete his usual expletives from the conversation; when one of Charles's dogs sniffed around his ankles, he unceremoniously kicked it away. Inner City Aid was doomed from that moment. In October 1988, the month of its promised relaunch, it was 'phased out to make way for other initiatives'.

In its first year of operation, Inner City Aid had raised just £33,000 of its £10 million target – much of it from a book of royal cartoons compiled to mark the prince's fortieth birthday by Charles Knevitt, who had given up his job as architecture correspondent of *The Times* to become its founder-director, and who now resigned in high dudgeon. Knevitt and many others who volunteered their time and energy to such causes still remain bitter at the prince's apparent indifference to their fate.[10]

Undeterred, Charles continued to cauterize his private woes by stepping up his public crusades. If his own private life had reached an impasse, from which he could see no way out, he would compensate by helping others to find the personal fulfilment he himself still sought. The Prince's Trust was doing just that for thousands of deprived youngsters every year; now, as he approached forty, Charles felt a need to return to a broader canvas, re-emphasizing his more global concerns to a self-indulgent world in danger of forgetting them. To him, architecture and the environment were, of course, interlinked; city planners and corporate executives were equally guilty of abandoning the greater long-term good to short-term gain for the few. The autumn of 1987 saw him go to war on two such fronts, one of which would eventually bear fruit, the other prove one of the most questionable interventions of his life.

A growing friendship with the ambitious young politician Chris Patten, minister for overseas development, saw the prince boldly allow himself to be used as a pawn in some government in-fighting on the ecological front. There were even suggestions that disenchanted civil servants had a hand in his ill-judged attack on Nicholas Ridley, secretary of state for the environment, over the dumping of toxic waste in the North Sea. In cahoots with Patten, the prince had inserted some heated passages into his speech, beyond the prepared text distributed to the media. He was playing a dangerous political game, which earned him private rebukes from other government ministers and further distanced him from their boss, Margaret Thatcher. It was subsequently insisted that Charles conform to the agreed rules of his constitutional remit, by submitting all future speeches to the relevant government department for approval before delivery.

Within months the prince retreated into the self-deprecating cocoon where he felt most comfortable. The tabloids had more fun the following February, when he chose another environmental speech to reveal that 'as I become older and more autocratic, I have banned the use of aerosols in my household'.[11] Another month, and he was back in the familiar defensive mode of pre-empting their attacks: 'There is still a prejudiced misconception in certain circles that people concerned with the environment, and what happens to this earth, are bearded, be-sandalled, shaven-headed mystics who retreat every now and then to the Hebrides or the Kalahari Desert to examine their navels and commune with the natives!'

His distinguished audience at a European environment conference laughed uneasily, awaiting some substantive contribution to the debate amid more crypto-Jungian reflections: 'There is a growing realization that we are not separate from nature; a subconscious feeling that we need to restore a feeling of harmony with nature and a proper sense of respect and awe for the great mystery of the natural order of the universe . . .' Then came the red meat:

> Many people are now aware of the problems and dangers of the possibly catastrophic climactic changes through air pollution; of the mass extinction of species threatened by the loss of tropical forests and other essential habitats . . . When we read that over the next sixty years, if we go on as we are doing, something like a third of all the forms of life at present living on this planet may be extinct, can we feel anything but a cosmic horror?'[12]

It was an ecological credo which he intended to hammer home. With his marriage in shreds, and Diana somewhat out of favour with her usually adoring public, Charles was feeling newly emboldened. That Christmas, he decided to return to the ramparts on architecture, with an intervention almost as dramatic as his 'carbuncle' speech about the National Gallery extension. This time it would concern the area around St Paul's Cathedral, scene of the marriage he would otherwise rather forget.

Since his Hampton Court speech had up-ended statutory planning procedures, major British developers had established the habit of showing the prince their plans at an early stage, for fear that he might sabotage them later. One such, Stuart Lipton, earning himself the nickname of 'Lip-service' for his pains, had taken the precaution of sharing with Charles the plans submitted by the seven finalists in one of Britain's biggest post-war design competitions: to rebuild Paternoster Square, the precinct beside St Paul's disfigured by the decaying 1950s office blocks of Lord Holdford (who had at the time received the Queen's gold medal for architecture).

Although the architects involved were a mix of Britain's finest – some modernists, some not, from Richard Rogers and Norman Foster to James Stirling – Charles loathed all their schemes on sight. To the prince, St Paul's was 'one of the architectural wonders of the world, the equal in architecture to Shakespeare's plays'. He had been 'deeply depressed' by his sneak preview of the plans, and became determined to do something about it. On 1 December

1987, as guest speaker at the annual dinner of the Corporation of London's planning and communication committee, he spared the usual pleasantries and plunged straight in: 'It is not just *me* who is complaining. Countless people are appalled by what has happened to their capital city, but feel totally powerless to do anything about it.' Then he rolled up his sleeves:

> What *have we done* to St Paul's since the bombing [of 1940]? In the space of a mere fifteen years, in the Sixties and Seventies, and in spite of all sorts of elaborate rules supposedly designed to protect that great view, your predecessors, as the planners, architects and developers of the City, wrecked the London sky-line and desecrated the dome of St Paul's. Not only did they wreck the London skyline in general. They also did their best to lose the great dome in a jostling scrum of office buildings, so mediocre that the only way you ever remember them is by the frustration they induce – like a basketball team standing shoulder-to-shoulder between you and the *Mona Lisa* . . .

There was some uneasy laughter as the prince, after a brief European *tour d'horizon* – 'Can you imagine the Italians walling-in St Mark's in Venice or St Peter's in Rome?' – reached his memorable climax:

> You have, ladies and gentlemen, to give this much to the Luftwaffe: when it knocked down our buildings, it didn't replace them with anything more offensive than rubble. We did that.

The Prussian general Carl von Clausewitz had called war the continuation of diplomacy by other means. Around St Paul's, said Charles, planning had turned out to be 'the continuation of war by other means'.

Holford's redevelopment of Paternoster Square in the 1950s had set the precedent for the subsequent 'destruction' of the city centres of Bristol, Newcastle, Birmingham, Worcester and many more. Did modern planners and architects ever use their eyes? They averted them now, under the lash of the prince's tongue, as he protested that 'large numbers of us are fed up with being talked down to and dictated to by the existing planning, architectural and development establishment'. They must seize this second chance to build something 'of real quality, of excellence next to so great a building, in the heart of our capital city' – perhaps even to convert London back into a 'city without towers' by the year 2000.[13]

For all the power of the prince's intervention that evening, the precinct of St Paul's approaches the year 2000 as nothing like 'a city of towers'. At Christmas 1997, a decade after his so-called 'Luftwaffe speech', the prince's continuing interest was responsible for the fact that Paternoster Square was an abandoned and derelict wasteland, long since forsaken by big business – a muggers' paradise unfit for habitation by the homeless, even by hoboes.

Charles's protracted involvement – his power of veto over modernist schemes, amid visions of a neo-medieval millennium – saw the site stand empty and neglected for ten years. He succeeded in his ambitions to exclude Richard Rogers's work from contention, then to see off the developers' chosen 'masterplanners', winners of a public competition, but failed in his attempts to replace them with an architect more to his own taste. In the process, the prince used his office to undo many years' work by leading British architects, notably Sir Philip Dowson's team at Arup Associates, while steering this huge project the way of his considerably less experienced protégé, John Simpson.

Somewhat against their will, Dowson and his colleagues bent over backwards to accommodate the prince, organizing a series of meetings to explain their thinking and two elaborate exhibitions in the cathedral crypt to bring their plans to life. Charles did not even visit the second exhibition. In his 1989 book, *A Vision of Britain*, it took him just two picture-captions to dismiss the immensely complex, sophisticated Arup plans as 'a rather half-hearted, grudging attempt to accommodate public concern about the national importance of this great site'. Given to dismissive one-liners about modern British architects, the prince accused Arup of wanting 'to put St Paul's in a prison camp, surrounding it with [a] spiky roof-line'.[14] Thus were many months of painstaking, expert work dismissed with a frivolous flick of the royal pen.

Behind the scenes, meanwhile, he was involved in machiavellian manoeuvring to steer ownership of the site the way of developers who would dismiss Arup and hire Simpson. This he achieved in October 1989, when the site was sold for £158 million to an *ad hoc* British–Japanese consortium calling itself Paternoster

Associates. A leaked memo to the prince from one of his architectural advisers, Dr Brian Hanson, revealed just how much time
and money Arup Associates were wasting by reluctantly courting
his approval. 'The absolute minimum requirement of the meeting',
Hanson suggested, 'is to show them YRH [Your Royal Highness]
is taking a *very* close interest in developments (which will unsettle
them).' In other words, in the gloss of the cultural commentator
Bryan Appleyard: Use your position to terrorize these people. 'The
word "dirty" does not even begin to capture the sheer cowardly
nastiness at work here.'[15]

Deyan Sudjic, then editor of the architectural magazine
Blueprint, described the prince's intervention – overturning a
democratic selection process, subverting statutory planning procedures, and denying the public any say – as 'a gross abuse of the
royal prerogative'. The prince was 'lurching from one half-digested
piece of received wisdom to another, abandoning each as he has
discovered a new enthusiasm, moving from fiasco to fiasco'. Like
others before him in other fields, Sudjic lamented that it had
become Charles's habit 'to adopt as his own the views of the last
person he has talked to'.[16]

Nonetheless, the scale of the prince's apparent victory in
Paternoster Square became clear in February 1993, when another
environment secretary, Michael Howard, announced that he would
not be ordering a public inquiry into the royally endorsed Simpson
scheme, declaring himself 'satisfied that the current proposals meet
the needs of this nationally important site'.

Despite Howard's compliance, and the granting of planning permission, it took another three years before the City fathers finally
abandoned the Simpson scheme as 'unworkable'. Ownership had
meanwhile passed to American developers, who unsurprisingly
introduced commercial criteria into the prince's architectural
equation, resulting in a compromise that was 'perilously close to
being a standard commercial development in Classical dress'. It
was the tenth plan to have failed in almost as many years since
Charles first vetoed the bold original plan which had excited
modernists, won public approval, and could by now have been
standing, enhancing the Thames waterfront beside Blackfriars
Bridge, a symbol of the City of London's prestige as the financial
capital of the world. By the end of 1996, nine years after his
Mansion House speech, even the editor of the prince's own

architectural magazine, *Perspectives*, described 'empty and forlorn' Paternoster Square as 'a national humiliation'.[17]

Under another new masterplanner, Sir William Whitfield, yet another team of architects was assembled, balancing Simpson with modernists acceptable to the prince, such as Michael Hopkins and Richard MacCormac. Had Simpson, wondered *The Times*, been retained as 'a mere sop to royal concern'? Not for nothing was the septuagenarian Whitfield nicknamed 'El Mellifluoso'; he had a knack for smoothing over troubled architectural waters. It took him just a year – while supervising the rebuilding of Windsor Castle after the 1992 fire – to come up with another plan acceptable to the prince. Not everyone was happy. Maxwell Hutchinson, a former president of the Royal Institute of British Architects, called the team behind the Whitfield compromise 'a motley crew of new boys and old-timers'.[18] The new £400 million scheme, now back in the hands of Japanese developers, Mitsubishi, reflected 'the higgledy-piggledy character of the City before the arrival of 1960s brutalism'.[19] By mid-1998, however, Mitsubishi was hopeful of approval by the City planners, successors of the dinner guests whom Charles had lambasted eleven years before. By 2002, barring further upheavals, this tortuous resolution of the prince's personal vision of the London skyline might at last be ready for inspection.

On his fiftieth birthday in 1998, however, the site was still standing derelict and empty, still a 'national humiliation', and a sore embarrassment to Tony Blair's supposedly 'cool Britannia'. But for Charles's unilateral interference, Arup's brave new scheme could have greeted the new millennium, showing off the work of Britain's greatest living architects to the world – perhaps even dispensing with the need to celebrate British creativity by spending £1 billion on the controversial Millennium Dome at Greenwich.

One man's minority vision, in short, had frustrated a nation's hopes and aspirations. If this latest scheme falls through, or fails to meet expectations, Charles can expect to pay a heavy price.

CHAPTER TWELVE

'WHY DON'T YOU LEAVE MY HUSBAND ALONE?'

ALL DIANA KNEW WAS THAT SOMEONE HAD BEEN KILLED. FOR SEVERAL minutes, as confused reports arrived at their Klosters chalet, the Princess of Wales was forced to adjust to the possibility that it might be her husband. It was Thursday, 10 March 1988, and Diana was bedridden with influenza, frustrated at being unable to join the royal party on the ski slopes. That morning had seen her friend the Duchess of York suffer a nasty tumble; three months pregnant, Sarah was resting in the chalet with Diana when a sudden rush of helicopters overhead seemed to carry portents of disaster. Over lunch, Charles had elected to lead the rest of their party down one of the most dangerous off-piste runs in the Alps, the Gotschnawang, locally known as 'the Wang'. There had been avalanche warnings posted that day – but then, as he joked, there always were.

Escorted by a Swiss policeman, the prince had set out with his perennial hosts and close friends, Charles and Patty Palmer-Tomkinson; thirty-five-year-old Major Hugh Lindsay, another close friend since his three years in royal service as an equerry to the Queen; and one of the most experienced of all Alpine guides, Bruno Sprecher (who had actually been hired to escort the Duchess of York). All were accomplished skiers, who had many times before enjoyed braving what Charles called the 'special dimension' of off-piste skiing – and all, by the prince's own account, were well aware of the risks they were taking. 'We all accepted,' he said, 'and always have done, that mountains have to be treated with the greatest respect ...'

It was a beautiful winter's day, with brilliant blue skies and near-perfect skiing conditions. After their first run, the royal party had just paused for breath when, 'with a tremendous roaring', as Charles put it, the avalanche was suddenly upon them. Slabs of snow 'the size of rooms' cascaded down around them. The prince, his policeman, Charles Palmer-Tomkinson and Sprecher all managed to ski to one side. But Charles could only watch with horror as Lindsay and Patty Palmer-Tomkinson were 'swept away in a whirling maelstrom as the whole mountainside seemed to hurtle past us into the valley below.' It was all over 'in a terrifying matter of seconds'.[1]

The two ill-fated members of the group had been swept over the edge of a precipice and fallen 400 feet before hitting a slope and hurtling another 400 feet down the mountain until they came to rest beneath the snow. Somehow, Mrs Palmer-Tomkinson survived, with multiple injuries that would never entirely heal. But Lindsay was killed instantly by the sheer impact of the speeding wall of snow. On duty in the Buckingham Palace press office, by cruel irony dealing with the first flood of enquiries, was his wife Sarah, six months pregnant with their first child. They had been married only the previous July.*

Charles had escaped death literally by inches. Back in the chalet, after helping dig Mrs Palmer-Tomkinson out, he was quick to endorse her husband's view that they should all return to the slopes as soon as possible, the very next day. 'It's what Hugh would have wanted,' said Charles Palmer-Tomkinson, to the prince's agreement. Recognizing that both were in a state of shock, an appalled Diana tried urgently to dissuade them. They should return to London immediately, she argued; to do otherwise would appear callous and disrespectful of Lindsay's memory. Not until her pleas were echoed by his press secretary, Philip Mackie, and a newcomer to his staff, Richard Aylard, could the prince be persuaded that his wife was right.

The Klosters tragedy was a turning-point for both of them. While Charles and the Palmer-Tomkinsons insisted on returning to the same resort in subsequent years, as the best psychological way to handle their continuing trauma, Diana would always refuse to

---

* Sarah Lindsay gave birth to a daughter on 14 May, two months after her husband's death. Eight years later, in 1996, she remarried.

go with them. Amid the appalling events of that day, as she packed Hugh Lindsay's belongings and gave her husband sound advice, she felt a renewed sense of self-worth, persuading herself that she had taken effective charge of a crisis that Charles himself was in no condition to handle. While he entered a prolonged period of depression and withdrawal, agonized with guilt over their friend Lindsay's death, Diana embarked on a long, slow journey towards recovery from her illness and emergence as a confident public figure in her own right.

The virulent strain of rivalry between them had been evident that January in Australia, where Diana had taken every opportunity to upstage Charles. At his old school in Melbourne, Geelong Grammar, the prince had been reluctantly persuaded to dust off his cello for the assembled photographers; Diana, astonishingly, strode right through the photocall to sit down at a nearby piano, where she began to play Rachmaninov, inevitably diverting all cameras her way. At more than one event during Australia's bicentennial celebrations, at which the Waleses were officially representing the Queen, the travelling press noticed the princess hitch her skirt an inch or two higher while her husband was greeting dignitaries or making a speech.

Yet again Diana stole his headlines, and marred his last chance of becoming governor-general, then under renewed discussion. Charles had responded positively to an initial approach from the current incumbent, Sir Ninian Stephen, only to find himself deemed 'inappropriate' by the Labour prime minister, Bob Hawke, who already had one eye on Australia's coming march towards republicanism. The episode dejected Charles, who took it as a personal affront.[2] His distaste for Australia and Australians, always lost on journalists mindful of how much he enjoyed his schooldays there, became all the more intense.

Appalled by his wife's flirtation with the press, the prince gritted his teeth through a joint visit to Thailand before travelling on alone to Africa, where he was joined by friends, including the Palmer-Tomkinsons and Ronald Ferguson, for a Serengeti safari. Their host was Geoffrey Kent, owner of the travel company Abercrombie and Kent, a polo-playing acquaintance who was fast becoming a close friend, not least because of his willingness to bear the expenses of trips like these, and the 'honour' of paying for the transportation of top-class polo ponies around the world for the prince's pleasure. Major Ferguson, whose role as the prince's polo manager had been enhanced by his daughter Sarah's marriage into the royal family, had yet to embarrass all concerned with a series of colourful indiscretions, from visits to London massage parlours to an ill-advised affair with a woman young enough to be his daughter.

Back home ahead of Charles, Diana resolved to build on the Klosters experience by finally conquering her illness – *en route* to confronting the 'other woman' who, in her view, had caused it. So she yielded to the demands of her former flatmate Carolyn Bartholomew that she surrender herself to the care of a specialist. At first Diana resisted, reluctant to confront the truth about herself, which she had so far managed to keep from the world; but Carolyn was a good enough friend to issue an ultimatum, telling Diana that she would go public about her bulimia unless she agreed to seek help. A call to the Spencer family doctor led the princess to Dr Maurice Lipsedge of Guy's Hospital, London, the same specialist who had treated her sister Sarah's anorexia ten years before, with whom she felt an immediate rapport – not least because he told her that her illness was not her own fault, as she believed, but her husband's. 'Is that going to reappear later?' Charles was still saying at mealtimes. 'What a waste!'[3]

Dr Lipsedge proved as good as his word by effecting a near cure within six months. Where Diana was used to making herself sick as often as four times a day, she soon reduced it to barely once a month – and then only at Highgrove, when Charles was entertaining the Parker Bowleses, or in other royal residences, when they were forced to mask their marital unhappiness for the benefit of his parents. After secretly reading books given to her by Dr Lipsedge, hiding them from Charles to avoid his scorn, she shared the common experience of many bulimics in realizing they are not alone, that others suffer from a condition they thought unique to themselves. Once persuaded of the external forces behind it, all relating to the state of her marriage, Diana began to recover her self-esteem.

Still haunted by the Klosters tragedy, Charles meanwhile took himself off to Italy again with Camilla, painting watercolours and indulging their mutual love of the countryside, before moving on to Turkey. The public was dismayed at his failure to return home when his three-year-old son Harry was rushed to hospital for an emergency hernia operation. By his own account, Charles offered to return but was reassured by Diana that it would 'not be necessary'. So he was not surprised to learn that she maintained an all-night vigil beside their son's bed, earning herself saintly headlines while he again suffered the indignity of being painted as a cold, absentee father.

As Charles approached his fortieth birthday, numbed by the state of his marriage, he felt that he was at least making progress on two of the crusades closest to his heart: architecture and the environment. The autumn of 1988 saw Chris Patten assuring him that his public pronouncements had played a role in the apparent 'greening' of Margaret Thatcher, who told her party conference in October, 'No generation has a freehold on the earth. All we have is a life tenancy with a full repairing lease.'

If it was empty rhetoric in her mouth, it was manna from heaven to Charles, who took to the airwaves that same month with a BBC documentary spelling out his architectural credo, *A Vision of Britain*, accompanied by a book of the same name. While his outspoken views struck a loud chord with the public, he again outraged the architectural profession, with whom he boldly renewed his protracted warfare.

A typical example was Colin St John 'Sandy' Wilson, designer of the new £500 million British Library in King's Cross, London, which Charles sneered at as 'an academy for secret police'. Knighted a decade later in 1998, as the embattled library finally opened to considerable acclaim, Professor Wilson said his recognition was 'no thanks' to the prince; it had 'not been easy to get over' Charles's careless dismissal of his building; the prince, who had laid the foundation stone in 1982, had since not even bothered to visit the site. It came as 'no surprise' to Wilson that, because of Charles's gibe, his practice was not subsequently shortlisted or even invited to compete for major projects such as the hundreds of buildings commissioned after the launch of the National Lottery. Eventually the practice was forced into liquidation. 'One was seen', said Wilson ruefully, 'as a bad bet for raising further funding.'

Emeritus Professor of Architecture at Cambridge, Charles's alma mater, Sir Colin merely professed himself 'flabbergasted' at the 'irresponsibility' of a Prince of Wales who fancied himself as a patron of the arts.[4] With a dignity reminiscent of the hapless 'carbuncle architect', Peter Ahrends, he left it to others to state the obvious. Charles had 'given his opinion freely, but in ignorance', wrote one commentator who had taken the trouble to visit the site, concluding that Wilson and his architect wife, Mary Jane ('M.J.') Long, were 'creating a building of beauty, civility, finesse and usefulness'. The visitor hoped the prince would feel able to 'eat his words, and humbly and publicly apologise'.[5] At the time of writing, Charles has finally deigned to visit the library, with Wilson graciously agreeing to show him around. But there was no reciprocal grace in the shape of an apology; that, too, would have been a princely first.

In 1988, in both book and television film, Charles laid down his personal 'Ten Commandments' of architecture, all relating to neo-classical style and practice. Four years later, he was to go so far as to found an architectural school, grandly named the Institute of Architecture, with lavish premises in Regent's Park, to put them into practice. He wanted its students, he said in a rare burst of Jungian self-awareness, to 'appreciate that there are certain time-less values which we can learn from the past and apply to the future . . . to learn that in order to be able to design with sensitivity and an appropriate sense of reverence for the natural surroundings, they first need to learn humility and how to submerge the inevitable egocentric tendencies that we all experience'.

In mid-1997, five years after its foundation, the Institute received only three applications for places in the coming academic year, and was forced to suspend operations pending a complete overhaul. The Prince of Wales was 'facing humiliation' as his Institute 'sank into disarray'. In a letter to the *Architects Journal*, one examiner – Martin Richardson – described its students' projects as 'inept, crude and lifeless . . . Their work is poorly drawn and desperately undistinguished, however becrested with the Prince of Wales' three feathers'. Behind the cream walls of its 'exquisite' Nash villa, in the view of John Welsh, editor of the journal of the Royal Institute of British Architects, the Institute bearing the prince's name had been 'reduced to the status of a Swiss finishing school for rich kids'.[6] In a variation on the same theme, another pundit dubbed it 'a finish-ing school for aesthetically-inclined young fogeys with a desire to recreate Renaissance Italy in the backyards of Blighty'.[7]

The following spring, as the Institute faced terminal crisis, Charles was reduced to naming an unrepentant modernist, Adrian

Gale, as its fifth director in six years. The supreme irony was that Gale had once worked for Mies van der Rohe, the prince's architectural *bête noire*, on the design that Charles had personally prevented Lord (Peter) Palumbo building at No. 1 Poultry, in the City of London. But Gale also happened to be a close friend of the new chairman of the Institute's governing council, Lady (Hilary) Browne-Wilkinson.* It could only appear, in the words of one observer, that 'everything the prince stood for had been defeated by the forces of modernism'.[8]

Over the years, clinging to his insistence on classical custom and practice, Charles's Institute had been forced to 'buy' students, with bursaries and grants costing £125,000 a year, and had been adjudged by the RIBA to fall short of the standards required for academic accreditation. What could have gone so wrong?

Gavin Stamp, who taught students from the prince's Institute at the Mackintosh School of Architecture in Glasgow, was in no doubt. 'The individual who gave his royal name to this school must surely be held responsible,' he declared in 1998. The Institute could never have been established without Charles's ability to raise millions from wealthy friends like the Sultan of Brunei. 'But he has failed to nurture his creation. Instead – like many of great wealth who are disconnected from reality – he seems all too ready to act on the advice of the last person he has talked to.'

That old, familiar charge again. But Stamp was speaking as one who had wished the Institute well, and wanted to see it succeed. 'It would seem in the nature of royalty to attract sycophants and careerists, and the pity is that the Prince of Wales has not listened to those who have the Institute's best interests at heart.' So what style of architecture was Charles actually advocating, beyond his penchant for dismissive one-liners about the work of modernists – even about the work of those, like Stirling, whom he fondly (and wrongly) imagined to be 'modernists'? It had become hard to say, apart from his well-known taste for 'easy-lookin' Classicism, with lots of columns and pediments', as exemplified by his friend Quinlan Terry, 'the tweedy conservative architect who had a nice line in designing new Georgian mansions for the very rich'. As the Institute underwent its umpteenth internal upheaval, with its entire

---

* At the time of her appointment, in 1998, Lady Browne-Wilkinson also happened to be the lawyer who had recently handled Camilla Parker Bowles's divorce.

board of governors dismissed and replaced, Stamp concluded sadly that it would 'perhaps have been better if the prince had never set it up, if he was not prepared to see things through . . . It is almost enough to make one a republican.'[9]

Those 'Ten Commandments' were also the guiding principle behind Charles's ambitious (and contemporaneous) plans to build a 'model' village on Duchy of Cornwall land at Poundbury, near Dorchester, in the heart of Dorset's Thomas Hardy country. For this project he originally called in the latest in his ever-changing succession of architectural gurus, a Luxembourg-born theorist named Leon Krier, biographer of Albert Speer, and noted for favouring 'monumental classicism'.

Charles, who had featured Krier's work prominently in his television film, had first enlisted him to advise on Simpson's scheme for Paternoster Square. Now he asked him to design a model for 'an alternative, kinder city which would somehow manage to be classical, community-based and green'. But things got off to a bad start when Krier arrived for a 'consultation' session with the locals carrying a set of already completed plans. 'We don't want to live next door to a factory. It's barmy,' said one local worthy, as public opposition grew to the prince's 'feudal' plans. 'Let him come and live here himself,' muttered another. 'See how he'd like it.'

Thanks to a combination of planning objections, local opposition and lack of finance, Poundbury hit the buffers in 1990, while a series of disagreements saw Krier storm angrily away. Gradually a scaled-down version of the scheme resurfaced, and a few rows of dinky princely cottages eventually came to pass, regardless of the wishes of those who would have to live there. In architectural terms, Poundbury was 'the equivalent of his embracing faddish diets and alternative medicine. As a model for a city it not only doesn't work, it is turning out to be unbuildable'. When the *Observer*'s Peter Dunn interviewed an elderly couple none too happy about the roundabout materializing in their cabbage patch, Charles paid them a hasty visit while the duchy wrote letters of complaint to the paper's editor. By 1996, the locals were up in arms as the council started demolishing historic buildings, some associated with Hardy, while continuing to favour the 'mock-period' royal village down the road.

As Poundbury's 100 houses trickled on to a reluctant market – a far cry from the prince's original target of 2,500 – a leading member of Dorchester's Civic Society lost patience. To John Walker, also a local antiques dealer, Poundbury was 'a tasteless pastiche of what Dorchester once looked like . . . It's not a village, it's a horrid executive housing estate. The only reason the houses have sold is because of the royal connection. It is HRH's theme park.' Already, after less than a year's occupation, the first 'For Sale' signs had begun to sprout, not just because of the 'uneasy' combination of traditional materials and modern embellishments. The HRH connection was also inflating prices, and supposedly happy Poundbury-dwellers were turning out to be property dealers with an eye to the main chance. Thanks to Charles, the historic town John Walker loved was turning into 'something out of *A Year in Provence*'.[10]

By his mid-forties, ten years after his first foray into the architecture debate, this part-Poundbury was all Charles had to show for his intermittent tirades on the subject. The future of his architectural school remained uncertain. 'Slammed by his enemies as a merely destructive critic, and challenged to do better than the modernists whose past mistakes he has so mercilessly catalogued,' as the *Sunday Telegraph*'s architectural correspondent put it, 'the prince has failed to come up with the goods . . . Given the extent of his personal wealth and of his influence, this seems more than unfortunate.'[11]

Charles's great-grandfather King George V, who as Prince of Wales showed no particular interest in architecture, managed as Duke of Cornwall to build his own 'model' village of handsome and durable neo-Georgian houses around the Oval, the Surrey cricket ground in Kennington, south London. The development began on duchy land in 1909, following complaints about seriously substandard housing. In 1992 the present Duke of Cornwall, scourge of so much twentieth-century architecture, was said to take a particular pride in his predecessor's achievement.

He must also have envied it. All Charles had to show for his own decade of subversive activism was a style of supermarket architecture ingloriously dubbed 'Caroline Tescoism'. As Brian Appleyard observed, 'His role in architecture has been more damaging than he can possibly realize . . . His ignorance of the real workings of real politics has resulted in a planning nightmare in which "Wrenaissance" belfries or cornices can be glued to any old hyperstore in the name of his whims.'[12]

Charles has declined all invitations to take part in public debate on his pet subject, preferring to exercise his prerogative as the nation's aesthetic arbiter more surreptitiously, with secret visits to developers and private conversations with the juries of competitions. 'The claim to be defending a democratic approach does not sit easily with his own inherited authority,' argued Sir Richard (now Lord) Rogers, architect of the Lloyd's Building in the City of London, the Pompidou Centre in Paris and the Millennium Dome at Greenwich. 'The prince might like to consider whether the charges of paternalism and unaccountability, with which he criticizes architects, might not more aptly be directed at his own way of doing things.'

As a man with 'strong public views about architecture, a high public profile and enormous private wealth', suggested Rogers, the prince enjoyed 'an extraordinary opportunity' to commission important buildings, but had 'yet to produce a noteworthy construction'. Where were the royal commissions to compare, for instance, with Inigo Jones's Queen's House for King James I, Nash's Brighton Pavilion for the Prince Regent, or the Crystal Palace in London for Prince Albert?

To Sir Richard, Charles's 'Disneyland' approach was defending a past that had never existed. 'If the conservative principles favoured by the Prince of Wales and his followers had been applied throughout history, very little of our 'traditional' architectural heritage would ever have been built.' Charles's insistence that buildings conform to the height of those around them, for instance, would have ruled out most of the great Gothic cathedrals, not to mention the massive Italian stone *palazzi* so favoured by the prince on his frequent excursions to paint watercolours. His argument that 'adventurous' work was 'certainly inappropriate in rural areas' would have deprived posterity of the very masterpieces of Palladio and Vanbrugh which he now cited as his ideal. Most of the great buildings in the classical and Gothic traditions which he now valued so highly were, as Rogers pointed out, 'in their own time, revolutionary'.

Most ironic of all, Wren's design for St Paul's – itself a watered-down version of his original scheme, rejected as too avant-garde – had been so controversial at the time that Wren had had to build an eighteen-foot perimeter fence around the construction site to prevent his critics from seeing and again frustrating his plans. Would a seventeenth-century Prince Charles have allowed Wren to proceed with his daringly modernist plans for St Paul's Cathedral? It seems highly unlikely.[13]

Those who enjoy dishing it out must also be able to take it. To a man surrounded all his life by sycophants and flatterers, the first waves of expert opposition to his views, from doctors, architects and teachers, had come as an unwelcome shock. Publicly voiced resentment that he was interfering in areas beyond his expertise unnerved the prince, as did the damage his assaults caused British businesses.

At times like these, Charles has always tended to crumple. 'There's no need for me to do all this, you know,' he told a radio interviewer in the mid-1980s. 'If they'd rather I did nothing, I'll go off somewhere else.' During a lunch designed to win over influential journalists, he went further:

> I've had to fight every inch of my life to escape royal protocol. I've had to fight to go to university. I've had to fight to have any sort of role as Prince of Wales. You're suggesting that I go back and play polo. I wasn't trained to do that. I have been brought up to have an active role. I am determined not to be confined to cutting ribbons.

Particularly sensitive to accusations that he should get 'a proper job', Charles was apparently 'incandescent with rage'. His tirade, according to one of those present, was delivered with 'frightening intensity'; the prince was 'either going to have a public function, or a nervous breakdown'.

By the time of his fortieth birthday, Charles's public work was drowning in tidal waves of negative publicity about his marriage. Equally damaging was his failure to give any central focus to what seemed like a different obsession every week. After books and television films on architecture and ecology, he went on to publish collections of his watercolours and his treatise on organic farming. The Palace had to fight to prevent tens of thousands of unsold copies winding up on the shelves of remainder shops. To the average Briton, Renaissance Man had become the pub bore; the crusader prince on his white charger had metamorphosed into Don Quixote on Rosinante, tilting with his polo mallet at politically incorrect windmills.

Charles and his admirers had reckoned without one of the crueller enigmas posed by the history of his office: that, given the constraints of the job, the more successful Princes of Wales have tended to be the less visible ones. 'Sensitive to criticism and prone to self-doubt', very like his great-grandfather, George V, in the description of his official biographer, Charles also had a short fuse and an even shorter attention span. His butterfly mind was easily distracted. Readily discouraged, he allowed frustration or overt opposition in one field to divert him too easily towards another.

Shrinking from private as well as public challenge, he still chose to surround himself only with like-minded advisers; notoriously bad at taking advice, he has now been through four private secretaries since Adeane. It became a characteristic part of this process that many initiatives launched with great fanfare during the 1980s, like Inner City Aid, were subsequently left to fend for themselves, often to wither and die. Without the prince's active support, such causes had little hope indeed.

The sole exception was the Prince's Trust, which has thrived since an idealistic Eurocrat named Tom Shebbeare arrived in 1988 to draw the prince's bewildering array of initiatives under its umbrella. More than 30,000 'disadvantaged' young people in Britain's inner cities started successful small businesses on grants from the Trust, which in many cases they were subsequently able to repay. By Charles's fiftieth birthday in 1998, the hundred most successful businesses supported by the Trust enjoyed a collective turnover of £60 million a year and employed more than 2,000 staff.

Ten years earlier, wishing as little fuss as possible to be made about his fortieth birthday, like most mere mortals, Charles decided to devote the only photo opportunity that day to the Trust, in the shape of a party with beneficiaries in a Birmingham train shed. That night, however, there was a glittering ball at Buckingham Palace, to which Diana invited her riding instructor, James Hewitt, and Charles invited his hunting companion, Camilla Parker Bowles. 'Now that I'm forty,' said Charles that day, 'I feel much more determined about what I'm doing.'[14] So, by now, did his wife.

While Charles busied himself with his public crusades, leaving her to develop a public life of her own, Diana was finally getting her act together. She dismayed many of her supporters, whether friends or distant admirers, by a sudden reliance on astrology to chart her future course. But it was all part of a 'more spiritual' approach to her own difficulties, as much as those of others, encouraged by such new friends as the Italian 'earth mother' Mara Berni, proprietor of one her favourite London restaurants, San Lorenzo. James Gilbey, who reputedly used the Knightsbridge restaurant as a 'safe' address for intimate letters to Diana, remarked that 'Mara and [her husband] Lorenzo are highly attuned, very perceptive and have seen a lot of unhappiness and frustration in Diana. They have been able to help her come to terms with her situation.'[15]

The princess dabbled in tarot cards, clairvoyance, even hypnotism. For once Charles could not be too scornful, as the Windsors themselves have a long tradition of attending seances and relying on 'alternative' methods of healing. Astrologers like Debbie Frank preceded psychotherapists like Susie Orbach as Diana's equivalent of Charles's Laurens van der Post. They played as crucial a role as therapists like Stephen Twigg in helping her to recover the sense of self-esteem banished by her bulimia.

Experiments with acupuncture, aromatherapy, diets of vitamin supplements and the meditative Chinese art of t'ai chi ch'uan were all part of the process, as was an increasingly strict physical regime, involving daily visits to the Buckingham Palace pool and sundry fashionable London gyms and 'exercise studios'.

In Andrew Morton's summary, based on Diana's own tape-recorded words:

> The counselling, the friendships and the holistic therapies she embraced during this period enabled her to win back her personality, a character which had been smothered by her husband, the royal system, and the public's expectations towards their fairy-tale princess. The woman behind the mask was not a flighty, skittish young thing nor a vision of saintly perfection. She was, however, a much quieter, introverted and private person than many would like to have believed.[16]

All but recovered from her bulimia, Diana began to relish the public-relations war in which she managed so effortlessly to get the better of her errant husband. It was, for the moment, a purgative form of revenge. Still deeming AIDS an 'inappropriate' cause for royalty, Charles declined to accompany her on a visit to New

York, where she hugged stricken children for the cameras at a hospital in Harlem, the 'black capital' of the United States. 'I feel so sad when I think about how I held that little boy in my arms,' she told reporters on the flight home. 'It was so moving. Maybe it's because I'm a woman travelling alone. It never feels so bad when my husband is with me.'

It was the first broadside in what would soon become open war. Appalled by this thinly veiled attack upon her husband, the Buckingham Palace press office issued a hurried statement, explaining rather clumsily that 'visiting Harlem Hospital was a very emotional experience for [the princess]. She has been working non-stop for two days and the full impact is only just catching up with her'. But the moral victory was Diana's. A few weeks later, in February 1989, she felt sufficiently self-confident to take on the root cause, in her eyes, of all her woes: Camilla Parker Bowles.

Charles was horrified when Diana insisted on accompanying him to the fortieth birthday party of Camilla's sister, Annabel Elliott, at the financier Sir James Goldsmith's house in Richmond, west London. Friends of Charles and Camilla had long become used to seeing them together, behind Diana's back, accepted in their own secret circles as a couple. So there was a distinct *frisson* among the forty guests when Diana arrived on Charles's arm. After dinner the princess scoured the party for her husband and his mistress, until she found them chatting in a side-room with one other friend. Diana asked both men, Charles included, to leave. She had something to say to Camilla. It began with, 'Look, I wasn't born yesterday.'

Seven years of pent-up fury proceeded to pour out of Diana, who made very clear to Mrs Parker Bowles her suspicions about the precise nature of her relationship with her husband: the hunting expeditions, the letters and phone calls, the weekends at Sandringham and Balmoral, the visits to Highgrove before and after her own arrival and departure – and the fact that the redial button on the phone in the prince's study always dialled her number.

'Why don't you leave my husband alone?' Charles's wife yelled at his mistress. Camilla, according to her friends, handled a very awkward moment with brutal panache, holding open the door for Diana and dropping a mock-curtsey as the princess made a haughty exit. Whoever won on points, this was a highly cathartic moment for Diana; however hysterical her outburst, it gave her morale a huge boost to have confronted her enemy, aiding the long process of healing mental wounds that had cut deep into her psyche.[17]

If she had won that battle, however, Diana was losing the war. Charles had virtually moved out of Kensington Palace, where she remained based with their sons, and spent all his spare time at Highgrove, where he no longer bothered to hide his relationship with Camilla from the highly embarrassed staff. At the nearby Parker Bowles home, Charles was known as the 'Prince of Darkness' because of the frequency of his late-night visits. At Highgrove, Mrs Parker Bowles would make herself scarce at week-ends, when Diana arrived with the boys, then reunite with Charles as soon as they had left to return to London. Sometimes, accord-ing to his valet, Ken Stronach, Charles and Camilla would make love in the garden while Diana was asleep inside. One of Stronach's 'secret' duties was to retrieve the prince's pyjamas the next morn-ing, and clean the grass-stains off them. 'There was mud and muck everywhere,' said the valet. 'They had obviously been doing it in the open air. It was a big risk, but he's blind to everything where that lady is concerned.'[18]

That May, Charles declined to accept an invitation from his father-in-law to accompany Diana to a sixtieth birthday party for Countess Spencer. He would, he told his wife by memo, be 'travelling'. She did not need to be told that his travelling com-panions, on a trip to Turkey, would be the Parker Bowleses. So she invited James Hewitt to accompany her to the party for Raine Spencer. 'With five hundred people there,' she told him, 'we'll be safe.'

Hewitt was soon to be transferred to Germany, to take com-mand of a tank squadron. Naturally pleased by his promotion, he had delayed breaking the news to Diana, rightly fearing that she would try to talk him out of going. The dashing captain had become a mainstay of her growing stability, and indeed self-respect; she expected him, as she did many others, to give her needs and wishes priority over his own. Once Hewitt finally told her of his imminent posting, the princess retreated into a sulk, refusing to take his phone calls. He eventually left the country without seeing her again.

While Charles and Camilla recklessly toured Turkey together, mixing private pleasures with public duty as the prince paid calls on the president and prime minister, Diana turned for solace to one of the knockabout friends from her Coleherne Court days, the car salesman James Gilbey. A sympathetic confidant on her own giggly wavelength, and a friend of long enough standing to arouse no suspicion, Gilbey became the latest repository of all Diana's woes, a new shoulder to cry on, privy to every detail of her miserable marriage.

Only he will ever know what else he became to the princess. Sex was certainly an item on their conversational agenda, on which the entire world was eventually to eavesdrop. As Gilbey chuckled with 'Squidgy' – his pet name for Diana – over the latest royal gossip, billing and cooing like two moonstruck teenagers, they could hardly suspect that British intelligence was taping their phone calls.

The same, it transpired, went for Charles. Mindful, ironically, of the worldly Mountbatten's advice never to write letters to ladies – they might 'fall into the wrong hands' – the prince felt no such inhibitions on his cellular phone. Mobiles, at the time, were still comparatively new and exclusive toys, a plaything of the rich and famous, apparently offering more privacy than conventional landlines in rooms where walls had ears. But sinister forces were already at work, eventually to humiliate both prince and princess by parading their innermost secrets to the widest possible audience.

It would be three years before their indiscretions in December 1989 would return to haunt them both, via transcripts of the 'Squidgygate' and 'Camillagate' tapes; but it was now, from the Cheshire home of his friend the Duke of Westminster, that Charles declared his undying love for Camilla, to the point of wishing to be reincarnated as her tampon, while 'Squidgy' worried aloud to James Gilbey about getting pregnant.

But still the world defiantly believed in the fairy tale, refusing to accept hints from the tabloid press that all was not well with the Waleses' marriage. The papers printed far less than their sleuths knew, fearful of libel suits from the 'happily married' Parker Bowleses, and still constrained by institutionalized respect for the monarchy. Given the loyalty of most proprietors and editors, mindful of the status quo and the allure of titles, a surprising degree of self-censorship still prevailed, as it had during King Edward VIII's affair with Mrs Simpson. This time around, however, the dam would eventually burst.

*

For the present, content that Camilla could compensate for Diana's inadequacies, Charles pressed on with business as usual. This was the height of his 'scattergun' period, when initiatives on architecture and the environment, holistic medicine and organic farming were not enough to occupy his restless spirits.

In February, while coping with the Diana–Camilla confrontation, he was also dashing off letters to the foreign secretary, Sir Geoffrey Howe, about the 'inhuman and diabolical' regime in Romania. In June, soon after his idyll with Camilla in Turkey, he turned his attention to literacy standards in schools, managing to alienate his own staff by complaining about their prose, in a speech itself less than stylistically immaculate.

'All the people I have in my office, they can't speak English properly, they can't write English properly,' he told a conference of business executives. 'All the letters sent from my office I have to correct myself. And that is because English is taught so bloody badly.'[19] The result was not merely more ribbing from the press, for his own imperfect English, but an angry delegation from his private office to protest at his high-handedness.

In June he launched his ill-fated plans for Poundbury; in July he received that roasting from Sir Richard Rogers. In August, while up at Balmoral with Camilla, Charles was dashing off more letters to government ministers on topics from stubble-burning to the 'greenhouse effect'. By December, two days after whispering in Camilla's ear how he wished he could live 'inside' her, he was publicly protesting about the language of the New English Bible and the 'crass' Alternative Service Book, urging a return to 'the more eternal values and principles which run like a thread through the whole tapestry of human existence'.[20]

As his office failed to keep pace with his enthusiasms, and he turned a deaf ear to advice about the need for focus, the prince lost another private secretary in Sir John Riddell, who returned to the City after five years in the seat vacated by Edward Adeane. The successor nominated by Charles, Major General Sir Christopher Airy, would last barely a year. As the prince's life seemed to spin out of control, there were other portents of the tidal wave of woes about to wash over the monarchy. Photos of Prince Andrew's daughters on the lap of his wife's American lover, Steve Wyatt, were discovered in a London flat vacated by the Texan millionaire.

Love letters from Princess Anne to a Palace equerry were found in a misplaced briefcase.

The marital difficulties of the Duke of York and the Princess Royal were suddenly as public as those of the Prince of Wales. But these were lesser characters in the royal soap opera. Divorce might be an option for his siblings, however unpalatable to their mother, but it was unthinkable for the heir to the throne.

Relieved to see the media spotlight switch to Andrew and Fergie, Anne and Mark and Tim, Charles took the chance to reassert his high seriousness with another documentary for BBC Television, this time a showcase for his concerns about the global environment, *The Earth in Balance*. A month before its transmission in May 1990, he felt secure enough to take another secret trip to Europe with Camilla; a month after, quite unexpectedly, his activity ground to a prolonged halt.

It was not the first time Charles had fallen off a horse, whether steeplechasing or playing polo, but it was by far the worst. A scar on his left cheek from a polo-pony kick, requiring twelve stitches, had long been visible evidence of his relish for physical risk as some sort of compensation for his intellectual frustrations. On horseback, as on the ski slopes, so determined was he to prove himself, to attempt feats in excess of his natural abilities, that amateur psychologists went so far as to interpret his refusal to heed the Klosters avalanche warnings as evidence of a death wish. Even since that brush with the fates he had carried on regardless, in the same macho vein, to the point where he was understandably described as 'an accident waiting to happen'.

During a hard-fought polo game at Cirencester, on 28 June 1990, it finally did. Losing his balance while going for the ball, Charles fell between two ponies, one of which ran over him, kicking his right arm hard as it went. Rushed to hospital in acute pain, the prince had suffered a double fracture of the arm above the elbow. After consultations with royal physicians, the Cirencester team set the fracture.

Still in pain a few days later, Charles consulted a Swiss surgeon, Dr Peter Matter, who had helped Patty Palmer-Tomkinson to her remarkable recovery from the Klosters avalanche. There ensued differences of opinion between Matter and the English medics, which saw Charles's arm strapped, unstrapped and restrapped, leaving him in agonizing pain throughout July and August, increas-

ingly depressed and unable to fulfil any engagements. At one point
Matter told Charles that, without an operation, he might never
again be able to salute, which steeled him to more radical treatment. In September he was admitted to the Queen's Medical Centre
in Nottingham for a series of operations that should perhaps have
taken place weeks, even months earlier.

As royal aides, from chefs and butlers to secretaries, moved into
a wing reopened and refurbished especially for the prince, so did
the two women in his life. Mrs Parker Bowles was careful to come
in female company, so that her visits went unremarked by the
press, and indeed by Diana, whom she was equally careful to
avoid.

Made to feel less than welcome by her husband, who was still in
acute pain and in very low spirits, the princess took to visiting
other areas of the National Health Service hospital, not least the
intensive-care unit. Here, for the first time, she discovered the satisfaction of hospital visiting, and her unique ability to bring comfort
to the suffering. To Diana it was second nature to keep in touch
with the patients she had befriended, following up her hospital
visits with letters and phone calls to monitor, perhaps even speed,
their progress. If it was a comfort to them, it was a revelation to
the post-bulimic princess, who had found her true vocation.

'Anywhere I see suffering,' she said, 'that is where I want to be,
doing what I can to help.'[21] While Charles languished offstage,
embarked on a long-drawn-out recuperation, his wife was showered with more positive publicity than ever, a neo-Florence
Nightingale who had found herself the public role that would
characterize the rest of her life. Now her crusade went beyond her
continuing quest for positive publicity to gall her husband, with the
princess making as many private as publicized visits to Great
Ormond Street Hospital for Sick Children, the Stoke Mandeville
centre for the disabled, and hospital wards all over the country,
notably those for AIDS patients. It was in one of these the following year, in the company of Mrs Barbara Bush, that she embraced
a terminal patient, who burst into tears while they were talking.
America's First Lady professed herself deeply moved by Diana's
ability to comfort the suffering, recognizing that it was the private
woman as much as the public princess who seemed to be blessed
with a special gift to respond to them so profoundly.

Only once that summer did Charles ask Diana to put on a show of togetherness – at a concert to mark the Queen Mother's ninetieth birthday, at which he conspicuously proceeded to ignore her. Some guests were sufficiently shocked to leak as much to a Sunday newspaper, moving some of Diana's friends to pained expressions of sympathy. 'Don't be so surprised,' she told them. 'He ignores me everywhere, and has done for a long time.' As summer turned to autumn, she remained at Kensington Palace with their sons while Charles continued to convalesce, in Camilla's care, at Highgrove and Balmoral. Reluctantly resigned to the fact that her husband did not want her around, Diana was surprised when he made no effort to see his children, who clearly missed him. When she let him know as much, Charles took to sending William and Harry occasional faxes about his progress.

His slow and painful recovery, in truth, had led to chronic depression. Some of his friends put it down to a mid-life crisis; others worried that Charles was on the verge of a nervous breakdown. Confronting the ruins of his marriage, beset by guilt about his children and cut off from his public work, the prince succumbed to a prolonged bout of acute self-pity. At this midpoint in his life, when he should have been able to savour some success to build on, his personal horizon was a wasteland of private and public failure.

He took little comfort from Diana's continuing refusal to admit that their marriage was beyond salvation. Only the child of a broken home could have fought on so stubbornly to salvage a relationship long past repair. When she paid an official visit to Edinburgh that October, she did not dare proceed to her husband's side at Balmoral. His moods when depressed frightened her, and she was not sure that her hard-won new sense of security would survive another bout of his scorn. Besides, she had no wish to confront Camilla, with or without her own husband, or any other of Charles's friends who might be there to comfort him, not least about her. So she again returned to London alone.

Towards the end of the month Charles finally came south to spend a weekend with his wife and children, then flew straight back to Balmoral. As October turned to November, even he could no longer justify his absence in Scotland, so he chose a night when Diana was on duty, hosting the president of Italy at a London art gallery, to slip back to Highgrove. At 11 p.m. that evening he was seen leaving the house in his plain Ford estate car, and driving over to the nearby Parker Bowles residence, whence he did not return until the early hours of the following morning. When Diana telephoned at midnight, to be told her husband was out, the discomfort of the Highgrove staff was tinged with enormous sympathy. 'When she asked where he was,' said the man who took her call that night, 'what could I say? In her heart, she knew all too well.'[22]

Still, after nearly six months out of circulation, Charles could not countenance a return to public life. With a policeman and a physiotherapist in tow, he took himself off to Provence, France, as the guest of the Baroness Louise de Waldner* at her château near Avignon. A photograph of him peering out of his bedroom window, wearing only a loosely tied dressing gown, his hair dishevelled and his arm in a sling, showed the Prince of Wales at a very low ebb.

It was four more months before Charles could contemplate the call of duty. By then he was suffering pain in his hip, from which bone had been taken for the operation on his arm. His long-standing back problem, stemming from a degenerative disc at the base of his spine, now also returned to haunt him. But he was well aware that he could not afford to stay away from the public scene much longer. Diana, as he saw it, had seized the chance to fill the vacuum with positive publicity of her own.

Bizarrely, his sense of humour suggested that he might make light of his prolonged absence by returning to the public stage wearing a false arm with a hook on the end, like Captain Hook in J. M. Barrie's *Peter Pan*. His staff were so desperate to dissuade him that they even – as a last resort, given what they knew of their relations – appealed to his wife to intervene. For the last time, Diana saved Charles from himself by pretending to lose the false arm *en route* to the engagement.

All she got in exchange, of course, were more muttered curses. However trivial this little episode, it was to prove Diana's last attempt to lend Charles her support. From now on a state of open warfare would exist between them.

---

* Mother-in-law of Oliver Hoare, a friend of both Charles and Diana, later to be at the centre of another phone call mystery. *See* p. 318.

PART FOUR

The War of the Waleses

CHAPTER THIRTEEN

'WHAT KIND OF DAD ARE YOU?'

IT WAS CHARLES WHO FIRED THE FIRST SHOT – IN ANGER. WORN DOWN by all the negative publicity, and stung by suggestions that he was a neglectful father, his patience finally snapped when a poll voting Diana the most popular royal, and himself the least, coincided with reports that he planned to ignore his wife on her thirtieth birthday.

In fact he had offered to host a party for Diana at Highgrove, and she had turned him down. When he encouraged friends to leak as much to her favourite newspaper, the *Daily Mail*, Charles unwittingly triggered the sequence of charge and savage counter- charge that would slowly but surely precipitate the end of their marriage.*

Earlier that year, in February 1991, the younger royals had come under fierce criticism for partying while Britain was three weeks into the Gulf War. 'This country is at war, though you would never believe it from the shenanigans of some members of Her Majesty's clan,' raged the *Sunday Times*. 'It is the exploits and public demeanour of the minor royals and nearly royals which causes most offence.'

While Britons were dying in action, Fergie, Duchess of York, had returned from the ski slopes to go 'playing with her gang, very publicly, at a high-spirited dinner in a London restaurant'; her husband Prince Andrew, a serving officer in the Royal Navy, had

* The Prince of Wales's office has long believed, through several changes of personnel, that 'the *Mail* and the *Sun* are the only papers worth leaking to'.[1]

been enjoying a couple of days' golf on a 'sunny Spanish links'; the Prince of Wales and his father had taken up arms, but only against innocent birds. 'Not even war, it seems, can stop the last shoot of the season at Sandringham.'

Charles's brother-in-law, Viscount Althorp, had recently confessed to an adulterous weekend in Paris, while his cousin, Viscount Linley, had graced the front page of a tabloid paper 'in fancy dress, wearing red lipstick and holding on to various males in drag'.[2] Linley had since absented himself to the Caribbean island of Mustique, whither his mother, Princess Margaret, had also been bound, until the Queen had 'grounded' her sister in Blighty for the duration.

Charles's wife had escaped criticism, not least because it was known that she had sought permission to pay a morale-boosting visit to British troops in the Saudi desert – a project her husband vetoed, in order to hijack it for himself. By July, however, the princess was still concerned that a celebration might seem inappropriate. Besides, she had no particular wish to spend her birthday grinning her way through the guffaws of the Highgrove set, no doubt including the Parker Bowleses.

That was why Diana had turned down his offer of a birthday party. Not, of course, that the *Mail* said so; on the contrary, the gist of its report, under the byline of its veteran gossip columnist, Nigel Dempster, was that Charles had made a tender, loving offer, which his wife had unreasonably refused. For Diana, it was not enough to leak her own riposte to the following day's *Sun*. It was now that she decided to let the world in on her private miseries, and began to make the tape-recordings that were to inform Andrew Morton's book *Diana, Her True Story* – revealing her bulimia, her quasi-suicide attempts, and her husband's long-running affair with Camilla Parker Bowles.

In time, after Morton's book had precipitated their formal separation, Charles would feel obliged to hit back with his side of the story via another journalist, Jonathan Dimbleby. Diana would cap that with a clandestine interview for BBC TV's flagship current affairs programme, *Panorama*, arguing that her husband was unfit to be king. In the protracted tit-for-tat crossfire over the next several years, their children would know inestimable suffering, and the institution of monarchy would be brought to its knees.

If it all began with that leak from Charles to the *Daily Mail*, the civil war between the Waleses was not really of his volition. In private, the prince had long since given up any hope of improving his marriage and was now reshaping his life around its short-comings, further frustrating Diana by walking away from her tantrums; in public, he still hoped to present some show of togetherness, well knowing how corrosive public sniping would be. When the birthday leak rebounded on him, because Diana was so much more the publicly popular of the two, he urged his friends to desist from further blackening his wife's name. He persuaded her to agree to a couple of joint appearances together; but these too backfired, as their body language could not conceal the depth of their antipathy. To make matters worse, Charles was beginning to lose the public-relations war on the professional as well as the private front.

As Diana began visiting the homeless – another distinctly unroyal cause she would soon make her own – Charles took the royal yacht to Brazil as a power base during the Earth Summit in Rio. His seaborne reception for politicians and businessmen, a mini-eco summit financed by the British taxpayer, attracted mini-mal coverage from a press far more interested in his wife's separate schedule. Amid his private staff, meanwhile, backstage politics over the trip led to the departure of yet another private secretary, Christopher Airy, to be replaced by the ambitious young Richard Aylard.[3]

Aylard was to prove a radical new broom, urging unprecedented media offensives upon his boss. As the new team settled in, how-ever, the prince remained dispiritingly gaffe-prone. On 22 April 1991, the eve of Shakespeare's birthday, a speech bemoaning plans to drop the Bard from the national curriculum led to an angry exchange with the education secretary, Kenneth Clarke, to whose office Charles had again failed to submit an advance text. A week later, in Madrid, Charles managed to speak out against gas-guzzling cars at the very moment his 8 m.p.g. Bentley was being driven 600 miles across Europe for his use in Prague. While Diana gained in public confidence, Charles was reaching the midpoint of a long trail of banana skins.

It dated back to 1988, when he deplored the 'irresponsible' use of aerosol cans and banned them in his household, while present-ing an enterprise award to a group of Rastafarians for spray-painting graffiti. And, for all Aylard's efforts, it would stretch well into the 1990s. In 1993, for instance, on a visit to the United States, the Prince of Wales managed to bemoan 'the technical ease of modern life, the effortlessness and speed of modern communication' within hours of stepping off a supersonic Concorde, pride of British Airways' fleet.

Britain's growing dissatisfaction with its monarchy was not entirely down to the state of the Wales marriage. The previous autumn, a new prime minister had entered 10 Downing Street with a vow to make Britain a 'classless' society. Moments before, upon formally taking office, John Major had gone down on bended knee to kiss the hand of the nation's supreme symbol of hereditary wealth and privilege.

The irony was apparently lost on Major, whose government managed more to exacerbate than to narrow class distinctions while he continued to talk of a nation 'at ease with itself'. As recession turned to slump, the growing armies of the British unemployed, homeless and bankrupt were not alone in resenting the private wealth of the maladroit monarchy they were expected to subsidize. The mood of the hard-pressed middle classes – their businesses failing, their homes repossessed in record numbers, their domestic budgets stretched to the limit – was to abandon their instinctive loyalty not just to the Crown, but to most of the major institutions at the heart of British life.

From the Church of England to the Bank of England, the House of Commons to the Old Bailey, Fleet Street to the BBC, schools to local government, the law courts to the police: each pillar of British society faced challenge and change as the average Briton's customary deference to authority gave way to a healthy, well-motivated scepticism. 'The gap between myth and reality is widening,' stated one journal. 'People are discovering . . . that judges are fallible and the police corruptible; that Parliament is neither representative nor sovereign; that many of the most important decisions affecting their lives are no longer made in Westminster but in Brussels, Washington or Tokyo, the boardrooms of multinationals and the dealing rooms of banks.'[4]

Also at stake were the fundamental verities upon which most British institutions rely: not just faith in the hereditary principle, but the self-regulation of the professions, the neutrality of the Civil Service, the integrity of the law, even the sovereignty of Parliament.

The growing influence of the European Union on every aspect of British life was forcing further reappraisal and self-doubt. Major's mission to carry the United Kingdom to 'the very heart of Europe' was supposed to serve as a final farewell to the splendours of Britain's imperial past. But it was a farewell many British institutions still seemed reluctant to take, none more so than the monarchy, caught napping through this sea change in British society, clinging to its eternal assumption that it was somehow above the fray, that it had a divine right to fiddle while its subjects burned.

Hence the furore over the conduct of the younger royals. And hence Charles's angst that all his concerns about the quality of human life, the individuality of each mortal soul, the need for a sense of community, of physical and spiritual self-help – such heart-felt anxieties, into which he had poured years of his own voyage of self-discovery, remained buried beneath the soap opera that was his crumbling marriage. But still the problems were all too often of his own making. Still he thought it was no-one else's business, and cursed the 'reptiles' of the press when he chose to spend April in retreat at Balmoral with Camilla while Diana went skiing with their sons – and happily complied with all the requests of photographers. Still he made the tactical error of underestimating her guile, ignoring rather than humouring her requests to play some role in his life.

A visit by Charles to Oman, for instance, in the hope of persuading the oil-rich sultan to invest in his Institute of Architecture, just happened to coincide with a stopover by Diana while she was making a separate visit to Pakistan. Her offer to extend her visit, in the hope of helping the prince's cause, was curtly rejected by her husband's staff on his behalf. By now, impatience with his wife's inconsistencies had turned to suspicion of her motives, making Charles reluctant even to share his schedule with her. Still Diana insisted that she meant well, that together they could constitute 'a great team', but Charles no longer trusted her. Amid such lost opportunities, however sound his judgement, the prince also lost his last few chances to prevent his would-be 'wife and helpmeet' – as his grandfather, George VI, once lovingly described his own wife, now the Queen Mother – fast turning into an avenging angel.

Herself tempted to call it quits, and embark on a long, complex journey out of the royal family, Diana decided instead on one last strategy to make the marriage work. She would stake out her own turf, carving out a public niche for herself, while trying to reach some accommodation with Charles by lending her public support to his causes. Her hope, of course, was that he would finally begin to take her seriously – if not as a private figure, then as public one – and thus, perhaps, show her some respect.

Still he remained wary. But he did allow her to persuade him, in his own interests, as she put it, to escort her to the 1991 FA Cup Final, reluctantly accepting her argument that it might do his public image some good to be seen showing an unwonted interest in his country's national sport. In the event, it was all too evident that Charles had merely permitted himself to be dragged along to the royal box. He pointedly ignored Diana throughout the game and made little effort to conceal his boredom. It was soon after this that his wife ordered separate notepaper for her own use, with her own royal cypher at the top, rather than using their joint insignia for her private and public correspondence – another warning sign whose significance eluded him.

As so often, Charles retreated into his shell, leaving the way clear for Diana to make further advances in the public-relations war. That June he could not dissuade her from attending Royal Ascot for only two of its four days, letting it be known that she was growing increasingly averse to the 'frivolous' aspects of the royal routine. As she meanwhile stepped up her visits to hospitals, the homeless, hostels for battered wives, that same month offered her an unexpected, heaven-sent opportunity to score a definitive public victory over Charles.

The prince was closeted at Highgrove, and Diana lunching with a girlfriend at San Lorenzo, when each received the news that their son William, then eight, had been involved in an accident at school. While he and some friends had been fooling around with some golf clubs, 'Wills' had suffered a serious blow to the head, and was now undergoing tests at the Royal Berkshire Hospital in Reading. By the time both his parents got there, from different directions, doctors were advising that William be transferred to London, to Great Ormond Street Hospital. Diana travelled with her son in the ambulance, with Charles following behind in his Aston-Martin.

On arrival, tests confirmed that William had suffered a serious fracture of the skull, requiring an urgent operation under general anaesthetic. There was a remote possibility of brain damage, his parents were advised, and of complications during the operation. The Prince of Wales declared himself satisfied that his son was in the best possible hands, and departed as planned to the Royal Opera House, Covent Garden, to attend a performance of Puccini's *Tosca* in the company of some environmental Eurocrats from Brussels. Diana, meanwhile, stayed at the hospital throughout the seventy-five-minute operation – 'the longest hour of my life', she called it – awaiting confirmation that all had gone well. She then spent the night at William's bedside, while Charles slept on the royal train *en route* to an environment conference in Yorkshire.

The next morning's papers angered them both, in their different ways. Diana was upset to see suggestions that her son was a closet epileptic, which, of course, was wholly untrue. Charles was enraged by reports that he was an uncaring father – 'What Kind Of Dad Are You?' asked the *Sun*'s front page – which, in the eyes of the country, was rather more debatable. In vain did he subsequently plead that he did not leave the hospital until entirely satisfied there was no more he could do; that the trip to the opera was an unavoidable public duty; that he had kept in touch with William's progress by telephone; and that Diana's all-night vigil was typically melodramatic. The damage was done. Few other parents in the land could imagine donning black tie and swanning off to the opera while their son was undergoing emergency surgery.

Not for the first or the last time, Charles's own upbringing was returning to haunt him. Would his own parents have cancelled a public engagement to hang around a hospital while any of their children underwent surgery? Probably not. So instinctive was the call to public duty, so deep-dyed the reluctant need to give it pride of place over private anxieties, that the prince again misjudged the public response, and Diana's ability to milk it for all it was worth. This was a grim, grown-up version of the Cherry Brandy Incident – a private ordeal which turned into a public nightmare. It would take him as long, if not longer, to live it down.

More of a spin doctor than any of his previous private secretaries, Aylard subsequently sent the prince a memo urging him to arrange some photo opportunities with his sons, to give the lie to the growing public myth that he was an uncaring father. 'I'll try!' scribbled Charles in the margin, rather desperately, aware of the difficulties of persuading Diana to allow him any such opportunity, and himself reluctant to use the children for advantageous publicity.[5] Few such chances presented themselves before Aylard talked him into co-operating on a lengthy television documentary in 1994; and even then, when Harry fell over in front of the cameras while playing at Balmoral, Charles was seen to sit frozen on a doorstep, unsure what to do, while one of his female companions ran to the screaming prince's rescue.

Was Charles an uncaring father? Of course not. Was he a less dutiful parent than Diana? Not in the eyes of his sons. Did he take a different attitude to parenthood from his wife, and indeed most parents of his generation? Absolutely, according to public opinion, as shocked by his priorities during the golf-club episode as by the frequently published statistics about how few days per year he spent with his children, compared with Diana, who organized her diary around them.

At this stage, it is true, Charles saw fit to schedule his children around his public engagements, still believing that duty came before pleasure, not seeing fatherhood as a duty more important than the royal imperatives that were his increasingly reluctant lot. It would take Diana's death, and a wholesale revision of his priorities, for Charles to take the view of most normal parents that his children, especially in times of trouble, were a priority that made life's other banalities pale into insignificance.

It was against this background of internecine strife that Diana's thirtieth birthday came and went – she spent it, in the end, with her sister Jane and their children – and the Waleses' tenth wedding anniversary loomed. 'What is there to celebrate?' she shrugged to a friend as the media expressed surprise at the lack of public festivities – not even a joint photocall to mark this milestone in the sometime fairy tale. Indeed, complained picture editors, it was becoming increasingly hard these days to get any photograph at all of them together.

Charles spent his wife's birthday closeted in his study, fighting a losing battle against the government's proposed defence cuts, which proposed mergers between various regiments of which he was colonel in chief. Despite all the angry letters he dashed off to the relevant government ministers, the prince was to find that his public stature had diminished to the point where even loyal Conservative Cabinet members no longer felt obliged to cower before royal protests. The episode is more interesting for the fact that the soldier in Charles, often drowned by the seaman and pilot, was always ready to spring into action on behalf of military tradition.

As far back as 1980, the mayor of the Welsh town of Bridgend could testify to Charles's cavalier correctness in such matters. When the mayor wrote to the prince with an indignant protest that the Welsh Guards had marched through the town without saluting the war memorial, Charles replied to the effect that there were no regulations requiring troops to do any such thing. As colonel in chief of the regiment, moreover, he found any suggestion of disrespect 'extremely offensive' to a regiment which lost over 1,400 officers and men killed in action in two world wars.

As if this were not rebuke enough, the poor mayor was indignantly urged to check his facts before complaining about a regiment which took great pains over its correctness and great pride in its associations with his principality. He made it very clear that he found it hard to put himself in the mayor's shoes.[6]

At times like this, Charles's strength of feeling could overcome his command of the English language he so publicly cherished. At others, it could cloud his political judgement, as when, more than a decade later, the future commander in chief used a major television interview to make the rash proposition that 'in this age of the free market' the British army should put itself up for auction to the highest bidder.[7]

By then, of course, the Tory defence cuts were duly going through, and Charles was forced to clutch at military straws in an unstable world increasingly beyond his ken, citing the hiring of a battalion of Gurkhas by his friend the Sultan of Brunei as an admirable precedent. At the time, during the agony attending the tenth anniversary of a wedding he deeply regretted, he seemed to reach out for any public issue capable of diverting his attention.

Diana, too, was temporarily diverted that summer of 1991 by a family row over the sale of Spencer heirlooms. Times were hard at Althorp, and her mother had meanwhile been left by her second husband, Peter Shand Kydd. The princess made less fuss than usual on their cruise aboard John Latsis's yacht, while calculating that Charles spent more time talking on the phone to Camilla than he did to her. She was happy to be left alone with the boys, sleeping in her own quarters, seeing little of the husband she had now come to loathe. Besides, there was more than her family's problems to distract her. One of her closest friends, Adrian Ward-Jackson, was dying of AIDS.

For six months Diana had secretly helped to care for Ward-Jackson, a governor of the Royal Ballet, who had also become deputy chairman of the AIDS Crisis Trust since being diagnosed HIV positive in the mid-1980s. Once he became bedbound, Diana was among his most frequent visitors, occasionally bringing the boys with her. 'Adrian loved to hear about her day-to-day work and he loved, too, the social side of her life,' said their mutual friend Angela Serota, a former dancer with the Royal Ballet, then married to the director of the Tate Gallery. 'She made him laugh, but there was always the perfect degree of understanding, care and solicitude. This is the point about her, she is not just a decorative figurehead who floats around on a cloud of perfume.' Ward-Jackson did not fear death. 'It was a great journey he was going on. The princess was very much in tune with that spirit . . . It was an intense experience.'[8]

Diana had promised Ward-Jackson she would be with him at the end. In August his condition deteriorated just as she was leaving for the cruise on Latsis's yacht; the princess made arrangements for an emergency helicopter home, but the emergency passed. On her return she went straight to his bedside in a London hospital – the same hospital where her sons had been born – *en route* to her statutory summer sojourn with her in-laws at Balmoral. On the evening of 19 August Angela Serota telephoned Diana there, as agreed, to say that the last rites had been administered; their friend might not live through the night. The last flight to London had already left, so Diana drove the 600 miles south, arriving at 4 a.m. in time to hold Adrian's hand and stroke his fevered brow. Her vigil, in the end, lasted three days and nights; Diana took to comforting other relatives of dying patients – 'God has taken our mother,' said one, 'but put an angel in her place' – before sharing Ward-Jackson's final moments in the early hours of Thursday, 23 August.

Trouble was brewing, meanwhile, back at Balmoral. In her hurry to head south on the Sunday evening, the princess had broken the sacred protocol of leaving without first seeking the Queen's permission. She had then lingered in London for several days over the kind of bedside visit the royals deemed worthy of an hour at most. Now she was staying on to make arrangements for her friend

Angela, packing her suitcase while she slept, and telephoning her husband in France to inform him of her travel plans.

When Diana returned to Scotland the atmosphere was frostier than ever. Charles took his family's side in suggesting she had made an unnecessary drama of one man's death from AIDS. At Ward-Jackson's memorial service a few weeks later, Diana was forbidden to sit with his family and friends, including Angela, on the left-hand side of St Paul's Church, Knightsbridge. Charles's staff insisted that, as a member of the royal family, she sit in their traditional place at the front of the church, on the right-hand side. Such absurdities only reinforced the change in Diana wrought by the whole experience. 'I reached a depth inside which I never imagined,' she wrote to Angela Serota. 'My outlook on life has changed its course and become more positive and balanced.'[9]

That September saw Harry join his brother William at boarding school, Ludgrove in Berkshire, leaving Diana alone in the 'empty nest' she now called her apartment in Kensington Palace. But the princess was fast developing her own circle of supporters, privy to the secrets of her marriage, who offered a wide range of positive advice. In Lucia Flecha da Lima, wife of the Brazilian ambassador to London, she had found a wise and forceful counsellor, as much a substitute mother as Mara Berni, while surrogate sisters included Angela Serota, her former flatmate Carolyn Bartholomew and the Hon. Rosa Monckton, managing director of the London branch of Tiffany's. Girlfriends on whom she relied less for wise counsel than light relief included Kate Menzies, Julia Samuel, Julia Dodd-Noble and Catherine Soames, ex-wife of Charles's friend Nicholas.

Like the royal staff, however, most of Diana's friends were to find themselves dropped and taken up again on the most baffling whims. 'She found it difficult to accept criticism,' conceded Rosa Monckton, whose friendship with Diana once ceased abruptly for four months after she had offered some constructive criticism. 'Then, as usually happened, she just picked up the tele-phone one day, said, "Rosa, how are you?" and off we went again.'[10] Rosa remained her firm friend to the very end, spending a week alone in Greece with the princess just a fortnight before her death.

Charles, too, had a loyal, tight-knit circle of friends to see him through this darkest year of his failing marriage. Nicholas Soames, now a rising Conservative MP, remained his oldest and most devoted ally, predating even Andrew Parker Bowles and Camilla – who was now chatelaine of Highgrove in all but name, hosting gatherings of the select coterie who visited in Diana's absence. Besides the Palmer-Tomkinsons and the Tryons, there was Camilla's sister Annabel and Norfolk neighbours Hugh and Emilie van Cutsem. Older figures like van der Post and Lady Susan Hussey, his mother's favourite lady-in-waiting, were also frequent visitors to Highgrove. When their presence coincided with hers, Diana tried to treat them with civility, but found them 'stuffy' and 'dull'. She was also aware that they considered her beneath them, tolerated as Charles's wife but not up to their level of smart sophistication.

They certainly found it highly amusing when Charles celebrated his forty-third birthday that November by taking his wife to see Oscar Wilde's play *A Woman of No Importance*. The other woman in his life at the time – apart, of course, from Camilla – was the *Mary Rose*, a warship sunk off Portsmouth Harbour in 1545, which had recently been recovered. Knowing the project to have been close to Mountbatten's heart, Charles became involved in the restoration work, and assumed the leadership of ambitious plans to build an appropriate museum.

But they ended in failure after he rejected the original design, then fell out with the architect whom he commissioned to produce an alternative, Professor Christopher Alexander of University of Berkeley, California. Charles had more success with his continuing campaign to defend Shakespeare's place on the national curriculum. With one of his lesser-known mentors, his former schoolteacher Eric Anderson (by now headmaster of Eton), he hosted a lunch for educationalists which led to the foundation of Shakespeare summer schools at Stratford-on-Avon, and which have since become an annual fixture under the auspices of the Royal Shakespeare Company.

Still, however, he would not give an inch on the domestic front. Later that month, December 1991, Diana was photographed in public tears as she left St James's Palace after a memorial service for the Romseys' daughter, Leonora Knatchbull, who had died of cancer at the age of only six. Six months earlier, Diana had held Leonora's hand on the balcony of Buckingham Palace, as together they watched the Trooping the Colour ceremony. But her tears that day were not just for a tragic little child prematurely taken from her parents. They were tears of rage because of the unexpected presence of Camilla Parker Bowles – who, as far as Diana knew, had only recently got to know the Romseys – at the intimate family occasion. In fact, Camilla was closer to the Romseys than Diana realized: Broadlands, where Mountbatten had once hosted clandestine meetings between the prince and his paramour, was now the Romseys' home, and so continued to be a 'safe house' for their secret trysts.

To Charles's intimate circle, Camilla's presence alongside his wife was another sign that he was no longer bothered about keeping their relationship secret. Diana knew all about it, after all; if she could not maintain her public dignity, that was her problem. The Princess of Wales alternated between rage and hysteria as she imagined the two of them laughing behind her back at her distress. Charles remained oblivious, strengthening his wife's resolve to continue her public work, while finding a way out of the marriage. She saw it as a domestic triumph that Christmas when the Queen went out of her way in her Christmas broadcast to remind her subjects that she had no intention of abdicating in Charles's favour. Though he knew in his heart that this would always be the case, the prince was distressed at this coded signal of his mother's displeasure, milked by the media as a public humiliation.

Only one more unscripted, impromptu scene remained before the drama that was the Wales marriage entered its final act. It came out of the blue three months later, when Charles and Diana were on a skiing holiday with their sons – not, at Diana's insistence, in Klosters, but in the Austrian resort of Lech. Here, on 29 March 1992, the princess received the news that her father had died. As she made immediate plans to return home, leaving her children in their father's care, Charles insisted on returning with her. Sensing the public-relations ploy implicit in his offer, Diana told him bitterly that it was 'a bit late to start playing the caring husband'.[11]

Charles had not originally intended to join his wife and children in Lech, having laid alternative plans to visit Milan that week. When he decided to fly in for the weekend, his staff ensured that photographers were alerted to his arrival at the Arlberg Hotel, via a radio-co-ordinated operation ensuring that his sons were waiting on the hotel doorstep, ready to fly into his arms for the cameras. There were more 'happy family' photocalls the next morning. The whole episode – part of Aylard's new 'charm offensive' to paint Charles as a caring father – thoroughly sickened Diana, who was now in no mood to let him in on her grief for her father. Even as she mourned, an untimely row ensued in the royal hotel suite, as Aylard and other members of Charles's staff took his part, insisting that Diana must let him accompany her home. But the princess would not be moved. Charles, she said, had made no effort in life to befriend his father-in-law, so she saw no reason why he should now be allowed to intrude on her family's private grief.

To the prince, this was not the point. He could not risk the negative publicity that would inevitably attend his bereaved wife's return home without him. Eventually Aylard prevailed upon the princess to let the Queen act as referee, extracting an agreement that she would abide by her mother-in-law's decision. Un-surprisingly, a phone call to Windsor resulted in a royal command that the couple fly home together. On their arrival at RAF Northolt, in a BAe 146 of the Queen's Flight, the media pack wait-ing on the tarmac noted that Charles came down the steps first, stopping at the bottom to chat with Aylard, while a gaunt-faced Diana struggled after him, carrying her own hand luggage. Sycophantic to the last, they duly reported next morning that Charles had loyally abandoned his holiday to support his wife in her moment of need.

In truth he drove straight off to Highgrove and Camilla, leaving Diana to mourn her father alone at Kensington Palace. Two days later, the prince could not even bring himself to drive up to Northamptonshire with his wife for her father's funeral. He took a helicopter from Highgrove to Althorp, the Spencer family seat, leaving Diana to travel from London without him. After the service he returned briefly to Althorp before returning to his heli-copter, pleading a prior engagement in London. That night, as Diana stayed with her grieving family, Charles was back at Highgrove.

Even during the few minutes he took to offer his condolences to Diana's family, Charles managed to leave a remarkably clumsy calling card. It is unclear whether he knew of the conflict of emotions assailing the new Earl Spencer, his brother-in-law Charles, who, unlike Diana, had remained estranged from his

During eleven years together the public kisses turned sour.

The birth of William in 1982 and Harry in 1984 offered brief bursts of happiness amid the gathering marital gloom.

Charles played polo to work off his frustrations. But frequent injuries led to depression. He found consolation, he confessed, in talking to his plants.

As the marriage collapsed, Diana sent a forlorn 'postcard home' from the Taj Mahal, while a solitary Charles painted watercolours. But they could not hide their unhappiness on official trips to Canada and Korea (*opposite*) and Australia (*overleaf*).

TO MAR
COMMENCEMENT OF
OF THIS BUIL
THIS STONE WAS
ON SUNDAY 13 FEBR
BY
THE HONOURA
HENRY BOLTE K.C
PREMIER OF VIC

After the marriage broke down, Diana poured out her heart to *Panorama*, while Charles returned to the arms of Camilla Parker Bowles.

As Diana won international awards for her humanitarian work (seen here in Angola, 1997, campaigning against landmines), Charles tried to recover from his unpopularity after the divorce.

Hunting has always been a joint passion for Charles and Camilla. But the prince cannot marry the 'love of his life' without the blessing of his sons.

Balmoral (*right*), summer 1997.

Charles escorted Diana's coffin home from Paris after her fatal crash in August 1997. On arrival at RAF Northolt, he was joined by the prime minister, Tony Blair, and Diana's sisters Jane and Sarah.

The day before her funeral, Charles and their sons moved among the sea of floral tributes from a nation paralysed by grief.

6 September 1997: Princes Philip and William, Earl Spencer, and Princes Harry and Charles march behind Diana's coffin to her funeral in Westminster Abbey (*opposite*).

Charles paid a touching tribute to his sons' courage at his first public appearance after Diana's death, in Manchester (*above left*). It was back to business as usual by the time he visited Sri Lanka in early 1998 (*above right*). In South Africa, November 1997, he relished a photocall with Nelson Mandela and the Spice Girls.

Canada, March 1998: six months after their mother's death, William and Harry begin to take over the spotlight from their father.

father at the time of his death. Either way, Charles Spencer was surprised at the style in which his sister's husband chose to couch his message of sympathy. 'You lucky man,' were the Prince of Wales's words of consolation. 'I wish I had inherited so young!'[12]

CHAPTER FOURTEEN

'WHY DON'T YOU GO OFF WITH YOUR LADY?'

FEBRUARY 1992 MARKED THE FORTIETH ANNIVERSARY OF ELIZABETH II'S accession to the throne, seen by Buckingham Palace as the perfect springboard for year-long celebrations, echoing the national euphoria that had greeted the Queen's silver jubilee fifteen years earlier, and deflecting national attention from the marital problems of her children. Helpfully, as he thought, her son and heir suggested a neo-classical fountain in his mother's honour in Parliament Square, to be funded by public subscription.

Amid the depths of a recession, with hard-pressed British tax-payers protesting about subsidizing the world's wealthiest woman, the Queen herself was quick to veto her loving son's idea. It proved a sound judgement on the monarch's part, as her personal mile-stone that February was obscured by the visible deterioration of Charles's marriage during a disastrous six-day visit to India. Beside the Taj Mahal, built by a seventeenth-century Mogul emperor for his wife, who had died in childbirth, the Princess of Wales posed poignantly alone, sending a deliberate 'postcard home', bearing the clear message that she now saw herself as an abandoned woman. Despite a longstanding public promise to take his bride to the Taj Mahal, made during his bachelor days, the prince had opted to remain behind in Delhi.

In vain did Charles's office plead that there was no room in his busy schedule to permit 'sightseeing' at the Taj Mahal. Neither press nor public could be convinced that a meeting with trainee Indian journalists was more important than a photo opportunity with his wife at one of the world's most celebrated symbols of marital love. And the price he paid for his wife's superior sense of public relations grew heavier two days later, on St Valentine's eve, when Diana agreed to present the prizes after a polo match in Jaipur – for which, as it was drily observed, the prince had somehow found time in his busy public schedule.

Among those due to receive a prize was her husband, who stood meekly in line with his victorious team-mates, awaiting his chance to be photographed with the world's most famous woman. When it came, with a hundred lenses poised, Charles naturally leant forward to kiss his wife on the cheek – strictly for public consumption. Diana waited until he was committed to the move, then withdrew her head at the last minute, leaving her husband kissing her earring. It was, in the words of one of those present, 'one of the cruellest, most public put-downs of any man by his wife, executed in front of a hundred professional cameramen and five thousand laughing Indians'. Diana had 'triumph in her eyes'.[1] The resulting photo made a powerfully negative image, prompting fevered discussions in Palace circles as to how much longer this public humiliation of the prince could be allowed to go on.

Diana's tricks were in part Charles's come-uppance for some machiavellian scheming of his own before the trip. On hearing that the Foreign Office was organizing his wife's public schedule around the issue of family planning, the prince had protested that he had himself wanted to 'spearhead' that particular issue. The FO planners did not dissent from Diana's pained comment that they should 'disregard the spoiled boy'. As one of those involved put it at the time, 'It's time he started seeing her as an asset, not as a threat, and accepted her as an equal partner. At the moment her position within the organization is a very loose one.'[2]

They were not to know that Charles was long since past that point. Instead, he consulted the eminent lawyer Lord Goodman about the woeful state of his marriage – purely, at this stage, to explore the legal options open to him. Lobbied by his closest friends, notably the Romseys and the van Cutsems, the Queen and Prince Philip rallied to their son's support, registering sympathy rather than disapproval for the first time in the long course of his marital woes. But soon these woebegone parents were distracted by domestic disarray on three simultaneous fronts.

The following month, to its own mortification, the House of

Windsor swept the first week of a general election campaign off the
front pages by announcing the formal separation of the Duke and
Duchess of York. The politicians had barely managed to complete
their election before their headlines were again stolen by the Prince
of Wales's failure to support his wife through her father's funeral.
But the woes of the Waleses were, for once, themselves being
upstaged. On the day that the Duchess of York left Britain for a
five-week holiday to the Far East with her so-called financial
adviser, taking her children out of school for the duration,
Buckingham Palace was obliged to announce that the Princess
Royal's divorce from Captain Mark Phillips had finally become
absolute.

As is his wont at moments of crisis, Charles felt overwhelmed.
His birthright was being rapidly devalued, perhaps even en-
dangered, yet he could see nothing that he could do to help. His
marriage, to him, was beyond salvation; besides, events in India
had proved that Diana could not now be trusted even to smile her
way through joint public appearances. Any other intervention
would have to be approved by his mother, whose oft-stated preference was that he try to stay out of the newspapers for a while.

Opting to keep a low profile, Charles escaped from it all by touring Britain's stately homes to gather material for a book on
Highgrove and its garden. He himself was only too glad to see the
back of Fergie, Duchess of York, who to his mind, as to his father's,
had besmirched the monarchy's dignity beyond the point of any
forgiveness. His wife, he knew, was more distressed at losing a
close friend from the family circle – her only fellow outsider, with
a uniquely shared perspective on the difficulties they faced.

Of late, however, Diana had carefully distanced herself from the
fellow 'Sloane Ranger' with whom she had once relished public
horseplay; the Gulf War episode had shown her that the public preferred its princesses statuesque, dignified and reticent. Once, the
two unhappy Windsor wives had plotted simultaneous exits from
the royal scene; now Diana, recognizing her loftier obligations as
mother of a future king, had let her friend 'go it alone'. If Fergie
was resentful, the bond between the two would soon be renewed
by Diana's own separation. In the meantime, Charles saw little
reason to offer his wife much sympathy over the fate of her sometime friend.

At the time, he was more concerned about what he saw as wilful

intrusion by Diana into a relationship he had hoped to develop
with Mother Teresa of Calcutta. Earlier that year, when she had
been hospitalized with a heart condition, Charles had instructed
Aylard to send flowers, ensuring that the card was signed by him
alone, rather than himself and his wife. Now Diana had avenged
herself by taking a trip to Rome to meet Mother Teresa. As he
berated his wife for what he saw as a spiteful intervention, their
voices grew so loud that they could be heard in the adjacent office,
where the inadvertent eavesdroppers thought they detected a chill-
ing note of finality in this latest domestic spat. 'It was', in the
words of one member of their staff, 'like a slowly spreading pool
of blood seeping out from under a locked door.'[3]

Even those of their staff naturally loyal to the status quo, and
thus to the prince, felt some sympathy as a tearful Diana begged
him to soften his attitude towards her, or else she would have to
'reconsider her position'. She fled from the room and ran upstairs,
sobbing, heading for the bathroom in the hope that the children
would not see her upset. By her account, however, Prince William
pushed some tissues beneath the door, saying, 'Mummy, I hate to
see you sad.'[4]

At the lowest ebb of their forlorn, fractious marriage, Charles
and Diana were both intent on trying to hide their difficulties from
their children, as keen as any other parents to spare them undue
suffering. Like all such couples, however, they deluded themselves
about the extent to which they could succeed. At the ages of nine
and seven, William and Harry were as sensitive as any other
youngsters to problems between their parents, which is, of course,
invariably more than the parents think. Charles's sense of a proper
distance between father and son, inbred by his own childhood,
proved useful for once in hiding his own unhappiness from his children, with whom his dealings proceeded on a perfectly normal
basis. Diana, however, could not help letting her suffering show,
taking them into her bed and smothering them in angst-ridden
mother-love. Charles, of course, was not to know this, until she
herself chose to reveal it to the world; nor can he be expected, like
any other father, to have considered it fair play. For the present,
however, both tried to maintain a façade of business as usual,
which meant putting a bold private face on increasingly
acrimonious public warfare.

It was now that Diana embarked in earnest on establishing her own separate public identity, constructing the private agenda that would earn her such goodwill, to offset what she saw as the crashingly dull public schedule that reflected Charles's priorities. That month, for instance, she delivered a passionate speech about AIDS, to a private gathering of media executives, within hours of doing her Palace duty by charming all comers as guest of honour at the Ideal Home Exhibition (to mark 'National Bed Week'). As he toured the Duchy of Cornwall, paying his annual round of landlord–tenant visits with few journalists in sight, Charles was effectively being sidelined – not just by his vengeful wife, but by the antics of his increasingly dysfunctional family.

That April, the Princess Royal was seen in public for the first time with her new beau, Captain Tim Laurence, while rumours abounded that the royals were negotiating the Duchess of York's silence. Into this bleak family album the Princess of Wales now pasted another forlorn 'postcard home', as she again allowed herself to be photographed travelling poignantly alone, this time at the Pyramids. Although she and Charles had flown out on the same aircraft, the princess disembarked in Egypt for an official visit while her husband proceeded to Turkey to see the Sufi whirling dervishes at Konya. Staff at a nearby luxury villa, lent to the prince by a wealthy Turkish friend, later revealed that he had been joined there by Camilla Parker Bowles.

It did not go unnoticed that the Prince and Princess of Wales returned from the same part of the world in separate aircraft of the Queen's Flight. When they then flew on to Spain, to represent Britain at the World Expo trade fair in Seville, their half-hearted show of togetherness fooled few. That weekend, in some ways mercifully, the years of pretence were at last ended, and the Wales marriage undone beyond the remotest chance of recovery, by the first of five torrid newspaper extracts from Andrew Morton's book, *Diana, Her True Story*. Because of Charles's affair with Camilla, the public now knew beyond any doubt, their future queen's marital miseries had been acute enough to make her ill, even to drive her to five desperate half-attempts at suicide.

For the prince, Morton's revelations were 'a humiliation of almost unendurable proportions'.[5] That June weekend, sensing what was coming, Charles had taken the precaution of inviting wise and loyal friends, Eric and Poppy Anderson, to join him at Highgrove.

He was astounded by Diana's apparent complicity in a book that paraded their marital miseries in such detail, giving so partial an account of their differences, exposing himself and Camilla Parker Bowles to public scorn and contempt.

His parents, for once, were in complete agreement with Charles that his wife's behaviour was inexcusable. That Sunday afternoon, as the public lapped up Morton's revelations, the prince boldly went to play polo, as usual, at Windsor Great Park, where his mother offered him significant public support by inviting the Parker Bowleses to take tea with her in the royal enclosure. Camilla was wearing a suit in Prince of Wales check.

At Windsor that evening, for the first time, the prince broached with his parents the once 'unthinkable' prospect of divorce. It was not a notion to which the Queen warmed. The following morning Charles met Diana at Kensington Palace to explore whether their marriage could now have any future at all. After a brief and very bitter exchange, both agreed it was quite beyond redemption. Although it would take six more painful months to come about, their formal separation was agreed in principle that morning.

That week, as fate would have it, also saw the beginning of Royal Ascot, traditionally a time for 'happy family' public appearances. At lunchtime Charles and Diana were obliged to ride side by side, grim-faced, in an open carriage to the annual ceremony of the Order of the Garter in St George's Chapel, Windsor. The next day, as the race meeting got under way, the royal family tried its usual tactic of 'business as usual', processing down the racecourse and waving to the crowds as if their world were as serene as ever. What was always in danger of becoming a surreal occasion got off to a distinctly unorthodox start, with the estranged Yorks and their daughters among the crowd waving to the surprised-looking royal cortège.

That afternoon, Charles's parents again offered him moral support by publicly rubbing salt in Diana's private wounds. Camilla, unsurprisingly, was nowhere to be seen; but the Queen saw fit to invite her husband, Andrew Parker Bowles, to join the royal family – including Diana – in the royal box. In full view of journalists, Prince Philip then ignored the princess as she walked past him, trying to hide her distress. The war of the Waleses, it seemed, had now been extended to include the rest of the Windsors.

At the end of the day, for the benefit of the cameras, Charles and Diana left Ascot together, only for the royal limousine to stop a mile down the road, in full view of the astonished royal press corps, so the couple could switch cars and go their separate ways. This procedure was repeated daily, as the nation debated the truth or otherwise of Morton's revelations. After three days of public torture, Diana herself resolved the issue by visiting her friend Carolyn Bartholomew, known to be one of his informants, and kissing her in front of photographers. It was her way of saying, 'Yes, it's all true.'

Two days later, moved by the warmth of her reception at an engagement in Southport, Lancashire, the princess could not stop herself dissolving into public tears. There followed a Windsor summit, at which Charles's parents would not hear any talk of separation. Instead, they demanded a 'cooling-off period' of at least three months, preferably six, during which the couple should 'try to resolve their differences'.

Besieged by hate mail, Camilla Parker Bowles fled to Venice with her sister. Asked about Morton's book, Camilla said, 'I haven't read it, but I will with interest when the time comes.' Her husband, meanwhile, denounced it as 'fiction, fiction'.

As the establishment closed ranks around the royals, the Archbishop of Canterbury fretted that 'the current speculation about intimate personal matters has exceeded the boundaries which should be observed in a society claiming to respect basic human values'. The chairman of the Press Complaints Commission, Lord McGregor of Durris, felt moved to borrow a phrase from Virginia Woolf, accusing journalists of an 'odious exhibition' of 'dabbling their fingers in the stuff of other people's souls'.

The very next day, McGregor was privately disabused by evidence from senior newspaper executives to the effect that the royals in question were orchestrating the dabbling themselves. He also received an apology from the Queen's private secretary, Sir Robert Fellowes, for misleading him 'in good faith' about his sister-in-law's involvement in the Morton book. (Fellowes also offered his resignation to the Queen, who declined to accept it.)

None of this emerged for six months, and might never have become public at all, were it not for leaks in January 1993 from Sir David Calcutt's report advocating legislation to curb press excesses. McGregor was forced to come clean – and John Major's government was sorely embarrassed – by evidence that Major and his Cabinet colleagues had been informed that the Prince and Princess of Wales had both been feeding information to the press throughout the period when both Palace and government had been blaming the media for invading the couple's privacy.

As long ago as May 1991, it emerged, McGregor had been told at a private dinner in Luxembourg by Lord Rothermere, owner of the *Daily Mail* and the *Mail on Sunday*, that the prince and princess had each 'recruited national newspapers to carry their own accounts of their marital rifts'. Later he had been told by Andrew Knight, executive chairman of Rupert Murdoch's News International (owners of the *Sun*, the *News of the World*, *The Times* and the *Sunday Times*), that Diana was personally 'participating in the provision of information for tabloid editors about the state of her marriage'.

'I took further soundings,' McGregor eventually revealed, 'and was satisfied that what Mr Knight told me was true.' Knight also told McGregor that it was Diana who had tipped off photographers about her visit to Carolyn Bartholomew, legitimizing the contents of Morton's book.

At first, McGregor accused both the Prince and Princess of Wales of 'using' newspapers to reveal details of their marital problems in what amounted to open warfare. Eventually he was prevailed upon to withdraw his charge against the prince, maintaining it solely against the princess, about whom he did not mince his words. Her actions, said his lordship, had 'seriously embarrassed' the Commission and undermined the purpose of his 'carefully timed' and 'emotively phrased statement'.

But his revised position, based on briefings from the Palace, did not ring entirely true with newspaper readers, to whom the princess had been declared guilty without evidence or trial. Lord Rothermere had asked for his evidence of press recruitment to remain confidential; it would never have become public but for leaks to the *Guardian*. To what, however, could Rothermere have been referring, beyond the leak from Prince Charles's friends to Rothermere's own employee, Nigel Dempster of the *Daily Mail*, about Charles's spurned offer to throw his wife a thirtieth-birthday party?[6]

Charles, unlike Diana, had lost control of his friends. Hers, so the argument went, had demanded her permission to tell all to Morton because they were seriously concerned about her mental and physical health. His, outraged at so one-sided an account of the marriage, defied his instructions to keep silent. McGregor's dutiful service to the Palace again rebounded on him as those unnamed 'friends of the prince' got back to work, adopting a new and ugly *ad feminam* line. To the London *Evening Standard*, 'one of Charles's circle' revealed that Diana was in 'a familiar state of nervous excitement'. This made her 'very dangerous'. The prince's camp could not 'carry on indulging her neurotic tyranny'. In the heat of the moment the *Standard*'s reporter, Rory Knight-Bruce, himself felt moved to abandon any pretence at impartiality: 'It is time for the Establishment to see off the woman who thought that she was more powerful than the royal family.' He then wheeled on another 'senior source in the Church of England' to call the princess 'a little girl lost'. But the anonymous cleric proceeded to let the side down with an apparent pang of guilt: 'She may be flirtatious – and she is, I've met her several times – but she is surely incapable of adultery.'[7]

The Morton furore showed Charles at his most remarkably phlegmatic, calmly carrying on business as usual while his world imploded on him. On 5 July, for instance, he found time to write to the colonel commandant of the Parachute Regiment, indignant that the troops who processed past him the previous day had been wearing T-shirts or 'scruffy' anoraks. 'At the risk of being a dreadful bore, and a frightful fusspot,' he expressed shock and amazement that any soldier from such a regiment could appear on parade so badly turned out.[8]

Perhaps the prince thought he could afford to relax. He had taken the precaution of hiring his own version of Andrew Morton, whose revelations were to start appearing the following day. After an approach from his private office, Charles's version of events was to be told in the *Today* newspaper – a mid-market rival of the *Mail* – under the byline of Penny Junor, a writer so doggedly loyal as to be unafraid of risking her own reputation to save that of the prince. In a tenth-wedding-anniversary book in 1991, as Diana poured her woes into Andrew Morton's tape-recorder, Junor had written that the marriage was 'actually very healthy'.[9]

Now, under the headline, CHARLES: HIS TRUE STORY, Junor told the world that Diana was 'a sick woman', whose conduct had been 'irrational, unreasonable and hysterical'. The marriage had deteriorated entirely because of her bulimia, which had 'caused her to distort the truth and to seek someone to blame for her misery, the prince himself', while also subverting their children against him. Charles had 'encouraged his wife to get treatment, to try to accommodate her whims and to cope with her jealousy, only to be met with tears and shouting'.

There was nothing, of course, for Diana to be jealous about. 'There is no doubt that Charles loves Camilla very dearly, but as a friend, and a friend he has had to rely on increasingly over the years to maintain his sanity.' That, insisted Junor, was the full extent of their relationship. 'The Prince of Wales was "not the adulterous kind".'[10]

'Why don't you save yourself a phone call and ring the papers direct?' Diana raged at Charles as the falsehoods peddled in his name continued to blacken hers.[11] For once, however, it looked as if the might of the British Establishment might not prevail. The British people were not going to surrender their beloved Diana without a struggle. When she visited the city of Liverpool in mid-1992, thousands of people turned out for a glimpse of her. In the same city, in December of the same year, just eight of his future subjects turned up to greet the Prince of Wales.

Refusing to give up, however hopelessly, the Queen's staff insisted that the couple go ahead, as planned, with their annual vacation on John Latsis's yacht, the *Alexander*. The Palace billed it as a 'second honeymoon', which Fleet Street graciously translated into a 'reconciliation' cruise. Charles invited the Romseys along, with his cousin Princess Alexandra and her husband, Sir Angus Ogilvy, to share the strain. For Diana this was 'the holiday from hell'; she had 'too many painful memories' of previous holidays aboard the same yacht. Again she insisted on separate quarters, taking her meals alone with the children, and again she picked up the ship-to-shore phone to hear Charles talking to Camilla.

Another inevitable row ensued. 'Why don't you go off with your lady and have an end to it?' she stormed. Charles walked out of the room in despair. The marriage, observed one of their fellow travellers, was 'all over bar the statement'.[12]

'We must not let in daylight upon magic.' It was 125 years since the journalist Walter Bagehot, in his classic work *The English Constitution*,[13] had warned of the dangers for the mystical institution of monarchy in becoming too familiar with its people. In recent years, largely thanks to the Waleses, that daylight had become a hole in the royal ozone layer.

As Charles and Diana went their separate ways for the summer, August 1992 saw the Duchess of York's topless frolics with her financial adviser beside a French swimming-pool, *devant les enfants*, earn her final banishment from Balmoral. Even a government minister, Alan Clark, felt moved to despair of the whole royal spectacle as 'vulgar and brutish'. The House of Windsor was in a turmoil widely seen as terminal. Comparing the duchess with Woody Allen, whose marital troubles surfaced that same week, even the super-sober *Sunday Telegraph* felt moved to conclude: 'There is no such thing as a free bonk.'[14]

These were dark days in Elizabeth II's forty-year reign. Charles's mother was far from amused by the extent to which her children were undermining all her work in maintaining the dignity of the institution in her care. Had the Queen been over-indulgent towards her offspring? How could she have allowed matters to reach the point where one daughter-in-law was revealed to have made five apparent suicide attempts while the other paraded topless on front pages the world over? With her only sister and her only daughter divorced, two sons *en route* and the third conspicuously unmarried, the Queen was presiding over a domestic shambles fast curdling to a constitutional crisis. 'If this were an ordinary family visited by the local social services,' wrote one columnist in *The Times*, 'the lot of them would by now have been taken into care.' Perhaps, he suggested, it was time to institute a formal ceremony called 'The Severing of the Ties', at which the royal family would also repay the public money lavished on all those weddings.[15]

On the surface, the House of Windsor's woes had been brought about by the failure of its younger male members to marry the right sort of women – or, perhaps, to treat them as the equal partners generally assumed to share most modern middle-class marriages. Buckingham Palace maintained its traditional, supposedly dignified silence on the subject, adopting its familiar if increasingly desperate optimism that this was just another storm which would blow over. The Crown's more vocal supporters meanwhile downplayed the crisis by invoking British history: many a reign had seen more scandalous royal conduct; the monarchy had survived far worse than this. Both camps, however, were overlooking fundamental shifts in British society during the present Queen's reign. If not yet a more genuinely democratic, egalitarian society, post-war Britain at least nourished such aspirations.

By 1992, a three-year recession declining into slump had sharpened class distinctions, bringing with it resentment against the Windsors' heedless pursuit of pleasure; and as Britain hesitantly progressed towards the heart of a federalist Europe, the Crown's constitutional role was in danger of erosion, if not extinction. Since the Gulf War antics of the junior royals, the pomp and circumstance of monarchy, in which Britons had traditionally taken such pride, had come to look like an incongruous symbol of Britain's imperial past – and currently the perquisite of a pampered, undeserving élite, oblivious to the hard times being endured by their fellow countrymen. The generation advancing towards the seats of power no longer shared the unthinking, tribal loyalty to the Crown engendered in its parents.

'Above all things,' Bagehot also wrote, 'our royalty needs to be reverenced . . . We have come to regard the Crown as the head of our *morality*.' With the ancient institution of monarchy buckling beneath the strain, July was to prove the cruellest month, beginning and ending with the Prince and Princess of Wales conspicuously apart on her thirty-first birthday and their eleventh wedding anniversary.

To counter the public perception that he was an absentee parent, Charles unprecedentedly took his younger son to school – an event considered momentous enough to lead the front page of the London *Evening Standard*. The most celebrated marital feud since Samson and Delilah was being conducted almost entirely in public, through the columns of the very tabloid press which the protagonists affected to despise. But the media blitz of Charles's friends did him little good. A *Daily Express* poll showed that the public squarely blamed the prince for his marital problems, still favouring Diana as far and away the most popular royal, 23 per cent ahead of Princess Anne, with the Queen herself in third place on 11 per cent and Charles a distant fifth on 9 per cent.[16]

To Diana, there was something sinister about the timing of the sudden release of the so-called 'Squidgygate' tape – the transcript of her conversation with James Gilbey on New Year's Eve, 1989. Under the auspices of the *Sun*, more than 60,000 Britons paid six figures in telephone bills to listen to that affectionate conversation – illicitly and illegally tape-recorded nearly three years before – in which he called her 'darling' fifty-three times, and she thought aloud, 'Bloody hell, after all I've done for this fucking family . . .'

Few believed the tabloid tale that the bugging was the work of a seventy-year-old retired bank manager, who sat all day in his garden shed idly taping other people's phone calls. Technical experts on both sides of the Atlantic testified that a recording so sophisticated – Gilbey was speaking from a car phone – could only have been an inside job. But who was trying to discredit Diana, and why? With no evidence to support her claim, the princess herself inevitably suspected her husband's office, knowing that Aylard and his staff had returned to their media offensive. 'It was [leaked] to make the public change their attitude towards me,' she said. 'It was, you know, if we are going to divorce, my husband would hold more cards than I would – it was very much a poker game, chess game.'[17]

As the prince retreated to Nottingham for laser surgery on his left knee, and Diana took the chance to be seen visiting hospices and the homeless, September saw widespread publication of a document purporting to be an internal Palace memo criticizing the princess, which was quickly exposed as a fake. But now, for the first time, one tabloid portrayed Diana's relationship with Hewitt as 'physical', while others reported that she had enjoyed six secret rendezvous with Gilbey at a 'safe house' in Norfolk. When Scotland Yard denied the story, apparently at the behest of the Palace, events had reached the point where Britons were surprised to find the Palace defending the princess.

Was the campaign to denigrate Diana being orchestrated by Charles's private office at St James's Palace? The prince still insisted that he had instructed his staff and friends to hold their peace. But the Duchess of York's mother, Mrs Susan Barrantes, was claiming that there was a concerted campaign to discredit her daughter, implying secret service involvement in the topless French photos. Few much cared about the decline and fall of Fergie, who continued to self-destruct with increasingly louche behaviour. For all the assaults on Diana's reputation, by contrast, the relentlessly negative coverage did little to diminish her public popularity. When she gave up her state-of-the-art Mercedes sports car that month, at the height of anti-German feeling over the sterling crisis, a caller to a London phone-in suggested that she should have 'kept the car and traded in the husband'.

For the first time, at the beginning of a long process that would climax in the week of Diana's death, a perceptible gap was beginning to open between the self-confidence of the Establishment and the indignation of the British people. However well intentioned, the black propaganda campaign on Charles's behalf was not working. Diana's unshakeable public popularity was seen at its starkest that October, when she escorted him to a service in Westminster Abbey marking the fiftieth anniversary of El Alamein, one of the most significant land battles of the Second World War. The prince must have anticipated what might happen. He knew that Camilla's father, Major Bruce Shand, who had distinguished himself at El Alamein, would be present. As he and his wife processed to their seats, with the press watching minutely, they had to walk straight past Camilla Parker Bowles. Charles gave her a formal little nod and a smile; Diana, of course, looked firmly the other way. The results were all too predictable. MEMORIAL DAY WRECKED BY CAMILLA, proclaimed the next day's *Sun*, anxious to make amends for the Squidgygate tape. PRINCESS SNUBS RIVAL AFTER SHOCK AT MEMORIAL SERVICE.

It was time, Charles decided, to try to get a grip on his press coverage. Within days he had written a lengthy memorandum to Aylard, setting out new policy initiatives on dealing with the media. 'However depressing the thought might be,' Charles wrote, 'I do think we must realise that certain sections of the media have now proved to their own satisfaction that sensationalised royal stories are one of the best ways of selling newspapers in a recession. There is every reason to suppose that they will continue to operate in a thoroughly unpleasant way . . .'

Insulated from the true values, however lamentable, of the world in which he lived, convinced that his private life was of less consequence than his public work, Charles clung doggedly to his ivory-tower approach to press relations. To him, the relative merits of Diana and Camilla were not a fit subject for public discussion, any more than his respective feelings towards either party. In the absence of any professional media advisers, he still remained locked in the damaging delusion that his marriage was not so much

a constitutional issue as 'sensational' material to newspaper editors
and their circulation managers, who would indeed 'continue to
operate' in ways he himself might well deem 'unpleasant'. In truth,
five years of Palace 'cover-up' was meeting its come-uppance.
Charles's way of acknowledging this was to recommend respond-
ing in a 'positive, self-confident and professional' manner,
emphasizing good news rather than bad, paying special attention
to approaches from film and television companies. To Charles,
the power of television to influence the public was the most
effective way of countering the external 'excesses' of the tabloid
press.[18]

The resultant 'special effort' – a source of some tension between
Buckingham Palace and St James's Palace – began to make itself
felt as October turned to November, and continuing speculation
over the Waleses' marital future overshadowed a gala evening at
Earl's Court, designed to celebrate the Queen's forty years on the
throne. The following evening, when Charles and Diana went to
the Royal Opera House to hear Placido Domingo sing *Otello*, it
was the first time in three years that they had attended the same
function together on two consecutive nights. Knighted newspaper
editors who should have known better were persuaded by St
James's Palace to use this remarkable statistic to run suddenly
optimistic articles about the couple's future. You only had to look
at the princess's smile, ran the captions; all the negative publicity
had been wrong. 'Why Charles and Diana are back together,'
cooed the *Daily Express*. 'Hopes rise', trilled the *Daily Mail*, 'of a
marriage on the mend.'

It took just three days for these fantasies to return to haunt the
Palace strategists, not to mention the editors. Early November saw
the royal press corps off with the Waleses to South Korea. The
princess had tried to pull out of the trip, but Charles had insisted
that she could not let down their hosts. Clumsily billed by his press
office as 'the Togetherness Tour', the visit saw the final death
throes of their marriage finally enacted before a world that
watched slack-jawed.

From the moment they landed in Seoul and emerged from their
aircraft with the aftermath of a row etched on their faces, neither
Charles nor Diana made much effort to hide their misery. So grim
were their looks throughout the five-day trip, so evident their
unwillingness even to speak to each other, that those same papers

who had just proclaimed the 'marriage on the mend' had no alternative but to christen them 'The Glums'. It was, as one of the press corps reported, 'a very public, and very humiliating, end to the love story of the century'.[19]

It was a miserable climax to the worst year of Charles's life. He had married the wrong woman, and was now paying a price he saw as cruelly disproportionate. Even he could not tell what the future might now hold; his destiny seemed to be spinning beyond his control. His sense of duty to the fore, he was prepared to sacrifice any chance of private happiness for public redemption. But now, as so often, emotional problems were accentuating his physical ones, and a recurrence of his back problem even forced him to make the reluctant decision to give up top-flight polo, a prospect that filled him with gloom.[20] Numbed by a sense of sadness, and of failure, he succumbed to another bout of deep, defeatist depression. As he flew from Korea to Hong Kong without his wife, who returned alone to London, the prince poured out his heavy heart in a letter to a friend, concluding, 'I don't know what will happen now, but I *dread* it.'[21]

On her return, with Charles at the other end of the earth, Diana chose to assert herself one last time. Earlier that week she had further established her own distinct identity, thanks to a forty-minute meeting with President Mitterrand of France – the first time in British history that a Princess of Wales had enjoyed any such 'summit' in her own right, with a senior foreign head of state. Now, back in London, she gave the keynote speech of European Drug Prevention Week. Not merely was it one of the longest public speeches she had ever given, another attempt to bulk out her public persona. Given its central theme – lavish physical affection upon your children and they will be less likely to look elsewhere for artificial substitutes such as drugs – the speech was also full of secret messages about her own dilemma, and the apparent inadequacies of her husband.

Herself well known to be a copious hugger of her sons, in contrast to their father, Diana seemed to be offering Charles veiled rebukes, in such phrases as, 'Hugging has no harmful side-effects . . . There are potential huggers in every household . . .' In passing, she also offered some private theories about his personal shortcomings, given a cold and formal upbringing utterly starved of physical affection:

> Children are not chores, they are part of us. If we gave them the love they deserve, they would not have to try so hard to attract our attention . . . Children who have received the affection they deserve will usually continue to recognize how good it feels, how right it feels and will create that feeling around them. We've all seen the families of the skilled survivors. Their strength comes from within and was put there by learning how to give and receive affection, without restraint, or embarrassment from their earliest days.

Significantly, in retrospect, she went on, 'If the immediate family breaks up, the problems created can still be resolved, but only if the children have been brought up from the very start with the feeling that they are wanted, loved and valued. Then they are better able to cope with such crises . . .'

If it was a message about Charles – at the time, before their formal separation, another cry for help – this heartfelt speech was also about herself. To the former Diana Spencer, her husband's friendship with Camilla Parker Bowles was but the latest and most devastating in the lifelong series of betrayals that had begun when her mother abandoned her at the age of six. To Aylard, meanwhile, the speech was nothing less than a betrayal of his master. Mindful of the prince's memorandum about positive media coverage, particularly on television, he negotiated special access for a respected TV journalist, Jonathan Dimbleby, who would spend the next eighteen months making a film and writing a book about the prince's public work and private beliefs. Son of the veteran royal commentator Richard Dimbleby, and himself chairman of the Council for the Preservation of Rural England, Dimbleby shared many of Charles's interests and enthusiasms; a great admirer of the prince, he set out to correct what he saw as gross public misperceptions of 'an individual of singular distinction and virtue'.[22]

Amid discussions with his wife about the fine print of their separation, Charles still found the time and emotional energy to protest to government ministers about matters close to his heart. One minute he was writing to the defence secretary protesting about his 'short-sighted' plans to cut back on regimental bands (which had played 'a crucial role' in the framework of the British army),[23] the next he was arguing with Diana about their plans for the forthcoming weekend. Charles had planned to hold one of his occasional weekend house-parties at Sandringham on the weekend of 20 November 1992, with a dozen or so guests down for three days of shooting, but Diana suddenly announced that she would be taking the children elsewhere. He pleaded with her to relent, or at least to let him have the children, but she proved adamant. The weekend house-party went ahead as planned; but for Charles this was one defeat too many. Five days later he asked Diana for a formal separation.

To Charles, this latest infuriating episode was the climax of a pattern of which the public knew nothing. Time after time Diana had frustrated his plans to spend time with their sons by altering her own plans to sabotage his. Apart from the natural frustration of any devoted parent, he was deeply hurt by the resulting public perception that he was a distant and uncaring father. It was this cruel charge, more than gossip about his triangular marriage, which chewed away at the prince as he steeled himself to the once 'unthinkable' prospect of separation, even divorce.

To him, the coming separation was unwelcome proof of failure in his duty to the Crown, which would have little noticeable impact on his daily way of life. To Diana, by contrast, the sadness was tinged with a sense of liberation, even renewal. In the days that followed, as she busied herself reassuring the children before the news was made public, her friends noticed a dramatic change in the princess. At last she was more cheerful and self-confident than they had seen her in a long time. Two months before, when the 'Squidgygate' episode had sapped her morale, she had seemed to lose the initiative in her long negotiations with her royal in-laws and their lawyers. Her sullen display in Korea, followed by the 'Camillagate' tape, had finally won her the independence she sought – but at what cost to her future credibility?

Then, to her rescue, came the House of Windsor's worst week for sixty years. As it happened, the Sandringham weekend that had proved the last straw for Charles turned out to be a multiple disaster for the prince and his family, as the Friday evening saw

Windsor Castle ravaged by fire. Charles rushed to the scene to console his mother, then returned to his guests at Sandringham. 1992, already the most traumatic year of Elizabeth II's reign, precipitating the House of Windsor's darkest hour since the abdication crisis of 1936, was not over yet. But the Windsor fire was widely taken as some sort of divine judgement, a *Götterdämmerung* reducing the tarnished British Crown to molten metal.

The castle, it transpired to universal astonishment, had not been insured against fire. In the ensuing furore over the cost of repairs, estimated at £60 million, it was pointed out that whereas Balmoral and Sandringham were the Queen's personal property, Windsor Castle was but one among six of her eight residences which belonged to the state. Yes, it was the Queen's favourite place of weekend sojourn, which she regarded as her real home; and yes, technically, it was a state museum; but no, in fact, only some of it was open to the public for some of the year. In other words, as it was succinctly put, 'While the castle stands, it is theirs, but when it burns down, it is ours.'[24] In a series of polls, nine out of ten Britons saw no reason why the taxpayer should foot the bill – as pledged by the government, in the courtly shape of the heritage secretary, Peter Brooke.

The Windsor fire was to prove a double disaster for the monarchy. Not merely did it expose the myth of the government's view of royalty, and indeed royalty's view of itself, as standing at the apex of a blindly loyal society which would rush without question to its aid. It also proved an urgent and irresistible catalyst for change – change of the kind the Queen had so long resisted. Four days later she volunteered the candid confession that 1992 had been an 'annus horribilis', a year on which she would not be able to look back with 'undiluted pleasure'. At what was supposed to be a celebratory lunch in her honour in the City of London's Guildhall, the grim-faced monarch made no specific mention of her children's marital troubles, or the public ill-feeling about her tax-exempt status; nor did she make any offer, as had been widely predicted, to contribute from her huge private wealth to the cost of rebuilding Windsor Castle. Her extraordinary speech was nevertheless the most honest and personal the monarch had ever delivered – a heartfelt confessional made all the more poignant by the throaty weakness of her voice, due to laryngitis inflamed by smoke inhalation at Windsor. Sadly, she croaked:

I sometimes wonder how future generations will judge the events of this tumultuous year. I dare say that history will take a slightly more moderate view than that of some contemporary commentators. Distance is well known to lend enchantment, even to the less attractive views. After all, it has the inestimable advantage of hindsight. But it can also lend an extra dimension of judgement, giving it a leavening of moderation and compassion – even of wisdom – that is sometimes lacking in the reactions of those whose task it is in life to offer instant opinions on all things great and small.

At the end of the Queen's speech, Prime Minister John Major leant conspicuously across their host, the Lord Mayor of London, to offer his sovereign what appeared to be a few words of reassurance. Forty-eight hours later, Major was on his feet in the House of Commons, announcing that the Queen had indicated her willingness to pay some taxes and to reduce the burden of her family on the taxpayer. Her gesture had the full support of her son Charles, who had himself made the same commitment. Though he convinced no-one, the prime minister went to some pains to stress that the Queen's 'request' to pay tax had been made 'some months ago, before the summer recess', and that the timing of his announcement had nothing to do with public reaction to financing the Windsor repairs. Buckingham Palace, describing the move as 'an appropriate step to take in the 1990s', said it had been mooted by the Queen as early as the previous July.

The prime minister's announcement was a watershed in the modern history of the monarchy's relations with its subjects. In a twentieth-century version of the Peasants' Revolt, the Queen's concession was a clear victory for what was soon to become known as 'people power', forcing further radical change on the monarchy in its quest for survival. Within a month, however, Major was back on his feet in the Commons with an even more momentous announcement.

On 9 December 1992, three days before a summit meeting on which he had staked his political future, the prime minister cancelled a meeting with Jacques Delors, the president of the European Commission, to make a statement to the House. Evidently, Major considered it of more importance to tell Members of Parliament in person that the heir to the throne and his wife had decided, 'with regret', to separate. At 3.30 p.m. he rose to make what his predecessor, Sir Edward Heath, later called 'one of the saddest announcements made by a prime minister in modern times':

> It is announced from Buckingham Palace that, with regret, the Prince and Princess of Wales have decided to separate. Their Royal Highnesses have no plans to divorce and their constitutional positions are unaffected. This decision has been reached amicably, and they will both continue to participate fully in the upbringing of their children.
>
> Their Royal Highnesses will continue to carry out full and separate programmes of public engagements and will, from time to time, attend family occasions and national events together.
>
> The Queen and the Duke of Edinburgh, though saddened, understand and sympathize with the difficulties that have led to this decision. Her Majesty and His Royal Highness particularly hope that the intrusions into the privacy of the prince and princess may now cease. They believe that a degree of privacy and understanding is essential if their Royal Highnesses are to provide a happy and secure upbringing for their children, while continuing to give a whole-hearted commitment to their public duties.

On an engagement in the north of England, Diana heard the announcement on the radio with 'deep, deep, profound sadness . . . The fairy tale had come to an end, and our marriage had taken a different turn'.[25] But Major did not seem content with merely ending the fairy tale. Two weeks after announcing the Queen's tax concession, the prime minister strove to secure the prospects of the heir to the throne by taking personal charge of the separation announcement, yet somehow managed to achieve the opposite. Not content with calling the immediate future of the Crown into some doubt, he contrived to talk his way into a deeper constitutional crisis. There was an audible gasp in the chamber as Major continued:

> The House will wish to know that the decision to separate has no constitutional implications. The succession to the Throne is unaffected by it; the children of the Prince and Princess retain

> their position in the line of succession; and there is no reason
> why the Princess of Wales should not be crowned Queen in due
> course. The Prince of Wales's succession as head of the Church
> of England is also unaffected.[26]

Major's addenda to the Palace's unadorned statement quite
avoidably opened a whole new can of royal worms. The prime
minister had chosen to make public, with the full authority of
his office, remarks confined by the Palace press office to off-
the-record, background 'Guidance Notes' distributed to newspapers and broadcasting stations. Was he really suggesting, for
instance, that the Supreme Governor of the Church of England,
whose canon is firmly fixed against divorce, could be crowned
alongside a queen long since estranged from her husband?
Could the Church, come to that, comfortably crown an adulterous
king?

Already in a state of schism, since its recent vote in favour of the
ordination of women, the Church of England was made to look
more hypocritical and less relevant than ever. Thanks to Major it,
too, was now enmeshed in the unenviable problems of the Crown.
In questioning the future of two major national institutions, the
prime minister raised issues that elbowed aside more humane
expressions of sympathy for the royal couple. What should have
been a poignant moment, whose implications could well have un-
folded with a gradual dignity, turned instead into a constitutional
spasm.

The details of Major's statement were based on talks he had held
some months earlier, when it was clear that the marriage was heading towards separation, with the Lord Chancellor, Lord Mackay,
and the Archbishop of Canterbury, Dr George Carey. It was
Carey's view that a formal separation within marriage 'would be
likely to win widespread understanding . . . By putting [the institution of marriage] above their emotions as individuals, the royal
couple would be widely admired for their dedication to serving the
public interest.' But the Archbishop added an important proviso:
that extra-marital affairs that might reach the newspapers would
'need to be avoided'.[27]

That evening, for the first and only time in her life, Mrs Camilla
Parker Bowles felt obliged to issue a statement to the press.
Speaking as a 'close friend' of the prince, she said, 'If something has

gone wrong, I'm obviously very sorry for them. But I know nothing more than the average person in the street. I only know what I see on television.'[28]

CHAPTER FIFTEEN

'THEY WILL FORGIVE ME'

TWO DAYS AFTER THE PRIME MINISTER HAD ANNOUNCED THE WALESES' formal separation, the Queen hosted a formal dinner aboard *Britannia* for European leaders attending the Edinburgh summit. It was a measure of Diana's continuing importance to the monarchy's future that the seating plan placed her with the Queen at the top table, between President Mitterrand of France and the British foreign secretary, Douglas Hurd.

Charles was relegated, along with Prime Minister Major, to table three. It was a rare moment of sharp public relations on the Palace's part, reluctantly reflecting public support for the princess as the wronged party in the marital breakdown. A poll that week showed 50 per cent saying that Diana had 'done most to improve the standing of the royal family over the last two years', compared with 29 per cent for the Queen and just 14 per cent for Charles. Asked who was responsible for the collapse of the Waleses' marriage, Charles was held to blame by twice as many respondents as Diana – 57 per cent 'sympathized most' with her, a mere 12 per cent with him.[1]

'God knows what the future will hold,'[2] Charles wrote that day to his friend Nicholas Soames, before travelling north to attend his sister Anne's remarriage at Crathie Kirk, beside the Balmoral estate, to Captain Tim Laurence, a self-effacing soldier formerly seconded to the Windsors as a royal equerry. Even that was marred by the need for a clandestine, almost conspiratorial ceremony, screened from press and public by a phalanx of royal Range-Rovers.*

Although the traditional family gathering at Sandringham that Christmas welcomed a new family member in the shape of Anne's new husband, more accustomed to eating downstairs with the staff, several more familiar royal faces were conspicuous by their absence. While the Princesses Beatrice and Eugenie joined their father, Prince Andrew, at the Queen's Christmas lunch table, their mother was exiled two miles away to Wood Farm, a cottage on the Sandringham estate, where King George V had once pored over the royal stamp collection.

For the first time in more than a decade, the Princess of Wales was also absent. Although invited to lunch by the Queen, Diana opted for the company of her brother and his family at Althorp. So Diana's Christmas was marred not merely by the unwonted absence of her father, but also of her children, who were at Sandringham at their grandmother's bidding. Every chance was seized for the Prince of Wales to be photographed out walking with his sons, teaching them to shoot (or, as their mother used to put it, to 'kill things'). Diana's absence was used by her foes to criticize her hitherto unimpeachable qualities as a mother; like it or not, the argument went, she should have put up with an uncomfortable Yuletide amid the royals for the sake of her sons. The consensus, however, was that the Palace had again miscalculated. So brutal a demonstration that the young princes were regarded as the monarch's grandchildren first, and Diana's sons second, smacked of all that was wrong with the House of Windsor. To *The Times*, it was 'the unacceptable face of monarchy'.

Within days William and Harry were back where the nation evidently believed they belonged: at their mother's side. After an unprecedented six days apart from her sons, Diana swept them off for a New Year vacation on the Caribbean island of Nevis. On the nine-hour journey on a scheduled British Airways flight, the princess travelled in an economy seat while her royal sons sat up front in first class. It was another typically shrewd piece of public relations – as was the deal she made with the paparazzi who besieged her holiday hotel: in exchange for a brief, relaxed photo session each morning, they would leave her in peace for the rest of

---

* In February 1997 Princess Anne's first husband, Captain Mark Phillips, married an American heiress, Sandy Pflueger, in an exotic ceremony at her family's estate in Hawaii.

the day. In the resulting deluge of public 'postcards home', the future King William and his brother looked much happier at play beneath the West Indian sun than they had amid the freezing formality of royal Norfolk.

So Charles's sons were away, mercifully, when his worst fears were realized on 12 January 1993. For some time Charles had been aware of rumours that a transcript of one of his late-night phone calls with Camilla had fallen into the wrong hands. Like Diana the previous summer, he too wondered who had chosen this moment to leak it, and why. British Intelligence could be assumed to have monitored many of his calls, as they do those of elected public figures as much as appointed or hereditary ones. But the royal family, of all figures at the apex of public life, could tradition-ally assume that the hidden forces at work in British society were loyal to their cause, working to protect them from embarrassments such as this. Was this another assumption he would now have to discard? The question of betrayal soon paled into insignificance beside his utter mortification at the contents of the transcript itself.

At first in Australia, then in America, then in newspapers and magazines all over Europe, the transcript of the 'Camillagate' tape was published in full.

'I want to feel my way along you, all over you and up and down you and in and out,' the future head of the Church of England told the wife of one of his oldest friends. 'I fill up your tank! I need you several times a week,' said the heir to the throne to Mrs Silver Stick-in-Waiting.

Most of the mainstream British press at first funked publication in full, not least because that very week they were fighting off the threat of legislation to curb press freedom. But photocopiers and fax machines whirred samizdat copies from Fleet Street to the City of London, from Whitehall to Downing Street, from Land's End to John o'Groats. The wonders of modern technology thus averted a repeat of the establishment conspiracy of 1936, when the rest of the world knew all about King Edward and his Mrs Simpson while the British were kept in ignorance. By the weekend, two British Sunday papers summoned the nerve to follow their Australian col-leagues in publishing the text in full.

'Oh, God,' moaned Fred to his Gladys, 'I'll just live inside your trousers or something. It would be so much easier.'

'What are you going to turn into?' she giggled. 'A pair of knickers or something?' Both giggled. 'Oh, you're going to come back as a pair of knickers!'

'Or, God forbid, a Tampax,' he ventured. 'Just my luck to be chucked down a lavatory and go on and on forever swirling round on the top, never going down.'

Even more damaging than the sex-talk, for the man aspiring to the nation's moral leadership, was the open, unashamed deception of his friend, the hapless Andrew Parker Bowles. 'Not Tuesday,' said Camilla. 'A's coming home.' Arrangements were then discussed for clandestine meetings at the homes of friends. Amid profuse declarations of love, the couple finally displayed a winsome teenage inability to hang up.

'Press the button,' said Camilla.

'Going to press the tit,' said Charles.

'All right, darling, I wish you were pressing mine.'

'God, I wish I was. Harder and harder.'

That weekend Charles was summoned to a summit with his parents at Sandringham. Never had the reputation of her son and heir, or indeed that of the monarchy, sunk so low. Although she had long known of Charles's friendship with Mrs Parker Bowles, and had even upset the Church by endorsing it, with her public embrace of Camilla, the Queen had never raised its precise nature with her son. Even with her family, she has a habit of avoiding personal conversations, preferring to stick to safer subjects such as the weather. On this occasion, however, Charles's behaviour amounted to family business. The future of what Prince Philip called 'the firm' was at stake. Upon Charles's arrival, Elizabeth II made it very clear to her son that she was distinctly unamused.

Previous Princes of Wales had, of course, kept mistresses, while also keeping the golden Establishment rule of not getting caught. This was one aspect of royal history that the historian in Charles had overlooked when he said to his wife one day, in a moment of exasperation, 'Do you seriously expect me to be the first Prince of Wales in history not to have a mistress?'[3] There was thus a certain retrospective romance to Edward VII's dalliance with Lillie Langtry, and a generous grace in his wife's invitation to his favourite mistress, Camilla's great-grandmother, to visit the King on his deathbed. But neither he nor his adulterous grandson,

Edward VIII, had been caught in public with their trousers down. Charles's love of his mobile phone was to prove far more damaging than his love of a homely Gloucestershire housewife, devoted enough to beg for sneak previews of his speeches.

Close to despair, the prince stage-managed a panicky newspaper campaign of damage containment via his ever-talkative staff and friends. THEY WILL FORGIVE ME proclaimed the front page of the *Daily Mail* on the heir to the throne's behalf, after an 'emotional' chat with 'a member of his circle'. Although twenty-seven more such tapes of Charles–Camilla sex-talk were rumoured to be in circulation, the prince apparently believed the worst was over. 'Things', he was quoted as saying, 'can only get better.' By 'distance and silence', his private secretary told *The Times*, he hoped to 'douse the fires of a nine-day wonder'. Time, his advisers believed, was on his side: 'He still has many years in which to prove his worth as the next monarch.'[4]

It was a claim that rang hollow in certain quarters, notably the habitually loyal Tory press, where a major recently drummed out of the Army for provoking 'unwelcome publicity' was permitted to wonder whether the same should not apply to his brother officer, the Prince of Wales.[5] Annex C of chapter sixty-two of the Army's General Administrative Instructions specifically forbade affairs with the wives of fellow officers; among eight statutes under which officers can be called upon to resign or retire for misconduct, rule D cited adultery with 'a spouse of a serving member of the armed forces'. The prince, as the nation was reminded, was colonel in chief of no fewer than seven regiments. 'You cannot have one rule for the serving army officer, and another for the honorary colonel in chief,' said a senior military man who preferred, for obvious reasons, to remain anonymous. 'The Army has got to lead by example, and Prince Charles is clearly not doing so.'[6]

At the time, the prince was still in hiding at Sandringham, considering his future tactics with his coterie of friends and advisers. On the same day that he and Mrs Parker Bowles both declined an invitation from the Press Complaints Commission to lodge a formal protest over the transcript's publication, he also remained silent on demands for his resignation from the Army. Not that he had become newspaper-shy. The previous day, his office had telephoned the *Observer* to deny a front-page story by its political editor suggesting that Charles had abandoned hope of becoming king. The same day's *Sunday Telegraph* led with a similarly sourced assertion that Charles's affair with Camilla was over, and that he would become celibate for the rest of his life. The prince would meanwhile be carrying on with his schedule 'as normal'; the very next day, as planned, he would be meeting local worthies in King's Lynn.

Alas, the meeting never took place, as he was struck down overnight by a convenient bout of gastroenteritis. Lest anyone wonder just how convenient, the Palace was quick to stress that numerous other Sandringham residents had caught the bug, including the Queen herself. After two days Charles was said to have made a full recovery. But still he cancelled his engagements, unlike his mother, also fully recovered, who accompanied her own mother to the local Women's Institute.

Charles did not dare show his face in public again until ten days later, when he visited a north London housing development. Buckingham Palace sent advance orders to the hosts that he did not want to meet 'too many people'. Children, especially, were to be kept away from the Prince of Wales 'because they tend to ask awkward questions'. They duly were. The following day, however, as Charles left a health centre in Whitechapel, east London, a Cockney pensioner shouted, 'Have you no shame?' Looking shaken, the prince climbed into his limousine and sped away. 'What right has he got to come to the East End after what he's been up to?' demanded the feisty old man, who refused to give his name to reporters. 'He's a disgrace.'

The damage was inestimable. At the beginning of February 1993, a Gallup poll in the *Daily Telegraph* showed that Charles's support was haemorrhaging in the propaganda war with his estranged wife. Where Diana remained the royal family's most popular member, on exactly the same figure as eighteen months before, Charles's approval rating had slumped from 15 per cent to just 4 per cent.[7] That weekend another poll for the *Sunday Times* showed that four out of five respondents thought that 'too many members of the royal family lead an idle, jet-set kind of existence'. Bookmakers cut the odds against the monarchy's abolition by the year 2000 from 100–1 to 8–1.[8]

Any doubts about the public significance of Charles's adultery had now been dispelled by the Church of England's second most senior clergyman, the Archbishop of York. Speaking while the Archbishop of Canterbury was abroad, and thus with the authority of the Church's 'day-to-day leader', Dr John Habgood said he certainly considered it a matter of public concern. 'Looking back over history, the nation has been extraordinarily tolerant of all sorts of behaviour among its monarchs, but all tolerance has its limits and I would not want myself now to say where those limits might lie.' A week later, from South Africa, the Archbishop of Canterbury signalled his agreement: 'We expect our leaders at every level to embody Christian values.'[9]

Although neither archbishop said as much, it was beginning to look as if Charles might have some difficulty finding a prelate prepared to crown him. There was much discussion of a 'revision' of the Coronation Oath. Said the Archdeacon of York, the Venerable George Austin: 'I've been a monarchist all my life, but I must say my support is not what it was. If Prince Charles divorces and remarries, I would have very great difficulties.' The prince's adultery would seem to 'disqualify' him from heading the Church of England, added the Revd David Streater, head of the Church Society.

Charles's 'nine-day wonder' did not look as if it was going to disappear quite as fast as he had hoped. Amid his constitutional woes, the prince had become the butt of humour as cruel as it was crude. When the American film of Morton's book was shown on British cable TV, to an estimated audience of 2 million, Tampax was the leading product advertised between segments. On American TV's *Saturday Night Live*, Mick Jagger dressed up as a bewigged butler to present 'Camilla' with a present from the Prince of Wales on a silver tray – a gift box of tampons. Thanks to Charles, Jagger told the BBC, the royal family were in 'a right old mess . . . They've shot themselves in the foot. There's not a lot you can say in their support.'[10] When a brief trip to the United States took Charles to Williamsburg, Virginia, the local radio rebroadcast the 'Camillagate' tape, dubbing him 'the phone-sex prince', and students at the College of William and Mary celebrated its tercentenary with 'Charles and Camilla slumber parties' – somewhat overshadowing their honorary fellow's sombre call for a return to 'traditional values'.

Among young British women, a 'Charlie' was now a synonym for a Tampax. One British tabloid carried a cartoon showing

Charles entering his greenhouse to find his plants begging, 'Talk dirty to us.'[11] As if this were not enough, the Privy Council reportedly endorsed arrangements whereby Princess Anne would become Regent if the Queen died before Prince William reached eighteen, the age at which he could accede to the throne. The plan had apparently been initiated by Prince Philip, 'who has accepted for some time now that his eldest son is not king material'.[12]

The look on Philip's face signified as much when he accompanied Charles to the scene of an oil-spill in the Shetland Islands. If Charles was putting a brave face on things, Philip found it conspicuously difficult to muster much more than a furious scowl.

As the prince gritted his teeth for a visit to Mexico, polls now showed that almost half his mother's subjects, 42 per cent, thought he should 'never become king'. Asked if he should take over the throne 'within the next couple of years', a resounding 81 per cent said no.[13]

On the fourth and last day of his visit to Mexico, at the invitation of some local farmers, the prince hooked up two oxen to an ancient wooden plough and determinedly steered it through two hard-wrought furrows. Another dream photo opportunity, duly relayed home by an unusually large posse of travelling press, though not, perhaps, with quite the effect intended. Blazoned in colour across the front pages, the pictures bespoke an uncomfortably apt metaphor for the prince's life at that moment. His marriage over, his reputation in tatters, Charles had many more long, hard furrows to plough before any reassessment could be made of his standing in Britain and around the world.

In the meantime, though drained by a combination of jet lag, polo and pollution, he chose the end of his visit to Mexico to clarify his immediate aspirations. The tour had included a meeting with 100 business leaders, from whom he had wrung promises of a wide range of environmental and social projects. It was the fourteenth such gathering under the auspices of his Business Leaders Forum, set up in 1990 primarily to offer assistance to the fledgling democracies of Eastern Europe.

Positively publicized back home, the Mexican tour had proved quite a contrast with that in South Korea three months before, where Charles's attempts to set up a waste-recycling programme had been obscured by saturation coverage of his failing marriage.

Given an unusually strong media escort on his Mexican tour, thanks to the 'Camillagate' embarrassments, even the tabloids were reporting his speeches, hammering home a call, as *The Times* distilled it, for 'sustainable development, quality of life and the need for a spiritual dimension in a technological age'. Charles left Mexico, according to briefings from his staff, convinced that 'his future lies as a leading player on the world environmental stage'.[14]

The prince had apparently taken a conscious decision to 'bury himself in his work' and 'rededicate himself to his perceived messianic role as an ecological prophet of the new world order'. A chastened new Prince of Wales would be re-presented for public approval in July 1994, on the twenty-fifth anniversary of his investiture as Prince of Wales – the peg for the book and film by Jonathan Dimbleby. On the ski slopes, at his various homes, even on the overnight sleeper from Scotland, a film crew was already at work shaping a mature, purposeful prince-with-a-heart to be presented for public re-evaluation, in the hope of winning back the affection and trust of the British people.

In the meantime, Charles's problem was that everywhere he went, even in Mexico, people tended to ask where his wife was. British children were told by the Palace advance party not to mention Diana's name; but the inevitable happened when an eleven-year-old Mexican girl tried to take his photograph. Charles asked her not to, bizarrely explaining that he did not photograph well. 'Diana does,' replied innocent little Maria, like a child in an H. M. Bateman cartoon, mentioning the unmentionable.

Would reed-bed sewage-disposal systems and Third-World waste-recycling plants prove enough to bring the British flocking back to their prince's banner, forgiving him his trespasses against their favourite princess? Diana was doing her best to prove otherwise. On 16 February 1993, while Charles was communing with rural farmers in Mexico, his estranged wife was effortlessly up-staging him again back home. As he, across the world, bemoaned 'a cynical disbelief in the relevance of the past to the present, in the value of what is traditional and timeless', she was talking in London about what was seen as a rather more urgent contemporary concern: 'Too many people have used AIDS as an issue to which they could add their own prejudices. If their views were voiced to help fight the disease, that would be fine. However, too often their attitudes reveal only a narrowness of mind and a sad lack of common humanity.'[15]

Was this another coded reference to Charles? If so, Diana had good reason. When the Princess of Wales arrived in Kathmandu a few days later, escorted by the overseas aid minister, Baroness (Lynda) Chalker, the Nepalese welcoming band owned up to some disappointment at 'instructions from London' not to play the national anthem. Travelling journalists were briefed to write that Diana had been 'snubbed' by the Nepalese royal family, who would not be hosting an official dinner in her honour.

Charles consistently denied that he had any knowledge of it, but visitors to St James's Palace were becoming increasingly aware of a 'dirty tricks' campaign by his staff to rehabilitate the prince by discrediting Diana.[16] 'I was now the separated wife of the Prince of Wales,' she said. 'I was a problem. I was a liability . . . This hadn't happened before.' Now she found that 'overseas visits were being blocked and letters going astray'. Diana's 'enemies' – the people 'on my husband's side' – were making her life 'very difficult'.[17] When the princess attempted to arrange a visit to British troops and refugees in Bosnia, under the auspices of the Red Cross, she was told that Charles's own plans to go there took precedence.

It was not like Charles to stoop to vindictiveness, but it was like a few of his friends, and some members of his staff, to do so on his behalf. It was another 'remarkable coincidence', as Diana herself put it, that a missing extract from the 'Squidgygate' tape surfaced just as she was making her own bid for solo glory on the world stage. Charles, at the time, was offering upbeat photo opportunities on the ski slopes of Klosters, 'getting up smiling' each time he fell down – to quote but one set of mid-market picture captions – and 'looking like a man again enjoying life'.[18]

The only way to proceed, as Charles saw it, was to get on with his new life and hope for the best. At his request, Camilla was getting on with the redecoration of Highgrove, expunging all trace of Diana. In London, meanwhile, the prince fulfilled a longstanding ambition by establishing his own press office in St James's Palace, independent of the Buckingham Palace machine. The busy public prince was thus more effectively contrasted with the softer, private side of Charles. That flying visit to British troops in Bosnia, for instance, and a dash to the bedsides of IRA bomb victims, were followed on Easter Sunday by a winsome appearance as a would-be Pied Piper in *The Legend of Lochnagar*, an animated television version of his story for children.

The previous Sunday, his mother had been persuaded to leave the parish church at Sandringham via the back door, so as not to crowd the photographers' view of Charles and his sons exiting by the front. Cynical though the Palace's tactics might appear, the prince's camp believed that they were beginning to work, and that Operation 'Caring Prince' was forcing Diana on to the defensive. Then, with the crudest of public gestures, Buckingham Palace contrived to give the game away.

Mid-April saw a memorial service in Warrington, Lancashire, for Tim Parry and Johnathan Ball, teenagers killed by an IRA bomb in the town's shopping centre two weeks before. In a grave misjudgement, the Palace overruled Diana's expressed wish to attend, announcing that it would instead be sending Prince Philip. Pressed for its reasons – and a response to the suggestion that Philip, not noted for his concern for children, was widely perceived as the royal family's least compassionate member – the Palace explained that this was a job for 'the most senior royal available'. In the absence of the Queen, 'who never attends memorial services, except those of very close friends', her husband was next in line.

This had not been its policy in the past; in 1988, for instance, pre-fall Fergie had been the official choice to attend a service for the victims of the Clapham train disaster. The Warrington ceremony, as one paper pointed out, was 'precisely the kind of delicate royal duty that the princess handles so well . . . Diana's presence in Warrington would have been the best possible advertisement for a united royal family desperately in need of some positive publicity. It would also have given the lie to the persistent rumours that staff of the "born" royals are out to reduce the princess's public work to an ineffective side-show'.[19]

Charles was not directly involved in the furore, but it did not reflect well on him or his family. The service went ahead without Diana, and with Philip in her stead. The night before, it became public knowledge that the princess had telephoned the parents of the two dead boys to offer her sympathy, and to express regret that she would not be able to join them for the service. 'She was ever so nice. It gave me a big boost to talk to her,' said Mrs Wendy Parry, who revealed that Diana, as 'one mother to another', had said she would like to have given her a hug. 'It is a great comfort that someone in her position should take the time to think of us,' said Maria Ball.

The wide airing given the bereaved parents' delight at Diana's phone calls did not deter friends of the Palace, such as Lord Wyatt, from trying to turn the episode against her. Careful to call her condolences 'genuine', to avoid losing his audience, Wyatt declared that they were 'mixed up with her vanity'. The princess was 'addicted to the limelight her marriage brought. It's like a drug. To feed her craving she'd do anything, even if it meant destroying the throne she solemnly swore to uphold.' With a disingenuous plea that he was 'far from anti-homosexual', Wyatt also took the chance for a passing sideswipe at the princess's work for AIDS victims: 'This elevates them to heroes to be copied by the young. It's well known that AIDS stems mainly from sodomy.'[20] Much more in keeping with popular opinion was the outspoken columnist Julie Burchill: '[Diana's] phone calls were utterly in character; Prince Philip's attendance was not . . . Day by day, despite their pathetic PR efforts, the [royal] family seems more and more to be the most unnatural, destructive and loathsome family since Charles Manson's homicidal gang of the same name.'[21]

The town of Warrington itself chose to settle the issue by inviting the princess to a charity concert for the bereaved families' appeal fund the following weekend. She was unable to go, but sent a message of condolence, offered a 'substantial donation' to the appeal fund, and promised to meet the families privately as soon as possible.

The Palace, by general consensus, had shot itself in the foot, undoing all its work to promote the newly 'caring' prince by a clumsy attempt not just to tarnish his wife, but to shut her out of her natural public habitat. It was a tactic which never looked like working with the British people, who had long since recognized Diana's genuine sense of compassion and her rare gift for expressing it. In an action 'quite typical of her', as Burchill wrote, the princess was 'yet again displaying the warmth and spontaneity which comes harder than speaking Swahili to the Windsors'.

A survey by the *Daily Mail*, which had mounted a huge operation to 'monitor' the royal couple 'in minute detail' throughout the four months since their separation, showed that Diana had attracted more than 9,000 spectators to her sixteen public appearances, while Charles had attracted barely 4,000 to his thirty-one. Diana, concluded the paper, had 'got the better' of Charles; the Palace's tactics were 'clearly not working' for the heir to the throne.

Where, meanwhile, had Charles been while his father attended the Warrington memorial service? In Spain, at the funeral of King Juan Carlos's father. Although Diana was spending the day alone at home – as by now, thanks to the Palace, the entire nation knew – the prince chose not to send their sons back to their mother during his absence, instead sticking rigidly to the schedule, by which they were with him until the following day.

Over the Easter weekend, the television début of his *Legend of Lochnagar* cartoon was marginalized by a current affairs programme that broadcast, for the first time in Britain, the 'Camillagate' tape. Indeed, the royal Easter at Windsor was further marred by a distinct absence of royals. Princes William and Harry were with their mother in London; Prince Edward was away ski-ing; Prince Andrew made a hurried exit to spend the day at home with his estranged wife and their children. Apart from Charles, only Princess Anne and her new husband, Tim Laurence, lined up alongside the Queen, Prince Philip and the Queen Mother for the traditional family photos – for which only one of the royal grand-children, Zara Phillips, was on hand. On Easter Monday, the Queen was spotted wandering Windsor Great Park on her own, deep in thought. She may well have been wondering if the 'Diana problem' was being handled in quite the right way.

That February, a despondent Charles had contemplated his future on a lone Caribbean cruise aboard *Britannia*. In his absence, the Princess of Wales took their sons to the Trocadero Centre in London's Piccadilly Circus. For several hours, amid crowds as astonished as they were delighted, the junior Waleses had fun under their mother's careful watch, enjoying the video games of 'Funland' alongside equally excited children their own age. Like the previous week's go-karting near Windsor, or their annual trip to the water slides of Thorpe Park, it was a great day out – of a kind they had never shared with their father.

Charles has never been known to take his sons with him to any public place frequented *en masse* by his future subjects, apart, of course, from polo fields. Thanks to his upbringing, and premature middle age, it would not even occur to him. The princess's Trocadero expedition was not merely a sign of the 'natural touch' that so endeared her to a vast and unshakeable band of followers, it was a deliberate display of the way royalty can behave if it chooses. Since her formal separation from Charles, Diana had consciously been pioneering a royal style then quite alien to her in-laws – an anathema to the House of Windsor, but a breath of welcome and long-overdue fresh air to its subjects.

Charles's three-day sunshine break that weekend cost the British taxpayer more than a million pounds. When Diana herself had been to the Caribbean the previous month, she had sat in the crowded economy cabin of a scheduled British Airways flight beside the lavatory, which made for even longer queues than usual. She had since used scheduled flights for her official visit to Nepal and a skiing holiday in Austria, just after Charles had travelled to and from Klosters by private jet. It would seem 'profligate', she told a friend, to use aircraft of the Queen's Flight.[22]

In February 1993, when the princess travelled to Cardiff Arms Park for the England–Wales rugby international – an official royal engagement, announced in the Court Circular – she passed up the chance to use the royal train, opting instead for a regular seat aboard British Rail's InterCity service. That weekend, she took her girlfriends Kate Menzies and Lulu Blacker, plus escorts and detectives, to the Royal Ballet at Covent Garden. Far from arriving in a chauffeur-driven royal Rolls, the party climbed happily out of a British-made Ford minibus, which soon became the norm for such visits. At Easter, when Diana took her sons to watch motor racing at Donnington Park, she was herself at the wheel of the family's Ford station wagon.

Instinctively, Diana was pioneering a British version of the Scandinavian-style monarchy, which was supposedly under discussion by the royal family's 'Way Ahead' group as one of a reformed House of Windsor's few hopes of salvation. As a tactic in the guerrilla war forced upon her by Buckingham Palace, it was a typically adroit piece of public relations. The minibus trip to Covent Garden, for instance, came within twenty-four hours of the prime minister's Commons statement detailing the Queen's proposed tax payments. Still dazzled by figures, Britain's twenty-five million recession-hit taxpayers had yet to wake up to the true extent of their monarch's future contribution to the Exchequer. Once they realized that it would come down to a mere 1 or 2 million pounds per annum, they began to feel much the same about building the Queen a new £80 million yacht as they had about footing the £60 million bill for the Windsor fire.

After more than forty years' service, the royal yacht *Britannia* was beyond yet another multi-million-pound overhaul. On the eve of the 1997 general election, however, a Tory promise to build a new royal yacht did not prove the vote-winner the party had hoped; on the contrary, Tony Blair made Labour's refusal to do so a campaign pledge, and *Britannia* was duly decommissioned within six months of his landslide victory. The royal family watched in tears.

To many observers, the Windsors showed more emotion over the loss of *Britannia* than they had over that of Diana only weeks before. It was a reminder of the savagery with which, five years earlier, the corporate might of the British Establishment had rounded on the Princess of Wales, within a month of her formal separation from the heir to the throne. As publication of the 'Camillagate' tapes threatened to damage Prince Charles's reputation beyond repair, leaders of every major British institution were urged to close ranks round the prince and set out to sideline his wife.

To Parliament and Church, the legislature and the armed forces, all of whom would one day swear oaths of allegiance to him, the prince's relationship with Mrs Parker Bowles was not the issue. It was Diana's failure to put up with it. 'The public are deceived in the princess,' declared John Casey, a historian at Caius College, Cambridge (whose chancellor is Charles's father). 'They will see that her friends are everything that is shallow and third-rate – a ghastly milieu where she fits in very happily. She will be diminished, especially when she loses her youthful looks.' Charles, to Casey, had 'long-term qualities', whereas the princess did not 'stand for anything'. The 'great question' about Diana and her friends was whether they had plotted to displace the rightful prince. 'If the public thinks that, it will very much turn against her.'

The conspiracy theme was taken up, without any visible sign of evidence, by Lord McAlpine, former treasurer of the Tory Party, then a big wheel in government circles. Accusing Diana of a propaganda campaign against the royal family, McAlpine proclaimed that she should not be 'allowed to enjoy the spoils of that victory'. Lord St John of Fawsley, master of Emmanuel College at Cambridge University, was sure she would not. 'I am reasonably optimistic that, having been through a difficult period, we are moving out of the shadows and into the sunlight . . . All the feeling of loyalty will constellate around the Prince of Wales as heir to the throne.'[23]

Charles kept his head down, communing with Camilla in the 'safe houses' of friends, as the forces of the Establishment went to war on his behalf. At times of crisis, when threatened with change or disruption on any significant scale, the senior echelons of British society can always be relied upon to rally round the status quo. Soon even Diana's own step-grandmother, the romantic novelist Barbara Cartland, disowned the princess for the crime of 'outshining' her husband. From the world of knighted media folk, Sir Peregrine Worsthorne rashly predicted that the 'electric charge' between Diana and the public would dissipate once she was perceived as Princess of Wales in name only: 'I don't see her carrying on as a star in her own right, as if she's got some momentous glamour of her own.'

At least Sir Perry had some cautionary words for the prince. Predicting 'a rather austere and unworldly' period of transition for the heir to the throne, he recalled the atonement paid by King Henry II for the murder of Thomas à Becket: 'The King ostentatiously had himself lashed on the steps of Canterbury Cathedral. Charles has got to find some equivalent.' But the Church of England was not bothered about penance. To the Bishop of Peterborough, the Rt Revd William Westwood, it was Diana's position that was 'perilous'. Unless she was careful, she would find herself greatly reduced: 'If you live by the media you should die by the media.' Charles had the continuity of his family's lineage and the necessary time to indulge in a period of reflection. 'My honest view is that Prince Charles should really move a bit out of the public eye. Doing ordinary things – openings and visits, that sort of stuff – wins people's hearts.' The former Lord Chancellor, Lord Hailsham, agreed : 'I think it best for the prince to be left alone. Let it simmer for a bit.'[24]

Charles continued to do just that, while now it was Diana's turn to suffer more grief, this time at the hands of her own brother Charles, who, amid the national debate, changed his mind about offering her the use of a cottage on the Althorp estate. The princess had looked forward to quiet weekends at the 'cosy nest' she would make out of the Garden House at Althorp. But Charles Spencer withdrew his offer because of the 'unacceptable levels of intrusion' that would inevitably result from the 'extra police presence, the inevitable cameras and other surveillance equipment'.[25] For several months the princess's relationship with her brother cooled.

At the time, she was anyway dealing with the much more pressing problems of any recently separated parent: reassuring the children. After one of their first weekends visiting their downbeat father, morose in the wake of the 'Camillagate' transcript, William and Harry returned to their mother full of questions about why he was so unhappy. Like any devoted mother, Diana herself was putting on an especially cheerful front to her sons, who could not fail to notice the contrast. She seemed all right, so why was Daddy so miserable? Was it all her fault? Diana reassured them that it was no-one's fault, least of all theirs. Their father can be expected to have told them much the same.

'The one thing we never fought over', she later confided, 'was the boys. It was an unspoken agreement between us. During the worst days of the marriage, when I threw a wobbly over something, Charles would just walk away, calmly turn his back and shut the door, leaving me hysterical, worse than ever. We tried to hide it all from the children, but I don't really know how much we succeeded. They were always sweet to both of us, but I suppose they knew things were bad. Children always do, don't they?

'I know I'm accused of smothering them in too much love, but I don't think a mother – especially a separated mother – *can* smother her children in too much love. Like Charles, who handles it all rather differently, I am just desperately concerned to minimize the effect on them. I want to make sure they feel secure. I'm terrified of their being damaged by all this. I suppose, in the end, it's impossible to avoid, but I pray they don't turn out as dysfunctional as our families. Yes, both our families . . .'[26]

Like all children of divorce, William and Harry will have felt reluctant to take sides. In most other imaginable ways, their feelings about their parents' separation will have been as desolate as those of any other children their age. Most such children are aware, however remotely, of problems between their parents, and can even feel relief when they are openly resolved in separation. Few such children, however, have to watch their parents' marital spats conducted in terms of public warfare. And the worst was yet to come.

CHAPTER SIXTEEN

'TIME AND SPACE'

FOR A QUARTER OF THE EARTH'S POPULATION, THE MONTH OF JUNE 1953 symbolized the dawn of a post-war age of unimagined promise. On the morning of Elizabeth II's coronation, her subjects awoke to the inspirational news that Mount Everest had been conquered by a British expedition – as if endorsing a poll showing that one-third of them believed the monarch to have been chosen by God. The editors of *Time* magazine, casting around for a figure to symbolize the hopeful spirit of the Fifties, nominated the twenty-six-year-old British monarch to 'represent, express and affect the aspirations of the collective sub-conscious' of the entire free world.

Forty years on, in June 1993, most of those aspirations seemed to have been cheated. After the false boom of the Eighties, the United Kingdom languished beneath the worst recession since the 1930s. Amid record numbers of homeless and unemployed, bankrupt and redundant, the monarchy too slumped into a seemingly symbolic decline. With the failure of the marriage of the heir to the throne, and all the public hope reposed in it betrayed by an ugly spate of mutual recriminations, the fortieth anniversary of the Queen's accession to the throne was marked less by retrospective rejoicing than a sudden and unexpected struggle for survival.

The Crown, like the country, had its back to the wall. Throughout the 1980s a festive succession of royal marriages and births had rendered the institution of monarchy as popular as at any time in its thousand-year history. Now that all those marriages had collapsed, and with them the royal ratings, Elizabeth II found herself ambushed by woes, and the stability of the Crown threatened as at no time since the abdication of her uncle, Edward VIII, in 1936. The royal melodrama had taken on Shakespearean proportions, as civil war between the future king and queen divided the nation, more in sorrow than in anger, into fiercely feuding camps.

At centre-stage was the world's most popular princess – cruelly wronged by her husband, to the majority, and schemed against by his coterie of cronies. A vandalized icon, a betrayed innocent, a manipulative hysteric: Diana, Princess of Wales, was many things to many people. But for the editors of *Time*, as for the vast majority, there was no doubt who had now come to 'represent, express and affect the aspirations of the collective sub-conscious'. Diana was 'another Joan of Arc . . . a feminist heroine'.[1]

At the beginning of June 1993, the fortieth anniversary of her mother-in-law's coronation, *Time*'s feminist heroine chose to draw up her will. Six months after her separation from her husband, Diana was advised that, though barely into her thirties, she should make arrangements for her children's future. The will she signed on 1 June 1993 was later described as a document drawn up by someone who 'did not expect to die in the near future'; it was a formulaic affair, with little serious thought given to the division of assets, goods and chattels. But it did have one distinguishing feature: a clause insisting that, in the event of her death, her husband should 'consult with my mother with regard to the up-bring, education and welfare of our children'.[2]

To be echoed in her brother's belligerent speech at her funeral four years later, Diana's 'express wish' was an overt rebuff to Charles, implicitly portraying him as an inadequate father. The truth at the time was that Charles was seeing less of his sons than he would have wished; when he did see them he tried to be as attentive and caring as any other father. The prince, according to Diana's camp, was an absentee parent more interested in spending time with his mistress, which precluded the presence of his children. Diana, according to the prince's camp, was still constantly up-ending their prearranged schedules, often at the last minute, to prevent him seeing them. It was a mutual stand-off about which the detailed truth will never now be known. What is known is that Charles, in the wake of his formal separation, was seeing more of Camilla than ever.

At first, in the immediate wake of the drama, the prince was super-careful. Fearful of calls being bugged, and aware of the public's hostility to Camilla, he cancelled their usual spring tryst at Birkhall, the Queen Mother's home on the Scottish estate. She and her husband, meanwhile, made several deliberate public appearances together, as much for the sake of their own children as the Prince of Wales's sagging reputation. That May, for instance, Andrew and Camilla arrived arm in arm at the Wiltshire wedding of Sarah Ward, daughter of Gerald Ward – one of the group at Annabel's back in 1972, when Charles and the premarital Camilla had danced the night away before returning to her flat.

By midsummer, however, as Diana signed the document that would eventually reveal her deep mistrust of her husband, Charles was under greater public pressure than ever, and thus in greater need of Camilla. A relentless spate of polls showed that an increasing majority of the British people now considered him 'unfit to be King', and wished the throne to pass straight to his son William. Although this was constitutionally impossible, without the (highly unlikely) agreement of the Queen and the prince himself, it was immensely damaging to his public standing, and a huge psychological strain on the man himself. So St James's Palace's disinformation machine, personified by those ubiquitous 'friends of Prince Charles' went back to work on the prince's behalf.

CHARLES GAVE UP CAMILLA TWO YEARS AGO ran the headline in the *Daily Express*, the one paper whose knighted editor could then be relied upon to print anything the Palace slipped its way, regardless of the hollow laughter on its own editorial benches. 'The prince', read the story, was 'beginning to grow in confidence as he puts the controversy of his marriage behind him'. Falsehood number one. 'There is nothing more that can come out about the prince's relationship with Camilla,' said a source 'close to' Charles. 'As far as we are concerned it's old hat.' Falsehood number two. 'The prince's relationship with Camilla has been over for more than two years, a full twelve months before Andrew Morton's book was published.' Falsehood number three. Paving the way for falsehood number four, the most shameless yet, implying it was all really Diana's fault. 'It was all so unnecessary,' said a 'high-ranking' source. 'All the humiliation, pain and heartache that followed could have been avoided. The prince ended his relationship with Camilla two years ago in the spring of 1991. He knew he had to give her up, and he did.'

But the 'dirty tricks department' wasn't finished yet. Referring to the so-called 'Togetherness Tour' of Korea, which had gone so badly wrong, Charles's 'friend' continued, 'After that trip he knew his marriage was finished, but suggestions that he again turned to Camilla are just not true. The prince feared that if he was ever seen with Camilla again, it would finally wreck his chances of becoming king. The people would not accept him.' So Charles had apparently held 'an emotional meeting' with Camilla, at which he had 'broken off their relationship'.

Now it became clear that Charles's 'friend' was making this up as he went along, and was heading towards another bright idea, even more despicable than pinning the blame on Diana. In the previous paragraph Charles 'knew his marriage was finished'; yet this post-Korea summit with Camilla now became a 'final effort to save his troubled marriage', since when he had 'stuck to his word' and avoided Camilla. There followed the paragraph showing that Charles's anonymous champion was prepared to stoop to anything – even, heaven forfend, a lie that also offended courtly chivalry – in the effort to save the prince's neck.

> In fact, it was 45-year-old Camilla, now beginning to lose her looks, who could not cope with being dumped by the man she cherished. She pursued him. In January, after the Camillagate scandal hit the monarchy even further, the prince made a gentleman's agreement with Brigadier Parker Bowles never to see his wife again.[3]

This was one of the lowest points in the lengthening catalogue of black propaganda on Charles's behalf: that the prince's 'friends' felt able to advance Camilla's 'failing looks' as proof positive that the prince had no alternative but to abandon her. With friends like these, the prince had no further need to be his own worst enemy. They even felt free to impugn his own honour with the lie about that gentleman's agreement with his fellow officer, the long-suffering brigadier.

So it was not entirely helpful that the brigadier's sister-in-law Carolyn now chose to confirm, in an interview with an Australian magazine, the widely known suspicions that the Parker Bowleses' marriage itself had long been one of convenience. 'Everyone knows Camilla and Andrew have an arranged marriage,' said Carolyn.

'Ever since they married they have had a fairly free life together . . . What they do suits them both very well.' Since the publication of the 'Camillagate' tapes, said her sister-in-law, Camilla 'just doesn't go out, except to private parties. Can you blame her? Imagine going out to the supermarket after you have had those tapes quoted at you in all the newspapers and magazines'.

Small wonder that Camilla's friends described her that summer as 'showing the strain'. Alarmed at the state of her health, just as Diana's friends had been twelve months earlier, they talked anonymously to the press of the 'intolerable strain' she was under. 'I am genuinely worried about her,' said one. 'The spark has gone out of her life, and she looks haunted and hunted.' Adding to the pressure on Camilla, who was looking older than her forty-five years, was the strain of maintaining the fiction that she had not seen Charles for six months – slightly out of synch with the Palace's fictional 'two years' – while in truth she was 'in touch' with him the whole time.[4]

When Camilla disappeared to India that autumn with two girl-friends, Emilie van Cutsem and Gerald Ward's wife, Amanda, her husband felt obliged to deny rumours that she had suffered a nervous breakdown: 'She is perfectly all right. She has gone away on holiday with a couple of other girls, that's all.' Soon after her return, she and Diana were both present at a memorial service for the Earl of Westmorland, the former Master of the Queen's Horse. This time, unlike the El Alamein service a year earlier, the two women managed to avoid each other. But the contrast between them could not have been more marked. Diana, newly liberated by life without Charles, looked stunningly beautiful and self-assured; Camilla, bowed down by the complexities of Charles's continuing presence in her life, looked to one observer 'shattered – almost old enough to be Diana's mother'.

As the great British public attempted to sift fact from fiction, opinion polls suggested that its instincts were sound. People did not believe the Palace's crude propaganda machine, assuming that Charles and Camilla were still very much an item – the very item, indeed, which had broken the heart and the marriage of the increasingly sainted Diana, the martyr-turned-comforter of the afflicted.

Winning the occasional battle, but losing the war, Charles spent most of 1993 maintaining a judicious silence. As Diana seized the chance for the kind of photo opportunities that were fast becoming her trademark – ladling food, for example, for suffering children in Zimbabwe – Charles was little seen or heard. He scored one private coup, which caused him some quiet, if cruel, satisfaction; Diana was visibly annoyed, on returning early from a holiday with her friends Lucia Flecha da Lima and Rosa Monckton, to find that Charles was using a junior member of his staff, Alexandra 'Tiggy' Legge-Bourke, as a surrogate stepmother to their sons. Harry's mother was especially upset by a front-page photo of her smiling son sitting on Tiggy's knee in a royal Range-Rover. In Diana's mind, Charles was using Tiggy to keep the boys happy while he blithely continued his normal routine, leaving them behind at Balmoral or Highgrove while he went shooting or hunting. But the boys seemed to like Tiggy, and Diana was forced, for now, to bite her tongue. Charles, meanwhile, continued to keep a very low public profile.

Or so it seemed. In 1993, according to official records, Charles undertook eighteen state functions, fifty charity events, twelve environmental and sixteen architectural engagements; attended eight occasions promoting healing and complementary medicine, twenty meetings involving the Duchy of Cornwall; visited Cambridge, Derby, Birmingham, Stoke-on-Trent, Yorkshire and Kent, as well as Mexico, Poland, Czechoslovakia, Turkey and four Gulf states. He founded the Prague Heritage Fund, took the chair of the Royal Collection Trust and also fitted in thirty-five miscellaneous functions 'promoting a range of good causes'.[5]

From his point of view, in other words, it was business as usual, worthy but dull stuff, unreported by a press still obsessed with his wife and mistress. Even to those around him, however, Charles's *faux-naïf* act was wearing a bit thin, as was his insistence on pursuing lost causes. On issues like architecture he had been so publicly discredited that there was little point in his spin doctors trying to draw attention to his speeches and engagements; much the same applied to holistic medicine and organic farming, princely obsessions of little or no interest to a public more concerned about his apparent betrayal of the world's most popular woman. A party to launch the Prague Heritage Fund was marred by his failure to appear in person, and his over-eager aides' hijacking of the occasion to discredit Diana; and his visit to Czechoslovakia was obscured by the use of that gas-guzzling Bentley. Even the chair-manship of the Royal Collections Trust, scarcely the most onerous of tasks, earned him little more than criticism about the Windsor wealth, its exploitation of visitors to Buckingham Palace to pay for the Windsor fire, and its failure to share the national art collection with the nation.

All occasions seemed to inform against Charles, or win him precious little of the positive publicity his press office craved. Too busy dealing with his private life, Aylard's propaganda machine was getting nowhere. While Jonathan Dimbleby and his film crew soldiered on – 'For a whole year,' said a senior figure at the Prince's Trust, 'it felt more like we were working for Dimbleby than for Charles'[6] – the results were still a year away, as was his twenty-fifth anniversary as Prince of Wales. While his aides ran out of ideas, Charles chose to pour his heart out to the prime minister.

In October 1993, out of the blue, a puzzled John Major suddenly received a letter bemoaning the public's loss of faith in people in public life. The Prince deplored as 'incredibly sad' the growing tendency to snipe at public servants as people with 'jobs for life' who waste the taxpayers' money. It is doubtful that Major, his mind more on the backbench revolt of his party's Eurosceptics, recognized this as a *cri de cœur* from a man who regarded himself as a much-maligned public servant, constantly accused of wasting tax-payers' money. But the PM's reply was suitably emollient, welcoming the prince's unexceptional remarks and blandly agreeing with him about 'the importance of the public services'.[7]

Major, in truth, was understandably playing a double game. Prompted by his foreign secretary, Douglas Hurd, who had been charmed by the princess and her quest to become an unofficial ambassador for Britain, Major held several sympathetic meetings with Diana and promised her his help. The prime minister suggested to Buckingham Palace that the princess might, with government support, prove a valuable asset to Britain on the world stage, using her global popularity to promote the country's image abroad and win valuable export deals for Britain. The Palace replied with an emphatic negative. That role, it firmly told Downing Street, was reserved for the heir to the throne.

So Charles now decided the time was right to break cover. On the eve of a trip to the Gulf states, on which he had invited along a *Financial Times* correspondent to report his work for British exports, he made a speech in Oxford 'praying' that the West could overcome its 'unthinking prejudices' against the Muslim religion and 'join forces with Islam' against Saddam Hussein's assaults on Iraq's Marsh Arabs.

Any attack on Saddam was likely to earn Charles favourable headlines, at the price of upsetting the Foreign Office, who accused him of jeopardizing the lives of three Britons then held in Iraq. But the speech went much further in its praise of Islam – 'part of our past and present, in all fields of human endeavour', which had 'helped to create modern Europe' and was 'part of our inheritance, not a thing apart'.

> More than this, Islam can teach us today a way of understanding and living in the world which Christianity itself is poorer for having lost. At the heart of Islam is its preservation of an integral view of the Universe. Islam – like Buddhism and Hinduism – refuses to separate man and nature, religion and science, mind and matter, and has preserved a metaphysical and unified view of ourselves and the world around us.[8]

Widely reported the next day, Charles's speech naturally had the Church of England muttering in its collective beard. Its future Supreme Governor seemed more intoxicated by Islam than by Anglicanism, on which, according to the Archbishop of Canterbury, he had 'given up'.[9] Charles's description of the 'unmentionable horrors' perpetuated by Saddam's regime, and the 'obscene lies' used to justify them, were meanwhile condemned by the FO as 'ill-judged', 'mistimed' and 'delivered without proper consultation'. Mrs Julie Ride, wife of one of the three Britons jailed for ten years for 'illegally entering' Iraq, said the prince's speech was 'not very helpful . . . His comments were pretty out of hand.'[10]

The prince's infatuation with Islam would soon lead him to form an advisory committee on Islamic matters, housed in his Institute of Architecture, thus blessing it with a much-needed financial boost from Middle Eastern potentates. Patron of the Oxford Centre for Islamic Studies, he first took an interest in the religion when the publication of Salman Rushdie's novel *The Satanic Verses* brought down a potentially fatal fatwa on the British writer in 1987. Perversely, perhaps, Charles came down on the side of the Ayatollah Khomeini, as he revealed in 1992 over dinner in Paris with the French philosopher Bernard-Henri Levy. The prince, according to Levy, launched into an attack on Rushdie, then approaching his fifth year in hiding, insisting that he was 'a bad writer'. Politely disagreeing, Levy conceded that Charles was entitled to his view. When the prince went on to protest that Rushdie was costing the British taxpayer too much, however, it struck the French philosopher as 'a bit steep'.*

'And the Crown of England?' Levy replied. 'Have you never asked yourself how much the Crown of England costs the British taxpayer?' Charles did not, apparently, come up with an answer.[11]

The membership of the prince's Islamic committee comprises a Roman Catholic and six Anglicans, including two bishops, as well as five Muslims. All are anxious to assert that the Prince of Wales is not, as is sometimes wondered, drifting towards conversion to Islam. 'People come up and ask me if he has become a Muslim,' says one of them, Dr Zaki Badawi, Egyptian-born principal of the Muslim College in London. 'I assure them that he is a very committed Christian, and there is no conflict at all between his Christianity and an appreciation of Islam.'[12]

But there are those in high clerical places who wish the prince was a more committed Christian than he appears. 'It would help if he loved the Church of England a bit more,' said the former Archbishop of Canterbury, Lord Runcie. The prince's views were 'so inconsistent . . . He would go in with the *Spectator* gang on "the lovely language of the Prayer Book", but then he would say, "Instead of interfering with politics, the Church should be creating centres of healing in the inner cities – ought to be bringing together the spiritual, the intellectual and the architectural" . . . I think he'd given up on the Church of England before I arrived [in 1980].' Although 'quite pious', Charles was 'deeply into Laurens van der Post spirituality . . . I don't think he took the Church of England very seriously.' The Archbishop's relationship with the prince was 'friendly', but 'I couldn't get much depth out of it. He is a mass of contradictions . . . so that the public don't really know where they are.'[14]

---

* France seems to bring out the worst in the prince. Also in 1992, the gourmet in him overcame the diplomat as he made an impassioned speech in favour of French cheese. Within months, back in France, the agronomist in Charles was mounting a defence of protectionist French farmers, thus compromising Britain's position in the already embattled GATT talks, and alienating the UK farming community, of which he considers himself an enlightened leading member. 'It was', to one observer, 'a characteristic contribution: well-meaning but, in political terms, breathtakingly ill-judged.'[13]

*

The night after his Oxford speech, Charles organized a 'Shakespeare evening' in the ballroom of Buckingham Palace, at which his own handwritten letters had secured the services of such titled luminaries as Sir John Gielgud, Sir Derek Jacobi and Dame Judi Dench. A celebration of his Shakespeare summer school for young would-be actors at Stratford, it took place before an invited audience of 'the great and the good', without one youngster, including his own sons, in sight. Diana, of course, would have stuffed the place with youth at the expense of those ageing grandees, and invited the cameras in to record the results.

It was a measure of the state of play, as the war of the Waleses moved towards its climax, that such an idea never even crossed the mind of the prince or his advisers. Not merely did they lack the princess's natural instinct for public relations; Charles's sense of royal propriety is such that it would not occur to him to invite schoolchildren to an event at the Palace that was portrayed as being laid on in their interests. As he sat down to dinner that night with theatrical knights and corporate fat cats, only too ready to give money to the Royal Shakespeare Company for the privilege of dining at the Palace, the prince was far more at home among the great and the good. To his authorized biographer, indeed, this was an evening quite out of character with the 'starchy formalities' normally associated with Buckingham Palace. The prince brought to the evening 'an élan ... redolent of the age of Prince Albert'.[15]

But this neo-Albert lacked the common touch. Everything he came into contact with seemed to be turning to base metal. Now Charles's plans for his 'model village' at Poundbury faltered seriously, to the point where he had to convene a weekend 'crisis' summit, while Diana regained the initiative in the battle for public attention. Although she had always benefited from the attentions of photographers, she was now complaining that they would not leave her alone. 'You make my life hell!' she had recently shouted at paparazzi who jostled her and the young princes as they left a London cinema. But the final indignity came that November, when she beheld the front page of the *Sunday Mirror*, adorned by a series of photographs of herself working out at her London health club. Dressed only in a revealing leotard, the princess was shown with her legs apart as she pushed up a shoulder press. The most voyeuristic photos of her yet published, they were also the least flattering; her emergent cellulite was but one detail of her naked thighs over which the nation pored that weekend. 'It was', in the judgement of one magazine editor, 'a crotch shot, plain and simple.'

She had, of course, been completely unaware that the pictures were being taken. The culprit turned out to be the gymnasium's manager, a New Zealander named Bryce Taylor, who had bored holes in the walls of his office to secure a scoop worth a six-figure sum. Against Palace advice Diana sued the *Mirror*, securing an injunction to prevent the paper or its daily sibling publishing more of Taylor's pictures. Amid the ensuing controversy, the princess won the support of Parliament, press and people against an editor who admitted he was a 'scumbag' and a photographer who was unrepentant. 'What I did was sneaky, surreptitious and pre-planned,' admitted Taylor. 'I don't make excuses. It was underhand. But if I told you I had an absolutely legal scam, which didn't hurt anyone and would make you a million pounds, wouldn't you say yes?'

On the eve of a court case in which Diana would have been grilled by one of Britain's most forceful barristers, Geoffrey Robertson, an Australian with republican sympathies, a settlement was reached in which Taylor was effectively paid off to disappear and keep his mouth shut. For Diana, accused by Charles's camp of courting the publicity, even co-operating with the photographer, it was more than she could take.

'Those pictures', she said, 'were horrid, simply horrid.' In early December, at a charity function at the Park Lane Hilton, the princess announced that she was withdrawing from public life. In a voice charged with emotion, she pleaded for some 'time and space' after more than a decade of incessant attention, both on- and offstage.

> When I started my public life twelve years ago, I understood that the media might be interested in what I did. I realized then that their attention would inevitably focus on both our public and private lives. But I was not aware of how overwhelming that attention would become, nor the extent to which it would affect both my public duties and my personal life, in a manner that has been hard to bear.

Over the next few months, she continued, 'I will be seeking a more suitable way of combining a meaningful public role with, hopefully, a more private life.' She could not be making this sort of statement without 'the heartfelt support' of the British public, whose 'kindness and affection have carried me through some of the most difficult periods' and whose 'love and care have eased the journey'.[16]

As the public bemoaned the apparent loss of its beloved princess, there were those who saw Charles's hand behind his troublesome wife's departure, albeit temporarily, from the public stage. In her speech Diana had referred to the support offered her throughout her ordeal by the Queen and the Duke of Edinburgh, but conspicuously failed to mention her husband. 'Did She Go or Was She Pushed?' was the question asked even by the magisterial *Times* newspaper.

In fact Charles had been forewarned of the speech by his mother, to whom Diana, as a matter of courtesy, had given advance notice of her intentions, and he had tried to talk her out of making it. Far better, surely, to phase out her public engagements, if she so wished, without 'grandstanding' in public like this. But Diana was adamant: she owed her public some explanation of her decision. 'The pressure was intolerable then,' she explained, 'and my work was being affected. I wanted to give one hundred and ten per cent to my work, and I could only give fifty. I was constantly tired, exhausted, because the pressure was so cruel . . . It was my decision to make that speech because I owed it to the public to say, "Thank you. I'm disappearing for a bit, but I'll come back." '

Besides, she added, it was always a good idea to 'confuse the enemy'. So who was the enemy? 'The enemy was my husband's department, because I always got more publicity, my work was more . . . was discussed much more than his. And, you know, from that point of view I understand it. But I was doing good things, and I wanted to do good things. I was never going to hurt anyone, I was never going to let anyone down.' They wanted to 'undermine' her, she said, 'out of fear', because 'here was a strong woman doing her bit, and where was she getting her strength from to continue?'[17]

All that remained, after his wife had left her adoring fan club in a state of shocked dismay, was for 'the enemy' to wonder publicly 'why someone so anxious for seclusion should have chosen to stage such a melodramatic exit'.[18]

*

Charles spent that weekend with Camilla at Highgrove. Their relationship remained so clandestine that few could know this, least of all the Venerable George Austin, Archdeacon of York, who nonetheless chose this moment to declare the prince unfit to be King. 'He made solemn vows before God about his marriage, and it seems – if the rumours about Camilla are true – that he began to break them almost immediately.'[19]

As the media floodgates opened again, with Austin's assault coming so hard on the heels of Diana's 'time and space' speech, the Palace could think of nothing to say. In due course, Austin would be crudely abused on Charles's behalf as 'a minor cleric of Pickwickian demeanour and modest accomplishments well-known for his eagerness to animadvert on public issues'.[20] At the time, the equally Pickwickian figure of Nicholas Soames again chose to fill the void left by the Palace, now preoccupied with the need for denials that Prince Andrew had AIDS or Prince Edward was gay.

Mustering all his new authority as a junior government minister ('a triumph', to one senior parliamentarian, 'of birth over ability'[21]), Soames dismissed the renewed calls for Charles to step aside in favour of William. Always ready to go out on a limb for his future king, as indeed when taunting female MPs in the chamber with sexist remarks, the portly son of the late Lord Soames – redolent, like his party at the time, of a bygone age – declared that 'being heir to the throne is not an ambition but a duty, and one which will befall him on a sad moment later in his life'. Charles would 'inherit the throne and that is the end of the matter', declared Soames, adding for good measure that Austin's 'hugely unrepresentative vapourings' had filled him with 'outrage and disgust'.[22]

Soames's own vapourings soon looked like a rather hasty rush to judgement. Among leading churchmen who boldly spoke out in Austin's support was the Revd Tony Higton, a member of the Synod of the Church of England, who had also 'reached the conclusion', albeit 'with great sadness', 'that Prince Charles is not fit to be the next King of England'. Higton spoke for many more reticent rank-and-file churchmen, mindful of the Scriptures, when he declared that Charles could become king only 'if he totally denies adultery with Camilla Parker Bowles'. If that were not possible, he should 'make a public expression of remorse and penitence', confirming that 'the romance was over'. Failing either of these options, 'I have to say that I think he is unfit to be king, and it would be better if the Crown passed straight to Prince William – provided he maintained the highest standards in his own private life.'

Higton conceded that both Church and people 'require higher standards from people in public places today than we did in the past', adding that he felt it his duty to take 'a firm stand' on adultery. 'I think it is very unfortunate if people in such high places as Prince Charles cannot behave morally.'[23]

Charges of hypocrisy were levelled, quite reasonably, at public figures who chose to pass judgement on the prince's morality in an age when more than a third of British marriages end in divorce, and most major institutions of British life, from Parliament to the Church itself, were constantly beset by sex scandals. Charles's problem was his putative role as Supreme Governor of the Church of England. History bore witness to countless adulterous princes and kings; but senior members of the Anglican Church, itself in a state of some disarray, felt the need to take a stand on the morality of the man next in line to become its titular head.

Yet again, Charles was caught in a timewarp fraught with irony; in previous centuries, whose values he cherished more than those of his own, his private life would have been far less likely to become the subject of public debate. As it was, Charles faced not merely the hostility of a Church struggling to justify its continuing existence, but a public whose natural loyalty to the monarchy, as a symbol, above all, of moral values, was severely stretched by his conduct.

On the day that Soames leapt to his defence, Charles made an official visit to Southwark, south London, to meet 'Gateway Project' volunteers providing job training and accommodation for unemployed and homeless people. The headcount of those waiting to see him was thirteen photographers, ten reporters and two members of the public. On the same day Diana was in Belfast, on a visit not announced in advance for security reasons. The count there was 30 photographers, 10 reporters and 160 members of the public. An opinion poll that month showed that now a negligible number of Britons, merely 3 per cent, blamed Diana for the break-up of the marriage. Only Fergie, the topless, toe-sucking, adulterous Duchess of York, commanded a lower public approval rating than the heir to the throne. A leading Labour MP, Frank Field, was calling for a committee of privy counsellors, chaired by the prime minister, to supervise the upbringing of Princes William and Harry.

It was a bleak midwinter indeed at Sandringham, with Diana spending Christmas Eve there with her sons but departing on Christmas morning after the family's annual parade to church. Back at Kensington Palace, she ate Christmas lunch alone off a tray, brooding about the beloved boys she had left behind with the alien Windsors. Next day she flew to Washington, to spend a few days with her friend Lucia Flecha da Lima, whose husband had been transferred there from London. 'I cried all the way out and all the way back,' said Diana, 'I felt so sorry for myself.'

It was the first time in her life she had ever travelled anywhere alone – 'a very strange sensation, liberating but rather frightening.' On the way home, Diana spent a night at the Carlyle Hotel, New York – the first time she had ever stayed alone in a hotel suite. 'No-one telling me what not to do. It was wonderful.' She discovered the joy of room service, cable TV, 'even' (giggling) 'blue movies'. Then the phone rang, and she realized there was no-one but her to answer it.

'Hello,' said the hotel switchboard, 'is that Lady Di?'

'No,' replied Diana.

'Sorry, ma'am, is that the Princess of Wales?'

'Yes.'

'Well, there's a man on the phone says he's your husband. Says his name is Charles Windsor and he's calling from a payphone down the block.' At this point, when telling her story, Diana would pause to insert a few footnotes: 'First of all, my husband' – the word was spat out venomously – 'never rings me. Second, he wouldn't know what a payphone is. And third, even if someone explained it to him, he wouldn't have any money in his pocket to put in the slot . . . So I took the call.'

Diana had worked out that some enterprising passerby had glimpsed her furtive flit from limo to lobby, done a double-take, and tried his luck from a local call box. In recognition of his enterprise she chatted to him for forty minutes, preserving his privacy by refusing to reveal what they talked about. What she loved about the story was the thought of this stranger subsequently doing the rounds of Manhattan bars, telling anyone who would listen: 'You'll never guess who I just talked to . . .'

'Yeah,' she would drawl the inevitable reply, 'and I'm the Queen of Sheba!'[24]

Charles might have been pleased to leave this dismal landscape, were it not for the lack of enthusiasm with which he contemplated another visit to Australia, reluctant to be drawn into its developing debate about abandoning the monarchy. On 26 January – Australia Day, celebrated as the anniversary of the arrival of the first British settlers in 1788 – the prince was standing at a microphone before a convivial throng in Tumbalong Park, in Darling Harbour, Sydney, waiting to present prizes to schoolchildren, when a young man suddenly ran towards the platform, apparently firing shots, and Charles's protection officer dramatically barged the prince out of his line of fire.

This 'demented' person – the prince's own word[25] – turned out to be one David Kang, a twenty-three-year-old student of Cambodian extraction, protesting about the plight of the 'boat people' in Australia; his 'gun' was in fact a starting pistol, and the 'shots' he was firing were blanks. But the prince was not to know that, nor indeed were the horrified spectators, one of whom thought, 'Oh my God, it's Kennedy all over again.'[26] Charles, testified another, 'had a bewildered look, but showed no sign of fear or panic'.[27]

'It's all right for you,' Charles told the audience, 'you've had a drink.' Later that day he duly delivered the keynote speech of his visit, arguing that it was the sign of 'a mature and self-confident country' to reconsider its constitutional arrangements. Back home in England, the Prince of Wales's grace under pressure generated the first positive headlines in as long as he could remember.

CHAPTER SEVENTEEN

'THE SADDEST DAY OF MY LIFE'

ON 4 APRIL 1900, WHEN A YOUNG ANARCHIST TOOK A POT-SHOT AT the Prince of Wales in Brussels, the future King Edward VII promptly telegraphed his mistress, Mrs Alice Keppel, to assure her that he was unharmed.[1] In Sydney almost a century later, his great-great-grandson telephoned her great-grand-daughter to say much the same.

It was proof positive, if proof were needed, that the Charles–Camilla relationship was on again, if indeed it had ever been off. During the prince's reluctant tour of Australasia, it emerged from his own staff that he had been 'in touch' with Camilla throughout, which rather gave the lie to a story that appeared while he was still there, the very weekend after the 'blanks' attack. Anxious to capitalize on the sudden spate of positive headlines, those tireless 'friends of Prince Charles' had been back in action. MY DUTY BEFORE LOVE, yelled the front page of the *Mail on Sunday*. PRINCE CHARLES SEVERS ALL LINKS WITH CAMILLA PARKER BOWLES.

Under the byline of Nigel Dempster, the recipient of those counter-productive leaks about Diana's thirtieth-birthday party, Charles was said to have 'renounced' his friendship with Camilla. 'He has decided to sacrifice his close friendship with the mother-of-two for the sake of his duty to the country,' wrote Dempster. 'The prince has resolved, after months of heart-searching, to remove any obstacle to his succession by finally severing their twenty-four-year relationship.' According to 'a royal confidant', the prince had made 'an irrevocable decision' on the matter. Charles recognized that, if he wanted to be king, which he did, 'there is no room in his life for Mrs Parker Bowles'. The prince had decided they must henceforth 'lead separate lives, which cannot cross at any point'. Camilla herself was said to be 'frantic'. She was 'very unhappy' about the fact that the prince was 'no longer taking her calls'.[2]

In fact, of course, the prince took her call in Australia that very day, to discuss that very story, about which he was furious. Charles was angry less about its inaccuracy than about the fact that his name was being mentioned at all in connection with Camilla's. There were those in his circle who were counselling him to abandon his mistress, as his only hope of public rehabilitation; the prince believed, quite rightly, that he could detect their hand behind the story. And they were defying his orders. Before leaving England, on a tour designed to restore some of his tarnished reputation at home, he had left strict instructions with both staff and friends to desist from leaking stories, however well intended, about himself and Mrs Parker Bowles. The disappearance of her name from the newspapers, especially in the context of his, was the prince's only chance to rise above the legacy of 'Camillagate'.

So the following month, when an Italian tourist burgled Charles's apartment in St James's Palace, his office sternly denied that those famous cufflinks with the intertwined 'C's were among his haul of jewellery. Those cufflinks, said the Palace, had never existed. Nor, it seemed to imply, had Mrs Parker Bowles.*

Camilla was being whited out of the public photos of the prince's entourage, while occupying pride of place at his side in private. They would ride with the Beaufort Hunt on alternate days, to avoid the least chance of being photographed together; she pottered about her garden while he played polo; unselfishly, she stayed away from her usual haunts, from social gatherings to race meetings, if he planned to attend. By night, however, or during those weekends when Charles's sons were with their mother in London, Camilla was still the mistress of Highgrove, the prince's openly acknowledged hostess at house-parties with their intimate circle.

In March he had a chance to make amends for the previous year's débâcle over the Warrington memorial service, as he

---

*In May 1998, when the stolen booty was finally returned to Charles by this latter-day 'Raffles', police listed the haul as including love letters from Camilla, five brooches, six gold buttons, a gold watch, two jewellery boxes, a clock – and five pairs of cufflinks.

happened to be on Tyneside when a deranged gunman invaded
Hall Garth School near Middlesbrough, stabbing a twelve-year-old
pupil to death and injuring two others. Charles altered his schedule
to divert to the school, where he arrived with a lavish wreath. For
ten minutes he spoke to the children and staff involved in the
attack, telling them how he had coped with the loss of
Mountbatten, and urging them not to bottle up their feelings. 'We
were very touched by his visit,' said the headmaster, Peter Smith,
'and the trouble he obviously took to make it right.' The next day's
headlines duly suggested that Diana had no monopoly on the
caring, compassionate face of royalty.

But Charles's respite was brief. The launch that month of his
architecture magazine, *Perspectives*, served only to draw attention
to the failure of Poundbury, just as its closure four years later (with
losses approaching £2 million as its circulation slumped from a
launch figure of 20,000 to barely 5,000) would highlight the continuing problems of his Institute of Architecture.

A speech that May denouncing the fad for 'political correctness',
in which he urged his future subjects to resist the forces of
'intellectual fanaticism', attracted much less attention than the loss
at Balmoral of his beloved Jack Russell terrier, Pooh. When Pooh's
sister turned out to belong to Camilla, who was said to be con-
soling the prince in his loss, it signalled the demise of the six-month
campaign to conceal her continuing role in his life. Again he began
to sink in the public esteem. This was a man who had now tried to
sell the nation two lies: the first about a happy marriage, the
second about a non-existent mistress. As so often in his life,
Charles was proving his own worst enemy.

And the following month, as if to dispel all doubt about his
capacity for misjudgement, he made the biggest mistake of his life
– volunteering for the role of prime prosecution witness, against
himself.

For eighteen months Jonathan Dimbleby and his team had been
toiling on a 600-page book and a 150-minute television film about
the prince. They had been granted almost unlimited access to every
department of his life, private and public, even his letters and
diaries. Officially, this unprecedented media event was designed to
mark the twenty-fifth anniversary of Charles's investiture as Prince
of Wales; unofficially, it was part of a long-term game plan,

masterminded by Richard Aylard, not merely to enhance the prince's tattered public image but to win acceptance for Camilla as his consort. It was also, of course, Charles's personal riposte to Diana's assault on him via Andrew Morton.

Both book and film covered the prince's public work to the point of tedium – an attempt to demonstrate, in Dimbleby's own words, that the prince was 'thoughtful, sensitive and intelligent', with a 'quick wit and a warm way', a 'daunting' range of commitments – a 'diligent' man, driven by 'a powerful sense of duty and destiny'.[3] But both broadcaster and prince had made a fatal miscalculation. Only ten seconds of those 150 minutes remained in the minds of the 14 million Britons who watched *Charles: The Private Man, The Public Role* on the ITV network on 29 June: the agonized moment in which the heir to the throne, would-be Supreme Governor of the Church of England, admitted that, yes, he had committed adultery with Mrs Camilla Parker Bowles. Camilla was the mainstay of his life – 'a great friend of mine . . . she has been a friend for a very long time, and will continue to be a friend for a very long time'.[4]

Thinking honesty the best policy, Charles was hoping to win the best of both worlds: respect for himself as a dutiful future king, devoting his time to the plight of the less fortunate, and thus indulgence of his private life, as a separated husband in love with another man's wife. Between them, Aylard and Dimbleby had persuaded him that the one could well lead to the other, if not at once, then in the longer term. It was a fatal misjudgement.

At the time, of course, Charles was still married to Diana, and Camilla to Andrew Parker Bowles. That in itself was enough to alienate most of his audience, the millions sufficiently loyal to the monarchy to expect him to set the nation some sort of moral example. Those who could not care less about his relationship with Camilla – people of their age, with less stringent moral standards – were also those indifferent to the monarchy, and interested in Charles merely as a celebrity in distress, an interesting case study in the art of the sales pitch. The vast majority, however, were fans of his wife, who could not forgive him the betrayal to which he now confessed, and could not believe he was rash enough to do so. The underlying irony, of course, is that honesty was to prove an effective policy for his wife, endearing her to the nation; in Charles's case, it had entirely the opposite effect.

The prince's version was that he had enjoyed three affairs with Mrs Parker Bowles: the first before her marriage in 1973, the second after she had her children, the third since 1986. This last, he insisted, had not happened until his own marriage had 'irretrievably broken down'. But it had happened. So that caveat, too, was soon forgotten as the prince himself caused a collective gasp around the nation, gave journalists licence to delete the dread word 'alleged' before the much more satisfying word 'mistress', outraged the most devout monarchists as much as the most rabid republicans, and launched a damaging debate in the Church of England which lasts to this day.

Whatever Everyman's view of Charles's public confession of adultery, it was the final indignity for Andrew Parker Bowles, the loyal courtier whose discretion had been stretched to extremes, but who was now publicly branded a cuckold. For two years Charles had asked him to postpone any thoughts of divorcing Camilla; the prince, as always, was anxious to preserve the status quo. The gallant brigadier, who also held the honorific post of Silver Stick-in-Waiting to the monarch, had endured public and private taunts; his heartier friends had taken to addressing him as 'Ernest Simpson'.

Some in his circle even thought he rather relished the notoriety. 'Having your wife bonked by the future King of England', as one put it, 'lends cachet.' But now his patience snapped. Whatever the prince's wishes, Parker Bowles had always intended to postpone his divorce until he left the army – an institution he loved, and to which he wished to cause minimal embarrassment. But his military career had now peaked; from commanding the Household Cavalry, he had been transferred to the rather unlikely command of the Royal Army Veterinary Corps.

The first non-veterinarian to be given the job in the corps' 200-year history, Parker Bowles found himself beset by more controversy when his appointment precipitated the resignation of its colonel commandant, Brigadier Robert Clifford, after more than thirty years' service with the RAVC. 'I have just been notified by the director that his successor is Colonel A. H. Parker Bowles OBE, late Blues and Royals,' wrote Clifford to the Ministry of Defence. 'As Officer Commanding Household Cavalry, Silver Stick-in-Waiting to HM The Queen and Steward of the Jockey Club, he is no doubt eminently qualified for the promotion, but he

is not a veterinary surgeon.' The clear implication was that the husband of Prince Charles's paramour had been found a role which
had 'less to do with his want of professional qualifications and
more to do with his extra-mural activities and friendships'.[5]

Now Parker Bowles was accused of 'ducking' foreign postings,
preferring, for reasons no-one could quite bring themselves to
spell out, to stay in London. As the Royal College of Veterinary
Surgeons joined in the dispute, forcing the Ministry of Defence to
limit his remit to 'management' rather than 'clinical' matters, the
brigadier felt understandably hard done by. His distinguished
service career was ending on a sour note, in a less than glamorous
posting, fraught with unseemly politics. Due to leave the army,
anyway, at the end of 1994, he now set in train legal proceedings
that would formalize his divorce from Camilla as soon as possible
thereafter.

Diana, meanwhile, chose to be seen out and about on the
evening of Charles's televised confessions, looking happy and self-
assured as she attended a glitzy fundraising dinner at the
Serpentine Gallery in Hyde Park. In a short, slinky black evening
dress, she greeted her friend Lord Palumbo with a kiss on the
cheek, then bubbled her way through a receiving line arranged by
the American magazine *Vanity Fair*. The princess, who had
declined Dimbleby's invitation to take part in the film, had also
turned down his offer of an advance screening. 'My first concern
was for the children,' she said. 'I wanted to protect them.' When
eventually she did see it, she added, 'I was pretty devastated myself.
But then I admired the honesty.'[6]

The logical consequence of Charles's adultery was their own
divorce – a subject on which he declined to be drawn. It was 'not
a consideration in my mind', he said; it lay 'very much in the
future'. Diana, too, would brook no mention of what she called
'the D-word'. She did not want a divorce, she argued, and she
would certainly not be the one to start proceedings. 'I'm not going
anywhere. I'm staying put,' she insisted, arguing that it was
Charles who had asked her to marry him, so it was he who must
make the first moves towards 'unmarrying'.

Again Diana cast herself in the role of victim. It sat awkwardly
with her new-found self-confidence, but it worked with her
adoring public, to the point where Charles found himself obliged
to return to the counter-attack. His irritation with Diana's huge

weekly bill for clothes and beauty treatments, which he was, of course, still paying, somehow found its way into the tabloid press. Diana's worst fears were being vindicated: the 'men in grey', alias 'the enemy', were back at work to discredit her.

That summer, the tabloids somehow got hold of the fact that she had apparently been making anonymous phone calls to the art dealer Oliver Hoare, an old friend of both the prince and princess. A mystery caller had been dialling Hoare's number, then hanging up if his wife answered the phone. Sometimes the caller stayed on the line without speaking, which alarmed Hoare and spooked his wife Diane. An expert in Islamic art – he had been on some of Charles and Camilla's trips to Turkey – Hoare at first feared the possibility of a terrorist assault on his family. So he called in the police, who tapped his phone and traced the calls back to Diana's private line at Kensington Palace, to her mobile number, even to her sister's home on weekends when the princess was staying there.

Diana steadfastly maintained her innocence, blaming the anonymous calls on a delinquent schoolchild, but only the most devout loyalists failed to accept her guilt. The clear inference was that she had been having an affair with Hoare, who had declined to press charges. When his ex-chauffeur spoke to the press of a 'love nest' in Pimlico, where the couple had enjoyed 'secret assignations over a four-year period', both denied it emphatically. 'What have I done to deserve this?' said Diana via the only journalist she felt she could trust, Richard Kay of the *Daily Mail*. 'I feel I am being destroyed.'[7] For a while the Hoare marriage collapsed under the pressure, but the couple were later reconciled. Charles looked on in dismay, worried at the effect on the children. 'They are the ones who will suffer from all this,' he was quoted as saying. 'It will all be played back to them when they return to school.' His once close friendship with Hoare was broken off, and has never been resumed.

Otherwise, Charles seemed to have found unwonted peace of mind since his separation from Diana. Friends spoke of him as happier, more relaxed, more confident and far less prone to bouts of depression. They had seen his sense of humour return, and with it a *joie de vivre* that had for several years been 'stifled by melancholy'.[8] His main problem that autumn was the book through which this approved self-analysis was communicated to the outside world, published, with singular ill-timing, just as the Queen left on an official visit to Russia, the first by a sitting British monarch since the 1917 revolution.

Back home, his mother's historic handshakes in the Kremlin were upstaged by Charles's portrayal of her via Jonathan Dimbleby as a cold, distant parent with whom he had never been able to share his troubles. He was 'emotionally estranged' from both his parents, craving affection that they were 'unable or unwilling to offer'. His father was a bullying tyrant who had pushed him into marriage with Diana against his own better judgement. Passages excised from the author's manuscript on the Palace's insistence contained even harsher judgements of Philip from his beleaguered son.

As for Diana, Charles's portrayal of her via Dimbleby is distilled simply by a few highlights from the book's index: 'volatile behaviour ... jealousy of Camilla Parker Bowles ... alleged suicide attempts ... resentment of the prince's interests ... attempts to control the prince's life ... self-absorption ... psychiatric help ... outshines the prince ... persuades the prince to drop some of his friends ... disagreements about the children ...'[9] The text described Diana as 'hysterical ... obsessive' and prone to 'violent mood swings ...' Through Dimbleby, to one observer, Charles made it clear that Diana was 'nothing more than a hired womb'.[10]

The prince's indiscretions hurt and enraged his parents, 'shocked and horrified and disappointed'[11] his wife, offended his siblings, agonized courtiers and bemused his future subjects. Their effect on his children can only be imagined. In the process he even managed to upset such dropped names as Barbra Streisand, once his 'only pin-up', who had recently raised hundreds of thousands for the Prince's Trust by breaking a twenty-eight-year absence from the stage to serenade him with 'Someday My Prince Will Come' at the Wembley Arena. He confided that, while Streisand no doubt still had great sex appeal to the masses, for him her charms had faded.[12] After permitting Dimbleby to share this with the world, Charles felt obliged to make amends by inviting Streisand to Highgrove for a weekend. Even his staff were amazed by the singer's advance demands: white flowers only in her bedroom, an omelette of egg whites for breakfast. But they talked philosophy deep into the night, and apparently made their peace.[13]

Five years on, both book and film are now referred to by Charles's staff simply as 'the Dimbleby débâcle'. Rarely one to take responsibility for his own mistakes, the prince would eventually pin the blame on the man who had talked him into it, Richard Aylard, whose own marriage had by then broken up amid the pressures of royal service. The same was true of his protection officer, Colin Trimming. Diana was not the only one to talk of a 'marital jinx' surrounding the Prince of Wales.

The beginning of 1995 saw the formal end of the Parker Bowles marriage; by the year's end, the brigadier was already remarried to an 'old friend', Rosemary Pitman. Another marriage which broke up that year was that of the England rugby captain, Will Carling, whose name had been romantically linked with the Princess of Wales. There was more to Carling's friendship with Diana, believed his wife, Julia, than the rugby coaching he gave her sons.

The princess panicked, and mounted a rearguard action via sympathetic journalists like Richard Kay, insisting that her relationship with Carling was innocent. 'I don't need a lover,' she said. 'I am happy on my own. I've got my children to keep me company, and my work to keep me going.'[14] Diana feared that such publicity would be used against her in the event of a formal end to her marriage; above all she feared losing custody of her children, like her mother before her. Still the princess insisted that she did not want a divorce, and still Charles maintained that nothing was further from his thoughts.

But the warfare was continuing, in a scrappy, spasmodic way, and few could see how divorce could be postponed much longer. Whatever damage it might cause the Crown was as nothing to the gradual corrosion currently taking place. There was no modern precedent for a divorce settlement between the heir to the throne and his potential queen, and the power of the Palace was never to be underestimated. Feeling that she was losing ground in the public-relations war, Diana secretly hatched the most daring coup of her young life.

One Sunday in early November 1995 the princess gave all her staff an unexpected day off. Against the advice of her closest friends, and behind the backs of her senior staff, she had decided to give a major interview to the BBC's flagship current affairs programme, *Panorama*. For some months a *Panorama* reporter named

Martin Bashir had been researching one of the programme's occasional specials on the monarchy; now, with the same lucky timing as Andrew Morton, he found himself with a major scoop on his hands.

Bashir and a minimal crew, equipped with specially lightweight compact cameras, slipped into Kensington Palace undetected that Sunday morning. Diana was alone apart from one trusted adviser and friend, the psychotherapist Susie Orbach. The princess had told no-one at the Palace of her plans, and the *Panorama* team had also maintained conditions of the utmost secrecy. Even after the filming, while the programme was being edited, its existence was kept from the BBC's governors, some of whom had close contacts with the Palace. Whether or not Diana was well advised to give the interview, the conditions in which it was made were proof positive of her fear of the power of those 'men in suits' whom she now dubbed her 'enemies'.

Diana did not inform the Queen that she had given the interview until a week before its transmission on Monday, 20 November. The BBC chose Charles's forty-seventh birthday, 14 November, to reveal its forthcoming scoop. Diana had deceived the two most senior members of her staff: her press secretary, Geoff Crawford, who felt obliged to resign at once (to return to Buckingham Palace, where he soon became the Queen's press secretary); and her private secretary, Patrick Jephson, who also departed within weeks, quitting the royal employ to enter public relations. The Queen's revenge was to terminate the BBC's sixty-year monopoly on the monarch's annual Christmas message, which would henceforth be shared with ITV, the commercial network.

Britain's electricity generating board quite rightly catered for a huge surge at 9.40 p.m., after the BBC news, that Monday evening in November. Made up with heavy eyeliner, to look browbeaten and defensive, Diana spoke with astonishing candour of her depressions, her eating disorders and her suicide attempts. Chronicling the slow collapse of her marriage, she said that Charles had made her feel 'no good at anything . . . useless and hopeless and a failure in every direction – with a husband who loved someone else'. He had taken a mistress, Camilla Parker Bowles, and then blamed her for getting upset about it. 'There were three of us in this marriage,' as she put it, 'so it was a bit crowded.' Charles had told her she was 'an embarrassment' to the royal family, and unstable enough to be committed to an institution.

The princess went on to admit her own adultery with James Hewitt, conceding that she was 'absolutely devastated' when his collaboration on a lurid book betrayed their secret. In one phrase she subsequently came to regret, she said she no longer harboured any hope or desire of becoming queen, but would rather be 'a queen in people's hearts'. Someone, she said, 'has to go out there and love people and show it'. The phrase stuck, becoming the butt of much satire before her death, and one of the epitaphs most favoured by the millions who mourned her. At the time, she felt it drowned out another message she took the chance to convey: that she wanted to be an 'unofficial ambassador' for Britain: 'I've been in a privileged position for fifteen years. I've got tremendous knowledge about people, and I know how to communicate, and I want to use it.'

She had allowed her friends to co-operate with Morton's book, she admitted – failing to reveal the truth that she herself had made secret tape-recordings – because 'I was so fed up with being seen as a basket-case. I am a very strong person and I know that causes complications in the system that I live in.' Questioned about the prince's attitude towards her within their marriage, she went on: 'I think that I've always been the eighteen-year-old girl he got engaged to, so I don't think I've been given any credit for growth. And, my goodness, I've had to grow.' Still maintaining that she did not want a divorce, Diana implied that her 'enemies' in the Palace were cornering her into one. They were trying to push her out of public life. But this was one princess who would not 'go quietly'. She would 'fight to the end, because I believe that I have a role to fulfil, and I've got two children to bring up.'

And did she think her husband would ever be king? 'I don't think any of us knows the answer to that. Who knows what fate will produce, who knows what circumstances will provoke?' It was a devastating rejection, couched in the most calculated terms. 'I would think that the top job, as I call it, would bring enormous limitations to him. I don't know whether he could adapt . . . My wish is that my husband finds peace of mind, and from that follows other things.' Yes, she suggested, because of this 'conflict', Charles might well be happier if he allowed the throne to pass directly to their son William.[15]

On the BBC's *Newsnight* programme, immediately after the

interview, Charles's friend Nicholas Soames denounced Diana's performance as 'toe-curlingly dreadful', suggesting that she was 'in the advance stages of paranoia'. But the popular response was overwhelmingly supportive. Twenty-three million Britons watched the interview – twice as many as had watched Dimbleby's film on Charles the previous year – which was later seen by more than 200 million viewers in around a hundred countries. Polls showed public support for Diana running at 85 per cent.

Among senior commentators, even the most devout monarchists were sufficiently impressed to take her side. In contrast to the princess, 'an exceptionally able woman in a group of not particularly able people', wrote Lord Rees-Mogg, its former editor, in *The Times*, Soames had appeared 'a blustering fool, a grotesque confirmation of everything she had been implying about the inadequacy and malice of the royal establishment'. Diana's performance had been 'one of the most formidably skilful political performances by a woman since Margaret Thatcher'. The public would sympathize with her position as 'a badly supported royal bride, with her postnatal depression which the royal family did not at all understand, with her distress at finding her husband was in love with another woman'. So wronged was Diana that, unlike Charles, she could even get away with adultery. As a 'neglected' wife, predicted Rees-Mogg, she would even be 'forgiven for having fallen for the dubious charms of the miserable Hewitt'.[16]

The historian Paul Johnson also called Diana a 'heroine', whose sexual indiscretions he too forgave because 'she was chaste when the prince began the adultery game'. Johnson went on to quote Jane Austen on Queen Caroline, the estranged wife of the unpopular George IV. 'She was bad, but she would not have become as bad as she was if he had not been infinitely worse.'[17]

Charles simply could not believe what Diana had done. It was billed, of course, as her reply to Dimbleby, which had in turn been his reply to Morton. The tit-for-tat went all the way back to his piqued leak about her thirtieth-birthday party, now more than four long years earlier. But this was an interview too far. The prince saw it as a gratuitous attack by the princess on himself and his family, even on the institution of monarchy, the princess as an urgently needed ploy to strengthen her bargaining position in the divorce negotiations. Whichever one of them was nearer the truth, it worked on both counts.

Elizabeth II had now had enough. It took less than a month for the Queen to write formal letters to both her son and daughter-in-law, on 17 December, arguing that it was now time to settle their differences 'amicably and with civility' by agreeing to a divorce 'sooner rather than later'. Leading clerics were dismayed by the spectacle of the Anglican Church's Supreme Governor not merely sanctioning, but actively encouraging divorce; yet the Queen had been advised by her prime minister, John Major, with the knowledge and support of the Archbishop of Canterbury, that the monarchy could not withstand much more of the Waleses' civil warfare.

Taken aback by the Queen's letter, Diana consulted her lawyers, who urged caution. Cancelling her plans to spend Christmas with the royal family at Sandringham, she wrote no immediate reply. Charles responded to his mother at once, and positively. If he had been pushed by his father into marrying Diana, he now appeared to have been pushed by his mother into divorcing her.

At stake, as the lawyers settled into months of bargaining, was Charles's bank balance as much as Diana's dignity and lifestyle. By now, the prince was ready to concede almost anything to rid himself of his turbulent spouse. What he most definitely did not want was more than the minimum contact with her necessary to stay in touch with his children. So Diana's request to share the facilities of his office in St James's Palace, where he would also make his home after the divorce, was high on his hit-list. She could stay in their marital apartment at Kensington Palace, which would also provide valuable continuity for William and Harry, but she should also establish her own office there. He, of course, would finance it.

Whatever 'lump sum' was finally agreed for the global settlement, he insisted that it must be paid in instalments. The Prince of Wales, according to public statements from his office, was not as well-off as people might imagine. In truth, his insistence on a 'drip-drip' financial settlement was his way of regulating Diana's public behaviour. If she broke the discretion clauses written into their agreement – if, God forbid, she wrote or authorized another book – he could cut her off without a penny.

The matter of her 'HRH' – those three magic letters signifying seniority in the royal pecking order, then meriting a statutory bow or curtsey – was one of supreme indifference to him. But it wasn't to Diana, who was told by friends that she had been careless to offer them as a bargaining chip for other more practical aspects of the settlement, especially a lump-sum pay-off rather than the humiliation of instalments. When the details leaked, even as the lawyers were still negotiating, there was a public hue and cry about the insult to their princess: the appalling potential prospect, for instance, of her having to curtsey to Fergie, ex-Duchess of York, whose divorce settlement was itself still under negotiation.*

The talks dragged on through Christmas, when Diana's impetuous nature got her into potentially deeper legal trouble. She was tired from an overnight trip to New York, where she had collected a Humanitarian of the Year award from Henry Kissinger, when she arrived at London's Lanesborough Hotel for what, this year, was something of a charade: the Prince and Princess of Wales's annual Christmas party for their staff.

Entering separately from Charles, Diana strode straight over to 'Tiggy' Legge-Bourke, whom she now resented sufficiently to believe that she, too, was having an affair with her husband. The room was naturally agog to see Diana head straight across the room towards her *bête noire*, and whisper in her ear. Whatever it was that she said – 'seven words' was all the newspaper-reading public were told – was enough to send Tiggy reeling from the room in tears. By the weekend, the prince's right-hand woman was publicly threatening to sue his wife.

With Charles's encouragement, Tiggy consulted one of Britain's leading libel lawyers, Peter Carter-Ruck, who promptly issued a statement deploring 'a series of false rumours which are a gross reflection on our client's moral character'. They were, of course, 'utterly without the very slightest foundation'. Charles was even prepared to countenance Tiggy mounting a lawsuit against his wife; but again it took wiser heads to counsel caution. Diana, they told him, would relish her day in court; there was no telling what soiled private linen she might choose to wash in public before the

*One of the reasons Diana's divorce proceeded so slowly was the determination of her lawyer, Anthony Julius of Mishcon de Reya, to use the Duchess as a 'canary'. When the princess asked him what this meant, Julius explained that miners used to dispatch canaries into the pits as a precaution against lethal gases; on the same principle, they would use Fergie as their legal 'stalking-horse'.

divorce settlement gagged her for life. Quietly, Tiggy was persuaded to let the matter drop.

In a gross breach of protocol, meanwhile, breaking a lifetime's habit of dealing promptly with all correspondence, Diana never replied to the Queen's letter of December. Three times she was nudged to do so by Her Majesty's private secretary, who also happened to be her own brother-in-law, but ten weeks elapsed without any response. All this time the lawyers' meters kept ticking, to the point where Charles himself intervened with a desperate letter to Diana, pleading for a meeting. Finally she agreed, but set strict terms. She would come to his office at St James's Palace, at 4.30 p.m. the following Wednesday, 28 February 1996, on condition they could meet alone. No lawyers, no aides, no flunkies. To the dismay of his staff, Charles agreed.

'They'll probably bug us, anyway,' snorted Diana as the last of her husband's staff backed reluctantly out of the room, where she and Charles then talked alone for forty-five minutes. By her own account, filtered to the world via Richard Kay, she told him, 'I loved you, and I will always love you because you are the father of my children.' The prince was horrified when this appeared in print the next morning. By his own account of the meeting, Diana's attitude was a more graphic version of her public threats on *Panorama* three months earlier: 'You will never be king. I will destroy you.'[18]

Later that afternoon, without warning Charles or the Queen, Diana issued a statement revealing that they had agreed to an uncontested divorce. It was, she said, 'the saddest day of my life'. Unilaterally, and thus most provocatively, she offered the world her own version of the conclusions negotiated with Charles:

> The Princess of Wales has agreed to Prince Charles's request for a divorce. The Princess will continue to be involved in all decisions relating to the children, and will remain at Kensington Palace, with offices at St. James's Palace. The Princess of Wales will retain the title and be known as Diana, Princess of Wales.

So furious was the Queen about Diana's pre-emption of Palace protocol that she gave aides rare authorization to leak her displeasure. The Queen was 'most interested', mused her spokesman, to hear that the Princess of Wales had agreed to divorce her son.

Her Majesty was even more interested, it seemed, in Diana's version of the details of the settlement, especially concerning the little matter of her title, which would naturally 'take time' to resolve.

In the event, it took four more months. Diana's lawyers began by asking for a lump-sum settlement of £50 million. But the complex legal negotiations went way past mere money and titles to jewellery, office space, even freedom of movement. The one matter about which there was never any argument, for all Diana's fears, was custody of the children – to be shared equally.

'The one thing I was terrified of', she constantly told friends, 'was losing the children. Once I knew they were safe, that the royal machine was not going to steal them from me, I didn't really care about anything else.' If a mite disingenuous, the remark was made with an almost scary passion. 'Not Charles,' she would say when she had calmed down. 'Not Charles, but his people. And his family – some of them.

'Not Margaret, who was always very nice to me, even defended me against the occasional tirades of my father-in-law. Nor Anne, who could be surprisingly supportive at times. Her relations with Charles have always been pretty strained, anyway. Nor, of course, the Queen, who behaved pretty impeccably throughout, would have me to tea from time to time to see how I was doing. I got the impression – though she never, of course, said so in so many words – that she knew her son was not an easy man to be married to. I think she thought I had been pretty hard done by. Okay, by now I'd done things that had upset her, like *Panorama*, but I always had the feeling she disapproved of his relations with you-know-who. Not the woman herself – the Queen, for some reason, rather likes her – but the way he handled the affair. She was devastated when it became so public. Still is, I think. I don't know that she would ever approve of Charles marrying her. And he wouldn't without her blessing.'

By now, Diana herself was past caring. Among her ever-changing circle of friends, she was famous for saying different things to different people, playing them off against each other for her own, often devious, ends. On this occasion, however, she chose to say, 'Oh, what the hell, let him go ahead and marry her. Why not? It might bother a lot of people – and I would watch all the fuss with some enjoyment – but it wouldn't bother me any more. I'm past caring.'[19]

Diana's post-marital title proved one of the most contentious issues. Though Charles still professed not to care, his father certainly did. Philip felt that Diana had unforgivably let down the 'family firm', and must be punished. He was outraged by her apparent demand that any future children by another man should bear hereditary titles. Nor could he forgive her for suggesting that Clarence House become her official residence on the death of the Queen Mother. Philip wanted Diana to be downgraded to Duchess of Cornwall, minus her HRH.

For a while, those three magic letters became a sticking point in the negotiations. As Diana reconsidered her previous offer to drop them – with widespread public support, as the mother of the future king – Charles's lawyers even made the absurd suggestion of HFRH, Her Former Royal Highness. Then one day, according to Diana, her son William said to her, 'I don't care what you're called. You're Mummy.' That settled it. She agreed to surrender her royal status, in return for a title very similar to her current one: Diana, Princess of Wales.

When the final terms were made public, Diana received a lump-sum settlement of £17 million (most of which Charles had to borrow from his mother), plus £400,000 a year for an office and staff separate from his. She was stripped of her HRH, formally expelled from the royal family, and her name deleted from the prayers said for them each Sunday in churches throughout Christendom. Letters patent to that effect were rather brutally published, on the Queen's personal instructions, in the 'noticeboard of the Establishment', the London Gazette.

The Prince of Wales was granted a decree nisi on 15 July, which became absolute on 28 August. The fifteen-year ordeal was finally over for both of them – if not for their children. Yelled the front page of the Sun, on Diana's behalf: BYE BYE, BIG EARS.[20]

PART FIVE

After Diana

CHAPTER EIGHTEEN

'I WILL NEVER REMARRY'

BACK IN 1993, AS CHARLES MOVED OUT OF THE KENSINGTON PALACE apartment they had shared for twelve years, the first thing Diana did was to change the locks – a purely symbolic gesture, as neither ever carried keys. At Highgrove, meanwhile, Charles himself lit an equally symbolic bonfire, on which he threw everything that reminded him of Diana, including many of their wedding presents. Staff were dismayed to see the prince sipping champagne as he watched objects not merely of some value, but of potential use to others, going up in smoke. Then he got Camilla to take charge of a complete refurbishment of the house, blotting out all memory of his former wife.[1]

That was at the apex of their mutual antipathy, when neither knew how the story of their 'fairy-tale' marriage would end. Now that they did, some three and a half years later, Charles went in for a further act of symbolism. At the end of August 1996, the weekend before his divorce became absolute, the prince took another step down the long road of trying to win his mistress public acceptance as his consort. After a telephone tip-off from 'a well-spoken woman', giving 'precise instructions' on how to find their 'remote Welsh love-nest', long-distance lensmen snatched the first photographs of Charles and Camilla together for twenty years.

The 'remote Welsh love-nest' was in fact a retreat in the hills of Powys, which the couple had been using undetected for some time: Glyn Celyn House near Brecon, the home of Camilla's former brother-in-law Nic Paravacini, a millionaire banker, and his second wife, Sukie.* So close did the journalists get that they were even able to describe, with irresistible innuendo, how Camilla was looking when she got up, an hour after the rest of the household, at 8.30 a.m. 'Her hair still tousled from the night before, she couldn't resist taking a lingering look across the valley from the window as she wrapped herself in a plain white dressing-gown.'[2]

Charles, according to a friend, was 'sick and tired of all the lies, and the running from one secret address to another . . . It looks tawdry and shabby.' Indeed it did, not least to the Church of England, whose senior clergy weighed in to warn the prince sternly against remarriage. The clerical consensus was voiced by the Bishop of Manchester, the Rt Revd Christopher Mayfield: 'Many Christians feel that a marriage, once made, cannot be ended, so remarriage is not possible. It would cause considerable unhappiness and bring tensions to the surface.' It would be 'highly anomalous' to have an admitted adulterer as Supreme Governor of the Church, agreed the Bishop of Woolwich, the Rt Revd Colin Buchanan. 'I don't think, quite frankly, the public could tolerate a Queen Camilla,' added the Bishop of St Albans, the Rt Revd Robert Taylor.[3] Even Charles's own vicar at Highgrove called on him to drop the title Defender of the Faith. It was time for the prince to show some 'penitence', said the Revd John Hawthorne of St Mary the Virgin, Tetbury. He could never remarry and still expect to become Supreme Governor of the Church of England.[4]

The British people expressed their collective view via an opinion poll summed up in one headline as GOD SAVE QUEEN ANNE.[5] They would rather change the constitution by promoting Charles's divorced and remarried sister, the Princess Royal, than contemplate Queen Camilla. The public mood was captured by Sir James Hill MP, chairman of the Commons constitutional committee: 'To walk out in public together at this stage is tantamount to sticking two fingers up to public opinion, which is still behind the Princess of Wales.' Added another Tory MP, David Evans: 'It is totally unacceptable for them to be seen together in public as a couple. They are both divorcees; it would be virtually flaunting his mistress. They have to behave like royalty, not like the rest of us . . . It will be goodbye to the royal family if this goes on.'[6]

As Charles became a free man, nonetheless, Camilla appeared to

---

* Paravacini's first wife was Andrew Parker Bowles's sister, Mary Ann.

be readying herself for a proposal. With the discreet help of a public relations adviser, she laid on a series of photocalls to make herself appear more human, the tip-offs to Fleet Street usually coming from that same 'well-spoken woman' who had alerted them to the prince's 'dirty weekend' in Wales. She was also said by friends to be taking unwonted trouble over her appearance. 'She has been dressing more smartly, tidying herself up . . . She is re-acting to the feeling that the Princess of Wales was always smart, but she was, frankly, a scruffbag.' Then her friends went quiet. 'We don't want to be ostracized if she becomes the prince's consort . . . We no longer joke about her being the prince's mistress. After all, she may become our future queen.'[7]

Camilla was conspicuously absent from Charles's side at Balmoral that week, despite being dubbed 'the love of his life' by no less a fig-ure than the constitutional historian, Lord Blake, a close friend and adviser to the Queen. Blake spoke up for the prince: 'If they are gradually seen together it will mean an acknowledgement of a liaison which has been going on for a very long time . . . Being seen together will gently start the process. Many people will be delighted if Prince Charles can find happiness in a new marriage.'[8] Again, the British public did not seem quite so sure. One newspaper poll showed 88 per cent against Charles marrying Camilla; another had 54 per cent demanding that, if he must marry her, he should renounce the throne.[9] 'The kindest thing might be for Charles to go quietly,' suggested the Guardian. His love for Camilla 'will have to survive persecution and humiliation on an epic scale . . . Who could seriously condemn the prince if he were eventually to come to the conclusion that the game is not worth the candle?'[10]

But Charles, for the present, had other priorities. As Diana avenged the loss of her HRH by dropping her royal patronage of a hundred charities, retaining only a 'big six', her public pronounce-ments carried an air of menace: 'I'm not going to be a recluse.' On the day her divorce became final, the princess defiantly flashed her wedding and engagement rings at the cameras when visiting the English National Ballet. Bowed down again by his own relentlessly negative publicity, Charles took his revenge by writing to forty shops and businesses: 'With effect from 2 September 1996, any expenditure incurred by or on behalf of Diana, Princess of Wales, should be invoiced directly to her office, Apartment 7, Kensington Palace, London SW1.'

Via the usual friends, meanwhile, he leaked his dogged determination to have both Camilla and the Crown: 'I will never give them up. Never.' His great fear, he was quoted as saying, was that Diana would hold him 'captive for years to come'. Every time he and Camilla appeared in public together, Diana would 'play to the cameras', looking wistfully at her wedding ring through red-rimmed eyes. 'It will never end until she finds someone else,' he was quoted as saying. 'It will go on and on.'[11]

Diana, as it happens, did appear to have found someone else, at least for the moment: handsome, wealthy, forty-one-year-old Christopher Whalley, whom she had met during her daily workouts at the Harbour Club in west London. The couple were even caught on closed-circuit camera together at Harvey Nichols, the fashionable Knightsbridge store where they liked to meet for lunch. But Prime Minister John Major, on his annual visit to Balmoral that September, cautioned the Queen that Charles should 'slow down' his rush to win acceptance for Camilla.

Suddenly, Charles's 'friends' changed tack yet again. He would 'reign alone – for the sake of the monarchy' was the new consensus whispered to the mid-market press. 'I will always put duty first,' Charles had apparently told his mother. 'HRH has no intention of remarrying,' said an unnamed senior courtier. 'It simply does not feature in his plans. Neither he nor Mrs Parker Bowles would do anything to undermine or damage the monarchy.' For once, Camilla herself chipped in with a leak to the lower end of the tabloid market, specifically the *Sun*, to the effect that she had vowed 'never' to marry Charles.

But they would continue meeting privately, indeed all but living as man and wife at Highgrove, except when William and Harry were there. Camilla's favourite hunter, Molly, had been stabled there for more than a year; her two Jack Russell terriers, Tosca and Freddy, had long known their way around the estate. Camilla's inherited wealth had been badly eroded by the crisis at Lloyds insurance, where she suffered disastrous losses as a member of no fewer than ten syndicates. After her divorce she had sold her marital home, and now lived with her elderly father in Ray Mill House, just twenty minutes away from Highgrove at Laycock, Wiltshire. The £850,000 lodge was purchased for her by a trust led by Lord Halifax, an old friend of the prince, who also happened to be married to the former wife of Andrew Parker Bowles's brother, Richard.

Three years before, at the time of the publication of the 'Camillagate' tapes, Camilla had come close to a nervous breakdown. At the time, according to her friend Charles Benson, she was 'shattered . . . It was akin to letting the general public into your bedroom'.[12] Now, as the inevitable divorces had resulted, the tape was remembered less for the Tampax than the touching late-night banter of two reckless lovers. So Camilla felt free to take her future boldly into her own hands. At Bowood House, the nearby Wiltshire home of her friends the Earl and Countess of Shelburne, she made her first public appearance as a charity worker, hosting an evening which raised £10,000 for the National Osteoporosis Society, founded to combat the 'brittle-bone' disease which had inflicted a painful, lingering death on her mother two years before. The invitation-only evening, strictly for loyalists from the forty square miles of hunting Gloucestershire nicknamed 'Beaufortshire' – or now, to some, 'Camilla-lot' – could not have gone ahead without Charles's tacit blessing. He was not present; but he was helping her in other, less visible, ways.

In October of the previous year Camilla had left a party at London's Ritz hotel separately from the prince, because of the scrum of photographers, but in one of his official cars, driven by his chauffeur, Andy Crichton. The following June she received the same VIP treatment to and from the thirtieth-birthday party of her godson Henry Dent-Brocklehurst, where, according to chums, she was looking 'unusually glamorous'. At Royal Ascot she drew gasps of admiration in a smart, fitted suit – no longer the dowdy country housewife of yesteryear. In September, within days of the Paravacini photo opportunity, she had smiled for pre-arranged cameras while picking up her children from her local railway station in Wiltshire.

Camilla was still the most reviled woman in England, according to frequent samplings of opinion, but she was clearly now trying to do something about it. 'The irony is that she is exactly the sort of person the British public admires,' said a friend since childhood, Broderick Munro Wilson. 'Where the Princess of Wales has been so clever is that she has manipulated the press and, because she is so photogenic, she has had a field day. So poor old Charles has turned out to be Big Ears and Camilla has turned out to be the Wicked Witch of Wiltshire, when nothing could be further from the truth.'[13]

Now, in mid-September, Camilla's statement to the *Sun* – to whose then editor, Stuart Higgins, she had long been close – considerately took the heat off Charles during the embarrassing indiscretions of Lord Runcie, the former Archbishop of Canterbury, that his marriage to Diana was 'arranged', that he had 'given up on' the Church of England, that he was into 'van der Post-type spirituality'. Lurking behind the 'new' Camilla, softening her image and helping out her prince from a distance, was the public-relations adviser Alan Kilkenny, a skiing friend of Charles, and his private secretary Richard Aylard.

But now it was also time for Aylard, the man who had advised Charles to confess publicly to adultery while masterminding Camilla's higher profile, to pay the price for the 'Dimbleby débâcle'. As constant polls continued to show huge public antipathy to Camilla, Charles fired Aylard as his private secretary, replacing him with a 'safe pair of hands' from the Foreign Office, forty-four-year-old Stephen Lamport, and a bright young spin doctor from the Press Complaints Commission, thirty-year-old Mark Bolland. 'As always,' Diana observed of Aylard's abrupt departure, 'when things go wrong, Charles blames anyone but himself.'[14] A 'new era of realism' at the Palace, according to strategic leaks that weekend, had 'friends of Charles' taking yet another new tack: now he would 'wait until his ex-wife remarries before making regular public appearances with Camilla'.[15] Of that, there was no immediate prospect.

October 1996 saw the wayward Fergie, Duchess of York, again relieving them all of the spotlight for a few weeks as two books about her, one by a psychic named Madam Vasso, the other by a supposed friend named Allan Starkie, revealed yet more extra-marital high jinx. The duchess had apparently made love to her Texan friend Steve Wyatt while pregnant with the Duke of York's child, even boasted of trying to brighten up her friend Diana's moribund sex life by teaching her how to use a vibrator within the sacred portals of Kensington Palace. The Queen convened a 'crisis meeting' over Fergie's mounting debts, now estimated at £5 million. The 'dirty duchess' was planning to write her own memoirs to get herself out of the red. What horrors would they contain?

Diana, Princess of Wales, was meanwhile carving her own niche as national carer-in-chief. Mid-October saw her at Harrods, chaperoned by its proprietor, her father's old friend Mohamed al Fayed, in support of the heart surgeon Sir Magdi Yacoub at a charity book launch. There had been much tut-tutting when Diana had been photographed in heavy mascara in an operating theatre, while watching Sir Magdi at work; she had since become close to him and his daughter. Why had she developed a penchant for attending open-heart surgery? 'Because I care. If I am going to comfort heart patients in hospitals, I need to know every detail of every stage of the process they have been through.'[16]

Some had other suspicions. The princess had recently been seeing a lot of a heart surgeon rather younger than Sir Magdi, Dr Hasnat Khan, whom she had first met the previous year through her acupuncturist, Oonagh Toffolo. When she flew to Pakistan to visit a hospital founded by Imran Khan, the cricketer turned politician who had married her old friend Jemima Goldsmith, she went out of her way to meet his family. Just how close was Diana to the dashing doctor? 'I want to marry him and have his babies,' she was quoted as saying when the tabloids began to run with the story. If this was indeed a romance, as was widely assumed, Diana was getting through many more men than her melancholy public persona might suggest.

But she was in no hurry to remarry. 'I'm looking for a man who understands what I'm about,' she told a lunch guest at this time. So what was she about? 'Caring. I'm about caring. I thought I'd married a man who understood that first time around, but I got it wrong. I'm not going to make the same mistake twice.' There were still traces of bitterness in Diana: Buckingham Palace was 'the leper colony', and the Queen Mother – who had part-engineered her marriage to Charles, and took his side when it broke down – was 'the chief leper'. But she was also, now the settlement had been reached, serenely self-confident: 'They can't get me now. In fact, I think they're frightened of what I can do to them.' Above all, she felt sure that her son William would be Britain's next monarch. 'Charles will never be king. My intuition has always told me that.'[17]

The Nation Decides, an American-style 'confrontational' television debate on the future of the monarchy, got 1997 off to a grim start for Charles. Amid much heckling from an unruly studio audience, as panels of experts struggled to argue the cases pro and con,

Camilla's name was jeered every time it was mentioned, and the notion of a Queen Camilla overwhelmingly rejected again in a huge, nationwide telephone poll. Charles himself fared little better, top of the poll for 'doing more harm to the monarchy than any other member of the royal family', and again voted less popular than his sister, Anne. More than a third of the nation – 36 per cent – thought he would make 'a bad king'. Almost half – 48 per cent – believed Britain would no longer have a monarchy in fifty years.[18]

Broadcast live from the set of the spectacular show *Gladiators*, at the National Exhibition Centre in Birmingham, the chaotic programme was stridently disowned by many of its participants. Charles and his staff thought they could afford to ignore it. But the show had attracted a huge audience, given republican arguments an unwontedly wide airing, and inflicted yet more damage on the dignity of the monarchy. Some sort of response was needed. Diana was in Angola, in photogenic pursuit of her global campaign against landmines, when Charles's 'friends' again briefed the Sunday papers that he had told the Queen he would 'never' marry Camilla. This latest reaffirmation of his intent to be king did not constitute 'any kneejerk reaction to a gimmicky showbiz event', said 'sources close to the prince'. He had made it plain to his mother that he intended to continue his relationship with Mrs Parker Bowles, and was 'contemptuous' of courtiers who had pleaded with him to abandon her.

Shortly after his divorce, it was now confirmed, Charles had indeed expressed the hope that he and Camilla might one day be able to wed. But public opinion was now making that prospect increasingly remote. 'He is determined that he will do his duty and become king when the time comes. That is his overriding concern,' said an unnamed privy counsellor described as 'particularly close' to the prince. 'But, equally, he is not going to discard the woman he loves.' Camilla herself was putting no pressure on him to marry her. 'The truth is that they have known each other too long not to have considered all the complications involved in their relationship.'[19]

The truth was, as it remains, that Charles saw no alternative to the status quo, whereby he and Camilla continue to maintain as close a relationship as possible in private, hiding it from the prurient public, from Church and State, even (until very recently) from his sons. There were more important priorities, which Camilla's public presence in his life could only derail. The prince's new support team was launching what it saw as a five-year campaign to regain him the respect and affection of the British people, targeting the Queen's golden jubilee in 2002 as the moment to complete his rehabilitation. By then the monarch would be seventy-six years old, and the prince himself fifty-three; it would be a highly appropriate moment for him to take over more of the sovereign's public duties, becoming 'king in all but name'.

Part of the strategy, now that the divorce had become final, was to put an overdue end to the corrosive 'war of the Waleses'. Ever more confident in her own detached public role, Diana herself seemed ready to agree to a rapprochement, forging a better liaison between their newly separate offices, co-ordination of their public work, even joint appearances for the sake of their children as much as the monarchy. At Christmas, they had been seen together publicly for the first time since the divorce, chatting amiably as they attended William's carol service at Eton. This was now billed as the harbinger of a new *entente*; whether *cordiale* or not, it amounted to 'the thaw of the Waleses'.

A meeting of Charles's advisers on the morning following his drubbing on the television debate agreed that it was crucial to improve the projection of his public work. Here was a man who spent most of his life doing unsung deeds for the good of the nation, as he saw it, and yet was perceived primarily as an adulterer who had betrayed the world's most popular princess. Post-Aylard, the new team established a Prince of Wales management committee, consisting of only two 'outsiders' beyond the prince's private staff: both in their mid-forties, Julia Cleverdon was chief executive of Business in the Community, and Tom Shebbeare director of the Prince's Trust. The following day, under Shebbeare's auspices, Charles made a speech in Edinburgh warning of the failure of many young people to achieve their true potential. He looked and sounded unusually uncertain of himself, while Diana strode confidently through Angolan minefields. But his speech that day was merely part of the means towards a more ambitious end. The monarchy, according to Shebbeare, was consciously 'moving from being an institution principally famous for ceremonial occasions to an institution principally of value for what it can add to the country through public service'.[20] Charles was to be the symbol of that sea change.

As, so it seemed, was Camilla, who now took on her first official charity role by becoming patron of the National Osteoporosis Society. The Queen had approved the idea 'in principle'; a fund-raising gala was planned for September, at which there were hints that Charles might even make his first formal public appearance at his lover's side. Insofar as she was setting herself up as a rival public figure to Diana, however, Camilla seemed doomed to failure. The enterprising princess had taken a camera crew with her to Angola, and was now the subject of a moving documentary about her compassionate aid work in a special edition of a respected BBC religious programme, *Heart of the Matter*. With a commentary spoken by Diana herself, the film was also shown, in shortened form, at the première of Richard Attenborough's *In Love and War*, a screen adaptation of Ernest Hemingway's *A Farewell to Arms*. It was Attenborough who had first involved Diana in the Red Cross appeal to rid the world of anti-personnel landmines, over 100 million of which were scattered about some sixty countries; in Angola, Somalia, Cambodia and Afghanistan, one in every 350 people was a landmine amputee, many of them children.

Now Diana wanted to take her campaign to Bosnia and Cambodia, but the risks were deemed too high. Besides, she was already walking through a hazardous enough political minefield at home. Denied the government recognition she craved as an am-bassador for Britain, the princess faced protests from Tory MPs that she was a 'loose cannon', whose landmine campaign had drawn her into the political arena in the run-up to a general election. Unlike John Major's Conservative government, Tony Blair's Labour opposition had pledged to work towards a world-wide ban. 'She is ill-advised and is not being helpful or realistic,' said a government minister, Earl Howe. 'Britain is one of the goodies on landmines and we are helping to draw up a sensible worldwide package. We do not need a loose cannon like her.'[21] But Diana refused to be deterred – 'I am a humanitarian figure. I always have been and always will be' – and the ensuing furore damaged the minister and his party much more than her.

A year later, six months after Diana's death, Charles's media advisers would be busy projecting him as a 'caring, compassionate prince', picking up the mantle tragically torn from his ex-wife. For the sake of the monarchy, a newly compliant Fleet Street would be only too happy to play along. 'Prince Charles showed his compassionate nature when he visited a hospice,' read the none too inspired caption on a front-page picture in the *Daily Mail* in April 1998, showing Charles joking with the parents of two-year-old Ryan Cuell, dying of a rare genetic disorder.[22]

Twelve months earlier, in the spring of 1997, Diana was filling that role far too effectively for Charles to go anywhere near it. So his relaunch team came up with the idea of portraying him as 'a Renaissance Man, scholarly and sensitive, but also an action man as happy on a horse as holding a paint brush'. The vehicle was to be a series of museum exhibitions, *Princes as Patrons*, starting in Cardiff in 1998 and culminating in a 'big show' either at the Victoria and Albert Museum or even Buckingham Palace itself to mark the Queen's golden jubilee in 2002.

'What's not often seen,' explained Richard John of the prince's Institute, 'is that all the Prince of Wales's interests are about rejecting the post-war material culture, where everything is about short-term gain, to thinking about the wider spiritual aspect.

> In this respect, they are very much of a piece. He has a very holistic vision. His interest in alternative medicine complements his interest in organic farming, for instance, and even his views on the built environment. He thinks about the broad picture – he is not thinking about the next five years, but the next fifty.

Although the show was 'certain to be dominated by the prince's watercolour paintings', ventured one arts correspondent with tongue firmly in cheek, other exhibits 'might range from maquettes of "good" architecture, like his village of Poundbury in Dorset; the blue ski-suit he has worn for the past twenty years; pictures of him talking to the plants at Highgrove; jug-eared mugs; and perhaps a selection of his favourite Status Quo and Three Degrees albums'.[23]

At the time, the notion of Charles as a neo-Renaissance patron of the arts still invited such satire. He was far better known for attending every meet of his local hunt during the preceding six months, for fear that 'we won't be able to do this much longer'. Such insensitivity to public opinion seemed to be causing backstage dissent among his Palace staff. 'We can change things around for the prince,' said one despairingly, 'but I doubt if the prince can change himself.'[24]

The debate between the traditionalists and the 'modernizers' behind Palace walls took on an added urgency in May 1997, as a historic general election ended eighteen years of Conservative rule and elected the eager young Labour Party of Tony Blair by the biggest landslide since 1832. Blair was committed to nothing if not 'modernizing' Britain and its ancient institutions. At first it was far from clear what attitude he would take to the monarchy. Already he had proved the Tories wrong to think that a new royal yacht would prove a vote-winner; on the contrary, for the first time in living memory, Blair had gained popularity by taking on the Palace, pledging repeatedly throughout the campaign that he would 'not spend £60 million of public money on a new royal yacht while there are people queuing for beds in hospital corridors'.

But he had also ordered his shadow Welsh secretary, Ron Davies, to apologize publicly for calling the Prince of Wales 'unfit to be king'. The future government minister was forced into an embarrassing public climbdown after saying on Welsh television on St David's Day, while Charles was touring the principality:

> We are told that he spends his time talking to trees, flowers and vegetables and so on, yet we know that he encourages his young sons to go into the countryside and kill wild animals for fun, for sport. I do not think someone like that is the sort of person the majority of people in this country would look up to and respect. You must ask yourself the question: Is he a fit sort of person to continue the tradition of the monarchy? I have come to the conclusion that he is not.[25]

Labour's victory seemed to bring an overnight spring to Britain's step, as a tired Tory era characterized by 'sleaze' and 'fat cats' gave way to a fresh new optimism. The new prime minister, the youngest since William Pitt in 1783, walked to the state opening of Parliament while the monarch arrived from the other direction in a golden coach. Some of Charles's staff, notably Mark Bolland, were alert to the nuances of 'new' Britain, soon to be known as Blair's 'cool Britannia'. But was the prince? In vain did his staff plead with him to attend the FA Cup Final, the year's biggest soccer match, two weeks after the election. Football bores him. It may be the people's sport, in a 'people's Britain' run by 'the people's party'; but Charles was not enough of a 'people's prince' to miss a Saturday afternoon in the country.

Charles had known Blair since his days as shadow employment secretary at the beginning of the decade. But his real link with the new government came via the longstanding friendship of its spin-doctor-in-chief, Peter Mandelson, and Tom Shebbeare, who had worked together at the British Youth Council twenty years before, jointly publishing a pamphlet entitled 'Youth Unemployment – Causes and Cures'. Through Shebbeare, Charles had known Mandelson since 1991, when he flattered the strategist behind the redesign of the Labour Party's logo by greeting him with: 'Ah, the red rose man!' Unlike many of his colleagues, who saw reform of the House of Lords as a direct route to reform of the Crown, Mandelson was a devout monarchist, a working-class boy who went weak at the knees in the royal presence. Reviewing a new book on the British constitution six months after the election, with all the authority of the new government's minister without port-folio, he wrote, 'I share the author's belief in the efficiency and value for money which the monarchy brings.' Mandelson went on to praise 'the strategic foresight seen in the meetings of the Way Ahead group' (comprised of senior members of the royal family and their staff), which 'show its commitment to operating as a modern constitutional force in the twenty-first century'.[26]

Thanks largely to Mandelson, and his special relationship with Blair, the Prince of Wales established a 'partnership pact' with the new government, by which he would be kept in closer touch with its work and play an active role in its plans to help unemployed young people into work. Blair professed himself 'very touched' by a long, personal letter he had received from Charles after his election victory, outlining the work of the Prince's Trust and expressing the hope that they could enjoy a close working relation-ship. The prince repaid the compliment in kind, with the unusual step of writing an article for a Sunday paper, in which he paid tribute to the government's 'new deal' for the 250,000 jobless people under the age of twenty-five, and welcomed its plans for a national 'citizen's service', in which young people would work with the sick, elderly and disabled, and help clean up the environment.

That same evening, in a television interview with Sir David Frost to promote the Prince's Trust, he accused the education system of 'failure', arguing that decades of 'fashionable' teaching had left generations of schoolchildren without the vital skills needed for work: 'I believe that education needs to rediscover those important features which have been abandoned in the past thirty or forty years . . . and I don't believe it has served young people at all well.' His Trust, in fact, had been 'picking up the pieces of a somewhat failed system'. For all the prince's chutzpah, derided in other quarters, the new education secretary, David Blunkett, welcomed Charles's 'enthusiastic commitment' to what appeared to be New Labour ideals.

In the process, the prince again appeared to be entering the political arena by endorsing the new government's policies, and, by inference, bemoaning those of the outgoing Conservatives. Just as his ex-wife was being accused of meddling in politics, so now was the heir to the throne. The usual litany of rent-a-quote Tory MPs, desperate at the time for any publicity at all, were typified by Michael Fabricant: 'The *raison d'être* of the royal family is to be above and separate from the antics of party politics.' Charles rode the storm with apparent ease. 'The prince manages to walk a very fine line between doing and saying interesting things without becoming involved in party politics,' said Shebbeare on his behalf. 'If anything is true, the Labour Party is copying us.' When Mandelson teased the prince that he was 'a secret Blairite', Charles replied, 'I gather Mr Blair is a secret me.' Privately, he argued that the government was stealing his ideas.

Charles and Blair laid plans to discuss their potential 'partner-ship' while both were in Hong Kong the following month to officiate at the colony's handover to China. But the prince's relaunch as a major national player, in harmony with the new government's social ideals, was pre-empted within a month of the election by a minor car crash on a narrow country lane near his home in Gloucestershire. A woman was left trapped in her car in a ditch after swerving to avoid another vehicle that came over the hill towards her 'like a bat out of hell'. The other driver, also a woman, had 'scarpered' – or walked away from the scene without checking on her condition. It was Camilla, apparently in a hurry to get to Highgrove.

Thus did the world discover that the Ford Mondeo which Camilla had been driving was leased for her by Charles. The first call she made on her mobile phone was to the royal protection squad; clearly, Mrs Parker Bowles was now officially regarded as a security risk. Equally revealingly, all inquiries about the crash were handled by Buckingham Palace. Police duly investigated, but few were surprised when no charges were brought against Mrs Parker Bowles for leaving the scene of an accident. Charles had planned to 'go public' about their continuing relationship by throwing a fiftieth-birthday party for her at Highgrove the following month. But the car crash inadvertently revealed, somewhat ahead of time, that his lover already had the entire royal infrastructure at her disposal.

Diana was also in trouble at the time, for taking her under-age sons to see a 15-certificate film *The Devil's Own*, which could be accused of glorifying the IRA. In vain did she score a diplomatic success in Washington, taking her landmine campaign to the Clinton White House, and extracting a promise of a review of US policy. Rushing home to attend a meeting of the All-Party Landmines Eradication Group in the House of Commons, the princess was told by the Palace to pull out at the last minute because of Tory protests. It was a non-partisan meeting, with speakers including Parliament's only independent MP, the former BBC war correspondent Martin Bell; but the new government had now declared a formal ban on British trade in landmines, a moratorium on their use by UK forces and the destruction of all British stocks by 2005, and committed Britain to working towards a global ban. Like Charles, Diana was in danger of appearing to endorse a government policy opposed by the Conservative Party. Declaring herself 'extremely disappointed and frustrated', she let it be known that 'It seems she cannot do anything without someone using it as an excuse to attack her.'[27] This would become a central theme of what were to prove the last few weeks of her life.

Still Diana saw her campaign as a humanitarian issue, not a political one. Two weeks earlier Clare Short, the new international development secretary, had been in the audience when the princess spoke about landmines at the Royal Geographical Society. Now the prime minister intervened, if belatedly, to support her right to have attended the Commons meeting. Wrote her friend and fellow campaigner Lord Deedes, a former Tory minister:

She has focused attention on an enormous human tragedy, in which precious few politicians showed any interest until her expedition to Angola . . . To quibble about the way she pursues this cause is sad and rather silly. The refugee struggling home and crippled by a land mine will not be unduly troubled about who convened a meeting in the House of Commons on behalf of him and his kind.[28]

Diana's own views were again articulated via her closest friend among sympathetic journalists, Richard Kay of the *Daily Mail*:

The great problem for Diana is that divorce has thrust her into a semi-detached royal existence – sometimes a member of the royal family, as in anything to do with William and Harry, sometimes not. To an extent this has suited her. It has allowed her to choose what she does and when she does it, who she sees and who she doesn't. But the cost of independence has been high, not only to her but also to the country. It is hard to imagine Charles with his smooth, well-oiled and efficient staff finding himself in the predicaments that have bedevilled Diana this week. (It is equally hard to picture the prince entertaining his bored sons on a wet Sunday by suggesting a trip to the cinema.) There is no doubt that Diana's old enemies within the royal household took great satisfaction from her discomfort over the IRA film.

But she could not appeal to the Palace for support. 'She has, after all, the not unreasonable belief that the stripping of her royal title demonstrated the Palace's attitude to her. They just didn't care for her.'[29]

A public auction of many of her royal gowns in New York the following week, which raised £3.5 million for her charities, now looked like a deliberate farewell to royal life. It was her son William's idea, wrote Diana in a preface to the catalogue, that she clear out her cupboards at the start of her new life as an ex-royal, raising yet more money for her chosen charities.

With Camilla's birthday looming, however, July began with the first British television documentary on Charles's long-term lover, followed by another debate, this time on a BBC religious affairs programme, as to whether she could marry the prince. For once

Charles was 'not unhappy' about 'mature discussion' of his private and public future. Even his sternest critics, like the Archdeacon of York, seemed at last to be taking a gentler line: 'As a private person, mistakes can be left behind.' The public was being 'softened up' for an eventual marriage, but the Church must make up its mind. 'The pretence that nothing is happening at all, when everyone knows perfectly well that it is a relationship, is damaging.'[30]

In his new-found confidence, as it transpired, the prince was still misjudging the public mood. Over the next two weeks, as Charles duly hosted Camilla's fiftieth-birthday party at Highgrove, and Diana took their sons on holiday to the South of France, there was an uneasy sense that events were slipping out of control. The British people could not believe that the heir to the throne was so openly flaunting his continuing relationship with the woman who had broken up his 'fairy-tale' marriage. Nor could they believe that Diana chose to accept the hospitality of Mohamed al Fayed, the Egyptian-born owner of Harrods, *Punch* magazine, Fulham Football Club and other quintessentially British institutions, who had admitted bribing Conservative MPs, and who was still fighting a long drawn-out, as yet unsuccessful battle to win the British citizenship he had been denied by the previous government.

Charles tried to balance the inevitable media blitz on Camilla – will he, won't he make her his queen? – with his own blitz of ministers in the new government, eight of whom he met in one week. But it was to prove another losing battle. The announcement of 'close links' between the Prince's Trust and Labour's 'welfare-to-work' programme – a 'new deal' for unemployed youth – was drowned out by copious coverage of the Highgrove party, where photographers were surprised to be allowed free rein at the gate. Camilla herself smiled graciously for the cameras as she swept past in Charles's chauffeur-driven car, sporting a sparkling new diamond-and-pearl necklace he had given her. It was 'a wonderful evening', according to her friend Jilly Cooper, the novelist. 'Camilla looked absolutely radiant. The most striking memory I have is of the full moon which arrived early and stayed. I think it's a sign.'[31]

Did the match now have the government's blessing? When a junior minister, Tony Wright, suggested as much, Tony Blair publicly dissociated himself, describing the idea as 'fictitious and fantastic'. Unknown to Charles, the prime minister soon hosted a weekend party of his own, at Chequers, his country residence in Buckinghamshire. William and Harry played football in the grounds with Blair's young sons while their father agreed to give Diana government blessing for the role she had so long sought as an ambassador for Britain. Thrilled by the prospect of an announcement in the autumn, the princess prepared for a three-day trip to Bosnia – forbidden by the previous government – to keep up the pressure on landmines.

Charles, too, was keeping up a furious pace on both fronts, private and public. To test the public response, his office let it be known that he and Camilla planned a summer holiday together at Birkhall, the Queen Mother's secluded home on the Balmoral estate. He would also be attending her first major public function as patron of the National Osteoporosis Society in September. Behind the scenes, Peter Mandelson was advising them both on how to proceed towards winning the public round to the idea of their marriage. As the *Church Times* solemnly discussed how to rewrite the Coronation Oath, to accommodate the first crowning in British history of two divorcees, the Archbishop of Canterbury felt moved to reiterate his view that it would cause 'a constitutional crisis'. In Australia for a Church convention, the Archbishop said, 'As in any other family, mistakes are made, and I often say our job is not to apportion blame . . . It is true that remarriage would create a crisis for the Church. This is well known, but Prince Charles has said he has no intention of remarrying.' The historian Paul Johnson, whose views Charles had long since learned to ignore, felt moved to declare, 'Charles must choose: Camilla or the throne.'[32]

Events were moving fast on all fronts that August, as all the major players in the gathering drama went their separate ways for a summer break. Charles took his sons to Balmoral, staging a rare photo opportunity amid the mountain streams to reassert his role as their devoted father. The two women in his life meanwhile left the same airport in different directions within twenty-four hours of each other. At 6.40 a.m. on 22 August Camilla flew out from Stansted aboard a charter flight to join the Marquess of Douro at his family's ancestral estate in Spain. Twelve hours earlier, bound for Nice aboard the al Fayed private jet, Diana had left Britain for what proved to be the last time.

*

On her previous holiday with the Fayed family, six weeks earlier, the princess had astonished the travelling press corps by racing her motorboat alongside theirs, clad only in a leopard-skin swimsuit, to harangue them furiously for disturbing her vacation. She ended with the tantalizing, if baffling promise that 'You'll get a big surprise with the next thing I do.' To long-time critics like the *Daily Mail*'s Lynda Lee-Potter, her behaviour was becoming 'increasingly erratic'. But what could Diana have meant by that 'surprise'? Could it have been what the world now discovered: that she had fallen in love with Fayed's son Dodi?

As the nation debated the eligibility of her latest suitor, not without a dash of xenophobia, Diana and Dodi enjoyed a week cruising the Mediterranean in the Fayed yacht, *Jonikal*. This time around, far from begging photographers to leave them in peace, Diana seemed quite happy to proclaim her new love to the world, lying in Dodi's embrace in her swimwear in the full knowledge that both amateur and professional cameras were trained upon them. She didn't even seem to mind when the inevitable picture spreads upstaged her flying visit to Bosnia. In one of the last phone calls she made, Diana told Rosa Monckton that life with Dodi was 'yes, bliss'.[33]

The princess had first met Dodi Fayed in 1986 at a polo match sponsored by his father, and again in 1991 at the London première of Steven Spielberg's film *Hook*, which Dodi part-financed. In 1997 both were guests at a dinner party hosted by Diana's stepmother, Raine, with whom she had recently been reconciled. Dodi's father had been a close friend of her own, and regarded himself as something of a 'father figure' to Diana after Earl Spencer's death. 'She would come and see me all the time. She would come shopping at Harrods, and have a cup of coffee and a chat.'

That June Diana had dined with Mohamed al Fayed after an English National Ballet performance of *Swan Lake*, which he had sponsored. When his wife discovered Diana had no plans for the summer, she had invited the princess and her sons to join their family aboard his yacht *Jonikal* in the South of France. 'She was so happy in St Tropez,' said Fayed, 'because it was as if she had rediscovered what family life is all about, the security it can bring you . . . She was great fun. She never stopped laughing and giggling for the whole fortnight.' Dodi had taught William and Harry to water-ski. The princess and her sons had all written Fayed thank-you letters. Diana's said, 'I miss you all enormously. I think your entire flock are hugely special,' William's that the *Jonikal* was 'an amazing piece of kit, and I loved sailing in it'.

After that first holiday, Dodi sent Diana bouquets of pink roses at Kensington Palace, and the princess was seen scuttling in and out of his London flat in Park Lane. A romance seemed to be blossoming. The following week the couple made a discreet trip to Fayed's Ritz hotel in Paris, travelling in the Harrods jet and staying in a £7,000-a-night suite. Together they looked over the Windsor villa in the Bois de Boulogne, which Fayed was converting into a family home. For them? To Dodi's father, it was 'as if they had been struck by lightning'. Both had suffered the trauma of watching their parents divorce while still small children – Dodi had been two when his parents separated, Diana six – and both, unusually, had been brought up by their fathers without a mother's full-time love and attention. 'They compensated each other for what they had both missed in life,' said Fayed. 'I think Diana liked the fact that he had such a gentle character and was caring. He in turn thought she was so kind.'[34]

During their second cruise aboard *Jonikal*, this time alone together, Dodi gave Diana a silver plaque inscribed with a love poem. She in turn gave him a silver cigar clipper and a pair of her father's cufflinks. Her 'blissful' week was spoiled only by another interview that went wrong, this time with the French paper *Le Monde*, conducted before she left but published on Wednesday 27 August. The princess had to interrupt her idyll with Dodi to deny that she had called the fallen Conservative government 'hopeless' over the landmine issue. She had, she insisted, been 'stitched up'; the quote had been written in since she approved a transcript of the interview by fax. She did not, however, deny describing the British press as 'ferocious'.

> It never forgives anything. It is interested only in mistakes. Every good intention is diverted, every gesture is criticised. I believe that abroad is different. There I am received with kindness, they take me as I am, without judgement, without lying in wait for slip ups. The reverse is true in Britain. I think in my position any sane person would have left long ago. But I cannot. I have my sons.[35]

Diana's discomfiture coincided with the news that Camilla Parker Bowles was to open a London office, with a full-time personal assistant, to deal with her public life. The significance of this announcement, so soon after the princess had established her own office at Kensington Palace, separate from Charles's, was lost amid media outrage at her statement that she would have left Britain if it were not for her sons.

That weekend, as Diana flew with Dodi from Italy to Paris, the British Sunday press proved her right with a vengeance. Diana's behaviour was 'disgraceful', spluttered Sir Bernard Ingham, former press secretary to Prime Minister Margaret Thatcher. She was 'part of Labour's plot to wreck the monarchy', although she didn't realize it because she and Dodi had 'more brass than brains'.[36] Her behaviour throughout the summer had been 'erratic and extravagant', according to the *Mail on Sunday* columnist Jessica Davies. The princess was 'suffering from a form of arrested development ... To repay [British] affection with her recent comments is not only disloyal, it is a gross dereliction of duty'.[37]

Under the headline SAD WILLS WANTS DI TO DITCH DODI, the *News of the World*'s royal editor Clive Goodman meanwhile reported that 'troubled Prince William will today demand that his mother dump Harrods heir Dodi al Fayed'. The fifteen-year-old prince was 'deeply unhappy' about his mother's affair, about which he had been 'worrying since he returned from the South of France holiday' where it began. Diana's son now planned to 'confront' her about the matter.[38]

William, alas, would never have the chance to 'confront' his mother about her relationship with Dodi, though both Ingham and Davies would be forced to eat their words.* Just as Britain's Sunday papers were being rushed around Britain, Diana was entering a Paris underpass with Dodi in a Mercedes being driven at high speed by a drunken chauffeur, with paparazzi photographers in hot pursuit.

---

* The first editions of these papers were retrieved from outlets throughout the country, and both columnists apologized the following Sunday. Davies's readers had been 'out for blood'. 'I am more sorry than I can say that I caused further unnecessary distress on a deeply sad day,' she wrote. 'If I could take the article back, I would.'[39]

CHAPTER NINETEEN

'GOODBYE, ENGLAND'S ROSE'

CHARLES WAS POLE-AXED BY DIANA'S DEATH. AFTER THE ORDEAL OF breaking the news to their children, who had been due to return to their mother that afternoon, he took a long, lone dawn walk around the Balmoral estate, trying to gather his very confused thoughts. His main emotion, apart from concern for his sons, was guilt. Guilt about all the bad blood between him and his ex-wife, guilt about the way things had turned out between them. 'I know him well enough', wrote his friend Clive James that week, 'to be sure that since last Sunday he has been on the Cross, and wondering whether he will ever be able to come down.'[1]

But Charles's guilt was tinged with fear – fear that, in death, Diana might prove as damaging to his future as she had in life. Already the crowds gathering outside Buckingham Palace, bearing the first ripples of a tidal wave of flowers, were showing signs of dissent. They were angry that the Palace flagpole was the only one in sight with no standard at half-mast, as angry with the Windsors as with the media for hounding the princess into an early grave. This was the family that had rejected her, a year ago to the week, who had stripped her of her royal title and deleted her name from the prayers for the royal family. Now, as Britons awoke to the numbing news, the first pictures they saw on television that morning showed the royals arriving at Crathie Kirk, near the Balmoral estate, for a service at which the Queen had instructed that Diana's name not be mentioned.

Charles was seen sitting between his two bereft sons in the back of a royal limousine, in a black tie but vividly green suit, staring fixedly ahead in silence. Could he not put his arms around them? Could he not, on this of all days, have spared them this ritual royal duty? The prince's instincts were ruthlessly compared with Diana's, and he did not emerge well. Later that day he flew to Paris to escort her body home, leaving their sons in the care of his parents at Balmoral. Among 'Diana's Army', the millions gathering on the streets to mourn her, who found their instinctive loyalty to the monarchy stretched to its limits, this brought the first mutterings of serious discontent. 'How dare he go to bring her home?' was a typical reaction. 'What a nerve. He's the man who ruined her life.'[2]

What would they have said if Charles had *not* gone to Paris? In death as in life, Diana had landed the prince on the horns of an insoluble dilemma. He was damned if he did, damned if he didn't. Showing that he cared by bringing her home himself, her coffin draped in a royal standard to which she was not strictly entitled, seemed on balance to be the right decision. If it was not the beginning of a display of public mourning, showing Diana's distraught public that he shared the scale of their grief, it was a token of respect that would disarm sterner criticism.

Amid the crowds who flocked to pay her homage, queuing in the rain all night to sign books of remembrance, keeping open-ended vigil with prayers and candles, bringing so many flowers that the country soon ran out, were many who would never normally attend royal occasions – refugees from the disenfranchized minorities on the margins of modern British life. People disillusioned by politicians and royalty alike had looked to Diana, it became clear, as their only true champion in what seemed an alien world. If she was to some extent an anti-Establishment figure, carving out a niche for herself as a royal rebel, even a royal pariah, she can never have known the depth of the chord she struck with all manner of social outcasts, their kinship born of parallel feelings of rejection.

As grief-stricken as the most devout of monarchists, they had lost their patron saint, a latter-day Boudicca of the oppressed. Deprived of her famous hugs, both literal and metaphorical, they sobbed and hugged each other. It was another of Diana's remarkable legacies, implanted in the national consciousness by ubiquitous images of her stroking and hugging sick children, taking them in her arms and cradling their heads on her breast. Tactile values, the importance of touch, were becoming a central part of her posthumous iconography.

As that extraordinary week wore on, and public rage with the Windsors mounted with each day that they remained secluded at Balmoral, Charles was the only member of his family to sense the true scale of the growing crisis. Friends in London with sharper political antennae hurried to telephone him in Scotland, with warnings of the public mood. The row over the empty flagpole, symbolic of ancient royal protocol with which Diana's mourners had no sympathy, was provoking ominous predictions about her funeral. The Queen might be booed; Charles himself might be subjected to abuse. After four days, as the tabloid press called desperately on the Queen to 'Show Us You Care', the prince was shrewd enough to admit that events were running beyond the control of his family, their advisers and indeed himself. On the Wednesday evening, 3 September, Charles telephoned the prime minister for help.

Tony Blair was handling his end of the crisis well. Within hours of Diana's death, on his own way to church with his family in his north-eastern constituency, Blair had skilfully caught the mood of the nation with an emotional tribute to 'the people's princess'*, a 'force for good in the world' with whom the British public had 'kept faith' – a deftly cryptic reference to her trials and tribulations, not least at the hands of Charles and the Windsors.

Now Blair decided to ride to the royal rescue. There was no truth in reports of angry disputes between Balmoral and London, which had Charles telling the Queen's private secretary, also his brother-in-law, to stick his protocol 'up your own flagpole'. The prince was completely at a loss as to how he or the royal machine should proceed. So concerned was he for his sons that, for once, he could not understand that their position robbed them of the right to grieve in private, that duty dictated some sort of public gesture. The Queen, after all, was not just Diana's ex-mother-in-law; she was the head of state of a country whose paroxysm of grief, however confused its motives, was causing the most remarkable public

---

*In a letter to the *Daily Telegraph* dated 16 September 1997, Vincent Phillips of Naburn, North Yorks wrote, 'The continuing myth that Tony Blair coined the phrase "The People's Princess" needs to be challenged. "The People's Princess" was actually the title of the chapter about Diana in Anthony Holden's 1993 book about the House of Windsor, *The Tarnished Crown*.'

scenes of her forty-six years on the throne. Charles had little alternative but to cave in to New Labour's sophisticated spin doctors. 'In effect,' as one Blair aide put it, 'he turned things over to us.'[3]

'We had to just keep our focus on the royal family itself, which was going through enormous difficulty and grief at the time,' Blair said later. 'We had to make sure they were properly supported. We had to try and keep our nerve. In a situation like that there are no rules and no training. You do what you think is right by instinct. I was very proud of the work my team did . . .'[4]

On the Friday, as if by magic, a Union Jack was hoisted to the top of the Buckingham Palace flagpole, then lowered to half-mast. The previous evening, at the gates of Balmoral, the entire family including William and Harry had made an appearance for the cameras, Charles holding his younger son's hand as they inspected the flowers laid there by well-wishers. The following afternoon, on the eve of the funeral, the Windsors finally came to London to move among the crowds, the presence of the young princes instantly defusing a week of mounting public anger. A bloodless revolution, it seemed, had been averted.

That evening, in a live television broadcast, the Queen paid tribute to her former daughter-in-law as 'an exceptional and gifted human being' who made 'many, many people' happy.

> In good times and bad, she never lost her capacity to smile and
> laugh, nor to inspire others with her warmth and kindness . . .
> I admired and respected her – for her energy and commitment
> to others, and especially her devotion to her two boys.

As the Queen's remarks rallied the nation back to the royal standard, and Charles could breathe a huge sigh of relief, the emotionally draining week seemed to have marked a genuine sea change in recent British history. With centuries of royal protocol cast aside in response to the public mood, bringing the House of Windsor down from its pedestal to share the grief of its subjects, Diana had signalled an end to stiff upper lip, to British inhibitions, to centuries of traditionally buttoned-up reserve.

But her death also unleashed deeper feelings overdue an outlet, aching to disprove Margaret Thatcher's dictum that there is 'no such thing as society'. As they roamed the streets of London in tears, the air pungent with the scent of a million flowers, Britons young enough to have been spared the Blitz had never felt such a sense of community. There was a feeling that the country had overnight become a warmer, more compassionate, more civilized place. Some, within months, would scoff, arguing that the response to her death had been 'disproportionate'; but few involved, from prime minister and prince to people on the streets of towns and cities all over Britain, doubted that many aspects of an outdated, post-imperial Britain had died with this uniquely contemporary figure.

The brief skirmish between 'people power' and 'Palace power', as the royals had seemed slow to share the nation's mourning, was an emphatic rejection of 1980s greed, 1990s mediocrity, and decades, perhaps centuries, of Establishment indifference. It was a louder echo of the events of 1 May, only three months earlier, when a young prime minister with all the charisma of a new JFK had been elected by a stunning landslide, giving Britain a sense of renewal, of escape from its past, after two decades of increasingly tired, heedless patrician rule. Was Britain finally escaping its imperial past, cramped by outmoded tradition, and looking with fresh young eagerness to a modernized, European future? So it seemed, thanks to the cult of Diana, as Blair pledged: 'Something must come of all this.'

Diana's funeral was attended, via television, by some 2.5 billion people around the world, getting on for half the earth's population. In London, the route of the procession had been lengthened to accommodate the crowds, again by public demand, and for fear that people might die in the crush. Thousands slept out on the streets overnight, knowing that nothing like this would happen again in their lifetimes.

Only 2,000 mourners could be crammed into Westminster Abbey, but at least they included as many true friends, colleagues and beneficiaries of the dead princess as the great and the good who are usually allowed to hijack these occasions. Again, 'people power' had won the day, ensuring that world leaders and European monarchs were less entitled to ex officio seats than people who had actually known Diana, cared about her, loved her. Before the day was through, they were to become part of another unexpected, quite unprecedented display of the popular will.

Women wailed, in a very unBritish way, as the coffin left Kensington Palace on its four-mile journey to the Abbey. As it passed Buckingham Palace the Queen, who bows to no-one, inclined her head towards her dead ex-daughter-in-law, the free spirit whose banishment from her family was now causing her such grief. As it passed St James's Palace, where it had lain all week, Charles and their sons joined the procession to walk solemnly behind it, flanked by Charles Spencer and Prince Philip. William could scarcely lift his head all the way, while young Harry braved his life's worst ordeal with remarkable composure.

After Diana's favourite passage from the Verdi *Requiem*, Elton John dragged the monarchy further towards the present day by singing a pop song, 'Candle in the Wind', his elegy for Marilyn Monroe, with new words specially written for his friend Diana, and a new title: 'Goodbye, England's Rose'. As its last strains died away, the applause from the crowd outside could be clearly heard in the Abbey. Then Diana's brother, Charles, unleashed a tribute that turned into a tirade, against the media who had dogged his sister's life, and the royal family who had tried to reclaim her in death. Before the world, he pledged to his dead sister that her 'blood family' would do all in its power to continue 'the imaginative, loving way' in which she had been bringing up her sons, 'so that their souls are not immersed by duty and tradition, but can sing as openly as you planned'.

As Charles Spencer's voice cracked with emotion, the applause outside began again. This time, despite the implied insult to Charles and the other senior royals in the midst of the congregation, it invaded the ancient Abbey, starting at the back, then creeping down the sides until the entire church, apart from the Windsors, was clapping. Even poor William and Harry, blinded by grief and untrained in royal protocol, joined in. Their father, according to observers, 'was seen to tap his thigh with his hand – whether in muted applause, or irritation, remains unclear – before composing himself'. The Queen and Prince Philip sat staring fixedly forward, in stony-faced silence. It was the nearest the House of Windsor had yet come to face-to-face rejection, the moment it knew that it must change to survive.

Again Diana was dictating Charles's agenda, even from within a stately coffin draped in the royal standard. The wailing continued afterwards, as it was placed in the hearse for the eighty-mile drive to Althorp. Crowds lined the entire route, right up the M1 motorway, throwing flowers in such profusion that the driver had to stop to clear the windscreen. By the time it reached her childhood home, its path strewn with floral tributes, the hearse's sombre black was garlanded in the bright colours of nature. The local girl beloved of the world was returning home for the last time. As she disappeared through the gates of the estate, offering the photographers the last pictures they would ever take of her, the curtain was drawn on a day of unique resonance. The will of the people had opened up a seismic fault beneath the thousand-year-old British monarchy, shaken to its foundations by the popular feeling for a free-spirited force of nature, loved all the more by the people for her rejection by the royals.

Charles and his sons travelled up by train with his brothers-in-law, Charles Spencer and Sir Robert Fellowes, to witness Diana's burial on an island in a lake at the heart of the estate, which she had loved in childhood – soon to become a place of pilgrimage, where her sons would be able to visit her in privacy whenever they wanted. Within hours that island too was carpeted with flowers, hiding the scars in the earth that had finally quenched her abundant spirit.

The royal family retreated to Balmoral that same evening, but it was to take days yet for Britain to return to anything remotely approaching normal. The signal, again by popular will, came four nights later at Wembley, the national soccer stadium, when a vital World Cup qualifying match was preceded by yet another minute's silence for Diana. The 100,000 crowd wept again, cradling their candles against the wind, as Elton John's elegy echoed around the country one more time.

But Elton John, soon to become Sir Elton, had himself said that day that it was now time for 'life to go on'. After ten of the most remarkable days in British history, the referee's whistle finally signified the freedom to stop talking about Diana in tones of hushed reverence, and to honour her memory with smiles, cheers and laughter. The England players, all wearing black armbands, dedicated their performance to her memory. They won 4–0.

By the end of the following week, Charles felt able to resume his public duties, taking a break from a busy day in Manchester to pay public tribute to his sons: 'I am unbelievably proud of the two of them, William and Harry. They are really quite remarkable. I think they have handled a very difficult time with enormous courage and the greatest possible dignity.' Bereavement was 'very difficult' for any family to handle, but 'perhaps you might realize it is even harder when the whole world is watching'.⁵ The boys had been 'hugely comforted' by some 250,000 letters of condolence.

There was, as yet, no public tribute to Diana or her work, no expression of regret at the way things had turned out between them. But Charles was still feeling his way. Pleasantly surprised that the wave of sympathy towards his sons was rubbing off on him, he had determined to proceed cautiously. There would be time enough to inch forward this latest, unexpected chance for personal rehabilitation; as yet he was content to play the role of anxious father, insulated more than he had dared to hope from the role of cruel, faithless ex-husband of a woman undergoing the fastest canonization in history.

At root, public opinion remained merciless. Diana's mourners apparently wanted the House of Spencer to succeed the House of Windsor at the earliest opportunity. A MORI poll for the *Sunday Times* now showed 60 per cent of Britons wishing Charles to step aside in favour of his fifteen-year-old son William, with 72 per cent graciously agreeing that the Queen should wait three years, until William's eighteenth birthday, to hand over the throne.⁶

Seemingly unperturbed, the prince proceeded with his public agenda, confident of government support. The chancellor of the exchequer, Gordon Brown, confirmed that Charles had personally persuaded him to lower to eighteen the qualifying age for cash grants to help the jobless start their own companies. More to the point, Tony Blair offered his public backing, offering to help 'sell' the prince's qualities to the doubting British public. 'He considers Charles a fellow moderniser,' ran the Downing Street briefing, 'whose instincts are more in tune with the public than has been recognised.'⁷

Compassion – with 'edge' – was the keynote of Blair's address to his party conference that month, the first by an incumbent Labour prime minister in almost two decades. That kind of compassion could now be reclaimed by Charles, both as social crusader and grieving father. Even the Church seemed to be echoing his deeper long-term themes, convening an emergency meeting of its House of Bishops to discuss the 'spiritual hunger' revealed by the mourning for Diana.

Within a month, as he began cancelling engagements to be with his sons, the polls perceptibly began to turn Charles's way. Seven in

ten Britons still believed the Queen should abdicate, 'handing over
to a younger royal rather than delaying the succession until her
death'; but a narrow majority (46 per cent to 44 per cent) now
thought Charles rather than William should succeed her. At 40 per
cent, those who thought Charles would make 'a good king' were
only 3 per cent less than those thinking he would make a positively
'bad' one. But the Camilla statistics were growing worse. More
than half the nation, 55 per cent, thought Charles should not
become king if he married Mrs Parker Bowles, with only 18 per
cent believing he should still become titular head of the Church of
England. A devastating 82 per cent still could not stomach the idea
of her ever being crowned queen.[8]

Of Camilla herself, as yet, there was still neither sight nor sound.
Diana's death had seen the cancellation of her planned summer
holiday with Charles, and indeed of her first appearance as patron
of the National Osteoporosis Society, with or without the prince at
her side. Charles was speaking to her by phone every day, telling
friends he needed her 'now more than ever', but avoiding the
slightest chance of being seen in her company. There was a minor
blip when Welsh taxpayers protested at footing the £30,000 bill for
a seven-foot, 400-yard fence under construction around the
Paravacini estate in Brecon, still one of the couple's favourite 'safe
houses' for secret trysts. Then, in early November, she was seen in
public for the first time since Diana's death, riding to hounds with
the Beaufort Hunt.

Charles could scarcely have been further away: in South Africa,
on a tour built around the unlikely conjunction of Nelson Mandela
and the Spice Girls. The long-planned visit coincided with Harry's
half-term, which the thirteen-year-old prince had been due to
spend with his mother, so Charles took him along for the ride.
Harry's presence lent a significant, sentimental boost to a conscious
'charm offensive' on Charles's part, joking with the travelling press
corps, good-humouredly gagging for the cameras when confronted
with bare-breasted tribal dancers, looking like a man 'with a huge
weight lifted from his shoulders'.

The resulting press coverage was the most positive he had
generated since Diana had first entered his life. It was ten years
since he had even acknowledged, let alone chatted with, the merry
band of reporters who follow him day in, day out. Their inevitably
grateful, wide-eyed dispatches omitted to mention that this was a

somewhat selective exercise, excluding those who had been closest to his ex-wife. But even they agreed to 'let that pass', suggesting that 'in time, Charles too may prove forgiving'.[9]

For those mindful of Earl Spencer's pledge that the 'blood family' would share the raising of Diana's sons, it was dispiriting to see young Harry accompany his father to a Johannesburg rock concert in a formal suit and tie; his mother, it was observed, would certainly have permitted, if not encouraged, T-shirt and jeans. But South Africa offered a watershed in Charles's rehabilitation, marking his first successful 'relaunch' amid the umpteen of the Diana and post-Diana years. All at once, the sycophantic media instincts that had always lain dormant broke back through the surface, with the right-wing monarchist press faithfully regurgitating the official lines of his spin doctors.

'Charles fights back,' declared the fogeyish *Spectator*, lamenting an era when 'the prime minister's wife neglects to curtsey to the Queen', but concluding that the prince was 'back in the ring, and it is going to be increasingly hard to land a punch'. Even the *Sun*, only begetter of 'the loony prince', anointed him – for no apparent reason beyond that cringe-making photocall with Mandela and the Spice Girls – 'Re-Born to Rule'. Could the death of Diana, wondered the *Guardian* more prudently, 'have had a liberating influence on our future king?'

Apparently so. In his one big speech of the trip, Charles took the chance, for the first (and, as yet, only) time, to pay public tribute to Diana's work for the causes close to her heart. He may, perhaps, have been swayed by her posthumous share in the award of the Nobel Peace Prize to the International Campaign against Landmines, which also saw 122 countries sign a worldwide ban in Ottawa that month. Among Charles's audience was not just Mandela but her brother Charles, Earl Spencer, a Cape Town resident, with whom the prince exchanged a few apparently cordial words. The resulting photographs served to conceal a complete *froideur* between the two, which dated from Spencer's Westminster Abbey tirade and would continue through the coming troubles of the Diana Memorial Fund.

At the end of his South African tour, Charles professed surprise that his very positive press coverage had described him, in essence, as 'a new man'. He was, he protested, 'the same as ever'. The truth was that Diana's untimely death had given him a chance, which he was seizing with a vengeance, to re-create himself as the 'caring, compassionate' prince of old – the earnest, well-meaning, if occasionally gauche figure he had cut before she ever came on the scene. The new 'media-friendly' prince – a jocular soul the press had not seen for twenty years – was such a success that Charles soon staged a reprise on a tour of Sri Lanka, Nepal and Bhutan, again chatting with reporters, even pausing to talk to ITN, then paint them a picture, while struggling up a steep mountain path.

Charles returned from South Africa a new prince. Within forty-eight hours he was pictured looking around furtively, almost as if he feared Tony Blair might be watching, when he again went out hunting, despite a huge recent Commons majority for abolition, as demanded by overwhelming opinion polls. But Charles, always content to ignore public opinion, could afford – in this case, literally – to ride his luck. Paradoxically, the rebranded prince could now revert to his old, heedless ways with apparent impunity.

Diana's death was proving, in terms of his public reputation, the biggest personal boost he could have hoped for. Now, with the help of his newly expert media manipulators, it was time to take the credit for modernizing the monarchy – converting an ancient, irrational institution into a slimmed-down, streamlined tourist attraction fit for the new millennium.

On 14 November 1997, Charles's forty-ninth birthday, the Queen kissed her son publicly for the first time in his life. This unprecedented public display of regal emotion – of the kind specifically disavowed by the Windsors during the mass mourning for Diana – took place aboard the royal yacht *Britannia*, poignantly moored on the Thames for a few farewell royal parties before its formal retirement the following month. Suddenly, as they adjusted to the post-Diana era, there was an air of change and renewal about the monarchy: Windsor Castle was reopening, restored to its former glories after the 'annus horribilis' fire, and the nation was promised a 'new look' Queen for her golden wedding anniversary the following week.

A week later, sure enough, HM went walkabout with her popular young prime minister, *en route* from an Abbey service to a Whitehall lunch. She smiled more than usual on such occasions; when handed a heart-shaped silver balloon, she did not, as usual, pass it without a second glance to a lady-in-waiting, but walked a few steps holding it for the benefit of photographers. For the first time in her reign, thanks to Downing Street's 'modernizing' machine, the Queen had 'ordinary people' at her lunch table that day: apart from her favourite jockey, Walter Swinburn, a Welsh guide leader, a woman police constable, a factory worker and a farmer.

Her tenth prime minister, born in the year of her coronation, paid his monarch tribute slavish enough to dismay his own political supporters as much as his opponents. Despite confiding that she had asked him not to be 'too effusive', Blair compared himself with Disraeli to Elizabeth II's Victoria, proclaiming, 'I am as proud as proud can be to be your prime minister today, offering this tribute on behalf of the country. You are our queen. We respect and cherish you. You are simply the best of British.' It was the end of all speculation that his ambitious programme of constitutional reform might soon offer Britain an elected head of state.

Recently, under Downing Street's spell, its hereditary monarch had visited a hostel for the homeless in London's King's Cross district, and a village in Oxfordshire with a high proportion of crime, unemployment and single mothers. Soon she would visit a pub and take her first ride in a London taxi. Was the Queen, and thus the monarchy, being 'Dianified'?

If so, part of the package for Charles was two more meetings with the Spice Girls, attending their film première that autumn and subsequently entertaining them to tea at Highgrove, driving the most devout monarchists to call for the institution's abolition before it modernized itself out of all credibility. As the teen-culture quintet pinched their future king's bottom and wiped their lipstick off his cheek, there were those who thought this too high a price to pay for the survival of an institution accustomed to hitching its coat-tails to rather more refined icons. For Charles, however, there was now the open-ended excuse that he was doing it all for his sons, especially Harry, inevitably rendering his critics pompous and mean-spirited. The rejuvenated prince, at times visibly, simply could not believe his luck.

The only setback during this virtual rebirth, so soon after Diana's demise, was the premature death that November of Dale, Lady Tryon, the former lover Charles had nicknamed 'Kanga', who had gone into a long spiritual and physical decline since Camilla had won their battle to remain the real love in Charles's married life. Once Charles had described Kanga as 'the only woman who understands me'; of late, since a mysterious fall from a hospital window had suggested signs of mental instability, he had been refusing to take her calls. During the final, troubled months of her life, when her marriage, too, collapsed, Lady Tryon repeatedly tried to get through to the prince, according to her cousin, Lady Elizabeth Anson, sister of Lord Lichfield, who revealed, 'He's not in contact with her, and her calls are not being taken by him.'[10]

Born with spina bifida, Dale Tryon had survived cancer of the uterus, only to succumb to severe depression. After breaking her back, she spent the rest of her life in a wheelchair, fighting gamely to rebuild her world before finally being defeated by septicaemia after an operation. It was very much to her credit that she had always spoken warmly of Diana, after recognizing that her own love for Charles was doomed; amid all her own suffering, she also remained devoutly loyal to the prince.

Like Diana, however, Kanga may yet have a powerful posthumous role to play in Charles's future. Somewhere out there, she confirmed shortly before her death, are 'lots' of letters Charles wrote her over the years. 'They have gone missing,' she said. 'I am very worried about it. I'm trying to get them back, but I haven't got anywhere.'[11] If ever unearthed and published, they would probably disclose the same surprising side to Charles's character as the notorious 'Camillagate' tape, which, amid its vulgarities, revealed a man capable of the tender, loving care that he could somehow never show his wife.

Kanga's death served largely as a reminder of the continuing 'Camilla problem' in Charles's otherwise newly promising path. A week after the prince's birthday, on the eve of his own golden-wedding anniversary, Charles's father made a speech paying touching tribute to his wife and the virtues of married life. The Duke of Edinburgh declared himself 'sufficiently old-fashioned' to believe in 'partnership in marriage'. It was 'essential' to the stresses and strains of royal life. Was this a hint that Charles should make an honest woman of Camilla?

If so, his son was not listening. Keeping her firmly out of sight, Charles had quite enough to occupy him on both the private and public fronts. As Diana's £21 million will was published, his attempt to use a legal loophole to save £8 million inheritance tax on her estate, which apparently had Blair's tacit approval, was sensibly vetoed by the former prime minister John Major, whom Charles had appointed his sons' 'guardian' to protect their legal interests. The precedent turned out to be dubious; but Major anyway felt it was inappropriate for the young princes, if not for their father, to be seen to attempt tax avoidance.

Himself exempt from inheritance tax, Charles soon had another unexpected lesson in how the other half actually live. On a visit to the offices of the *Big Issue*, the newspaper which champions, and is sold by, the homeless, he found himself in conversation with a former Hill House School contemporary, Clive Harold, who had fallen on hard times. 'So there you are,' said the magazine's founder, John Bird. 'Shows what life can throw up – one guy who's done really well and one who turns out to be the Prince of Wales.'[12] The occasion subsequently moved Charles to write an article for the paper about the 'dreadful problems' of homelessness – a symptom rather than a cause of people's problems, he argued, often the result of unemployment, low educational achievement or drink or drug problems. 'We live in an increasingly material world in which people's identity is determined so often only by the job they do and the money they earn, rather than by what they contribute to society.'[13]

As his children's first Christmas without their mother approached, it was the other Charles who was suddenly attracting all the unwelcome headlines: their uncle, Earl Spencer, whose lurid divorce hearings in South Africa revealed him to be a serial adulterer who had, ironically enough, shown little sympathy for his own wife's eating disorder. The halo that had hovered over Charles Spencer since his dramatic speech at his sister's funeral slipped more than somewhat, as the nation learned it had been subjected to a moral homily from a man whose own moral values were distinctly suspect. Those who had promised to police his pledge about the 'blood family' playing a role in Diana's sons' upbringing felt obliged to reconsider their priorities. Besides, Spencer had shown no immediate inclination to sell up in South Africa and return to England in order to be nearer his nephews, apart from visits to his ancestral estate, Althorp, to supervise construction of a Diana museum.

The Spencer sisters had been to visit William and Harry at their schools, but their uncle had even failed to take the opportunity to return home a few days early to meet up with Harry while he was visiting South Africa. Before a week-long skiing holiday with their father at New Year, in their mother's least favourite resort of Klosters, the boys spent their first Christmas since their mother's death at Sandringham, with their father and grandparents, bravely greeting members of the public as they processed to church on Christmas morning. In her annual message to the Commonwealth, their grandmother spoke of the 'almost unbearable sadness' of Diana's death, a source of 'shock and sorrow'.

Her sons, it seemed, were bearing up much better than might have been expected. Screened from publicity, with the British press on its best behaviour, William and Harry were fast growing closer to their father than they might ever have had the chance to do if their mother had lived. William had always hated the cameras that Diana's arrival inevitably brought with her; that much he was now spared, as he seized the chance to deepen his bond with Charles. Harry, too, relished the opportunity to catch more than the occasional glimpse of the busy public figure who happened to be his father. By cancelling engagements to be with his sons, Charles was earning far greater public popularity than he could ever have done by carrying them out. A dramatic poll proved as much over Christmas, showing that 61 per cent of Britons were now 'satisfied' with the way the prince was doing his job, as compared to 46 per cent just before Diana's death, with only 29 per cent 'dissatisfied', as opposed to 42 per cent.[14]

Given such causes for self-confidence, the Windsors now began rather brutally to sever their remaining links with other aspects of Diana's life. Charles Spencer was already neutralized, and his sister Sarah under criticism for the Diana Memorial Fund's ill-advised endorsement of margarine tubs, dolls and scratchcards. Now the Queen publicly snubbed Mohamed al Fayed by dropping Harrods as sponsor of the Royal Windsor Horse Show, which had been his passport to an annual meeting with her in front of the cameras.

Fayed, who had built a permanent shrine in Harrods to Diana and Dodi, and was still pursuing his application for British citizenship, felt moved to protest that he had been badly treated. 'I think it's bad manners,' he said, revealing that he had been frozen out by both the Windsor and the Spencer families since Diana's death. He had written a letter of condolence to Charles Spencer, and had it hand-delivered to Althorp, but received no reply. Among more than a million letters he himself received from all over the world were expressions of sympathy from the Queen, the prime minister and the Archbishop of Canterbury – but none from the Prince of Wales, Prince Philip or Charles Spencer. He had not been allowed, he complained, to contact William and Harry. 'Does this show compassion and respect? I don't think so. It's disgraceful.'[15]

Charles was again wiping the Diana slate clean. The New Year saw him move his sons with him into a new London home: York House, a self-contained, five-bedroom section of St James's Palace, previously used by the Duke and Duchess of Kent. On a poignant final tour of their former home at Kensington Palace, the boys chose their favourite belongings from their rooms, and their favourite souvenirs of their mother, for transfer to a London base with their father which they had never had before. The prince meanwhile announced that he would be 'streamlining' his charities in order to spend more time with his sons. But still they had not met Camilla Parker Bowles.

Diana had died believing that Charles would never marry Camilla – always, to her, the woman who had broken up her marriage. The princess took the view that Charles preferred the 'forbidden fruit' of an affair. 'Maintaining the status quo', she said, 'suits him perfectly,' adding mischievously that Charles 'is always happier when he has two women on the go'.[16] That status quo was now taking on a degree of permanence, with Camilla moving into St James's Palace as well as Highgrove, maintaining a wardrobe of clothes at Charles's London home, and spending several nights a month there, but always when William and Harry were not around. Six months after Diana's death came the strongest sign yet that the prince now wished Mrs Parker Bowles to be recognized as his consort.

On the weekend of 14–15 March 1998 the prince hosted his annual 'cultural' house-party at Sandringham, his family's Norfolk estate, with Camilla on hand as his official hostess. Sandringham being his mother's property, this could not have happened without the tacit endorsement of the Queen, who herself tactfully spent the weekend at Windsor. Among the guests, apart from close royal friends like Lord Jacob Rothschild and Lady Susan Hussey, was Peter Mandelson, the government minister who had now become the couple's tactical adviser. Viscount (John Julius) Norwich was on hand to lead poetry readings to a select audience, hand-picked for Charles by the American cultural socialite Drue Heinz, including the novelist Piers Paul Read, the writer William Shawcross, the conductor John Eliot Gardiner and the playwright Peter Whelan.

After a formal dinner on the Friday evening, the prince's guests spent Saturday morning on a tour of local churches, led by the octogenarian Lady Harrod, widow of the economist Sir Roy, an authority on Norfolk church architecture. There was an unscheduled 'drop-by' at a village hall, startling Cub Scouts in the midst of a cookery competition, before a barbecue lunch in a secluded log cabin on the 25,000-acre estate. An afternoon visit to nearby Houghton Hall, seat of the Marquess of Cholmondeley, was followed by a dinner of organic chicken in a light sauce, washed down with the finest wines from the Highgrove cellar. For the post-prandial movie, curiously, Charles rejected *The Full Monty*, the home-grown hit of the moment, in favour of a lightweight confection called *Princess Caraboo*, whose storyline about a fantasy princess may well have put some guests guiltily in mind of Diana.

On Sunday morning Camilla stayed behind to avoid the cameras as most of the group attended divine service at the church of St Mary Magdalene. Peter Mandelson also remained at Sandringham, to work on his ministerial papers. A round of stiff gin and tonics preceded a luncheon of venison, an afternoon at leisure, and a dinner of crab and sea bass, to background music from students of the Royal College of Music. Guests wore evening dress, with the prince in his distinctive scarlet-and-blue 'Windsor jacket'. Over brandy and liqueurs, Norwich read from Browning, Kipling and Betjeman.

As they took their reluctant leave on the Monday morning, guests were given a box of Highgrove chocolates to take home. 'This is a dream, and it's terrible when it ends,' said one. Another, meeting Charles for the first time, mused, 'I've never met such a bitter man. He spent most of the weekend complaining about his miserable lot.' To those guests who knew Charles well, Camilla's presence had seemed essential to help him relax; although looking 'older since Diana's death and, if possible, more careworn, [he] seemed cheerful and content'.[17]

It was the last the couple would see of each other for a month, as Charles headed off to Canada with his sons, before taking them to Balmoral for the Easter holiday. In Vancouver, where they undertook two days of engagements before a skiing holiday, the crowds were bigger, younger and more animated than expected. Teenage girls screamed hysterically at the sight of William, as if he were a pop or film star; still only fifteen, he was visibly unnerved by his first taste of the kind of idolatry his mother had bequeathed him. To a press that had pledged to leave the young princes in peace, allowing them the last few years of comparative freedom they would ever know, there was a distinct element of paradox in the Palace's use of them to generate positive headlines for their father.

Privately, William himself questioned the work done by the advance party who had planned the visit. He had not been expecting these mob scenes, nor much welcomed them. Still camera-shy, he was already showing signs of his father's youthful reluctance to take inherited, built-in celebrity for granted. The unease on William's face, suggested that he, too, might prefer the chance to earn such acclaim in his own right, via dutiful public work, rather than merely as his mother's son.

Still in pain from a knee operation, Charles was pleased to let his sons take the strain, encouraging them to play to the cameras by donning the jackets and caps of the Canadian ice-hockey team, recent heroes of the winter Olympics. It would be years yet before he himself succeeded to 'the top job', as Diana called it, yet already the baton was visibly passing to the next generation. His own hard-won identity was being blurred by his new role as his children's father – sole keeper, ironically, of his ex-wife's true flame, the sons who meant more to her than any other legacy. In death, it seemed, Diana was beyond criticism; in life, as a result, so were her sons. Charles could only look on with pleasure. He had no alternative but to subsume his royal role in theirs.

But there was, as always, a dissenting minority to deal with as the first anniversary of Diana's death approached, and with it a slew of commemorative books, articles and TV programmes. Those who felt the reaction to her death disproportionate, arguing that the cult of Diana was the hallmark of a culturally sick nation, found a cheerleader in Anthony O'Hear, professor of philosophy at Bradford University. Diana's death, argued O'Hear, had precipitated a 'defining moment' in British history, for all the wrong reasons; the public response had symbolized 'the elevation of feeling, image and spontaneity over reason, reality and restraint'.

On September 6 [the day of Diana's funeral] feeling was
elevated above reason, caring above principle, personal gratifi-
cation above commitment and propriety, and what Tony Blair
called 'the people' over rank, tradition and history . . . What
we had in that week was a potent mixture of popular culture
and undogmatic religiosity, as the sacrificial victim was
canonised.[18]

O'Hear's charges of 'fake sentimentality', of 'child-like self-
indulgence', again gave Charles and Blair common cause. While
the prime minister called O'Hear a 'snob', arguing that it was
'insulting' to condemn people for openly showing their emotions,[19]
the Prince of Wales expressed concern about the anguish the resulting controversy might occasion his sons. Charles, according to one
of his staff, 'thought the way she was canonised was way over the
top – and this attack on her by some nutty professor from Bradford
no-one had ever heard of is just as bad . . . All Charles wants is for
him and his sons to get on with their lives without reading "Diana
this" and "Diana that" every day.'[20]

There was little hope of that. The very papers which condemned
the 'tacky' commercialization of Diana's memory, and which had
entered a formal pact to leave her sons in peace, still sought every
opportunity to maximize sales with her name or face on their front
pages, offering Diana posters, Diana roses, extracts from Diana
books by the most minor figures in her life. At the time, for
instance, the *Daily Mail* was serializing a biography of the princess
by the American housewife who had briefly employed her as a
nanny in the months before her engagement.

Things would get worse before they would show the slightest
sign – after the orgy of publicity on the first anniversary of Diana's
death – of getting better, let alone allowing the princess to rest in
peace. The Spencer family embarked on apparent civil war, as her
brother Charles condemned the recent commercial decisions of the
Diana Memorial Fund, led by his sister Sarah. He called for the
Fund to be wound up, despite his own pledge to donate the pro-
ceeds of a rock concert at Althorp on what would have been
Diana's thirty-seventh birthday, and indeed from the 'theme park'
– complete with quasi-religious temple – he opened, at steep admission prices, near her grave. Furious that his sons were dragged into
the row, the Prince of Wales let his office reveal that William and

Harry had declined an offer to spend two weeks of their summer vacation with their Spencer uncle and aunts. They would rather stay with their father and his family at Balmoral.

And who could blame them? The war of the Waleses was in danger of giving way to civil strife between the Windsors and the Spencers. In death as in life, Diana seemed determined to haunt her ex-husband, dogging his every step towards public success and private happiness.

CHAPTER TWENTY

'THE PEOPLE'S PRINCE'

WHEN CHARLES, PRINCE OF WALES, MEETS RANDOM MEMBERS OF THE public, the odds are that his opening conversational gambit will be, 'What do you do?' It is the very question, ironically enough, most people would like to ask him.

What exactly *does* Charles do? In the absence of any reply from the man himself, the question most likely to infuriate him was recently answered on his behalf.

> We know he fronts charities and agonises over his and all our futures. He also rides to hounds, drives a gas-guzzling Aston-Martin (among a flexing of brutish muscle cars), blasts birds from the sky, potters in his lovely Gloucestershire garden, was the spouse of England's Rose, and wrings his hands over the state of British architecture.

A liberal journalist straining to be fair – Charles had, after all, 'tried his best to change the face of these sceptred isles' – the *Guardian*'s Jonathan Glancey could not help but wonder, 'Where did it all go wrong?'

> Few doubt that his heart has been in the right place, yet many believe he has been blinded by a peculiarly narrow vision that would have us all living in Georgian-style villas – pediments with everything – and turning our backs on the work of modern British architects, designers and inventors whose reputation worldwide has soared in the last twenty years. [1]

This 'fading royal blueprint' is endorsed by another seasoned observer, who sums up Charles as 'dreamy, ineffective and hopelessly unrealistic to an almost infantile degree . . . His ideas tend to emerge flavoured with something of the all-embracing gullibility of a New Age catalogue.' To the cultural commentator Bryan Appleyard, Charles is 'anti-progressive, fearful of the effects of unbridled profiteering, suspicious of technology and possessed of an inchoate yearning for some sort of holistic vision.'[2]

If these impressions of Charles are typical of the 'chattering classes' who now run Britain, including his own contemporaries among middle-aged, middle-class 'baby-boomers', the outlook elsewhere is hardly much rosier. To the countless devotees of the royal soap opera, who flocked back to Kensington Gardens on the first anniversary of Diana's death, the heir to the British throne will always be the man who undervalued, betrayed and discarded the prototype princess of the modern age.

As the father of her children, a lone parent nursing his sons through their grief, Charles is now spared the more vicious strain of criticism that flourished while Diana lived. But there are still many to whom no amount of worthy public work can ever banish the memory of his treatment of his wife, even among older, traditionally minded Britons with tastes and views similar to his own. The continuing presence in his life of Camilla Parker Bowles is a constant reminder of Diana's marital unhappiness. The public prince, in short, has been undone by the private one.

In vain can the heir to the throne, like other public figures in a *laissez-faire* but hypocritical, intrusive age, expect his public role to be detached or even distinguished from his private life. The high office to which he aspires, spiritual as well as temporal, carries stern moral obligations that render his personal self-conduct a more relevant test of his credentials than that of any other public official, elected or unelected, hereditary or self-made. It is an unenviable lot, conferred by accident of birth, which offers no obvious, compensatory means of escape.

At the same time, the insistence of the Windsors on continuing to live at public expense, although one of the world's wealthiest families, confers obligations beyond mere financial accountability – which is still, despite recent concessions, little more than cursory. It renders them answerable for their conduct, both private and public, to the taxpayers who subsidize – to the tune of some

£100 million ($160 million) per annum – their immensely lavish lifestyle around eight palaces and castles.* As hereditary Duke of Cornwall, living off the £4 million annual revenue from the £25 million turnover of his inherited estates, Charles is blinkered to consider himself exempt from this debate.

The prince's exemption from capital gains and other universal taxes, notably inheritance tax, is in itself a uniquely privileged position, granted to no other subject of the Crown. But the tide of constitutional reform working its way towards the monarchy, mindful of calls for a referendum on its future, will soon pause to reflect on the fine line between Crown and state ownership – of a vast, Ali Baba-scale treasure trove, from the Crown jewels via the Crown estates to the royal art collection. Prior to inheriting it all, the prince would be well advised to regard his inherited assets as a temporary if long-term loan from a 'people's Britain' that may, one day, seek to negotiate their return.

Luckily for the private prince, if not, perhaps, for the public one, Charles is largely insulated from such thinking, and from the true depth of public feeling about him, by the deference that still cocoons British royalty. Wherever he goes, in private and in public, the prince bathes in a feel-good foam of fawning sycophancy, a curious combination of respect for his office, of nervous excitement at meeting a celebrity, of awe at encountering a real, live picture-book prince. The transcript of a focus group's candid comments on the royals is the nearest he may ever get to being told, to his face, what many of his future subjects really think of him. In the unlikely event that any of them ever gets the chance to do so, candour would be covered by confusion, nuance by nerves, forthrightness by the sheer fascination of so tight a focus on so familiar a face.

It is another mixed blessing of being born royal that the usual rough edges of human interaction are smoothed over by a gloss of politeness, best behaviour, reluctance to rock the royal boat and fear of putting a foot wrong. Not since Mountbatten has anyone except Charles's wife, and occasionally his father, given as good as they have got, face to face. He tends to surround himself with like-

---

* Buckingham Palace, St James's Palace, Kensington Palace, Clarence House, Hampton Court Palace and Holyrood House in Edinburgh are maintained at state expense. Balmoral Castle and Sandringham House, Norfolk, are the Windsors' private property.

minded advisers, and to drop those who venture to disagree – to shun challenge, in other words, to dodge dissent. So his real trouble is that he tends to think, with the eager assent of those around him, that he is always in the right.

Roman emperors retained soothsayers not merely to predict their futures, but to whisper in their ear, amid all the head-spinning acclaim, regular reminders that they were merely mortal. Like King Lear's Fool, they enjoyed a licence not granted to other royal retainers: to speak home truths, however uncomfortable, without too much fear of royal retribution. These are not perquisites in which our contemporary royals care to indulge, for all the Queen's own acknowledgement, in her golden-wedding speech, that 'deference' can 'obscure' public opinion.[3]

It took banishment by his daughters, and the shock of naked exposure to the elements, for Lear to recognize his failure to identify with his subjects – to attempt to look at life, let alone endure it, from a less privileged point of view. Not until stripped of his royal support system was the old man finally capable of perceiving that a king is as much a 'poor, bare, forked animal' as the humblest citizen of his realm.[4]

As a self-professed lover and champion of Shakespeare – patron, indeed, of the Royal Shakespeare Company – Charles would do well to heed this elemental lesson. At present he rests content with wallowing in Henry V's self-indulgent lament:

> What infinite heart's-ease
> Must kings neglect, that private men enjoy![5]

But Charles is no Prince Hal (nor the obsequious Nicholas Soames, for all his girth, a Falstaff). A few more licensed fools at his court, a few more ventures onto storm-blasted heaths without the protection of his royal cocoon, and he might yet find ways to prove himself worthy of his birthright.

For the foreseeable future, the mystical power of the status quo will spare Charles any such desperate remedies, and the essential conservatism of British public life, even under a supposedly 'radical' New Labour government, will continue to red-carpet his inexorable progress towards the throne. The monarchy, as its champions keep reminding us, cannot survive without the goodwill of its people; yet those people may be forgiven for occasionally begging leave to doubt it, as they watch the very British institutions whose existence depends on the monarchy fight to protect it from popular dissent.

So Charles is probably well advised to maintain his patrician habit of ignoring public opinion, knowing the minimal impact it is likely to have on his preordained life. Not until the inmates take over the asylum, or politicians bow to the popular will, is there any chance of a candid, no-holds-barred appraisal of his suitability to become Britain's head of state. The law says he will, so he will.

It is a backdrop against which he has recently begun to thrive. The death of his former wife may have been a disaster for their children, but it was undeniably a blessing in scant disguise for Charles. In the eighteen months before his fiftieth birthday, the most turbulent period of his turbulent life, the prince found himself twice blessed. The one living obstacle to his private happiness and public fulfilment was unexpectedly removed; and, in the ensuing moment of crisis, a secure, popular government decided to promote him as 'one of us'. Just as Charles was on his knees, uncertain where to turn, the timely conjunction of these two quirks of fate proved the making of him.

As befits a man oft described as 'born middle-aged', the Prince of Wales thus approached his fiftieth birthday in finer public fettle, and better private spirits, than had seemed true for two decades – since the day, in fact, Diana first intruded on his Camilla-oriented life. He may, in his own words, be 'a bit of a crock': during 1998 chronic back pain returned to haunt him after he had fractured a rib in a hunting fall, while further cartilage trouble obliged him to undergo more 'keyhole' surgery, this time on his right knee. Such is the price he must pay, like his chronically arthritic father before him, for a lifetime in the saddle. Of late, in conditions of great secrecy, the prince has also been consulting a specialist about how to overcome troublesome memory lapses.

Spiritually, however, Charles is in better shape than he has been for many years. The responsibilities forced upon him by Diana's death, with its cruel and lasting impact on his sons, have visibly restored his sagging self-confidence. The chance to be himself again, to attempt to win back his public standing, has seen him reborn in mid-middle age. As he finally puts private responsibilities before public duties, human priorities before archaic rituals, Charles has undergone a remarkable transformation.

The human qualities well known to his inner circle, for all the battering they took during the Diana years, have come back to the fore. If not entirely at peace with himself, he is more so with the world around him. Throw in the shrewdest advisers he has had since his youth, extending beyond his own office to the inner councils of government, and you have a public figure suddenly and unexpectedly at the peak of his powers, bloodied but unbowed by his past, with cause for unwonted optimism about his future.

Fifty, moreover, suits Charles. Robbed of anything approaching a normal childhood or youth, torn in early middle age between a wayward wife and a devoted mistress, he developed a hangdog air that made him look older than his years. Now, as he enters his sixth decade, he has finally caught up with himself.

His fiftieth year, after the shock of Diana's death, proved one of the happiest and most fruitful of his life. His first as a quasi-widower, enjoying the reflected public sympathy directed at his sons, he was summarily 'modernized' by the government's slick rebranding department – gift-wrapped as a caring, compassionate prince, as contemporary, if not quite as 'cool', a symbol as any of Blair's brave new Britain, right at the heart of non-controversial national policy-making.

The estimable work of the Prince's Trust, largely unsung in its three decades of helping disadvantaged youth into gainful employment, has found a true soulmate in New Labour's welfare-to-work programme. As it shifts into top gear, the prince has been receiving public plaudits from the prime minister and the chancellor of the exchequer, almost as if he were a potential member of the Cabinet.

Herein, of course, lurk hidden dangers. If the heir to the throne identifies himself too closely with contentious government policy, even monarchists as staunch as the Conservative opposition would feel obliged to protest. In the case of welfare-to-work, however, Charles can always take a leaf out of Diana's book by declaring it less a political cause than a humanitarian one. Those rent-a-quote Tory backbenchers who denounced the late princess over her anti-landmines campaign seem rather less likely to criticize Charles for helping ease UK unemployment. However much the prince may bond with Tony Blair, it remains hard to see chums like Soames denouncing him from the opposition benches as 'a loose cannon', let alone as being 'in the advance stages of paranoia'.

For now, more than ever, Charles has all the unshakeable might of the British establishment on his side. Ideologically, this modernizing prime minister may be a closet republican, with each of his proposed constitutional reforms posing implicit threats to the royal prerogative. But the pragmatic politician in Blair, as instinctive about public opinion as was the woman he dubbed 'the people's princess', knows Britain is not yet ready for him to take on the monarchy. Roughly a third of its subjects still support it passionately; a third would be happy to see it go; and the other third couldn't care less. Compared with a mere decade ago, when its support ran consistently in the high eighties and nineties, these are disastrous figures for the House of Windsor. But they are not yet a mandate for constitutional upheaval undoing a thousand years of British history.

Incongruously, if necessary, Blair's current mission is to take a 'new', 'young', 'modernized' Britain to the heart of Europe, with a constitution anchored in an institution as antiquated as it is irrational. While depriving hereditary peers of the vote, he is paradoxically eager to shore up the only other hereditary office in the land.

Blair may spare unsteady old men from having to walk backwards in the royal presence. He may get the future king to open Parliament in a suit – Savile Row rather than Armani – instead of ermine robes. He may even substitute a Rolls-Royce – proud symbol, until its sale to the Germans, of British engineering at its very best – for that Ruritanian coach and horses. But an elected rather than hereditary head of state is way down his list of priorities. As even his republican backbenchers ask, anxious to see through lesser constitutional reforms, 'Why unleash a whole load of opposition?'[6] Blair's cosmetic surgery on the monarchy, moreover, seems likely to enhance its popularity, making fundamental reform, let alone abolition, rather more difficult for any genuinely radical successor.

Unthinkably, until its recent woes, the monarchy over which King Charles III hopes to preside has already agreed to make bowing and curtseying voluntary. It is doing away with ancient domestic titles from Silver Stick-in-Waiting to the Gentleman Steward of the Dessert Pantry, and even the grace-and-favour residences that go with their jobs. It has agreed to submit some of its accounts to Parliament for inspection. It has been persuaded to slim down the number of family members supported by the state, and to grant women equal status in the line of succession to the throne. While learning to live without its private yacht, if not yet its private train, planes and helicopters, it is admitting television cameras to its state banquets, its investitures and its garden parties. The Queen, unprecedentedly, is being 'miked' for sound.

Buckingham Palace has even succumbed to the New Labour fetish for 'focus groups', commissioning a firm of pollsters to sound out public opinion with an eye to its long-term future. A 1998 report that Britons saw the monarchy as 'stuffy', 'remote' and 'out of touch' steeled its nerve to further surface change, even to head-hunting a professional spin doctor to bring public opinion to heel, with a reluctant (and, in truth, dubious) Charles apparently in the vanguard of the 'modernizers'.[7]

For once, the ever loyal Nicholas Soames was being less than helpful when he accused Tony Blair of trying to 'bully' the royals into reforms 'in the name of new Britain', to 'bounce' them into discarding traditions in the name of 'cool Britannia'. Urging the Labour prime minister to be 'extremely cautious' in his advice to the Windsors, the former Tory defence minister described some of the new agenda as 'outrageous', notably the change in the law – publicly approved by the Queen herself – to give daughters equal rights of succession.* To Soames, this was 'nonsense' typical of the Blair administration.[8] To Charles, it was one of the planks on which the platform of his survival was being built.

So his birthright appears safe, if in a more populist guise, at least for the lifetime of this government, whose years in office will see his shy young son William grow to manhood, ready for his own launch into public life as an apt symbol of a new century, a new millennium. A second term for Blair would also see Charles's mother reach her golden jubilee, only thirteen years short of break-ing Victoria's record as the longest-reigning monarch in British history. The Queen, as Charles well knows, will never abdicate. She will gradually hand over to her son certain public rituals, including

---

*The real reason for this surprising innovation, in the wake of Diana's death, was to fore-stall the nightmare prospect of ex-HRH 'Fergie', Duchess of York, becoming the next Queen Mother. In the event of a multiple accident befalling Charles and his sons, his brother Andrew would become heir to the throne, with his daughters Beatrice and Eugenie next in line. Under the new law Andrew's claim could be pre-empted by his older sister, Anne, the Princess Royal.

arduous foreign visits, Commonwealth conferences and the State Opening of Parliament. Abdication, however, remains a dirty word in Buckingham Palace, for ever associated with the crisis of 1936, when it signalled a dereliction of duty. Abdication would also, as his father has pointed out, set an awkward precedent: if the Queen were to hand over to Charles at a certain age, would he in turn be obliged to step aside for William? Abdication, believe the Windsors, would rob the monarchy of the very last vestige of its already eroded mystique, devaluing it as a pensionable job like any other, to be set aside at retirement age. The Queen and her heir both believe that the role of sovereign is a sacred trust from God, for which she was anointed in her coronation, at which she swore vows lasting unto death.

So Charles's role for the foreseeable future, as for his entire life so far, is that of glorified understudy, waiting in the wings until the leading role becomes available, on a day which will, of course, carry great sadness for him at the same time as delivering his longed-for destiny. Until it comes, he must continue to face up to the prospect of being a grandfather in his seventies before inheriting the job to which he has been heir since the age of three.

Nor will the prince himself ever step aside, as is so often suggested, in his son's favour. Who can seriously suggest that William would contentedly usurp his father? Whole forests could now be spared by outlawing all future opinion polls and media debate on these two subjects. They are not negotiable, and never will be.

In the meantime, Charles's role at fifty has subtly shifted, from crusading public prince to protective private father, tending his sons through a private mourning commandeered by the rest of the world. Diana's death hijacked his public identity, converting him primarily into the father of their sons, robbing him of his previous status as a flawed private individual with worthy public aims. It is this transformation, from cruel ex-husband to poignant father, which has disarmed criticism and seen his approval ratings rise.

If Diana's death has done anything else for Charles, beyond removing his most powerful and effective critic, it has freed him up to be master of his own destiny again. This grim twist in the tail of the soap-opera script, leaving him in sole charge of the long-term storyline, has also freed him to be himself. His ex-wife's demise has bequeathed Charles, an introspective man prone to self-pity, a monstrous burden of guilt that he may never quite be able to shed. But her disappearance from his life, as well as that of an adoring nation, has also returned him to the centre of a public stage uncomplicated by her presence.

Whatever the future held for Diana, she was always going to have a complex, largely negative impact on public perceptions of her former husband. In death, as in life, she still may, freeze-framed for ever as the beautiful young mother, a force for good on the world stage, whom he betrayed and discarded. Such attitudes will never fade among 'Diana's Army', the millions who brought flowers to mourn her, who resented his family's apparent reluctance to share their huge outpouring of grief, and who now resent his expressions of thanks for sympathy aimed less at him than at his sons. So what, in conclusion, can he do about his apparently insoluble 'Camilla problem'? Or, in the words of one close to the late princess, 'She's got him, you know. In death, when it comes to Charles, Diana has achieved everything she aimed at in life.'[9]

In the mid-1950s, while serving at his country's embassy in London, Prince Bertil of Sweden met and fell in love with a Welsh ballerina named Lilian Craig. His father, King Gustav, would not allow them to marry because Lilian was a divorcee. Bertil took her back with him to Sweden in 1957, but she was never allowed to sit near him at royal functions or appear in official photographs. For twenty years the couple lived 'a shadowy, half-married life', until 1976, when Gustav's death finally enabled Bertil, at the age of sixty-four, to marry the love of his life. Only then, as a fully fledged princess, could she take her rightful place at his side.[10]

When Bertil himself died twenty years later, in January 1997, at the age of eighty-four, Charles and Camilla took a particular interest in his poignant story. Determined to avoid a similar fate, they embarked on the high-risk strategy designed to win her public acceptance as his consort. Only Diana's death forestalled their plans to take a summer holiday together, regardless of the consequences, before the prince appeared loyally at his paramour's side on her first public appearance as a Diana-like charity worker.

After the tragedy in Paris, all their plans were put on hold. Far from making it easier for Camilla to meet and befriend Charles's sons, Diana's death made it far more difficult. Charles's new status as lone parent of the world's most poignantly bereaved children placed a wider gulf than ever between Diana's sons and Camilla. Nor were the British public much keener than William and Harry to see Charles and Camilla renewing their romance. So they were again forced to resort to subterfuge.

On 27 January 1998, for instance, Camilla rose early to join the Beaufort Hunt near her home at Laycock, Wiltshire, and drove over to Highgrove to collect her horse, Molly. But her subsequent outing proved frustrating, as the hounds found it difficult to pick up the fox's scent in the muggy morning air.

At 1 p.m., after a few unproductive hours, Camilla and Molly discreetly peeled off from the hunt. Half an hour later, the Prince of Wales joined it at Charlton Down, a mile from Highgrove. The hounds had just picked up the scent, and Charles was able to enjoy an exhilarating chase lasting three hours. There are few things he and Camilla would rather share than the fun of the chase; but freelance photographers, as always, were roaming the fields and thickets.[11]

The prince is 'fed up to the back teeth', he has told friends, with the continued need for deception in his relationship with Camilla, which has even seen him resort to hiding in the back of his own car, driven to her home by his protection officer. Charles desperately wants to be able to take Camilla in her own right to Balmoral, to Klosters, even to Windsor. He wants her to win his sons' acceptance, which is, of course, the key to eventual public approval. Within a year of Diana's death, to the dismay of those still mourning her, that delicate process finally began when a chance meeting between Camilla and William at St James's Palace on 12 June 1998, nine days before his sixteenth birthday, led to a lunch hosted by Charles and eventually a tea à deux – a process soon to be repeated with Harry. In the fullness of time, one photograph is all it would take – one image of the boys smiling in Camilla's company, offering her presence in their father's life their unspoken blessing – and public opinion would soon swing round. No doubt Mandelson and his close friend Mark Bolland, the expert spin doctors in Charles's private office are already working on it. If not, they should be. Once William and Harry are seen appearing to okay Camilla, even 'Diana's Army' might relent.

For those poor boys, of course, it is an agonizing choice. Camilla is the one woman who can make their father happy, but she is also the woman who made their beloved mother so unhappy. It seems probable, as they grow older, that they will find it in their hearts to forgive, if not to forget. The more they are Windsorized – or, in truth, de-Spencerized – the more they will see that it is in the interests of the monarchy, as much as their own family circle, to have a contented, fulfilled Prince of Wales, rather than the moody, put-upon figure Charles cuts without his Camilla.

The prince would, of course, find it very difficult, if it comes to it, to choose between Camilla and the Crown. 'Heaven forbid it ever reaches that point,' says one friend.[12] What does the prince see in Mrs Parker Bowles, apart from the fact that it is hard to imagine a woman less like Diana? 'She mothers him,' says one veteran royal-watcher, who has noticed a 'strange, almost animal-like attraction' which Charles seems to derive from the way she lives her life. 'She is frankly not the most pristine of women,' he continues, quoting one so-called friend as muttering, 'You're never quite sure whether they're today's knickers she's got on.' Camilla's house, according to another, is always 'a bit of a mess . . . I don't think she goes to the hairdresser, and most of the time she can't be bothered to dress up.'[13]

Such sleazy backchat is one of the prices Camilla must pay, and Charles, too, for betraying Diana, a universal wife and mother more highly regarded, even revered, than either of them can ever hope to be. 'Which one would you rather go to bed with?' asked a British tabloid recently, above a photograph of Camilla next to a horse. 'I think he would just love the world not to be mean about her,' says their friend Patty Palmer-Tomkinson. 'It's a very courtly kind of love – a kind of chivalry. The prince worries like mad about her . . . He longs to do more for her and give her something of what he has.' Their relationship is now 'umbilical', according to another longstanding friend of Camilla, the society designer Nicky Haslam. 'It's not calf love, it's hooks into the heart,' as he puts it. 'It's like a rope attached to her. There's something very, very strong from her to him . . . I think it's much stronger than sex. It's a great need, this love.' A more worldly, perhaps hortatory note is struck by Camilla's public relations adviser, Alan Kilkenny: 'It's unseemly for the heir to the throne to have this divorced woman as a bit of stuff. I think people will think the less of him for not looking after her.'[14]

But the couple's problems are more profound than mere proprieties. Diana's death was an earthquake that opened up a seismic fault beneath the monarchy, a lightning-flash that illuminated deep, underlying changes in British society. It did not, as has been argued, provoke those changes; it merely revealed that Britons had begun, until then imperceptibly, to shed many of the national traditions and characteristics they supposedly held dear.[15]

The scenes of mourning for Diana were an epitaph more apt than many realized. The feelings released by her death were those she would have devoted her life to releasing. For the princess, ironically enough, loathed the inhibition and buttoned-up formality supposedly endemic in a country she otherwise held dear. 'Why must the British pride themselves on their emotional restraint?' she once asked. 'It's so unnatural, so psychologically unhealthy. Look what it's done to Charles: he's an emotional cripple. It's not his fault, it was the way he was brought up. Forced to hide his feelings, persuaded it was somehow unmanly to let them out, which has left him incapable of showing his feelings, let alone understanding them.' That was why she liked America and Americans so much: 'so warm, so open, so candid, so genuine.'[16]

So it was another irony that conservative commentators sneered at the response to her death as the 'Americanization' of Britain – meaning not a display of false emotion, but a display of any emotion at all. But beyond those public displays of strong and genuine emotion, which would have delighted (and astonished) Diana, was a readiness to dispense with formality, reserve, archness, deference and all those other indigenous traditions which add up to an in-built conservatism about the status quo. Combine the popular demonstrations of the week before Diana's funeral with the landslide election of a populist government four months before, and you have a flexing of public muscle to which all pillars of the establishment, not least the monarchy, must adapt to survive.

Hence the new, media-friendly prince, who kisses his brother in public, puts his arms round his sons, touches AIDS patients. Is this the 'Dianification' of Charles? His minders would like to think so. But he will never establish the same rapport as the late princess enjoyed with the adoring press corps, let alone the same love affair with the camera. Though a conscientious father, he will never be as genuinely 'touchy-feely' with his sons. Nor will he be as hounded in private, as no photograph of Charles will ever command the same galactic sums as one of Diana.

Unless, of course, it is with Camilla. For now, however sceptically, we must take the prince at his word that he will put duty first, and not inflict the divorced Mrs Parker Bowles upon a hostile nation as its future queen. But Charles, in turn, must also understand that the British people will not long tolerate, as he hopes, the present impasse – a closet affair, conducted behind closed doors in the country houses of loyal aristocratic chums. Like all the other aspects of monarchy which Charles supposedly shares Blair's eagerness to modernize – its scale, its finances, its remoteness and its arcane rituals – that kind of royal conduct belongs to a bygone era.

As he contemplates life after fifty, Charles must therefore square up to a decision that will affect the rest of his days: marry Camilla or renounce her. Were he to risk public wrath by making an honest woman of her, with twenty years for his future subjects to warm towards the 'non-negotiable' love of his life, Blair's government would not stand in his way.

Disestablishment of the Church of England, if it proved one of the consequences, would fit as well with Blair's 'modernization' programme as with Charles's ecumenical outlook. A multi-denominational coronation, with Camilla at Charles's side as his official consort, whether crowned or uncrowned, would be a logical launch to the new Caroline era – a mere caretaker reign, after all, before the glorious accession of the idolized King William V.

If, on the other hand, Charles were to abandon Camilla for the sake of the throne, he would stand accused of ruining his lover's life as well as his late wife's. Which might well cramp even New Labour's style in portraying him as a caring, compassionate prince, man of his times enough to declare the £1 billion Millennium Dome officially open.

So which path will the post-fairy-tale 'Prince Charming' choose? Upon that fateful decision hang his public hopes of a happy and glorious reign, let alone his private chances of living happily ever after.

BIBLIOGRAPHY AND SOURCE NOTES

The bibliographies of my two previous biographies of the Prince of Wales (1979 and 1988, as detailed below) extend to almost 100 volumes, a number of which are timeless, many now woefully dated, and some considerably more reliable than others. To spare the reader an extended version of that list here, given the recent boom in the production of royal books, there follows a shortlist of the key volumes consulted for, and most quoted in, the present work. The editions cited are those consulted by the author. Publication details of other books quoted in the text are given in full in the source notes. All newspapers cited are London-based unless otherwise specified.

Dimbleby, Jonathan: *The Prince of Wales* (London: Warner Books, 1995).
Holden, Anthony: *Charles, Prince of Wales* (London: Weidenfeld & Nicolson, 1979).
  Charles (London: Weidenfeld & Nicolson, 1988).
  The Tarnished Crown (London: Bantam Press, 1993).
Lacey, Robert: *Majesty* (London: Hutchinson, 1977).
Morrah, Dermot: *To Be a King* (London: Hutchinson, 1968).
Morton, Andrew: *Diana, Her True Story – In Her Own Words* (London: Michael O'Mara Books, revised edition 1997). *
Pimlott, Ben: *The Queen* (London: HarperCollins, 1996).
Wilson, Christopher: *A Greater Love* (London: Headline, 1994).

* This third edition of Andrew Morton's *Diana, Her True Story* was published after the princess's death with a new section (pp. 23–69) entitled *In Her Own Words*, comprising the transcripts of tape-recorded interviews she made in 1991–2, whose existence Morton concealed during her lifetime. In the source notes that follow, I have distinguished between Diana's own words and Morton's by referring to her first-person testimony under the initials IHOW.

CHAPTER 1: 'It was not to be' (pages 5–14)

1   Author's interviews outside Buckingham Palace, 31 August 1997.
2   *You Decide*, BBC1, 22 July 1997.
3   Confidential interview; source requests anonymity.
4   *The Times*, 24 December 1997.
5   Tina Brown, *The New Yorker*, New York, 15 September 1997.
6   Morton, p. 133.
7   *Guardian*, 12 August 1997.

8   *Express*, 12 August 1997.
9   Anthony Holden, *Charles at Forty*, ITV, London, Sunday 13 November 1988.
10   HRH The Prince of Wales, *A Vision of Britain* (London: Doubleday, 1989), p. 10.
11   Dimbleby, pp. 141, 167.
12   Ibid., pp. 336, 687.
13   C speech, 19 December 1989.

CHAPTER 2: 'No, not you, dear' (pages 15–32)

1   David Niven, letter to the author, 4 September 1978.
2   Morrah, p. 5n, and *The Lineage and Ancestry of HRH Prince Charles, Prince of Wales*, 2 vols (London: Charles Skilton, 1977).
3   Dalton, unpublished diary, 14 November 1948, q. Pimlott, p. 156.
4   Hansard, 16 November 1948.
5   Ibid.
6   C, conversation with author, 1978.
7   Morrah, p. 8.
8   Ibid., p. 8.
9   Cecil Beaton, *The Strenuous Years, Diaries 1948–55* (London: Weidenfeld & Nicolson, 1973), p. 17.
10   James Pope-Hennessy, *Queen Mary* (London: George Allen & Unwin, 1959), p. 616.
11   Pimlott, pp. 161–2.
12   Holden, *Charles, Prince of Wales*, p. 59.
13   *Daily Express*, 6 June 1953.
14   Holden, *Charles, Prince of Wales*, p. 70.

CHAPTER 3: 'A thoroughly average pupil' (pages 33–53)

1   Hansard, 28 June 1894.
2   Dimbleby, p. 39.
3   Holden, *Charles, Prince of Wales*, p. 72.
4   Morrah, pp. 39–40.
5   Morrah, p. 53.
6   Lord Altrincham, 'The Monarchy Today', *National and English Review*, August 1957.
7   Dimbleby, pp. 33–4.
8   An exhaustive history of Cheam School can be found in Edward Peel, *Cheam School from 1645* (Gloucester: Thornhill Press, 1974).
9   Foreword by HRH The Duke of Edinburgh to Peel, ibid., p. xi.
10   Peel, op. cit., p. 181.
11   *Evening Standard*, 16 August 1957.
12   Morrah, p. 59.
13   See Dimbleby, p. 44.
14   Holden, *Charles, Prince of Wales*, p. 102.
15   Queen to Eden, 16 January 1958, Avon papers, q. Pimlott, p. 262.
16   *The Times*, 28 July 1958.
17   BBC Radio 4, interview with Jack de Manio, *Today*, 1 March 1969.
18   Author's confidential conversation with courtier, 1978.
19   Morrah, p. 80.
20   Holden, *Charles, Prince of Wales*, p. 106.
21   Peel, op. cit., p. 257 and Morrah, p. 80.
22   Holden, *Charles, Prince of Wales*, p. 107.
23   *Radio Times*, 25–31 July 1981.
24   Peter Beck, letter to author, 23 January 1979.
25   Morrah, p. 82.

CHAPTER 4: 'He hasn't run away yet' (pages 54–76)

1   Pimlott, p. 262.
2   BBC TV interview, 26 June 1969.

3   Holden, *Charles, Prince of Wales*, p. 113. More detail on Gordonstoun can be found in Adam Arnold-Brown, *Unfolding Character: The Impact of Gordonstoun* (London: Routledge & Kegan Paul, 1962).
4   William Boyd, *School Ties* (London: Penguin, 1985), p. 11.
5   Ross Benson, *Charles, The Untold Story* (London: Gollancz, 1993), p. 53.
6   Ibid., pp. 52–3.
7   Patrick Pelham-Jones, *Redbook*, USA, March 1964.
8   Holden, *Charles, Prince of Wales*, p. 116.
9   Morrah, p. 87.
10   See Dimbleby, p. 76.
11   Basil Boothroyd, *Prince Philip* (London: Longman, 1971), p. 124.
12   Colville to *Time*, New York, q. Morrah, p. 104.
13   Ibid., p. 106.
14   C letter, 8 February 1964.
15   Ibid., p. 79 & fn.
16   Boyd, op. cit., pp. 21–3.
17   C letter, 8 February 1964.
18   Author's interview with Rt. Revd Robert Woods, 22 February 1979.
19   2 December 1965.
20   Author's interviews with David Checketts, 1977–8.
21   Morrah, pp. 127–8.
22   Morrah, p. 130.
23   C press statement issued via Checketts, August 1966; Morrah, p. 136.
24   BBC Radio 4, interview with Jack de Manio, *Today*, 1 March 1969.

CHAPTER 5: 'They don't know what I'm like' (pages 77–93)

1   Heseltine memo, undated.
2   Author's interview with Sir Harold Wilson, 1977, and Rt. Revd Robert Woods, 1979 and Morrah, pp. 138–40; *also* Lacey, pp. 324–5.
3   Holden, *Charles, Prince of Wales*, p. 136.
4   BBC Radio 4, interview with Jack de Manio, *Today*, 1 March 1969.
5   Dimbleby, p. 133.
6   Author's interviews with Lord Butler, 1978 and Hywel Jones, Trinity College, Cambridge, 1978 and 1988.
7   Author's interview with Lord Butler, 1978.
8   Dimbleby, p. 134.
9   Author's interview with Lord Butler, 1978. Butler's revelation that he had 'slipped' Lucia a key to the master's lodge, after the prince had 'asked if she might stay [there] for privacy' – subsequently confirmed to the author in writing – caused something of a stir on the publication of *Charles, Prince of Wales* in 1979 (p. 199), moving Buckingham Palace to indignant denials.
10   Author's interviews with Dr Dennis Marrian, Trinity College, Cambridge, 1978 and 1988.
11   Author's interview with Lord Butler, 1978.
12   C letter to Mountbatten, July 1968.
13   Holden, *Charles, Prince of Wales*, p. 143.
14   *Daily Sketch*, 13 March 1969, and author's correspondence with Edward Millward, 1979.
15   Joint BBC–ITV interview, 26 June 1969.
16   Pimlott, p. 392.
17   Joint BBC–ITV interview, 26 June 1969.
18   Author's interview with George Thomas MP, 1978.
19   Author's interviews with Checketts and Marrian, 1977–8.
20   Author's interview with George Thomas MP, 1978.
21   C letter, 9 October 1969.
22   Dimbleby, pp. 220–1.

CHAPTER 6: 'So how about it?' (pages 97–119)

1 Dimbleby, p. 220.
2 Nigel Dempster and Peter Evans, *Behind Palace Doors* (New York: Putnam, 1993), p. 69.
3 Ibid., p. 65.
4 Wilson, pp. 17–18.
5 Sir Philip Magnus, *King Edward VII* (London: John Murray, 1964).
6 Giles St Aubyn, *Edward VII, Prince and King* (New York: Atheneum, 1979), pp. 378–9.
7 Theo Aronson, q. Wilson, p. 18.
8 Richard Hough, *Edward and Alexandra* (London: John Curtis/Hodder & Stoughton, 1992), p. 189.
9 Magnus, op. cit., p. 260.
10 *Sunday Times*, 6 July 1997.
11 *Camilla*, written and presented by Christopher Wilson, Channel 5, 3 July 1997.
12 Dimbleby, p. 220.
13 C letter to Mountbatten, 19 March 1973.
14 C letter, December 1972.
15 C letter, 27 April 1973.
16 C letter, 20 May 1973.
17 Dempster and Evans, op. cit., p. 76.
18 Wilson., p. 60.
19 C memo to Checketts, 10 July 1976.
20 Sir John Wheeler-Bennett, *King George VI* (London: Macmillan, 1958), p. 294.
21 For more detail on C's service career, *see* Holden, *Charles, Prince of Wales*, pp. 171–88.
22 *Evening Standard*, 7 January 1975.
23 C to author, 1978.
24 C interviewed by Kenneth Harris, *Observer*, 9 June 1974.
25 Dimbleby, pp. 315–16.
26 Stephen P. Barry, *Royal Service* (New York: Macmillan, 1983), p. 170.
27 C speech to Parliamentary Press Gallery, House of Commons, 1975.
28 Wilson, p. 65.
29 Holden, *Charles, Prince of Wales*, p. 203.
30 *Daily Express*, 17 June 1977.
31 Dempster and Evans, op. cit., p. 87.
32 IHOW, p. 31.
33 Dimbleby, p. 337.
34 IHOW, p. 31.

CHAPTER 7: 'Somebody to look after you' (pages 120–136)

1 IHOW, p. 23.
2 Anthony Holden, *Their Royal Highnesses* (London: Weidenfeld & Nicolson, 1981), p. 30.
3 IHOW, p. 30.
4 Ibid., p. 23.
5 Ibid., pp. 23–4.
6 *Daily Mail*, 6 February 1993.
7 IHOW, p. 27.
8 IHOW, p. 30.
9 Interviewed by James Slazenger, *Woman's Own*, January 1978.
10 IHOW, p. 30.
11 Morton, pp. 98–9
12 Kitty Kelley, *The Royals* (New York: Warner Books, 1997), pp. 246–7.
13 Dimbleby, p. 335.

14 C letter to Mountbatten, 25 April 1973.
15 Mountbatten letter to C, 14 February 1974, and C to M, undated, March 1974.
16 C diary, 27 August 1979.
17 C letter to Mountbatten, 27 November 1978.
18 C diary, 27 August 1979.
19 Dimbleby, p. 307.
20 Author's conversation with Whitaker, 8 June 1998.
21 IHOW, p. 32.
22 Morton, p. 102.
23 Ibid., p. 105.

CHAPTER 8: 'Whatever love means' (pages 137–159)

 1 *Daily Mail*, 11 April 1980.
 2 *Private Eye*, April 1980.
 3 Wilson, pp. 73–4.
 4 Dimbleby, p. 363.
 5 Holden, *Charles, Prince of Wales*, p. 182.
 6 Morton, p. 110.
 7 In Dimbleby, pp. 338–9.
 8 Author's conversation with Whitaker, 8 June 1998.
 9 Morton, p. 112.
10 IHOW, pp. 33–5.
11 *Sunday Mirror*, 16 November 1980.
12 Author's conversation with Edwards, 24 May 1998, and Robert Edwards, *Goodbye
    Fleet Street* (London: Coronet, Hodder & Stoughton, 1988), pp. 169–83.
13 Wilson, p. 83.
14 Letter to *The Times*, 2 December 1980.
15 Author's conversation with Whitaker, 8 June 1998.
16 IHOW, p. 36.
17 Dimbleby, p. 335.
18 *Independent on Sunday*, 13 December 1992.
19 IHOW, p. 34.
20 Ibid., p. 35.
21 Ibid., p. 36.
22 Ibid., p. 37.
23 Ross Benson, *Charles, The Untold Story* (London, Gollancz, 1993), pp. 156–7.
24 Elizabeth Longford, *Royal Throne* (London: John Curtis/Hodder & Stoughton, 1993),
    p. 73.
25 *Daily Mail*, 6 February 1993.
26 *Panorama*, BBC1 Television, 20 November 1995.
27 Morton, p. 119.
27 Dimbleby, p. 346.
29 Benson, op. cit., p. 164.
30 IHOW, p. 37.
31 Nigel Dempster and Peter Evans, *Behind Palace Doors* (New York: Putnam, 1993),
    p. 39.
32 Dimbleby, p. 346.
33 IHOW, p. 39.
34 Ibid., pp. 40–1.
35 Morton, p. 124.
36 IHOW, p. 41.
37 Dimbleby, p. 348.
38 Morton, p. 125.
39 Dimbleby, p. 348 fn.
40 IHOW, p. 42.

CHAPTER 9: 'Like a lamb to the slaughter' (pages 163–182)

1 Humphrey Carpenter, *The Reluctant Archbishop* (London: Sceptre, 1997), pp. 222–4.
2 Walter Bagehot, *The English Constitution* (London: Fontana/Collins, 1963), p. 85.
3 IHOW, p. 42.
4 C letter, 3 August 1981.
5 IHOW, p. 42.
6 C letter, 3 August 1981.
7 IHOW, p. 42.
8 Dimbleby, p. 355.
9 Ibid., pp. 355–6.
10 *Panorama,* BBC1 Television, 20 November 1995.
11 IHOW, p. 43.
12 Dimbleby, p. 356.
13 IHOW, p. 43.
14 Ibid.
15 Ibid., p. 44.
16 Ibid.
17 Wilson, p. 97.
18 Dimbleby, p. 357.
19 Ibid., p. 359.
20 *Panorama,* BBC1 Television, 20 November 1995.
21 Morton, p. 133.
22 Dimbleby, pp. 399–400.
23 Ibid., p. 367.
24 *Panorama,* BBC1 Television, 20 November 1995.
25 IHOW, p. 37.
26 C speech to British Medical Association, 14 December 1982.
27 *Panorama,* BBC1 Television, 20 November 1995.
28 C letter, 10 October 1982.
29 *Panorama,* BBC1 Television, 20 November 1995.
30 Ibid.
31 C letter, 4 April 1983, and *Panorama,* BBC1 Television, 20 November 1995.
32 *Panorama,* BBC1 Television, 20 November 1995.
33 *Mail on Sunday,* 24 July 1983.
34 Dimbleby, p. 405.
35 IHOW, p. 51.
36 Ibid.

CHAPTER 10: 'Why can't you be more like Fergie?' (pages 183–201)

1 Holden, *Charles* (1988), p. 137.
2 Tina Brown, *Vanity Fair,* New York, September 1985.
3 Stephen P. Barry, *Royal Service* (New York: Macmillan, 1983), pp. 232–5.
4 IHOW, p. 47.
5 Dimbleby, pp. 432–3.
6 A fuller account can be found in Holden, *Charles* (1988), pp. 161–6.
7 Private source present at dinner.
8 Kenneth Powell, *Sunday Telegraph,* 4 October 1992.
9 Author's conversations with Ahrends, Manser and other architects.
10 Holden, *Charles* (1988), p. 138 (private source).
11 Private source.
12 Speech to IoD, 26 February 1985.
13 *Manchester Evening News,* 23 October 1985.
14 IHOW, p. 52.
15 Anthony Holden, *Daily Mail,* 1 May 1985.
16 C speech to annual general meeting of Scottish branch of Business in the Community, Edinburgh, 26 November 1985.
17 C letter, 6 November 1985.

18   Dimbleby, p. 471.
19   Edward Jay Epstein, *Dossier: The Secret History of Armand Hammer* (London: Orion Business, 1998), reviewed in the *Sunday Times* by Tony Allen-Mills, 15 March 1998.
20   Neil Lyndon, *The Times*, 24 September 1996, and conversation with author.
21   D to author, Kensington Palace, 9 October 1996.
22   *Express*, 14 March 1998.
23   C speech at Prince George, British Columbia, 4 May 1986.
24   C speech at Harvard University, 4 September 1986.
25   IHOW, p. 58.
26   D to author, Kensington Palace, 9 October 1996.
27   C letter, 18 November 1986.
28   C letter, 11 February 1987.

CHAPTER 11: 'I just want to be with her' (pages 202–216)

1   *Panorama*, BBC1 Television, 20 November 1995.
2   D to author, Kensington Palace, 9 October 1996.
3   C letter, 24 October 1987.
4   Wilson, p. 121.
5   Author's conversation with James Whitaker, 8 June 1998.
6   C letter, 24 October 1987.
7   Dimbleby, p. 460.
8   Holden, *Charles* (1988), p. 174.
9   Dimbleby, p. 455.
10   Author's conversations with Charles Knevitt and others involved, 1987–8 and 1992–3.
11   C speech at the Environment Awards to Industry, 23 February 1988.
12   C speech at European Year of the Environment Eyecatcher Awards, 22 March 1988.
13   C speech at the annual dinner of the Corporation of London's planning and communication committee, Mansion House, London, 1 December 1987.
14   HRH The Prince of Wales, *A Vision of Britain* (London: Doubleday, 1989), p. 71.
15   *Sunday Times*, 18 August 1991.
16   *Sunday Correspondent*, 30 September 1990.
17   Giles Worsley, *The Times*, 26 September 1996.
18   *Sunday Times*, 16 November 1997.
19   *The Times*, 22 November 1997.

CHAPTER 12: 'Why don't you leave my husband alone?' (pages 217–237)

1   C press statement, 12 March 1988.
2   See Dimbleby, p. 497.
3   Morton, p. 162.
4   *The Times*, 31 December 1997.
5   Peter Dormer, *Independent*, 2 June 1993.
6   *Sunday Times*, 24 August 1997.
7   Jonathan Glancey, *Guardian*, 21 January 1998.
8   Gavin Stamp, *The Times*, 7 March 1998.
9   Ibid.
10   *Sunday Express*, 26 October 1996.
11   Kenneth Powell, *Sunday Telegraph*, 4 October 1992.
12   *The Times*, 9 December 1992.
13   Richard Rogers, 'Pulling Down the Prince', *The Times*, 3 July 1989.
14   *The Times*, 14 November 1988.
15   Morton, p. 163, and other sources.
16   Morton, pp. 166–7.
17   IHOW, pp. 62–3, and other sources.
18   *News of the World*, 15 January 1995.
19   C speech to business executives, 29 June 1989.
20   C speech as patron of the Thomas Cranmer Schools Prize, 19 December 1989.
21   Holden, *Diana, a Life and a Legacy* (London: Ebury Press, 1997), p. 17.

22 Author's private conversation with former member of Highgrove staff.

CHAPTER 13: 'What kind of dad are you?' (pages 241–255)

1   A familiar quote among the royal 'rat-pack' to this day.
2   *Sunday Times*, 10 February 1991.
3   See Dimbleby, pp. 605–6.
4   *Independent*, 28 November 1992.
5   Interpretation disputed between Morton, p. 184, and Dimbleby, p. 578n.
6   C draft letter, 14 August 1980.
7   C interviewed by Dimbleby, ITV, 29 June 1994.
8   Morton, p. 172.
9   Ibid., p.176.
10 Rosa Monckton, *Sunday Telegraph*, 7 September 1997.
11 D to author, Kensington Palace, 9 October 1996.
12 Nigel Dempster and Peter Evans, *Behind Palace Doors* (New York: Putnam, 1993), p. 217.

CHAPTER 14: 'Why don't you go off with your lady?' (pages 256–278)

1   James Whitaker, *Diana vs Charles* (New York: Signet, 1993), p. 227.
2   Morton, pp. 191-2.
3   Patrick Jephson, former private secretary to the Princess of Wales, *The New Yorker*, 25 August–1 September 1997.
4   Morton, p. 183.
5   Dimbleby, p. 573.
6   Holden, *The Tarnished Crown* (1993), pp. 267–8.
7   *Evening Standard*, 26 January 1993.
8   C letter to Lt Gen. Sir Michael Gray, 5 July 1992.
9   Penny Junor, *Charles and Diana* (London: Headline, 1991).
10 *Today*, 6 July 1992.
11 Morton, p. 218.
12 Morton, p. 219.
13 Walter Bagehot, *The English Constitution* (Oxford: OUP, 1933) p. 100.
14 *Sunday Telegraph*, 23 August 1992.
15 Bernard Levin, *The Times*, 5 February 1993.
16 *Daily Express*, 13 July 1992.
17 *Panorama*, BBC1 Television, 20 November 1995.
18 C memo to Aylard, 23 October 1992.
19 Whitaker, q. Wilson, p. 147.
20 See Dimbleby, p. 511.
21 C letter, 8 November 1992.
22 Dimbleby, p. 688.
23 C letter to Malcom Rifkind, 16 November 1992.
24 Janet Daley, *The Times*, 24 November 1992.
25 *Panorama*, BBC1 Television, 20 November 1995.
26 Hansard, 9 December 1992.
27 Dimbleby, p. 597.
28 Wilson, p. 148.

CHAPTER 15: 'They will forgive me' (pages 279–295)

1   *Daily Express*, 2 December 1993.
2   C letter to Soames, 11 December 1992.
3   Richard Kay, *Diana, The Untold Story*, serialized in the *Daily Mail*, January–April 1998: part five, 22 February 1998, p. 90.
4   *The Times*, 13 January 1993.
5   *Sunday Telegraph*, 24 January 1993.
6   *Sun*, 25 January 1993.

7   *Daily Telegraph*, 9 February 1993.
8   *Sunday Times*, 14 February 1993.
9   *The Times*, 1 February 1993.
10 *Entertainment Express*, BBC1 Television, London, 12 February 1993.
11 *Sun*, 19 January 1993.
12 *Today*, 18 January 1993.
13 *The Royal Debate*, Sky TV, London, 16 February 1993.
14 *The Times*, 19 February 1993.
15 D speech to National Aids Trust, 16 February 1993.
16 See Holden, *The Tarnished Crown*, pp. 259–61.
17 *Panorama*, BBC1 Television, 20 November 1995.
18 *Daily Mail*, 3 March 1993.
19 Ibid., 8 April 1993.
20 *News of the World*, 11 April 1993.
21 *Mail on Sunday*, 11 April 1993.
22 D to author, San Lorenzo, 1993.
23 *Sunday Times*, 24 January 1993.
24 Ibid.
25 Morton, pp. 228–9.
26 D to author, Kensington Palace, 9 October 1996.

CHAPTER 16: 'Time and space' (pages 296–311)

1   *Time*, 30 November 1992.
2   Last will and testament of D, dated 1 June 1993, published London, 2 March 1998.
3   *Daily Express*, 7 June 1993.
4   Wilson, pp. 176–7.
5   Dimbleby, p. 657.
6   Author's private conversation with a Charles aide, 1998.
7   C letter to John Major, 15 October 1993.
8   C speech in Sheldonian Theatre, Oxford, 'Islam and the West', 27 October 1993.
9   Humphrey Carpenter, *The Reluctant Archbishop* (London: Sceptre, 1997), p. 221.
10 *Sunday Telegraph*, 28 November 1993.
11 *La Règle de Jeu*, Paris, reported in the *Independent on Sunday*, 31 January 1993.
12 *Daily Mail*, 6 January 1997.
13 Bryan Appleyard, *The Times*, 9 December 1992.
14 Carpenter, op. cit., pp. 221–4.
15 Dimbleby, p. 560.
16 D speech to the Headway National Head Injuries Association, 3 December 1993.
17 *Panorama*, BBC1 Television, 20 November 1995.
18 Dimbleby, p. 652.
19 *Today*, BBC Radio 4, 7 December 1994.
20 Dimbleby, p. 650.
21 Roy Hattersley, *Observer*, 5 April 1998.
22 *Daily Telegraph*, 8 December 1994.
23 Wilson, p. 183.
24 D to author, Launceston Place, 1994.
25 C foreign journal, 26 January 1994.
26 Teresa Powell, *Sun*, 27 January 1994.
27 Robert Milliken, *Independent*, 27 January 1994.

CHAPTER 17: 'The saddest day of my life' (pages 312–328)

1   Richard Hough, *Edward and Alexandra* (London: John Curtis/Hodder & Stoughton, 1992), p. 203.
2   *Mail on Sunday*, 30 January 1994.
3   Dimbleby, p. 681.
4   *Charles: The Private Man, The Public Role*, ITV, London, 29 June 1994.

5   Wilson, p. 172.
6   *Panorama*, BBC1 Television, 20 November 1995.
7   *Daily Mail*, 22 August 1995.
8   Dimbleby, p. 686.
9   Dimbleby, pp. 735–6.
10 Kitty Kelley, *The Royals* (New York: Warner Books, 1997), p. 462.
11 *Panorama*, BBC1 Television, 20 November 1995.
12 C diary, 19 March 1974.
13 Kelley, op. cit., p. 463.
14 *Daily Mail*, 11 October 1995.
15 *Panorama*, BBC1 Television, 20 November 1995.
16 *The Times*, 21 November, 1995.
17 *Daily Mail*, 21 November 1995.
18 Ibid., 29 February 1996.
19 D to author, Kensington Palace, 9 October 1996.
20 *Sun*, 29 August 1996.

CHAPTER 18: 'I will never remarry' (pages 331–351)

1   Anthony Holden and Richard Kay, *Daily Mail*, 4 December 1993.
2   *News of the World*, 25 August 1996.
3   *Sunday Telegraph*, 25 August 1996.
4   *The Times*, 26 August 1996.
5   *Observer*, 25 August 1996.
6   *The Times*, 26 August 1996.
7   *Sunday Telegraph*, 25 August 1996.
8   *The Times*, 26 August 1996.
9   *Mail on Sunday*, 1 September 1996.
10 *Guardian*, 28 August 1996.
11 *News of the World*, 1 September 1996.
12 *Camilla*, Channel 5, London, 3 July 1997.
13 *Sunday Times*, 1 September 1996.
14 D to author, Kensington Palace, 9 October 1996.
15 *Sunday Telegraph*, 6 October 1996.
16 D to author, Kensington Palace, 9 October 1996.
17 D to author, Kensington Palace, 9 October 1996.
18 *The Monarchy – The Nation Decides*, ITV, 7 January 1997.
19 *Express on Sunday*, 12 January 1997.
20 *Sunday Times*, 12 January 1997.
21 *The Times*, 15 January 1997.
22 *Daily Mail*, 23 April 1998.
23 *Sunday Telegraph*, 9 March 1997.
24 *Daily Mail*, 25 April 1997.
25 *The Times*, 2 March 1996.
26 Books section, *Sunday Times*, 15 June 1997.
27 *The Times*, 26 June 1997.
28 Lord (W. F.) Deedes, *Daily Telegraph*, 26 June 1997.
29 *Daily Mail*, 26 June 1997.
30 *Heart of the Matter*, BBC1 Television, 6 July 1997.
31 *Sunday Times*, 20 July 1997.
32 *Daily Mail*, 6 August 1997.
33 *Sunday Telegraph*, 15 February 1998.
34 Fayed interviewed in the *Daily Mirror*, 14 February 1998.
35 *Le Monde*, Paris, 27 August 1997.
36 *Express on Sunday*, 31 August 1997.
37 *Mail on Sunday*, 31 August 1997.
38 *News of the World*, 31 August 1997.
39 *Mail on Sunday*, 7 September 1997.

CHAPTER 19: 'Goodbye, England's Rose' (pages 352–371)

1   *The New Yorker*, 15 September 1997.
2   Author's interviews outside Buckingham Palace, 31 August 1997.
3   Anthony Holden, *Express*, 13 November 1997.
4   Blair interviewed, *Daily Mirror*, 20 March 1998.
5   *The Times*, 19 September 1997.
6   *Sunday Times*, 14 September 1997.
7   *Mail on Sunday*, 28 September 1997.
8   *Daily Mail*, 18 October 1997.
9   Anthony Holden, *Express*, 13 November 1997.
10 Nigel Dempster, *Daily Mail*, 17 November 1997.
11 *Hello!*, August 1997.
12 *Sunday Telegraph*, 7 December 1997.
13 *Big Issue*, 16 February 1998.
14 *The Times*, 24 December 1997.
15 Fayed interviewed in the *Daily Mirror*, 13 February 1998.
16 Richard Kay, *Daily Mail*, 7 July 1997.
17 Author's interviews, and the *Sunday Times*, 22 March 1998.
18 Professor Anthony O'Hear, essay in 'Faking It: The Sentimentalisation of Modern Society', edited by Digby Anderson and Peter Mullen (Social Affairs   Unit, London, April 1998).
19 *Sunday with Adam Boulton*, Sky TV, London, 19 April 1998.
20 *Express on Sunday*, 19 April 1998.

CHAPTER 20: 'The people's prince' (pages 372–385)

1   Jonathan Glancey, 'Adrift in a Modern Age', *Guardian*, 21 January 1998.
2   Bryan Appleyard, *The Times*, 9 December 1992.
3   QEII golden-wedding-banquet speech, 20 November 1998.
4   Shakespeare, *King Lear*, III, iv, 101 (Oxford edition).
5   Shakespeare, *Henry V*, IV, i, 233–4 (ibid.).
6   Denis MacShane MP, *Newsweek*, 11 May 1998.
7   Anthony Holden, *Express on Sunday*, 8 March 1998.
8   *Daily Telegraph*, 14 March 1998.
9   Author's private conversation with friend of D, 1998.
10 *Daily Mail*, 28 January 1997.
11 *Sunday Times*, 2 February 1997.
12 Author's private conversation with friend of C, 1998.
13 James Whitaker, *Diana vs Charles* (New York: Signet, 1993), p. 53.
14 Allison Pearson, 'Love in a Cold Climate', *The New Yorker*, 1 August–25 September 1997.
15 I have shamelessly stolen the 'lightning-flash' concept from my friend Peter Hennessy, Professor of Contemporary History at Queen Mary and Westfield College, University of London.
16 D to author, Kensington Palace, 9 October 1996.

INDEX